Coming Home to New Orleans

Coming Home to New Orleans

Neighborhood Rebuilding after Katrina

Karl F. Seidman

OXFORD
UNIVERSITY PRESS

OXFORD
UNIVERSITY PRESS

Oxford University Press is a department of the University of Oxford.
It furthers the University's objective of excellence in research, scholarship,
and education by publishing worldwide.

Oxford   New York
Auckland   Cape Town   Dar es Salaam   Hong Kong   Karachi
Kuala Lumpur   Madrid   Melbourne   Mexico City   Nairobi
New Delhi   Shanghai   Taipei   Toronto

With offices in
Argentina   Austria   Brazil   Chile   Czech Republic   France   Greece
Guatemala   Hungary   Italy   Japan   Poland   Portugal   Singapore
South Korea   Switzerland   Thailand   Turkey   Ukraine   Vietnam

Oxford is a registered trademark of Oxford University Press in the UK
and certain other countries.

Published in the United States of America by
Oxford University Press
198 Madison Avenue, New York, NY 10016

Library of Congress Cataloging-in-Publication Data
Seidman, Karl F.
Coming home to New Orleans : neighborhood rebuilding after Katrina / Karl F. Seidman.
p. cm.
Includes bibliographical references and index.
ISBN 978-0-19-994551-1 (cloth : alk. paper)—ISBN 978-0-19-994552-8 (eletronic text)
1. Community development—Louisiana—New Orleans—Citizen participation.
2. Neighborhood planning—Louisiana—New Orleans—Citizen participation.   3. Urban
renewal—Louisiana—New Orleans—Citizen participation.   4. City planning—
Louisiana—New Orleans—Citizen participation.   5. Economic development—Louisiana—
New Orleans—Citizen participation.   6. Hurricane Katrina, 2005—Social aspects.   I. Title.
HN80.N45S35 2013
307.1′40976335—dc23
2012033086]

ISBN 978-0-19-994551-1
ISBN 978-0-19-994552-8

1 3 5 7 9 8 6 4 2
Printed in the United States of America
on acid-free paper

For
Deborah and Sarah

CONTENTS

List of Tables   *viii*
List of Figures   *xi*
Preface   *xv*

1. The Flooding of New Orleans   *1*
2. Whither New Orleans?   *18*
3. Broadmoor Lives   *60*
4. A Village Rebuilds   *108*
5. A Tale of Four Neighborhoods   *158*
6. Neighborhoods and City Rebuilding   *254*

Acknowledgments   *295*
Appendix   *297*
Notes   *301*
Acronym Guide   *345*
Bibliography   *349*
Index   *365*

TABLES

2.1   Budget and UNOP projects included in Citywide
        Strategic Recovery and Redevelopment Plan (CSRRP)
        submitted to the Louisiana Recovery Authority   *38*

2.2   Louisiana's allocation of Community Development
        Block Grant (CDBG) disaster recovery funds   *45*

2.3   Timeline of events surrounding the evolution of
        Louisiana's Road Home Program   *46*

3.1   Key traits for Broadmoor and New Orleans residents in
        2000   *63*

3.2   Number of Broadmoor Plan projects by category and
        priority level   *74*

3.3   Partners for the Rosa F. Keller Library and Community
        Center   *86*

3.4   Broadmoor Development Corporation funding in its
        first three years   *92*

3.5   Number of Broadmoor housing units assisted and
        value of assistance under state government and
        Volunteer-Based Home Rebuilding Programs   *96*

3.6   Funding gap for new home construction   *97*

3.7   Change in Broadmoor population and housing units,
        2000–2010   *99*

3.8   Change in Broadmoor population by race,
        2000–2010   *100*

3.9   Broadmoor population change by Census tract,
        2000–2010   *102*

3.10   Share and changes in Broadmoor homeowners and
        renters, 2000 and 2010   *102*

3.11   Comparison of Broadmoor and Hollygrove
        neighborhoods   *103*

3.12   Funding for Broadmoor's rebuilding: nonfederal and
        federal funds, through mid-2010   *104*

4.1   Key traits for Village de L'Est and New Orleans'
        residents   *111*

4.2   Road Home and small rental property housing
        assistance to Village De L'est   *132*

4.3   State Community Development Block Grant
        (CDBG) recovery assistance to Village de L'Est
        businesses   *135*

4.4   Change in Village de L'Est population and housing
        units, 2000–2010   *150*

4.5   Change in Village de L'Est housing tenure,
        2000–2010   *151*

4.6   Change in Village de L'Est population by race,
        2000–2010   *151*

4.7   Repopulation and homeownership rates, New Orleans
        East neighborhoods   *152*

5.1   Key traits for four neighborhoods and New Orleans,
        2000   *160*

5.2   Change in Faubourg St. John population and housing
        units, 2000–2010   *170*

5.3   Change in Faubourg St. John population by race,
        2000–2010   *171*

5.4   Faubourg St. John population and housing change by
        Census tract, 2000–2010   *171*

5.5   Share and changes in Faubourg St. John homeowner-
        and renter-occupied housing units, 2000 and
        2010   *173*

5.6   Change in Mid-City population and housing units,
        2000–2010   *192*

5.7   Change in Mid-City population by race, 2000 and
        2010   *193*

5.8   Change in Mid-City population by Census tract,
        2000–2010   *193*

5.9   Share and changes in Mid-City homeowner- and
        renter-occupied housing units, 2000 and 2010   *195*

5.10   Federal financial assistance to Mid-City   *196*

5.11   Change in Tremé population and housing units,
        2000–2010   *220*

5.12   Share and changes in Tremé owner- and renter-occupied
        housing units, 2000 and 2010   *221*

5.13   Change in Tremé population by race, 2000 and
        2010   *222*

5.14   Tremé population change by Census tract,
        2000–2010   *222*

5.15   Displacement impacts of the LSU/VA hospitals   *232*

5.16   Change in Lower Mid-City population and housing
        units, 2000–2010   *242*

5.17   Change in Lower Mid-City population by race, 2000 and
        2010   *243*

5.18   Change in Lower Mid-City population and housing by
        Census tract, 2000–2010   *243*

5.19   Share and changes in Lower Mid-City owner- and
        renter-occupied housing units, 2000 and 2010   *245*

5.20   Four neighborhoods' 2010 population and housing
        recovery rates   *246*

6.1   2000 homeownership rates and 2010 recovery
        indicators for six neighborhoods   *258*

6.2   Grassroots rebuilding contributions across six
        neighborhoods   *265*

A.1   Road Home Program   *297*

A.2   Small Rental Properties Program (SRPP)   *298*

A.3   Alternative Housing Pilot Program (AHPP)   *298*

A.4   Small Firm Loan and Grant Program   *298*

A.5   Technical Assistance to Small Firms   *298*

A.6   Louisiana Bridge Loan Program   *299*

A.7   Public Facilities and Infrastructure   *299*

FIGURES

2.1   Parks and Open Space Map from Bring New Orleans
Back (BNOB) Commission's Urban Planning Committee
report   *24*

2.2   Meeting schedule and process for Unified New Orleans
Plan   *31*

3.1   Location of Broadmoor within New Orleans   *62*

3.2   Age distribution of residents, Broadmoor and New
Orleans in 2000   *63*

3.3   Broadmoor Street Map and Sub-Areas   *67*

3.4   Broadmoor Redevelopment Plan Committee
Structure   *68*

3.5   Community meeting and plan preparation phases for
Broadmoor's planning process   *72*

3.6   Diagram of Broadmoor's Partnership Implementation
Strategy   *75*

3.7   New Andrew H. Wilson Charter School   *90*

3.8   Inside of Wilson School with section of Former School
Wall   *90*

3.9   Broadmoor African American and white repopulation
rates by Census tract   *101*

4.1   Location of Village de L'Est within New
Orleans   *109*

4.2   Number of Village de L'Est Residents who emigrated to
the United States, 1975 to 2000   *110*

4.3   A typical street in Village de L'Est   *112*

4.4   Mary Queen of Vietnam Church   *114*

4.5   Site used for FEMA Trailer Park and proposed for senior
housing project   *119*

4.6   City Hall Demonstration against the Chef Menteur Landfill   *125*

4.7   "Viet Village" logo from business directory cover   *134*

4.8   New business façades on Alcee Fortier Boulevard   *136*

4.9   Tulane's clinic and the new community health center site   *145*

4.10   Site Plan for expanded urban farm project   *147*

4.11   Blighted apartment complex on Chef Menteur Highway in November 2010   *149*

4.12   Vacant and fenced Versailles Arms apartment Complex in November 2010   *150*

5.1   Location of Broad Street neighborhoods within New Orleans   *159*

5.2   Diversity of housing in Faubourg St. John   *161*

5.3   Faubourg St. John businesses on Ponce de Leon Street   *162*

5.4   Fair Grinds Coffee House   *164*

5.5   Vision Plan created by the Faubourg St. John Neighborhood Association   *165*

5.6   Alcee Fortier Park   *167*

5.7   Faubourg St. John 2010 homeowner and renter repopulation rates Census tract   *169*

5.8   Faubourg St. John African American and white repopulation rates by Census tract   *172*

5.9   Mid-City historic houses on South Clark Street   *175*

5.10   American Can Company: Site of the permanent Mid-City library branch   *181*

5.11   Morris Jeff Community School temporary site on Poydras Street   *184*

5.12   Comiskey Park, fenced and still closed in late 2010   *186*

5.13   Wise Words Community Garden   *189*

5.14   Lindy Boggs Medical Center complex   *190*

5.15   Crescent Club Apartments on Tulane Avenue   *191*

5.16   Mid-City African American and white repopulation by
        Census tract   *194*

5.17   Tremé's historic architecture: Shotgun homes on
        Governor Nichols Street and a large home on tree-lined
        Esplanade Avenue   *198*

5.18   Interstate 10 bisecting Tremé along Claiborne
        Avenue   *200*

5.19   Main Entrance to Louis Armstrong Park under repair in
        2010   *201*

5.20   Belles of the Bayou businesses on Bayou Road   *207*

5.21   Comparison of original Lafitte design with the plan for
        its redevelopment   *217*

5.22   Faubourg Lafitte under construction along Orleans
        Avenue in November 2010   *217*

5.23   Tremé African American and white repopulation rates
        by Census tract   *223*

5.24   Residential street in Lower Mid-City   *226*

5.25   Sites for Veterans Affairs and LSU hospitals   *232*

5.26   Sites for new LSU teaching hospital from
        Tulane-Gravier Neighborhood Rebuilding Plan   *234*

5.27   Historic home on VA hospital site being prepared for
        relocation   *238*

5.28   Cleared VA hospital site viewed from Tulane Avenue
        facing Galvez Street and the LSU hospital site   *239*

5.29   Lower Mid-City African American and white
        repopulation rates by Census tract   *244*

6.1   Model of neighborhood rebuilding capacity   *275*

PREFACE

In September 2005, like many Americans, I was shocked by the flooding and devastation that followed Hurricane Katrina, its human toll and the flawed response of the United States government. After many discussions with students and colleagues at MIT about what these events meant for New Orleans, the Gulf Coast region and national policy, I discovered several opportunities to get involved in the rebuilding effort. I was contacted by Ivan Miestchovich, Jr., a professor at the University of New Orleans, about the digital use of my textbook so that his fall class could be offered online while the university facilities were closed. I readily agreed and we then discussed the possibility of our spring classes collaborating on projects to assist with the rebuilding effort. During this same time, I had conversations with Long Nguyen, a colleague in Boston, about his emerging work to assist the Gulf Coast Vietnamese American communities. From these and other conversations, for our spring 2006 courses, Ivan and I established six projects on which students could work with public sector and community-based organizations in the New Orleans region. Over the next six years, I continued and broadened my activities in New Orleans, working on rebuilding plans and projects in several neighborhoods with community-based groups and economic development organizations. This work has included several projects with the Mary Queen of Vietnam (MQVN) church and community development corporation in New Orleans East, assisting the Broadmoor Development Corporation on its housing development plans, and ongoing work with Broad Community Connections (BCC) to revitalize the Broad Street corridor, including coteaching a class that prepared the plan that led to BCC's formation.

Through this work, I witnessed the role that residents and their community organizations played in rebuilding New Orleans. Under difficult physical conditions, considerable personal stress, and challenging political circumstances, local citizens joined together and took the lead to rebuild their neighborhoods. At the same time that they were reestablishing their personal lives and rebuilding their homes, these residents worked through neighborhood associations, churches, and other grassroots organizations to create rebuilding plans, organize resources to help their neighbors return, undertake improvement projects, start new schools, and envision and act on new ways to transform their city. The work of these grassroots organizations has been a vital part of the rebuilding of New Orleans. It should be included as part of the historical record and can inform our learning about how cities recover from a large-scale disaster.

I have written this book with two aspirations. The first is to document the work of grassroots organizations in rebuilding six neighborhoods. The accounts of rebuilding in these six neighborhoods are largely told from the perspectives of leaders and participants at the major community organizations involved in their neighborhood's recovery. The narratives focus on brief histories of these organizations, their goals and efforts around rebuilding, and the specific projects and activities undertaken. An appraisal of these rebuilding efforts and their outcomes for each neighborhood is provided that draws on 2010 Census data, the opinions of the grassroots leaders, and the author's own judgment. As such, the book does not provide a complete picture of rebuilding in each neighborhood. It addresses major governmental actions and projects that have shaped rebuilding, but does not capture all the investments and activities of governmental bodies. It also does not cover the activities of many nonprofit and community organizations involved in social, cultural, recreational, and social service activities that likely contributed to restoring community life but did not directly focus on neighborhood rebuilding. New Orleans received extensive recovery assistance from many parties: national organizations such as the Salvation Army, state and local affiliates of groups like Habitat for Humanity, and volunteer efforts by churches, universities, corporations, and others. These efforts are only documented to the extent they were highlighted by local leaders or played a central role in the work of community-based organizations.

The second aspiration is to draw lessons from New Orleans's recovery and the experiences of these six neighborhoods to inform future city rebuilding efforts after major disasters. The concluding chapter presents my views on these lessons and their implications around four issues: (1) what grass roots efforts and neighborhood scale rebuilding contribute to citywide rebuilding; (2) how neighborhood rebuilding can be undertaken when local capacity is largely in volunteer-based organizations; (3) integrating neighborhoods and citywide rebuilding plans; and (4) proposals to address flaws in federal policy for large-scale disaster recovery. The summation and contrasting of rebuilding in individual neighborhoods found at the end of chapters 3, 4, and 5 provides additional observations on the recovery process that may be useful to practitioners, policy-makers, and others interested in postdisaster recovery and urban community development.

A brief explanation of the time period covered in this book is also warranted. It is intended to cover the first five years of rebuilding efforts after Katrina, from August 2005 through fall 2010. However, the nature of events and sources of information made it impossible to use an exact time frame for the narratives in each chapter. In some cases, important milestones or events that occurred after this period are discussed. On the other hand, data from the 2010 US Census of Population and Housing is for April 2010, five months before the five-year anniversary of Katrina. Since the book focuses on the nature and broad accomplishments of the grassroots rebuilding, I don't believe these discrepancies in time periods of event and data covered make a material difference in documenting and drawing conclusions and implications what happened in these six neighborhoods.

CHAPTER 1

⌘

The Flooding of New Orleans

On the morning of August 24, 2005, a tropical depression over the Bahamas gained strength to become a tropical storm named Katrina.[1] The next day, the storm increased in intensity; moving westward, it swelled to hurricane force before making landfall on the southern coast of Florida between Miami and Fort Lauderdale on the evening of August 25. Katrina quickly passed over Florida, weakening somewhat before entering the Gulf of Mexico early the next morning. Over the next two days Katrina intensified and, on August 28, grew to become a Category 5 hurricane, ultimately reaching a speed of 175 miles per hour with hurricane force winds that extended for 90 miles and tropical winds as far as 200 miles from the storm's eye. At this point, Hurricane Katrina was 170 miles from the mouth of the Mississippi River and heading toward the Louisiana and Mississippi coast—New Orleans was likely to receive a direct hit. On its path to landfall over the next 18 hours, Katrina weakened and changed course, moving due North to bring it slightly eastward of New Orleans. It arrived near Buras, Louisiana, around 6 a.m. on August 29 as a Category 3 hurricane with maximum wind speed of 127 miles per hour,[2] and then made a second final landfall three hours later at the Louisiana–Mississippi border, slightly weaker at 120 mph. Although its winds diminished, Katrina did not shrink in size—in fact, it covered over 400 miles of the Gulf Coast with hurricane or tropical storm force winds.

New Orleans, 20 miles east of Katrina's eye as it passed, experienced a less intense storm but one that still hit the city for hours with hurricane-strength winds and heavy rainfall. Winds toppled trees, removed and mangled street signs, stripped windows off high-rise buildings, and tore off parts of the Superdome.[3] The eastern parts of the city experienced the worst of the storm, with some recorded gusts of over 115 miles per hour. As recounted by Anthony Wells in the book *Nine Lives:*[4]

> What happened was, the wind started up 'long about nightfall. Well, I been in wind before, shit. But this time, man, it got louder and louder till you didn't think it could get no worse. But it did, man. Stronger. Screaming like a thousand whistles. And we're up on the second floor, so the whole place is shaking…It went on and on. The lights was still on until, I don't know, sometime late, a lightening bolt hit the transformer over by the canal and that motherfucker lit up the whole sky. BOOM! Blue fire-red, purple, and green fire. The lights blinked on and off, and then, bam, everything went dark.

Wind and rain were only part of the problem, and actually the less disastrous of Katrina's instruments. Katrina produced storm surges that reached 24 to 28 feet near St. Louis Bay on the Mississippi Coast. Around New Orleans, the storm surge was less severe—15 to 19 feet in New Orleans East and 10 to 14 feet on the southern shore of Lake Pontchartrain—but it inundated New Orleans' levees. As the wall of water overflowed and eroded levees and stressed flood walls, breaches occurred and large sections of flood walls and levees gave way, causing massive flooding of the city. Part of the recipe for the levee failures included an extensive system of engineered waterways created to reduce the time and distance that ships had to travel between the Mississippi River and the Gulf of Mexico.[5] As Katrina produced the storm surge, the Intracoastal Waterway and Mississippi River Gulf Outlet (MRGO) funneled the rising waters into the Industrial Canal, a connector between the river and MRG0 system, adding to the water's height and pressure—pressure that proved far too much for the levees to contain.[6]

In less than four hours, multiple levees and floodwalls failed and water surged into the city.[7] In the early morning of August 29, the first flooding occurred as the storm surge, funneled by the shipping channels, overflowed and created breaches in the levees along the Intracoastal Waterway, flooding most of New Orleans East. This same surge soon entered the Industrial Canal, first pushing water over the canal's floodwalls and levees and then causing breaches in floodwalls on the canal's eastern and western sides. Along the eastern levee, the storm surge lifted and forced a 200-foot-long barge through the wall and into houses in the Lower Ninth Ward—helping to create a football field-sized gap.[8] By 8 a.m. water gushed into the Lower Ninth Ward and St. Bernard Parish, pushing houses off their foundations and causing extensive flooding that rose to the roof line of many homes.[9] Over the next two hours, levee breaches along two other canals flooded areas adjacent to Lake Pontchartrain and released the lake's swollen waters into New Orleans. First, floodwalls along the east side London Avenue Canal failed, flooding the Gentilly neighborhood. Next, several breaches along the 17th Street Canal opened up a massive flow of water into the Lakeview section of New Orleans that continued into other sections of central New Orleans and Metairie in neighboring Jefferson Parish. With these breaks in the walls that normally kept Lake Pontchartrain and Lake Borgne at bay, much of New Orleans became an extension of the lakes. Water rushed into the city over the next three days, flooding sections of the city that were below sea level and continuing until, on September 1, the flood waters reached the level of the lakes.[10]

Eighty percent of New Orleans flooded.[11] In large parts of the city— particularly its low-lying eastern and northern sections closest to the lakes—floodwaters were 8 feet or higher. Flood levels in a large swath of the Lower Ninth Ward exceeded 10 feet and much of neighboring St. Bernard Parish had flood levels from 6 to 10 feet with a few areas over 10 feet. Most of Gentilly and Lakeview reached maximum flooding above 8 feet, with the sections closest to Lake Pontchartrain under more than 10 feet of water. Large portions of central New Orleans that extended 2 1/2 miles east from the Jefferson Parish line almost to the Superdome and 5 1/2 miles south from below City Park into the prosperous Uptown neighborhood had 4 to 8 feet of flooding, as did several neighborhoods west of the Industrial Canal. Flooding in other more fortunate neigh- borhoods was less than 4 feet. The only areas that did not flood were the high ground along the Mississippi River, known as the "sliver by the river," and Algiers—the one section of New Orleans on the Mississippi River's west bank.

A HUMAN CATASTROPHE

The immediate aftermath embodied heart-wrenching tragedy, marked by a delayed and flawed government emergency response and heroic rescues of the city's stranded residents. Events riveted the nation's attention as they were reported in newspapers, on television, and in blogs and e-mails across the Internet.[12] Statistics are telling but only outline the extent of the human suffering. Katrina was the deadliest United States hurricane in over 75 years. There were at least 986 and perhaps as many as 1,440 deaths,[13] with many concentrated among New Orleans residents and the elderly. The average age of Katrina's victims was 69 and half of the deaths occurred among people 75 and older. New Orleans residents accounted for 73 percent of Katrina's death total—perhaps among the most tragic of the aftermath statistics, the city's black residents were far more likely to have died in the flooding than were whites. Death was an early and final consequence of the breaches and flooding. Almost two-thirds of Katrina-related deaths resulted from drowning and injury; a majority of these occurred at the sites of the worst breaches and flooding—the Lower Ninth Ward, Lakeview, Gentilly, and St. Bernard Parish.

On the morning of August 28, New Orleans Mayor Ray Nagin ordered a mandatory evacuation of the city soon after the National Hurricane Center had upgraded Katrina to a Category 5 storm. Despite this order, tens of thousands of people remained.[14] Some undoubtedly chose to ride out the storm to protect property, look after pets, or care for immobile family members, while others believed that the forecast was being overstated. Many residents[15] could not leave due to the lack of a car and the absence of an organized evacuation system.[16] Recognizing this problem, city government opened the Superdome as a refuge for those unable to evacuate.[17] By that evening, close to 20,000 people gathered there.[18] Others remained in their homes, becoming stranded and often threatened with drowning as the city flooded, with water levels rising over 8 feet and as high as 20 feet in some areas. Thousands had to be rescued via boat and helicopter by the Coast Guard, the National Guard, other emergency personnel, and private citizens. While this rescue effort moved people out of harm's way, its ad hoc nature caused many people to be dropped off on high ground, stranded without water, food, and shelter for many hours. They were left to find their own way to emergency shelter and medical care, which in some cases took days.[19] The experience of Harvey and Renee Miller, as recounted by McQuaid and Schleifstein in *Paths of Destruction,* reveals the disorder and ordeal faced by thousands of people during the evacuation:

> After being dropped off at the interstate overleaf, the Millers walked up to the medical station, then waited in line for a spot in the back of one of a line of pick-up trucks and vans waiting to take evacuees to the staging area about a mile west in Metairie. When they got there, the sight was horrific. Thousands of people were waiting, crowding around a handful of buses. There was no organization, no toilets, just chaos. Helicopters were landing every few minutes, disgorging more people into the mob. Every half hour or so, a few buses would leave and more would take their place. People would crush in around them, pushing to get on. The Millers tried repeatedly to get on, but when they reached the front they were turned away because of the dog (Monet). At one point, a National Guardsman offered to shoot Monet for them—humanely—if it would get them on a bus. They declined.

In the course of a night spent sleeping next to the interstate, the couple was separated, with Renee bused to Lafayette, Louisiana, and Harvey sent to Houston, Texas.[20]

Conditions in the Superdome worsened as more stranded people took refuge in the days after Katrina. Provisions for water, food, sanitation, medical care, and security were grossly insufficient. The wind had ripped off part of the roof, causing debris to fall inside. The loss of electric power meant sweltering heat, while low lighting was provided by a back-up generator.[21] After the storm, the National Guard supplied Meals Ready to Eat (MREs) but evacuees who had escaped disparate situations had to wait in long lines to obtain them.[22] Health conditions were particularly bad. The Superdome had originally been designated as a shelter for those with health problems; evacuees increasingly arrived with health problems created or exacerbated by the storm. Others came with chronic health conditions that worsened as they ran out of or lost their medications.[23]

On August 30, the city's Convention Center was opened to provide additional emergency shelter, creating another location that soon became overwhelmed by the challenges of overcrowding, inadequate food and water, crime, and sanitation. Moreover, the Convention Center was opened without provision for security and had not been recognized by FEMA as needing food and water.[24] The next day, Governor Blanco and FEMA announced plans to evacuate people from the Convention Center and Superdome. Long-delayed federal assistance to support the evacuation finally arrived on Thursday, September 1, three days after Katrina, with 300 National Guardsmen. Over the next five days, a large-scale, federally-mandated evacuation of New Orleans' remaining residents took place. More than 42,000 people were moved by bus or airplane to locations across the country. Houston was the largest recipient of Katrina evacuees, sheltering some 15,000 people in the Astrodome and another 11,000 in the Reliant Center.[25]

In all, Katrina forced the relocation of some one million people from the Gulf Coast. All of New Orleans was evacuated, with the exception of military and emergency personnel. The rapid evacuation under crisis conditions left many families separated for days or weeks, often unaware of their loved ones' location or survival. For some families separated by the evacuation and with their residences (and most possessions) destroyed by the storm, reunification was not possible for many months. Thousands of adults and children were reported missing after Katrina and Rita. It took over six months to resolve the 5,192 cases of missing and separated children from hurricanes Katrina and Rita,[26] with the final missing child, four-year-old Cortez Stewart, reunited with her family in Houston on March 16, 2006:

> During the storm, 4-year-old Cortez was with her godmother, Felicia Williams, and they became separated from Cortez's mother, Lisa Stewart, and her five other children. As families were evacuated out of New Orleans, Cortez and Felicia landed in Atlanta and Lisa and her family found themselves in Houston. For months both Lisa and Felicia were trying to locate each other but to no avail... until the National Center for Missing & Exploited Children... tracked down information about Felicia through her previous employer and then used computer databases at NCMEC to locate Felicia's family members in Georgia. With the active assistance of the U.S. Postal Inspection Service, NCMEC secured the proper address and phone number for Felicia in Atlanta and successfully resolved the case.[27]

ECONOMIC AND PHYSICAL LOSSES

Katrina and the flooding of New Orleans resulted in many lost lives, widespread dislocation, and much suffering. These human conditions cast a long shadow on the city as New Orleans' residents had to rebuild their lives and reunite their families, and in far too many cases grieve for lost family and friends, as they confronted the challenge of rebuilding their city. But as the immediate human suffering caught the nation's attention, the long-term problem of the city's rebuilding still loomed.

The scale of physical and economic losses faced by the city and its residents presented the greatest trial for New Orleans and raised confounding questions about if and how New Orleans could be rebuilt. While lives and families can be restarted in many locations, a city and its culture are necessarily tied to a place. Rebuilding a city requires reconstructing the physical place. For New Orleans, a city whose unique life and culture are entwined in a landscape, architecture, and history centered around its neighborhoods, rebuilding meant not only attending to the massive physical task but restoring the city's cultural and social life to those neighborhoods.

Katrina, Rita, and the resulting flooding produced physical destruction and economic losses on a scale far beyond past disasters. More than 90,000 square miles of the Gulf Coast were affected (an area larger than Great Britain). Over 300,000 homes were destroyed and another 200,000 were damaged. An early report from the Congressional Budget Office estimated economic losses to be from $70 billion to $130 billion. Other studies projected higher losses ranging from $150 to $200 billion.[28] Louisiana suffered the greatest losses among the Gulf Coast states and New Orleans clearly faced the most severe losses as the state's largest city, with 80 percent of its area flooded. Not only was New Orleans inundated with water, but the flooding remained, with water seeping into buildings, streets, and pipes for many weeks as the levee breaches were plugged and the city's essential pump stations were repaired and brought back on line to pump 225 billion gallons of water out of the newly formed "Lake New Orleans"—a project that was not completed until October 14.[29]

Widespread damage permeated every sector of the city—housing, schools, hospitals, businesses and commercial buildings, infrastructure, and of course, the troubled flood control system, as summarized in the Unified New Orleans Plan:[30]

Nearly 80% of the housing stock in the City was destroyed or severely damaged, the flood protection system was obliterated, the water and sewerage treatment and distribution systems were rendered useless, and electricity and communications were all but wiped out.

Hurricane Protection and Flood Control System

The first and most critical issue for New Orleans (and the region) was repairing and restoring the extensive system of levees, flood walls, pumps, and other infrastructure that protected the city from floods and hurricanes. The lack of a functioning system affected residents' and investors' confidence in returning to and rebuilding the city. Clearly, repairs were needed to remedy the extensive destruction and damage to the flood and storm protection system. This project alone involved replacing 25 miles of damaged walls and levees and repairing another 195 miles.[31] But Katrina also demonstrated that the prestorm system did not meet its promised function of protecting New Orleans from a Category 3 hurricane[32] so upgrades and improvements to the system would be needed at considerable time and cost. Finally, restoration of the region's coastal wetlands, which were eroding at a pace of 25 square miles per year and had lost another 217 miles of coastal lands due to the storms, was equally important.[33] These wetlands serve as protective buffers from storm surges—without restoration any surges from future storms were likely to become still larger and, once again, render the hurricane protection infrastructure ineffective. In late 2005, the cost to rebuild and correct failures in the existing flood control system to restore Category 3 storm protection was estimated at over $3 billion. To provide Category 5 hurricane protection and extensive restoration of coastal wetlands, a far greater investment was needed, on the order of $20 to $30 billion.[34]

City Infrastructure

All of the core infrastructure systems that support a contemporary city—water supply, sewers, electric and telecommunications distribution, and transportation—were heavily damaged by Katrina and the ensuing flood. Wind and fallen trees decimated overhead conduits for cable, telephone, and electric power. The force of the storm surge and extensive flooding by salt water from Lake Pontchartrain that sat for weeks in pipes, pumps, and other underground conduit systems led to extensive corrosion and damage to distribution systems for drinking water, sewage, and natural gas. The cost for short-term repairs to the sewer and water system alone was estimated at $1.9 billion, with long-term restoration over 25 years projected at $5.7 billion.[35] Streets, which were in poor repair before Katrina, were further corroded by the flooding.[36] Traffic signals and street signs also needed to be restored. Restoring public transportation—critical to a city in which 27 percent of residents did not own a car—posed another challenge. The Regional Transit Authority lost over half of the transportation vehicles used in New Orleans and faced widespread damage to its lines, facilities, and other equipment.[37]

Housing Damage

Perhaps the most severe damage and economic losses to New Orleans involved its housing stock.[38] Over 134,000 houses and apartments were destroyed or damaged by the hurricanes and flooding—71 percent of the city's occupied housing units. Almost three out of four homes in the city would need some level of repair or complete rebuilding. Substantial rebuilding would be needed for over 100,000 of these properties—the 85,889 classified by FEMA as having severe damage and another 21,500 with major damage.[39] An even greater level of housing damage was indicated by aerial surveys conducted immediately after Katrina by GCR, Inc., a New Orleans planning firm. GCR's survey revealed almost 109,000 housing units with over four feet of flooding, which is twice the two-foot flood level needed to meet FEMA's severely damaged definition. Counting only occupied units, as FEMA did, yields at least 98,111 severely damaged units—15 percent above the federal estimate. This number ignores the many homes affected by two to four feet of flooding. The Louisiana Recovery Authority estimated the statewide cost to rebuild and repair damaged housing and replace lost household items at $27 to $35 billion. The bulk of this investment was needed in New Orleans, where 60 percent of the housing units with major or severe damage were located.[40]

Many neighborhoods were in far worse condition than indicated by the citywide damage levels. GCR's survey identified 21 out of 71 neighborhoods where all or almost all (over 85 percent) of housing units had been flooded with over four feet of water. According to HUD's housing damage estimates for 14 districts within New Orleans, six had at least 75 percent of their housing units damaged, with the Lower Ninth Ward, New Orleans East, and Village de L'Est having the most widespread wreckage. In these locations, 84 percent, 90 percent and 91 percent, respectively, of occupied homes were damaged and at least two-thirds of these had severe or major damage.

Damage was more widespread among owner-occupied properties compared to rental properties and was far more common for African Americans than for whites, reflecting New Orleans' residential pattern in which black households were more likely to be in low-lying areas whereas white households were concentrated in higher elevation neighborhoods. The 134,000 damaged housing units were almost evenly divided between owner-occupied and rental units, but 76 percent of New Orleans' owner-occupied housing was damaged compared with 67 percent of rental apartments. Moreover, two-thirds of owner-occupied homes had severe damage, according to FEMA standards, compared to 51 percent of rental housing. Using the 2000 Census, GCR mapped flood levels by the race of property occupants and found that 76 percent of the population in areas that received at least four feet of flooding was African American while 39 percent was white. Despite this racial disparity, some higher-income, predominantly white areas had deep flooding, most notably Lakeview, as did some Asian (Village de L'Est) and mixed racial neighborhoods (Mid-City).

Schools, Health Care, and Public Facilities

As with all buildings in New Orleans, schools, medical facilities, and other public buildings were severely damaged after Katrina. Rebuilding them would be especially challenging and costly since many of these facilities were in poor condition before the storm due to many years of deferred maintenance.

Schools were in especially bad shape, with estimated capital costs of $500 million before Katrina.[41] Over 80 percent of the city's school buildings flooded and more than 50 percent of these facilities incurred major damages in excess of 25 percent of their replacement value. Another $600 to $800 million was needed to address storm and flood damage to school buildings and their contents.[42]

In the aftermath of Katrina and with the city's evacuation, all hospitals in New Orleans were closed and most health care providers left the city. This created the dual challenge of rebuilding facilities and bringing health care practitioners back to New Orleans.[43] Lengthy delays in reopening hospitals and health clinics, on top of other return-related obstacles, threatened to lead many of the city's doctors, nurses, and other practitioners to consider permanent relocation. The greatest medical rebuilding need was restoration of the city's largest medical complex, the Medical Center of Louisiana at New Orleans (MCLNO), which was closed with extensive damage. This included Charity Hospital—a major primary care provider for uninsured and Medicaid patients—and University Hospital—a major teaching hospital and the region's only trauma center.[44] Rebuilding and reopening this critical medical center was especially complex, given its size, cost, and the mix of pre-Katrina disrepair and storm damage.[45] Another seven acute care hospitals and ninety health clinics were also closed, with their ability to reopen entangled in a triad of uncertainty over the city's repopulation, the return of their staff, and funding for repairs.

In addition to restoring these critical education and health facilities, New Orleans risked losing many valued community amenities, including parks, libraries, and cultural and recreation facilities. These included 260 nonprofit cultural buildings that were destroyed or badly damaged, eight damaged public libraries whose contents were destroyed, and the landmark City Park that had $42 million in estimated damages.[46]

Business and Economy

New Orleans businesses incurred the same destruction of property and lost inventory as did residents, but their return and the restarting of the city's economy depended on restoring their market and their workforce, along with their physical assets. An early study estimated total business losses from Katrina at $21.1 billion for commercial structures and $36.4 billion for commercial equipment.[47] Although no city-level loss estimate for businesses was conducted, New Orleans companies undoubtedly represented a good share of these impacts given the city's size and extent of flooding. Whether caused by physical damage or other factors, many New Orleans firms and their associated jobs disappeared in the wake of Katrina. The city lost 105,000 jobs in the last quarter of 2005—about two out of every four jobs in pre-Katrina New Orleans.[48] Over 33 percent of the city's employers went out of business in the six months after Katrina, with the failure rate for the smallest enterprise even higher at 42 percent.[49] For employers seeking to reopen, recruiting workers and the lack of population and services were as significant obstacles as securing necessary rebuilding funds.[50]

New Orleans also needed to restore a market for business in order to rebuild the economy. For many small businesses, the market would depend on residents' return but also meant convincing tourists and conventions to return to New Orleans, since one in six city jobs relied on tourism.[51]

City Government

With the city literally in ruins, its future population uncertain, and the loss of economic activity, New Orleans immediately confronted a financial crisis as city revenues evaporated. Prior to Katrina, New Orleans collected $39 million per month in taxes and fees; in the eight weeks after the storm, it collected only $2 million—largely from a casino that was required to make fixed payments despite being closed.[52] New Orleans depended heavily on sales taxes and tourism for its revenue and there was little likelihood of this revenue rebounding in the foreseeable future. The city also had $2 billion in outstanding bonds;[53] failure to make payments on this debt—particularly $650 million in general obligation bonds—could result in bankruptcy. In light of this ominous fiscal situation, Mayor Nagin made drastic cuts in city government and laid off 50 percent of the city's workforce in October.[54] As New Orleans confronted the greatest threats to its existence and the Herculean efforts needed to rebuild, the city government's capacity to tackle these challenges and to restore a semblance of basic services was waning. One example of this dilemma was the City Planning Commission, which, according to the city charter, was responsible for preparing rebuilding plans after disasters.[55] With post-Katrina budget cuts, the commission's already overextended staff was reduced from twenty-nine employees to seven.[56]

REBUILDING NEIGHBORHOODS AND NEW ORLEANS

This litany of devastation illustrates the enormous rebuilding needs that confronted New Orleans as flood waters receded in September. With destroyed, flooded, and wind-damaged buildings across most of the city, downed trees and power lines, cars and boats strewn about, and a stinking brown film coating everything, the visual landscape raised doubts about how New Orleans would rebuild even before the hard facts and figures of rebuilding were known:

> The water had just receded when we came back... It's a dead zone. There are, of course, no people. Trees, branches and debris were everywhere. There was this

really bad smell, a mixture of sewerage and death is what it smelled like. It was a very foul strong smell. Everyone's homes were destroyed.... The only people you really saw were the National Guard who were either patrolling the area by air or by land or were at their posts.[57]

It was like a bomb went off... You could walk into anybody's house anywhere in the city...I drove around a bit...power lines were down. All the streets were profoundly littered with downed trees. There was a horrible brown film on everything... everything is dead, there was no sound, no birds...I was thinking about what we would do with our house and our city.[58]

The scale of the problem was overwhelming, requiring reconstruction on an unprecedented scale for any US city. How long would such a massive rebuilding take and where would a near bankrupt city and its residents and businesses find the billions in capital to finance such massive investments? How many residents would return after such a traumatic ordeal and with the city's continued vulnerability to flooding? Would businesses return and key institutions rebuild before knowing when and how many residents would return and which parts of the city would be rebuilt? If businesses, the city, and other institutions waited to rebuild, would residents return without schools for their children, health care services, and stores to supply vital goods and services? If too few people returned or only those with the financial means to risk rebuilding, would the city be left without the bars, social clubs, restaurants, musicians, parades, and festivals that were central to life in New Orleans?

These questions confronted New Orleans' leaders, and faced its residents, property owners, and business owners in September 2005. They are telling in two respects. First, coordinating the rebuilding of virtually an entire city is extremely challenging and critical. Rebuilding homes without schools, health care, and stores leaves residents without the services needed to stay in a location. If businesses return at a much faster pace than residents, they will lack workers and those dependent on local customers will not survive. Any failure to rebuild critical infrastructure precludes the return of most residents, businesses, and nonprofit organizations. To bring back the jobs, people, infrastructure, services, and amenities required to restore a vibrant city, New Orleans would need to rebuild all these sectors.

Second, restoring neighborhoods would be central to rebuilding New Orleans. Cities are built around neighborhoods—the places where people not only live but weave the fabric of social connections and engage in routines of daily life. Nowhere is this truer than in New Orleans where multiple generations of extended families often lived in the same neighborhood and social and cultural life revolved around churches, social clubs, and businesses inlaid among densely packed low-rise housing. This strong attachment to place among New Orleans residents is shown by Chamlee-Wright and Storr in their study of Ninth Ward residents and the factors that nurtured this connection:

> The distinct sense of place interview subjects describe is not one particular attribute, but a combination of interlocking elements, including thickly woven social networks based on friends, family, neighbors and church membership, particular foods and music perceived to be "distinctly New Orleans," Second Line funeral processions, and a climate hospitable to outdoor social gatherings ranging from casual conversations on the porch to neighborhood barbeques and block parties.[59]

A city's postdisaster recovery can be viewed as occurring on three levels: (1) individual household and enterprise actions to return and rebuild; (2) restoring neighborhoods as residential and social centers; and (3) city-wide reconstruction of infrastructure systems, restoration of public services, and recovery of the economic base. Public policies focus on the first and third levels: relief and rebuilding aid to individuals and businesses; and large investments to restore public infrastructure and facilities. However, the intermediate neighborhood scale is quite important to the rebuilding process. In fact, the most immediate environment influences individual rebuilding decisions. Moreover, a neighborhood's size and cohesion make it a feasible basis for coordinating rebuilding investments related to core public services such as schools, libraries, parks, health and social services, and the like. Finally, community-based organizations that focus on neighborhood issues and improvements are a potential source of capacity and resources to accelerate recovery. The focus of this book is on New Orleans' rebuilding at this intermediate neighborhood scale and how grassroots community-based organizations approached and contributed to this aspect of the city's recovery.

RELATIONSHIP TO EXISTING RESEARCH

Extensive research exists on post-Katrina New Orleans, including considerable investigation of the recovery process.[60] This recovery research covers a range of topics, though with limited work that provides a detailed picture of rebuilding at the neighborhood level, and it examines the contributions of grassroots organizations to the recovery process. Several authors have examined New Orleans' recovery planning process, including the detailed account by Olshansky and Johnson in *Clear as Mud* and analyses of the shortfalls in the process.[61] Another body of work concerns the challenges and problems in federal recovery programs and in the intergovernmental coordination of recovery aid.[62] There is also considerable research on recovery progress and difficulties and innovations in particular sectors such as education, health care, criminal justice, housing, and the like, including how well New Orleans' recovery process has addressed long-standing failures and racial and economic inequities.[63] Other studies address repopulation citywide and in specific neighborhoods and identify and analyze the factors that influenced differential repopulation across groups and geographies, including much lower repopulation rates for the city's black residents.[64]

Research on neighborhood-scale rebuilding has accompanied studies on citywide recovery and intergovernmental processes. Scholars have typically focused on an individual neighborhood, often addressing a specific aspect of recovery or examining how pre-Katrina racial and economic disparities impacted recovery progress.[65] In her article on recovery through early 2008 in the black middle-class neighborhood of Pontchartrain Park, Gafford concluded that these households encountered similar financial barriers to rebuilding as those in low-income neighborhoods, and linked this situation to a legacy of racial discrimination and inequality.[66] Bates and Green detailed how racial and neighborhood disparities in flood damage, insurance levels, property assessment practices, and the administration of homeowner recovery aid impacted housing rebuilding in the Lower Ninth Ward.[67] Another study examined how differences in the social resources provided through personal networks impacted neighborhood recovery in two heavily flooded New Orleans neighborhoods—the poor Lower Ninth Ward and affluent Lakeview.[68] It was found that Lower Ninth Ward residents were far less likely than Lakeview residents to receive assistance from their personal networks just prior to Katrina, during their displacement, and during recovery efforts.[69] The large-scale displacement among the poorer Lower Ninth Word residents eroded their personal networks and thus the network's capacity to serve as a recovery resource. In the epilogue to his study of struggles over identity, settlement, and development during the Tremé neighborhood's 300-year history, Crutcher discussed early recovery plans, decisions, and projects that affected the neighborhood evolution after Katrina.[70]

Several researchers have examined the relatively fast recovery within New Orleans' Vietnamese community. Leong and her coauthors linked rebuilding progress to social and cultural resources from the community's religious faith and history of repeated relocation and recovery that dates back to North Vietnam in the 1950s.[71] Chamlee-Wright explained how the

Vietnamese Catholic church fostered community rebuilding through the strengthening of ethnic, religious, and community bonds and its capacity for exercising communitywide coordination and political action.[72] Tang examined the interracial relations and areas of political solidarity between the Vietnamese community and black population in New Orleans East neighborhoods.[73]

This book contributes to this post-Katrina research by deepening understanding of the grassroots rebuilding process at the neighborhood scale. Expanding upon prior studies, it documents the rebuilding initiatives undertaken by community-based organizations across multiple neighborhoods and examines what these grassroots efforts contributed to the recovery of individual neighborhoods. Through detailed narratives of how community activists and resident-based organizations undertook neighborhood recovery, it reveals different agendas and approaches undertaken across neighborhoods along with the challenges incurred and key capacities and resources that contributed to rebuilding progress.

By examining the grassroots rebuilding process and its contribution to neighborhood-scale recovery, this work also informs the larger field of postdisaster recovery planning, policy, and implementation. Considerable research has been devoted to characterizing types of disasters, defining and understanding the overall recovery process, and informing how to plan and undertake recovery more effectively, including ways to mitigate future risks.[74] Researchers and recovery agencies are increasingly attentive to the role that community-based initiatives and organizations can play in the recovery process. Picou, Brunsma, and Overfelt emphasized that community mutual aid represents a "therapeutic process" that can counteract the corrosive effects of disasters on individuals and communities.[75] Other researchers have pointed to how community-based capacity to assist in rebuilding is an asset to help restore community livelihood systems and to improve the effectiveness and impact of recovery efforts.[76] The neighborhood cases presented in the ensuing chapters provide empirical evidence of the tangible contributions made by grassroots efforts to recovery and identify factors that serve to strengthen or inhibit grassroots capacity and outcomes.

Given the focus on "grassroots" recovery efforts at the neighborhood scale and considerable attention paid to recovery planning, it is important to clarify the meaning of these key terms as used in the balance of the book. Grassroots recovery (or rebuilding) refers to activities and initiatives undertaken by resident-based organizations focused on rebuilding a defined neighborhood. Grassroots organizations include established neighborhood associations, other place-based volunteer groups with a specific issue or activity focus, place-based religious congregations, and staffed organizations focused on improving a specific neighborhood with resident-based governance.[77] It also includes new organizations within these categories formed after Katrina to address neighborhood place-based recovery. Although primarily resident-based, grassroots efforts can also incorporate other neighborhood parties such as local businesses, non-residential property owners, and other nonprofit organizations. Neighborhood refers to a residential subsection of a city in which people live, form economic, cultural, and social relationships, and experience a sense of coherence or identity.[78] The New Orleans City Planning Department initially designated 68 neighborhoods and boundaries in 1980, which were later increased to 76.[79] The city's boundaries corresponded to neighborhood definitions held by many community-based organizations, but in some cases views on a neighborhood's identity, boundaries, and name varied among organizations working within the city-defined neighborhood. The neighborhood boundaries used in this book correspond to the New Orleans City Planning Department definitions; instances in which neighborhood definitions varied or were contested are discussed in individual narratives. Although the term "planning" has many meanings, and different traditions and approaches abound within the professional planning field,[80] when used in reference to neighborhood-level plans undertaken by or in conjunction with community residents planning is defined as a process that involves local residents and other stakeholders in articulating shared goals, conditions, and outcomes for their neighborhood and defining specific investments, projects, activities and other actions to be undertaken in pursuit of those goals. The desired changes and actions under a plan need not be limited to the physical and built environment; they can address social and cultural aspects, economic and human capital development, political organization and power, health and safety and other conditions that affect residents' quality of life.

OVERVIEW OF BOOK CHAPTERS

This book is about the rebuilding of New Orleans at the neighborhood level and the overall role of neighborhoods and community-based capacity in rebuilding cities after major disasters. This exploration recounts the process of grassroots rebuilding in six neighborhoods, drawing implications and lessons from their experiences. The six neighborhood narratives focus on descriptions of perspectives, activities, and accomplishments of grassroots neighborhood organizations and assessments of recovery outcomes roughly five years after Katrina. In several neighborhoods, major projects or initiatives that have shaped the area's recovery are included in the rebuilding narrative. Since neighborhood rebuilding occurred in the context of official citywide, state, and federal disaster recovery actions, chapter 2 summarizes how the official top-down process unfolded, and how it influenced events at the neighborhood level. Chapters 3 and 4 provide detailed narratives on rebuilding efforts in Broadmoor and Village de L'Est, respectively, which were characterized by early and deliberate grassroots efforts to rebuild on a community-wide scale and to create community-based capacity to implement a recovery agenda. Chapter 5 contrasts different experiences—both process and outcomes—across four neighborhoods in a central section of New Orleans in order to provide a more complete picture of variations in neighborhood recovery and critical factors that influenced its nature and extent. In the concluding chapter, the contributions of grassroots initiatives to citywide recovery and the interrelationships between neighborhood and citywide rebuilding are discussed; concluding thoughts are offered. The book closes with several recommendations for addressing shortfalls in federal policies on community recovery from massive scale disasters.

CHAPTER 2

❦

Whither New Orleans?

After Katrina passed and stranded residents were evacuated, the city began to tackle the immediate need to repair the many breaches to its levees and flood walls, find and recover hundreds of stranded bodies, and begin the cleanup of omnipresent storm and flood debris.[1] As early efforts focused on these critical tasks, the larger question of how and if New Orleans would rebuild was backstage, overshadowed by the immediate relief and repair work and held at bay by the incredible scale of the undertaking. It soon emerged to occupy the center stage for almost two years as the city's elected leaders and residents struggled to provide the official answer: a formal recovery plan for New Orleans. If the city's elected leaders, residents, businesses, and institutions were the ultimate decision makers on New Orleans' rebuilding process, their decisions were shaped by policies, rules, and resources controlled by others—how insurance companies settled claims, what minimal elevation standards the Federal Emergency Management Agency (FEMA) set to qualify for flood insurance, the amount and type of aid Congress would provide to rebuild, and the myriad rules imposed and decisions made by federal and state officials and their consultants on exactly how to allocate the federal rebuilding dollars. New Orleans' rebuilding emerged from the combined results of an official "top down" process that set the rules and guideposts and provided much of the funds needed to accomplish it, and "bottom-up" decisions by individuals, entrepreneurs, and organizations to rebuild in specific places and ways. The top-down process began swiftly with actions by city leaders to quickly craft a rebuilding plan and gain federal implementation funding but soon became engulfed in conflicts, mistrust, policies, and bureaucratic rules and processes that slowed the creation of a formal recovery plan as well as the flow of rebuilding funds. It was around and in response to this top-down system that the grassroots neighborhood rebuilding efforts of New Orleans' citizens took shape.

With such widespread destruction and after a complete evacuation of the city, the New Orleans public and its leaders confronted three central questions:

> Would people and businesses return to the city, and if so, then which parts of the city would or should be rebuilt?
> Where would the funds for rebuilding come from and what assistance would the federal government provide?
> What should be different in a rebuilt New Orleans and how could the rebuilding address some of the city's past social, political, economic, and environmental problems?

The first two questions concerned the fundamental viability and form of a rebuilt New Orleans—who would populate it, where rebuilding would occur, and how households, businesses, and city government would secure the required investment. The third question spoke to the possibilities for a new New Orleans: using the rebuilding process to change many of the city's flawed systems and institutions, reverse its trajectory of decline, and reverse its historic race-based economic inequality.

New Orleans began to tackle these questions when the very future of the city was in question. With the scale of destruction, the continued hurricane and flood risks, and questions about the cost and funding to rebuild, the weeks and months after Katrina were marked by uncertainty about whether enough people would return to have a viable city anywhere near the pre-storm scale. There were also doubts about the economic viability of the city, which rested so heavily on tourism. Entwined with the return of people and tourism was the fiscal fate of the city government—would it have the revenues to provide services, could it afford to keep servicing the entire city, and how would city service delivery decisions affect repopulation? President Bush tried to assuage these fears when he pledged federal funds to help rebuild the city and the Gulf Coast region, but a federal promise was not very reassuring given the levee failures and abysmal relief and emergency response after the storm. If these concerns were not daunting enough, the city's leaders and residents also had to put their own lives back together while they considered how their city might be rebuilt. Needless to say, New Orleans was in a state of considerable anxiety and stress as it contemplated how to rebuild.

PLANNING, PLANNING, AND MORE PLANNING

Creating a recovery plan was a logical way to prepare for rebuilding. [2] The scale of damage and price to rebuild dictated that every part of the city could not rebuild at the same time. Every water and sewer line; every road, bridge and streetcar line; every school, library, police station and firehouse; and every park and playground could not be rebuilt simultaneously. The city was unlikely to have sufficient funds; even if it did, the time needed to assess damage, determine what to repair and what to rebuild, engineer and design the improvements, and complete construction indicated that the work needed to occur in phases. In the fall of 2005, it seemed likely that the extent and pace of rebuilding would differ across the city and, thus, where and when to rebuild public facilities would vary by neighborhood. There was also the question of how to rebuild a better city—one with less risk of future flooding, better schools and services for its population, expanded and more equitable economic opportunities for its residents, and more responsive and accountable public and civic institutions. Another matter was how to assist the full range of people, institutions and enterprises displaced by the storm—renters and property owners, people of all races, those with more or less damage to their property and those of varied incomes and resources—to return to New Orleans if they so wished. A rebuilding plan provided a way to sort out these questions: to set priorities for public investment, define policies and actions that promised pathways to a better city, and find the ways and means to facilitate fairness in the opportunity to return and rebuild one's life.

A second reason for a plan was to encourage private action and investment to rebuild. Thousands upon thousands of families, businesses, and organizations faced a decision about whether to return to New Orleans and invest in rebuilding. A plan promised to create the confidence to return and rebuild by detailing what actions and investments the government and other critical parties would take and increase the prospects for carrying out these actions by creating a plan that was endorsed by New Orleans citizens, key institutions, and elected officials.

The last, and perhaps most urgent, reason for a recovery plan was to secure federal assistance. If the size and contour of federal assistance was uncertain in the early fall months of 2005, there was no doubt that a plan would be required to gain this assistance. With the scale of rebuilding that New Orleans faced, the city was likely to need special federal aid beyond that authorized under standard disaster recovery programs. With such exceptional assistance, federal bureaucracies were unlikely to dispense large amounts of public funds without a plan for how the funds would be spent (especially to a city and state with a history of government corruption). The precedent for a plan was evident in recent federal responses to disasters— the federal disaster funds appropriated for New York after the September 11th attack were predicated on the state's submission of an Action Plan.[3]

With these compelling reasons to craft a city rebuilding plan, New Orleans' leaders quickly took steps toward creating this plan. Soon after the storm, business leaders and economic development agencies set up temporary offices near the state capitol in Baton Rouge and initiated discussions on reopening the French Quarter in 90 days and how to initiate rebuilding plans.[4] Mayor Nagin met with a delegation of these business leaders and others in Dallas on September 10 to discuss rebuilding and pledged to appoint a body to plan the city's recovery.[5] On September 30, the mayor formally announced the formation of the 17-member Bring New Orleans Back (BNOB) Commission and charged it with creating a rebuilding plan for the city.[6] Earlier in September, the City Council had announced its intention to appoint an Advisory Committee on Hurricane Recovery, but this committee was short-lived and never developed any proposals.[7]

Plan A: The Bring New Orleans Back Commission

The Bring New Orleans Back Commission was the first attempt to craft a rebuilding plan. The commission consisted of 17 members appointed by Mayor Nagin with diverse backgrounds and expertise including a city councilor, business people, academics, religious leaders, and others. Mayor Nagin was careful to appoint a racially balanced commission, particularly in light of early comments made by some local business people that Katrina provided an opportunity to rebuild without so many poor people.[8] At its first meeting on October 10, 2005, the commission formed seven committees to conduct research on and prepare recommendations in the following areas: Education, Infrastructure, Economic Development, Health and Social Services, Culture, Urban Planning/Land-Use[9] and Administration/Government Effectiveness. Each committee was led by a commission member and included volunteers with expertise in the subject area. Many committees were also supported with research assistance from universities and consultants.[10] Acting with all due haste, the BNOB committees completed their initial work in three months and issued final reports in a series of public presentations from January 11 to January 20, 2006. The fast pace of the commission's work and the fact that many residents and business owners had not yet returned to the city and, if back, were preoccupied with rebuilding their lives and homes, meant that the BNOB's deliberations were not based on the participation and views of many ordinary citizens, associations, and businesses. Instead, they were dominated by a small group of government, business, and civic leaders working with professional planners, consultants, and experts.[11] This approach was designed to move quickly to show Washington that the city had a plan to rebuild and thus accelerate the provision of federal rebuilding dollars, with more detailed and participatory planning to come later.[12] However, the role of white business leaders in the commission, its expert-driven process, and the lack of public education and participation fostered considerable distrust of its motivations and recommendations.

While the BNOB Commission's seven committees addressed the city's pre-Katrina conditions and rebuilding needs across a wide range of issues and presented many valuable ideas and recommendations, the main action and controversy revolved around the Urban Planning Committee, chaired by Joe Canizaro, a real estate developer with strong ties to the Bush White House. With privately donated funds, the Urban Planning Committee hired the planning firm Wallace Roberts Todd (WRT) and commissioned the Urban Land Institute (ULI) to assist with preparing its recommendations.[13] ULI is a membership-based nonprofit organization that studies and conducts education on land-use and real estate matters and is well known for sending expert panels to visit cities and prepare recommendations typically around urban revitalization and redevelopment matters. ULI sent a panel of 50 experts to visit New Orleans from November 12–18, 2005, during which time they toured the city, interviewed 300 residents, and held a public meeting. The expert panel issued its preliminary report on November 18 and a final version in December.[14] This report made many recommendations across the seven areas covered by the BNOB committees, but its main proposals were: creating a new Crescent City Rebuilding Corporation[15] to receive federal funds and oversee rebuilding; establishing a financial oversight board for the city; implementing a diversified economic development strategy; using a regional approach to address transportation, environmental issues and economic development needs; using a strategic and phased approach to rebuild the city; and providing fair compensation to those who could not rebuild. The recommendation for phased rebuilding suggested that different parts of the city had different degrees of damage and, thus, would rebuild at different paces and with varied needs for public investment to reconfigure and reuse properties.[16] The exact language from the December report summary was:

> Rebuilding should happen in a strategic manner, encouraging those areas that
> sustained minimal damage to begin rebuilding immediately and those areas that

have more extensive damage to evaluate the feasibility for reinvestment and proceed in a manner that will ensure the health and safety of the residents of each neighborhood and proceed expeditiously.[17]

Although the ULI report did not propose reducing the size or footprint of the city, its recommendations sparked concern about plans to shrink the city and prompted considerable public discussion about reducing New Orleans' size to limit exposure to the risks from massive flooding and efficiently provide services needed for the city to return.[18] The view that some means were needed to decide which areas of the city would come back and would have enough population to warrant investment in new facilities and public services was clearly at the forefront of the Urban Planning Committee's thinking. To address this perceived need, Joe Canizaro, Chair of the BNOB Commission City Planning Committee, proposed letting people return and rebuild in all parts of the city and then reassessing which areas were viable. "At the end of three years, we'll see who is there," Canizaro said to *The Times–Picayune*, "And if a neighborhood is not developing adequately to support the services it needs to support it, we'll try to shrink it then."[19] However, not everyone agreed with this notion. Several city councilors were concerned about their neighborhoods' ability to return and rebuild, and the Katrina Survivors Association, organized by the community organizing group ACORN to advocate for those displaced by Katrina, demanded the right to return for all of the city's dislocated residents.[20]

On January 11, 2006, the Urban Planning Committee presented its report to a large audience at the downtown Sheraton Hotel. Relying on many ideas from the ULI report, the committee proposed a four-part "Citywide Framework for Reconstruction" that addressed: (1) flood and stormwater protection; (2) transit and transportation; (3) parks and open space; and (4) neighborhood rebuilding. The flood and stormwater plan proposed consolidating local levee boards into a single body, independent oversight of the Army Corps of Engineers, closing the MRGO, and expanding internal city stormwater retention and management. A transit plan proposed creating a new regional light rail system to connect the city to employment centers and the airport and, ultimately, to extend to Baton Rouge. In the parks and open space section, the committee called for creating parks in every neighborhood and using parks to retain and manage stormwater—an idea proposed earlier in the ULI report. A map was included (see Figure 2.1) with large dotted green circles in flooded parts of the city designated as "Potential Areas for Future Parkland" to represent this idea. The neighborhood rebuilding plan recommended building more temporary housing to

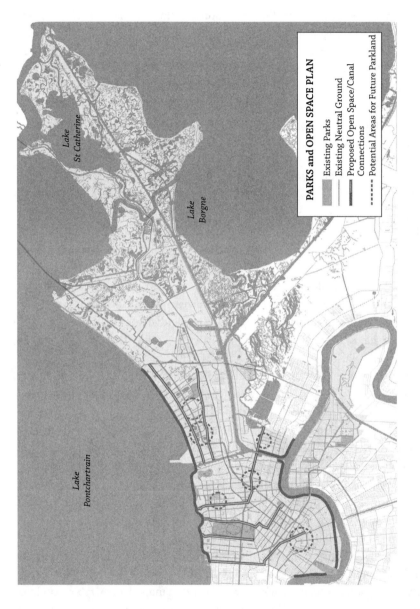

Figure 2.1.
Parks and open space map from Bring New Orleans Back (BNOB) Commission's Urban Planning Committee report
Source: Image Courtesy of WRT.

allow displaced residents to return and creating neighborhood planning teams to prepare more detailed rebuilding plans for each of the city's 13 planning districts by May 2006. It also proposed consolidating neighborhoods with insufficient population to ensure "equitable and efficient service delivery." Further, it divided the city into two areas: (1) Immediate Opportunity Areas that suffered little or no flooding and in which rebuilding and development would be accelerated; and (2) Neighborhood Planning Areas that were deeply flooded and had heavily damaged buildings, for which a neighborhood planning process would be conducted to determine the future of each neighborhood, including identifying which residents planned to return and determining that the "population needed to support facilities and services" would come back. The report suggested that a neighborhood would need to show that at least 50 percent of its former residents would return to demonstrate its viability for rebuilding.[21] It also recommended creating a Crescent City Recovery Corporation with a ten-year life span to receive federal recovery funds, issue bonds to raise additional funds, acquire and receive property, and implement redevelopment plans. Most controversially, the committee called for a moratorium on issuing new building permits in heavily flooded and damaged areas until FEMA issued new required Base Flood Elevations,[22] neighborhood plans were completed, and utilities and public services were available.

Strong opposition greeted the Urban Planning Committee proposals from the minute of their release. The city council announced its opposition to the plan just before its formal release. A large audience of close to 1,200 people attended the report's release on January 11 with many voicing opposition to the building moratorium and the idea that every resident would not have the right to return to their original neighborhood.[23] Press coverage fueled further opposition. The Times–Picayune published a map summarizing the plan and described it as calling for "vast reworking of the city's neighborhoods and housing patterns" and included large solid green dots for areas that the committee had indicated as "potential areas for future parkland" and labeled them "Approximate areas of expected to become [sic] parks and greenspace."[24] This map created the impression that the BNOB Commission was proposing that large parts of flooded neighborhoods would be converted to green space and thus that rebuilding would not be allowed. As public opposition to the Urban Planning Committee proposals grew, some city councilors advocated rebuilding the entire city and Mayor Nagin expressed his opposition to a building moratorium.[25]

Neighborhood and civil rights organizations contested the BNOB Commission proposals, contributing to the ultimate abandonment of its rebuilding plan. Opposition began well before release of the January report, when neighborhood residents organized protests at the commission's public hearings.[26] After January 11, protests asserting the right of all residents to return and rebuild in their own neighborhoods took place in several neighborhoods, including a march through the Lower Ninth Ward on Martin Luther King Day.[27] Civil rights groups, including the NAACP, the Urban League, and the African American Leadership Project, were particularly active in opposing the BNOB plan and advocating for no reduction in the city's footprint and the right of all residents to fully participate in the city's recovery.[28] Since poor and black residents were concentrated in the heavily flooded Neighborhood Planning Areas for which rebuilding would be delayed and subject to future planning, the BNOB plan raised vital civil rights issues: that recovery for poor and black neighborhoods would be slower and would receive less resources than other parts of New Orleans, or that it might not happen at all. To address these justice concerns, the African American Leadership Project (AALP), a network of African American organizations and leaders formed in 2002–2003, developed the Citizen's Bill of Rights to help ensure that displaced low-income and African American residents would be included in the city's rebuilding, and with an emphasis on reducing past inequities. AALP's efforts, which began in fall 2005, led to the adoption of the Neighborhood Rebuilding Equity Ordinance by the City Council and Mayor Nagin in April 2006. This new law established as city policy the timely inclusion of all neighborhoods in the city's rebuilding, delivery of city resources based on need, a commitment not to shrink the city's size or population, and the equitable awarding of rebuilding contracts and jobs to include city residents, locally based firms, minority- and women-owned enterprises and nonprofit and community development organizations.[29]

Beyond local political opposition, the failure of the BNOB Commission rebuilding plan was ensured when two federal actions that were cornerstones of the plan did not materialize. New Orleans anticipated that FEMA would provide funding for 13 neighborhood plans and their integration into a final citywide rebuilding plan. City officials believed they had a commitment of FEMA funding to complete such a plan, which was consistent with FEMA's recent policy to support local vision and planning as part of the recovery process.[30] By mid-March, however, it became clear that FEMA would not provide funding for the neighborhood planning process.[31] A second pillar of the BNOB plan was the creation of a federal rebuilding authority to purchase and assemble properties from owners who did not want to rebuild and convey them to developers for rebuilding. This federal agency, proposed by Louisiana Congressman Richard Baker, was expected to provide the legal basis and funding to assemble property for redevelopment in heavily damaged areas anticipated in the BNOB Commission plan and to be implemented through the proposed Crescent City Recovery Corporation. By early February, the Bush Administration expressed its opposition to Baker's proposal and the prospects for this rebuilding tool died.[32] In spring 2006, New Orleans lacked a rebuilding plan that could gain local popular and political support and faced uncertainty about the size and nature of any federal rebuilding aid that it would receive. Mayor Nagin's attempt to quickly create a framework plan that would provide a basis for direct federal aid and establish a roadmap for rebuilding had failed.[33]

Within the BNOB Commission, New Orleans' political, business, and civic leaders confronted some of the perplexing challenges facing the city in the months after Katrina. They sought to secure progress in rebuilding the city while addressing concerns about future flood risks and while seeking a process to coordinate investment in services and facilities to rebuild strong neighborhoods. Outside urban planning, other committees developed innovative proposals to reform key city systems.[34] Since these ideas and plans were not developed through dialogue with local residents, businesses, and organizations that would make rebuilding decisions, they were often poorly communicated and failed to gain public and political support. The lack of dialogue also led the BNOB leadership and the planners, developers, and engineers who advised them to misread and greatly underestimate the commitment to rebuild among the city's residents and business owners. It was this commitment that later fueled rebuilding in many neighborhoods that BNOB Urban Planning Committee viewed as having quite uncertain futures.

Despite its failures, the BNOB Commission had a lasting legacy on the city's rebuilding. The notion that neighborhoods would have to prove their viability and the belief, based on the green dot map, that if a neighborhood failed to do so it would become green space generated a groundswell of grassroots opposition and initiatives that prompted many neighborhoods to create their own rebuilding plans and take the recovery into their own hands. This proved to be one of the strongest and most consequential forms of grassroots protests of the BNOB Commission's vision of New Orleans' rebuilding process.

Plan B: The Lambert Plan

The failure of the BNOB process did not end efforts to create a rebuilding plan but did shift the initiative to the New Orleans City Council. City council members preferred a planning process to support rebuilding efforts for all New Orleans neighborhoods in contrast to the BNOB Commission's concern for efficient service delivery and protecting returning residents from future flood risk. In December 2005, the council passed a resolution to initiate a neighborhood planning process; by February it had found $3 million in unused federal Community Development Block Grant dollars to fund the project. The council contracted with two firms, Lambert Advisory and SHEDO LLC, to work with 49 of the city's 73 neighborhoods that had incurred at least two feet of flooding to prepare their own rebuilding plans. Several neighborhoods already had begun crafting their own rebuilding plans and the city council effort, officially the New Orleans Neighborhood Rebuilding Plan but better known as the Lambert Plan, ensured that each flooded neighborhood had assistance in preparing its own plan and provided citywide coherence to the budding grassroots planning efforts. A second goal was to prepare a list of priority projects for federal and other recovery funds.[35]

After selecting several other firms to assist them, the Lambert team worked with neighborhood residents and organizations across New Orleans from April to September 2006 to prepare the 49 neighborhood scale plans and combine them into an overall plan that included citywide policy proposals to address common priorities and issues across neighborhoods. One focus of the Lambert process was to engage local residents in defining the goals and priority rebuilding projects for their neighborhoods. Neighborhood planning typically entailed three phases, with a local public meeting held during each phase. In the first phase, residents reviewed information on current neighborhood conditions; in the second phase, residents reviewed planning concepts and set short- and long-term neighborhood goals; and in the third phase, they chose specific projects to advance their goals and classified them as critical early action, medium-term, and long-term projects.[36] Additional meetings were held in Atlanta, Baton Rouge, and Houston to gain input from displaced residents still living in those cities.[37] By focusing on residents' ideas and goals for their own neighborhoods, the Lambert Plan provided an important antidote to the professional and top-down BNOB process and helped nurture resident trust in the planning process and optimism about the potential to rebuild.

The final New Orleans Neighborhood Rebuilding Plan was released on September 23, 2006, almost 13 months after Katrina hit. It included individual plans for 46 neighborhoods and a citywide summary that proposed several policies to support rebuilding across neighborhoods. Key proposed policies included:[38] (1) implementation of a lot-next-door program to allow property owners the first right to buy adjacent lots that the government obtained when an owner decided not to rebuild; (2) allowing seniors to apply home rebuilding funds to new multi-unit condominium buildings in lieu of rebuilding their prior single-family home; (3) use of incentives and federal Community Development Block Grant (CDBG) funds to rebuild neighborhood retail centers; (4) targeting of certain funds for reinvestment in the city's poorest neighborhoods; (5) accelerated efforts at demolition and debris removal to clean up still widespread storm and flood rubble; and (6) expanded code enforcement and demolition to control and remove blighted properties. The estimated cost for all projects included in the 46 neighborhood plans was $4.4 billion, with $2.5 billion alone for the critical early action projects.[39] Since this plan did not address citywide rebuilding needs in several areas, such as infrastructure and public schools, $4.4 billion undoubtedly underestimated the full costs to rebuild neighborhoods. And by not addressing these key facilities, residents did not confront how to either set rebuilding priorities or coordinate efforts to address the set of investments needed to rebuild their neighborhoods.

The New Orleans City Council approved the New Orleans Neighborhood Rebuilding Plan on October 27, 2006, but then had to amend it the following week since the original version omitted a plan for the Broadmoor neighborhood, prepared separately under the leadership of the Broadmoor Improvement Association. Its next stop was the Louisiana Recovery Authority (LRA), the state agency established in September 2005 to receive federal assistance and oversee rebuilding efforts statewide, which approved the plan on November 6, 2006.

The LRA's action, however, was purely ceremonial since the Lambert Plan had been superseded by the announcement on July 5, 2006, that a new rebuilding plan would be completed under a process jointly agreed to by Mayor Nagin, the City Council, and the LRA.[40] This new plan was named the Unified New Orleans Plan for its status as the single citywide rebuilding plan that would be endorsed by all the governmental bodies needed to secure federal recovery funds.

Although the Lambert Plan did not become the official city rebuilding plan, it generated momentum for grassroots participatory planning, and many proposals developed under the Lambert process found their way into the final UNOP. In some neighborhoods, such as Mid-City (see chapter 5), the Lambert process provided the structure for residents' creation of a local rebuilding plan that had a life of its own.

Plan C: The Unified New Orleans Plan

The basis for the Unified New Orleans Plan (UNOP) emerged from four months of negotiations to merge the BNOB Commission and Lambert Planning processes and secure funding for an expanded and more inclusive planning process.[41] A catalyst for these negotiations was the Rockefeller

Foundation, which agreed to provide $3.5 million to fund the planning effort.[42] The Louisiana Recovery Authority also had a strong interest in seeing a single plan emerge to provide a blueprint for channeling federal recovery dollars to New Orleans. Representatives of the LRA, Rockefeller Foundation, Greater New Orleans Foundation, City Planning Commission, and parties in the BNOB and Lambert efforts met over several months to work out a structure and process for conducting a unified planning process to be funded largely by the Rockefeller Foundation. Before a final agreement was worked out, Requests for Qualifications were issued in June 2006 to select consultant teams to assist with a citywide plan and to help prepare neighborhood and district plans.[43] Preliminary agreement was reached on a nine-person body, the Community Support Organization (CSO), to oversee the planning process; it would include one member appointed by Mayor Nagin, one appointed by the city council, a third by the city planning commission, a fourth by the Greater New Orleans Foundation, and five citizens representing each of the five city council districts. A press release, issued on July 5, 2006, announced that the LRA, mayor, and city council had agreed to the main points of the UNOP process. Progress continued as consultant teams were selected in mid-July and the first two planning meetings occurred on July 30 and August 1, but not without further conflict and confusion. Paul Lambert resisted efforts to incorporate his process into UNOP, including taking out an ad in *The Times–Picayune* on August 3 in which he stated that the UNOP plan should avoid a duplication of work by focusing on those parts of the city not covered by the New Orleans Neighborhood Plan. Appointments to the CSO were also delayed by city councilor concerns over who would be appointed to represent their district. Moreover, the official Memorandum of Understanding (MOU) that committed the city's leaders to undertake a single rebuilding planning process remained unsigned for weeks after the July 5 announcement. It was not until August 28, 2006—the day before the first year anniversary of Katrina—that the MOU was signed and the final CSO membership announced.[44] A full year after the storm, New Orleans was now set to embark on a process—jointly sanctioned by the state government, city council, and mayor and funded by private foundations[45]—to create a formal rebuilding plan.

In mid-August, a process was designed for UNOP to complete a citywide plan and 13 district plans by mid-January 2007.[46] This process was similar in design to the three-phase approach used for the Lambert Plan: phase one would assess current conditions and identify overall recovery needs, visions and goals; the second phase would involve identifying recovery scenarios and projects to address the vision and goals, and the third phase would decide on a recovery plan with a prioritized list of projects. Four district-level meetings would be held so that community residents could deliberate and make decisions associated with each phase. UNOP differed from the Lambert process in two key respects: it would prepare plans for all city neighborhoods and districts, and it would address critical citywide rebuilding issues, such as flood control and city infrastructure, services, and zoning. In fact, it was the citywide plan that would meet the LRA's requirement for a city recovery plan with a list of priority projects for funding.[47] A separate consultant team was charged with preparing the citywide plan, and three citywide congresses would be held to address the municipal scale issues and common concerns that emerged from the district level planning. Figure 2.2 summarizes the UNOP planning schedule.

Despite a tight four-month timetable to complete UNOP, the planning teams worked hard to gain the participation of the city's residents, particularly those still displaced and living elsewhere. This was a logistical challenge given the dispersion of residents across multiple cities. AmericaSpeaks was hired to address the technical issues involved in holding the community congresses simultaneously in multiple cities with interactive communication links so that displaced residents could be active participants in at least this critical part of the process.[48] AmericaSpeaks was hired too late to prepare for the first community congress, held in the New Orleans Convention Center on Saturday, October 28. Fewer than 300 people attended, many of whom were planning consultants, observers, and media. The meeting primarily focused on consultant presentations and data on the current state of the city across a range of issues. AmericaSpeaks did provide keypads to all participants that allowed them to record answers to various questions and document the characteristics of meeting participants. These data identified who was not well-represented at the meeting—young people, African Americans, and residents from several districts. This information spurred extensive outreach

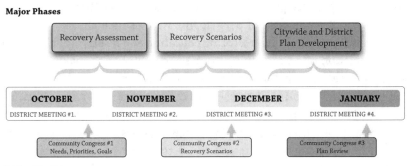

Figure 2.2.
Meeting schedule and process for Unified New Orleans Plan
Source: UNOP Citywide Plan, Figure 1.2.

and communications to reach unrepresented and displaced residents. Efforts included rebroadcasting the first community congress in several cities, an advertising campaign, a mailing to 120,000 displaced residents and outreach to faith-based groups aimed at gaining much greater and representative participation at the next congress.[49] Major preparations were undertaken to organize and run an unprecedented multicity deliberative planning meeting.[50] Facilities and communications equipment were provided for a simultaneous meeting in five cities: New Orleans, Baton Rouge, Atlanta, Houston, and Dallas. A satellite connection allowed simultaneous viewing of the meeting in each of the five cities. Each table in the meeting rooms in these five cities was equipped with a laptop computer with individual keypads to record voting on different issues and was staffed with a trained meeting facilitator. Child care, meals, transportation, and translation to Spanish and Vietnamese were all provided to help as many people as possible to attend and fully participate in the congress. The event was also broadcast live on the Internet, with viewing at libraries and public buildings in 16 other cities.

All these efforts paid off, as the second congress on December 2 attracted 2,366 participants—two-thirds of whom attended the four sites outside New Orleans.[51] Participants also were representative of the city by race (63 percent were black), income (half had pre-storm incomes below $40,000), and city district, although only 30 people under 20 years old attended. The congress achieved its goal of getting residents' opinions and preferences on key rebuilding issues, such as reducing flood risk, providing affordable housing, and priorities for reopening education and health care facilities. Participants expressed a strong preference for letting homeowners decide for themselves where to rebuild and for using incentives and building standards to reduce the flood risks. Participants also favored incentives to encourage people to rebuild close to each other and to buy and renovate blighted properties. Other policies or goals that received support from a large majority of participants were using financial incentives to build affordable housing, restoring education and health facilities based on repopulation rates, combining facilities to reduce costs, making schools a cornerstone for neighborhood rebuilding and improving school quality. The results of the voting at the second congress set some guideposts for the citywide UNOP plan: using incentive-based policies to promote safer rebuilding, promoting the clustering of new facilities and residential development, and making schools a centerpiece to bring back neighborhoods.

A third community congress occurred on January 20, 2007. A less elaborate production, it still involved sites in four cities (New Orleans, Atlanta, Dallas, and Houston) and almost 1,300 attendees. Based on the AmericaSpeaks polling, attendance was representative of the city's

pre-Katrina racial and economic composition and one-third of the participation occurred via sites outside New Orleans.[52] At this last public meeting
before UNOP was finalized, the focus was on presenting the priorities and
core citywide programs and policies in the draft plan and gaining citizen
input via small group discussions and keypad voting. Information was also
provided on the next steps to gain official approval for the plan and the
role of the city and other entities in its implementation. As with the earlier
congress, there was strong support for strengthening levees and restoring
wetlands to provide greater flood protection and a stated desire for better
schools and the use of schools as community centers. Participants overwhelmingly endorsed the plan, with 91 percent agreeing that the UNOP
plan should go forward. This was quite an accomplishment given the public
distrust of rebuilding planning after the BNOB Commission.

Two clear principles underpinned UNOP: the right of all residents
to return to New Orleans and a commitment to rebuild in all parts of
New Orleans. The idea of shrinking the city's footprint or consolidating
neighborhoods to reduce flood risk and provide more efficient service delivery was off the table. UNOP planners, however, sought to ensure that the
plan addressed flood risk and that this issue was included in rebuilding
discussions that occurred at district meetings and the citywide congresses.
Flood risk was discussed at the first citywide congress and the district planning analyzed this risk with maps that showed site-by-site property elevations and the extent of flooding after Katrina as part of their initial recovery
assessment.[53] Discussing flood risk and creating specific policies and plans
to reduce future risks were quite different. Risk reduction measures had to
be acceptable to residents and politicians who supported the right to rebuild
throughout the city and were distrustful of policies that might restrict this
right. The second community congress provided some guidance on how to
walk this tightrope with residents' preference for using incentives to spur
safer rebuilding.[54] UNOP consultants ultimately embraced this approach
with proposals for voluntary incentive programs to encourage residents to
elevate their homes and to cluster rebuilding within neighborhoods facing
the greatest risk of future flooding. They developed proposals for two programs to provide incentives for homeowners to rebuild in ways that would
reduce future flood risk.[55] One program would provide a grant beyond what
the state's Road Home Program paid to cover any additional costs to elevate
a home to meet FEMA's Base Flood Elevation (BFE). A second program provided a similar grant for the additional expense to demolish a slab-on-grade
home and rebuild a new home within FEMA BFE and design guidelines.

Planners also sought to address the thorny question of how to priori-
tize rebuilding investments in light of different flood risk and repopulation

rates across the city. Like the ULI and BNOB Commission before them, UNOP planners viewed New Orleans as comprising sub-areas with critical differences across these dimensions that warranted different actions. They classified the city into three "policy areas": one with either lower flood risk or higher repopulation rates, a second with either moderate flood risk or moderate repopulation, and a third with either the highest flood risk or slowest rate of repopulation. However, they turned the BNOB Commission proposals on their head by proposing that rebuilding investments should be the greatest in the areas with the greatest future flood risk or lowest repopulation rates. Their notion was to give the greatest aid to neighborhoods facing the greatest barriers to rebuilding and to use this as a guiding framework for the citywide plan.[56] A Cluster New Orleans Neighborhood Program was proposed to deliver special rebuilding assistance in neighborhoods with the highest flood risk or lowest repopulation rates with "funds and technical assistance to help residential property owners, neighborhood-serving small businesses and renters to return and rebuild in more sustainable clusters within their neighborhoods."[57] As with the home elevation programs, the proposal would provide incentives to voluntarily cluster rebuilding investments.

UNOP, completed in January 2007,[58] encompassed a 510-page *Citywide Strategic Recovery and Rebuilding Plan* and 13 district plans. The heart of the citywide plan was a recovery framework and a summary of 95 recovery projects.[59] In the recovery framework section, the overall vision and seven goals[60] that guided the plan are defined and the three flood risk/repopulation rate policy areas are presented along with how rebuilding priorities and strategies vary in each area. The project summary section organized projects into 13 sectors or types of rebuilding projects (e.g., Hurricane/Flood Protection, Housing, Transportation, etc.). The plan for each sector included a statement of the problem, overall rebuilding strategies, the specific projects (and policies and programs) to be funded and implemented, how the projects will apply across the three-city policy areas, and a rough estimate of spending for each project within the short-, medium- and long-term phases. A separate appendix provided a one-page summary sheet on each of the 95 projects along with its priority level.[61] The cost for all 95 projects was set at $14.4 billion, with $4.1 billion to be spent in the short term (one to two years) and the remaining $10.3 split divided into a $6.8 billion medium-term phase covering years three to five and a final $3.5 billion long-term phase for another five years. For a city in financial crisis, this was a daunting figure; however, UNOP failed to directly address how to fund the plan. It summarized the recovery funding that had already been allocated to New Orleans; presented three ideas for maximizing funds from federal disaster recovery programs; and provided a two-page list of federal and state government agencies, private foundations, and city tools as potential funding sources. Thirteen pages of tables distributed the costs for each project across the short-, medium-, and long-term phases. No details were provided on how specific projects would be funded: the individual project summary sheets had a section on costs but no information on funding.

UNOP implementation was covered in a separate section that proposed forming a Parish Wide Recovery Committee to coordinate recovery efforts across the dozen or so city agencies responsible for rebuilding programs and projects. The primary operational responsibility for implementation would rest with the Office of Recovery Management (ORM), newly created in December 2006 with its first Executive Director, Dr. Edward Blakely,[62] beginning work in January just as UNOP was finalized. ORM's mission under UNOP was to "lead in the preparation of action plans for the multiple agency participants in the council to adopt and implement, and oversee the financing and implementation strategies for all public recovery initiatives."[63] UNOP's implementation section acknowledged the large expansion in city staffing and resources that was needed to implement its ambitions plan; a table summarized—by short-, medium- and long-term phase—$470 million in additional resources required by major city agencies to augment their implementation capacity.[64] The short-term amount, at $158 million, was over one-third of the city's then $411 million operating budget. No details were provided on how the city might secure such funds. There were also no details on how New Orleans city government, in the wake of massive layoffs after Katrina and with a poor track record in managing federal programs and delivering public services (its school system was under state control and its housing authority under federal receivership), would gain the organizational capacity to implement 95 new large and complex programs while it rebuilt over 800 damaged public facilities.[65]

UNOP provided New Orleans with a plan that addressed all of the city's neighborhoods, affirmed the right of every resident and neighborhood to return, and provided a list of key rebuilding projects with the associated costs and priority levels. Perhaps most importantly, it shifted the public perception (and associated politics) of rebuilding planning from a process in which the city elites and outsiders were seeking to transform the city in their image to one in which residents had a strong voice in setting rebuilding policies and priorities. As a workable and honest guide to how New Orleans could rebuild it fell far short.[66] A $14 billion list of programs, policies, and projects without a viable way to be funded and the institutional means for implementation could not serve as the basis for rebuilding. Since UNOP participants, planners, and residents alike did not confront New Orleans' real financial and institutional constraints and make choices within these constraints nor create real actionable plans to overcome these constraints, UNOP functioned as a record of the city's aspirations for rebuilding rather than a true plan for rebuilding. In its basic purpose of creating a prioritized list of projects for federal recovery funds it also fell short. Available funds were insufficient to pay for some individual projects let alone the full $14 billion.[67] The real decisions on how to deploy the city's far smaller pool of recovery funds still needed to be made.

From $14 Billion to $442 Million: Target Area Plan and State Approval

At a city hall press conference on December 5, 2006, Mayor Nagin announced the appointment of Ed Blakely to head a new Office of Recovery Management—the first city government office devoted exclusively to overseeing rebuilding efforts. Blakely brought a distinguished academic career in city planning, serving as the chair of urban planning departments at three universities, along with practical experience advising Oakland's mayor on post-earthquake disaster recovery and in politics as a candidate for mayor of Oakland. As he began his job in January, Blakely had to craft an actionable plan from UNOP to move the city's recovery efforts forward. Blakely accepted UNOP as a "done deal,"[68] but this still left the question of how to implement the massive plan; a question that boiled down to which UNOP projects should be implemented first with money available to the city in the near term and in which neighborhoods should these funds be invested. According to ORM's Director of Infrastructure and Environmental Planning:

> The goal was to put the UNOP plan in a practical view. The UNOP plan was a long list of desires without clear priorities in terms of funding, or how much money was available. One thing that UNOP did have was prioritization. For each type of project, it was either a low, a medium, or a high priority. It did do some priorities. The problem is that there wasn't enough specificity in terms of if you had money on the table, what is funded first. It wasn't sequenced. The costs of the projects were only ballpark estimates, not real costs. So the idea was to actually put some meat on the bones of UNOP. The state required us to write a recovery plan that was the implementation of UNOP. That document is called the Long Term Community Recovery Plan, and ORM put that together.[69]

Blakely toured the city by bicycle to better understand conditions and identify neighborhood centers and activity areas that could spur revitalization with private rebuilding investments. Meanwhile, ORM staff sifted through the Lambert, UNOP, and other plans to capture key priorities, projects, and ideas for rebuilding and analyzed data on resettlement patterns. Through a series of meetings, Blakely and his staff created an approach that combined several large scale investments to jumpstart rebuilding in heavily damaged areas with smaller investments to add momentum to areas with faster rates of rebuilding and repopulation. The result was a $1.1 billion plan, announced by Nagin and Blakely at a morning press conference on March 29, 2007 that focused recovery dollars in seventeen Target Recovery Zones.[70] The seventeen zones were divided into three categories: (1) two heavily damaged Rebuild Zones (New Orleans East and the Lower Ninth Ward) would get $145 million, or almost half of the $316 million targeted to the zones; (2) six Redevelop Zones would share $115 million; and (3) eight Renew Zones would receive the final $55.9 million. A key tenet of Blakeley's strategy was to focus on commercial areas as a means to stabilize neighborhoods and generate private investment to rebuild. In fact, much of the funding was programmed for loans, grants, and incentives designed to spur private investment.[71] Despite the emphasis on target areas in the presentation and media coverage, most of the $1.1 billion plan ($742 million) was devoted to citywide blight elimination and rebuilding programs.[72] Unlike UNOP, ORM identified four specific sources of money to fund their plan: $117 million in federal recovery funds provided under the CDBG program already allocated to the city by the LRA; $325 million from state funds set aside to cover the 10 percent local match for FEMA public assistance funding that Congress was considering waiving; $260 million from the sale of city bonds authorized before Katrina; and $300 million from new bonds to be backed by city-owned blighted properties.[73]

After ORM released its Target Recovery Zone plan, the City Planning Commission completed its review of UNOP and approved it on May 22, 2007. UNOP was now before the City Council for final action along with the Target Zone Plan, which represented a near-term plan for UNOP implementation. However, neither plan met the LRA's requirements under its Long-Term Community Recovery Program—the program to distribute a portion of the federal recovery funds provided under the CDBG program (discussed in more detail below) directly to parishes for recovery efforts. The plan submitted to the LRA had to show how the specific funds allocated by the LRA would be spent to support Long-Term Recovery. New Orleans' ability to issue the $560 million in bonds included in the ORM plan was in doubt so the $1.1 billion plan had to be further whittled down to the $442 million in CDBG and 10 percent waiver funds available from the LRA. Using its Target Recovery Zone plan as the foundation, ORM prepared this final Citywide Strategic Recovery and Redevelopment Plan (CSRRP), which was then adopted by the city council on June 21, 2007, and the LRA on June 25th. According to Blakely,[74] several factors shaped decisions on what to include in the CSRRP budget. One consideration was to prioritize infrastructure, housing, and commercial development that could not be funded with FEMA public assistance. A second factor was addressing priorities expressed in neighborhood meetings for job creation, blight removal, and improved streets. Finally, funds were allocated to activities, such as blight removal and target area investment, which were deemed critical to repositioning the entire city for recovery.

The CSRRP allocated the $442 million to eight project categories and listed the specific UNOP projects to be funded in each of the eight categories.[75]

Table 2.1. BUDGET AND UNOP PROJECTS INCLUDED IN CITYWIDE STRATEGIC RECOVERY AND REDEVELOPMENT PLAN (CSRRP) SUBMITTED TO LOUISIANA RECOVERY AUTHORITY

Rebuilding category	CSRRP Budget	Included UNOP Projects: Number, Name, Recovery Value (High, Medium, Low) and Estimated Cost
School facilities and programs	$45 million	59—Repair and renovate existing school facilities or construct new facilities: high; cost to be determined
Recreation facilities	$65 million	88—Repair and renovate regional parks: medium priority; $24 million
		90—Repair and renovate neighborhood parks: medium priority; $5 million
Community facilities	$70 million	61—Neighborhood community centers: medium priority; $57 million
City roads and infrastructure	$80 million	23—Repair/restoration of high-priority major roads: high; $84 million
		24—Repair/restoration of high-priority minor arterial roads: high; $83 million
		25—Repair/restoration of high-priority collector arterial roads: high; $24 million
		27—Repair/restoration of high-priority local roads: medium; $4 million
		65—Sidewalk, streetscape and neutral ground improvements: medium; $240 million
Libraries	$16 million	84—Renovate main library and safeguard city archives: high; $34.5 to 36 million
		85—Repair, renovate or build new regional libraries: medium; $20 million
		89—Repair, renovate or build new neighborhood libraries: low; $35 million

Table 2.1, taken from the CSRRP, lists the eight plan categories, their allocated funds, and associated UNOP Projects. It also allocated 40 percent of the $442 million for projects in Target Recovery Zones, which the CSRRP presented as implementation of the UNOP neighborhood cluster development strategy. This pared-down version of UNOP included 19 of the 95 original UNOP projects funded at 10 percent of the estimated short-term costs and 3 percent of the $14 billion total. Most of the included UNOP projects were designated medium recovery value and the CSRRP budgets across the eight categories varied quite a bit from the UNOP cost estimates. For example, the budget for recreational facilities was $65 million compared to a $29 million estimate in UNOP, while $70 million was budgeted for four housing, blight reduction, and neighborhood recovery programs with UNOP cost estimates of $156 million. Neither of the two flood risk mitigation programs, included as high priorities in UNOP, was funded in the CSRRP budget. Although the city was pursuing other monies to implement UNOP projects, especially FEMA public assistance funds, the CSRRP constituted the main source for short- and medium-term recovery funds and thus the de facto rebuilding plan. ORM and city officials had now set priorities that UNOP had failed to set but did so without the public participation process that had been a hallmark of UNOP.

Twenty-two months after Katrina, New Orleans now had an official rebuilding plan that met state and federal requirements and $442 million to fund its implementation.

THE TORTURED ROAD TO FEDERAL ASSISTANCE

In his address to the nation from Jackson Square on September 15, 2005, President George W. Bush said, "And tonight I also offer this pledge of the American people: Throughout the area hit by the hurricane, we will do what it takes, we will stay as long as it takes to help citizens rebuild their communities and their lives."[76] Translating those words into action turned out to be a long and arduous process, especially for the homeowners, businesses, and local governments in dire need of federal assistance to rebuild. Federal assistance, after congressional and presidential approval, had to make its way through the federal bureaucracy, state agencies, and private contractors to reach the local recipients who would spend it on rebuilding. Although intended to accelerate the rebuilding of Gulf Coast communities, the billions in federal aid provided after Katrina have been marked by complex bureaucratic rules, conflicts over administrating these rules, and poor management. The result has been long delays in receiving federal assistance, sometimes as long as five years, and barriers to using the funds as state and local officials desired, further slowing New Orleans' rebuilding. If the city's leaders and citizens expected the federal government to underwrite their rebuilding plans, they soon learned that federal funds were unpredictable and came packaged in red tape. Uncertainty about and delays in receiving federal dollars not only slowed government action, it affected tens of thousands of residents and businesses who needed to make rebuilding decisions to move on with their lives.

Federal disaster aid comes in many forms, delivered by different federal agencies and programs. The legal basis for federal disaster aid is set in the Robert T. Stafford Disaster Relief and Emergency Assistance Act, a 1988 law named for the Vermont senator who helped write and enact the law. Under the Stafford Act, federal aid is triggered by a presidential disaster declaration in response to a governor's request.[77] Once a declaration is made, federal emergency assistance and longer term recovery aid is available through several programs under the Federal Emergency Management Agency (FEMA) that fall into three categories.[78] The first category is aid to individuals and households (Individual Assistance) which includes emergency assistance for temporary housing, food, unemployment assistance, and other survival needs. One aspect of this was a provision to provide cash assistance of $2000 to every household in Mississippi and Louisiana impacted by the storm.[79] While vital to helping people cope following the displacement and loss of personal belongings after the disaster, emergency aid does not fund rebuilding. Another component of Individual Assistance is home repair grants that support rebuilding by helping to fund the repair of damaged homes. The second category is Public Assistance (PA), which reimburses governments, tribal entities, and some nonprofit organizations for restoring damaged public facilities and infrastructure. This federal disaster recovery program helps to rebuild shared community facilities, such as schools, libraries, parks, and hospitals, as well as publicly-owned infrastructure. With the extensive damage to New Orleans' public buildings, transportation system, and water, wastewater, and sewer infrastructure, FEMA PA funds were a critical rebuilding resource for the city. A third category is the Hazard Mitigation Grant Program. It provides funds to state governments to reduce future disaster risks and associated losses. Beyond FEMA, the Stafford Act provides for a Disaster Loan Program run by the Small Business Administration (SBA). Disaster loans come in two forms: (1) physical disaster loans fund permanent rebuilding of damaged property by households, nonprofit organizations and businesses of any size; and (2) economic injury loans which are for small businesses to address operating losses from a disaster.[80] Although not directly part of federal disaster response programs, the federal flood insurance program pays claims for flood damages to insured property owners. Since much of the post-Katrina damage was due to flooding and private insurance generally does not cover flood damage, federal flood insurance was a critical rebuilding resource.

Stafford Act programs have proven insufficient to address the widespread damage accompanying major disasters. In these situations, congress has supplemented Stafford Act aid with special appropriations under the Community Development Block Grant (CDBG) program. Congress did this after the World Trade Center attack in 2001, the Oklahoma City bombing in 1995, and three prior natural disasters dating back to Hurricane Andrew in 1992.[81] Congress continued this pattern after Katrina, appropriating $19.7 billion in CDBG funds to aid rebuilding in five Gulf Coast states hurt by hurricanes Katrina and Rita—Louisiana, Mississippi, Alabama, Florida, and Texas. These funds were provided in three separate congressional appropriations. Congress passed the first one on December 30, 2005 (four months after Katrina) for $11.5 billion, of which $6.21 billion went to Louisiana.[82] A second $5.2 million appropriation occurred almost six months later on June 15, 2006 following considerable pressure from Gulf Coast states when it became apparent that the initial appropriation was too small to address home rebuilding needs. Over 80 percent of these funds went to Louisiana. The third and final $3 billion appropriation, dedicated to Louisiana's home rebuilding needs, was approved on November 13, 2007, over two years after the storms.

The Community Development Block Grant program, administered by the US Department of Housing and Urban Development (HUD), dates back to 1974 when congress consolidated multiple federal programs into a single block grant to cities.[83] Cities decide how to deploy CDBG funds to address local priorities, but these uses must primarily benefit low- and moderate-income persons,[84] and spending must conform to myriad federal rules and regulations. The CDBG program was not designed for disaster recovery, and adapting it to this purpose has posed challenges for both HUD and state and local governments and necessitated many waivers from federal requirements. These problems were well-documented after the World Trade Center disaster.[85] Congress took some steps to address the dissonance between CDBG goals and disaster recovery in its authorization for Gulf Coast recovery funding. It lowered the share of funds that had to benefit low- and moderate-income persons from 70 percent to 50 percent, eliminated caps on spending CDBG funds to provide public services, and allowed the Secretary of HUD to grant other waivers, but kept intact all fair housing, nondiscrimination, labor standards, and environment review requirements.[86] HUD's notice on the recovery CDBG funds' availability, process, and rules, issued in February 2006, also waived several minor administrative, financing, and reporting requirements.[87]

In addition to the formal disaster recovery programs, several federal policy developments influenced recovery aid to New Orleans, often with important consequences for the city's rebuilding. One key change, initiated after the September 11 attacks on the World Trade Center, was greater reliance on private investment to spur recovery through the use of federal tax incentives. As part of the post-September 11th recovery aid, Congress passed the Job Creation and Worker Assistance Act of 2002, which created multiple tax benefits designed to stimulate business investment in the section of lower Manhattan heavily affected by the terrorist attacks designated the Liberty Zone.[88] Seven specific tax incentives were provided, including employee tax credits, increased deductions from taxes for property investments, and the provision of $8 billion in bonds with interest payments that are exempt from federal taxes to finance new commercial and residential real estate development and utilities.[89] Congress and the Bush Administration repeated this approach after hurricanes Katrina, Rita, and Wilma; the GO Zone Act of 2005 provided almost identical tax incentives along with special allocations of Low Income Housing Tax Credits (LIHTC) to raise private capital to rebuild rental housing.[90] Over $23 billion in tax-exempt bonds and tax credits were authorized for the designated GO Zone (of which $12.5 billion was for Louisiana)—a scale of investment that exceeded the total recovery CDBG appropriations at an estimated cost to the federal government of $3.5 billion.[91]

Using bonds and tax credits to fund recovery investment had several consequences for rebuilding investment. First, it favored large projects and companies rather than helping small businesses and small property owners.[92] Second, it made recovery investments more dependent on both the strength of the local real estate market and on conditions in private capital markets. As a result, many of the heavily damaged areas in New Orleans (which were often poorer and had a higher share of black residents) were unable to make use of the large tax-exempt bond resource.[93] Moreover, as credit markets collapsed in 2007, it became very difficult to sell tax-exempt bonds and housing tax credits—a situation that stalled many recovery projects.[94] Ultimately, New Orleans was unable to use much of its tax-exempt bond resource, returning $750 million of its allocation to the state at the end of 2009.[95] The rebuilding of rental housing was also hard hit since investor demand for LIHTCs declined steeply after the financial crisis. By mid-2008, only 18 percent of the almost 11,787 housing units in Louisiana that had been allocated Low Income Housing Tax Credits were completed.[96] In New Orleans, 41 percent of these tax credit projects had not closed on their financing and thus were unable to start construction.[97] Developers in a few neighborhoods managed to overcome these barriers to complete projects, which added to the greatly needed supply of rental apartments.

Federal recovery policy also imposed fiscal burdens on state and local governments that lost large portions of their tax base and revenue due to the property losses and economic decline after the hurricanes. Under FEMA's Public Assistance Program, governments had to pay for 10 percent of the cost of recovery projects. Moreover, they had to advance the funds to construct projects and then were reimbursed by federal funds. These requirements were designed to prevent fraud and waste, but they were a real burden for local governments and delayed the start and completion of public infrastructure and facilities. As discussed later, it was especially problematic for New Orleans and required a special state arrangement to provide the city with monies to undertake public recovery projects. While the federal government had waived the 10 percent local match requirement after the World Trade Center attacks and Hurricane Andrew, there was no such waiver soon after Katrina.[98] It was not until May 2007, when Congress included the waiver in an amendment to a supplemental spending bill for the Iraq War,[99] that state and local governments in the Gulf Coast received comparable treatment and much-needed financial relief.

A final hallmark of federal recovery policy was utilizing state governments to administer and allocate federal recovery assistance. In addition to adding a layer of government review and red tape to the distribution of funds, this meant that critical decisions on how to use recovery grants and tax incentives rested with state government authorities and followed state priorities. As explained below, a Louisiana state authority set the priorities for the use of its multibillion dollar award of recovery CDBG funds and worked with other state agencies to design specific recovery programs. State agencies were also responsible for awarding almost $8 billion in tax-exempt bonds and $170 million in low-income housing tax credits to private firms and developers. Since most of Louisiana's (and other states') funding went to statewide programs, the ability to adapt and tailor recovery funding to local conditions and needs was limited.[100] Furthermore, states largely awarded their tax-exempt bond allocation to projects on a first-come, first-served basis without targeting communities and neighborhoods with the greatest damage and recovery needs.[101] Louisiana did change its policies in September 2007 to target half of its remaining tax-exempt bonds to the most heavily damaged parishes.[102] However, this change failed to address the mismatch between the recovery bond tool and conditions in hard-hit areas noted above that often made their use infeasible. Consequently, almost one-third of the bonds targeted to these severely damaged parishes were returned unused to the state.

Because of their size and key role in filling insurance gaps to rebuild public and community facilities, the FEMA Public Assistance and Community Development Block Grant funds were especially important to the rebuilding effort. CDBG appropriations funded homeowners to rebuild when insurance settlements fell short, and provided the only funds New Orleans received to implement its long-term recovery plans. Public Assistance was essential to rebuilding the city's decimated buildings and infrastructure and fully utilizing this program was a focal point for the city government's rebuilding efforts.[103] Although quite promising on paper, and despite the efforts to make CDBG funds more flexible, these two programs proved difficult to use and generated long delays in securing rebuilding funds for both the City of New Orleans and community-based neighborhood organizations.

CDBG RECOVERY FUNDS

Under the CDBG appropriation, the decisions on how to use this federal assistance and administrative oversight rested with each state government. Governor Blanco created the Louisiana Recovery Authority (LRA) in October 2005 to oversee state recovery efforts. The LRA was charged with creating a spending plan for the initial $6.21 billion and preparing the Action Plan needed for HUD for review and acceptance before the state would receive any funds.[104] Louisiana's Action Plan, summarized in Table 2.2, devoted 70 percent of the CDBG funds to housing programs and another 19 percent to rebuild damaged state buildings and government infrastructure. Most of the $4.4 billion allocated to housing in the First Action Plan was for the Road Home Program that provided grants to homeowners to cover storm property damage that exceeded funds recouped from insurance settlements. Initial estimates for the cost of the Road Home Program proved far too low and the program ultimately totaled over $8 billion.[105] One consequence of devoting most of the CDBG funds to homeowner assistance was that little of the CDBG funding was available to local communities to fund their rebuilding plans and priorities. The LRA allocated $700 million or 6.7 percent of its total CDBG funding to local governments for long-term recovery projects[106] of which $411 million went to New Orleans.[107]

Although the Action Plan was approved by HUD in May 2006, it took additional time to work out the details of specific programs with HUD to

Table 2.2. LOUISIANA'S ALLOCATION OF COMMUNITY BLOCK GRANT (CDBG)
DISASTER RECOVERY FUNDS

Spending Category	First Action Plan—2006 Amount	Second Action Plan—2007 Amount	Combined Amount Both Action Plans
Infrastructure	$1,187,500,000		$1,187,500,000
Economic development	332,500,000		332,500,000
Housing programs	4,370,000,000	3,608,800,000	7,978,800,000
Administration	310,000,000	41,200,000	351,200,000
Planning	9,500,000		9,500,000
Technical assistance	500,000		500,000
Unallocated	0	550,000,000	550,000,000
Total	$6,210,000,000	$4,200,000,000	$10,410,000,000

Source: Louisiana Office of Community Development, *Action Plan for Use of Disaster Recovery Funds*, April 11, 2006 and Louisiana Office of Community Development. *Proposed Action Plan for Disaster Recovery Funds Allocated by P.L. 109–234*, May 24, 2007.

ensure compliance with CDBG regulations. Still more time was needed to select private contractors or nonprofit organizations that handled applications and assistance payments for most programs. Finally, the processing of applications, calculation of assistance amounts and issuance of payments also took time, with Road Home Program grants subject to long delays. Frustrations with delays under the Road Home program led the Louisiana House of Representatives to vote 97–1 for a resolution demanding the governor to terminate its contract with ICF, the private firm hired to administer the program.[108] By December 2006, the Road Home program had over 90,000 applications but had paid grants to only 94 homeowners.[109] Two years after Katrina, 50,000 applications had been closed out[110]—still less than half of the 120,000 homeowners eventually assisted under the program. With these multiple bureaucratic steps and delays, most businesses[111]and homeowners did not receive any assistance from CDBG funds until 2007 or 2008, two to three years after their losses occurred. There were also claims of racial discrimination under the Road Home program. A lawsuit filed by two fair housing organizations and several home owners alleging that the program's formula, which capped grants at a home's pre-Katrina value, resulted in much smaller grants for homeowners living in poorer areas than those in wealthier (and typically whiter) neighborhoods, even for very similar homes in which the costs to rebuild were the same.[112] Under a 2011 settlement reached with the federal and Louisiana governments, $62 million in additional grants were provided for homeowners seeking to rebuild in areas in which Road Home grants had fallen short of their reconstruction costs.[113]

ICF took much of the heat for delays in disbursing Road Home grants, but navigating CDBG rules also slowed and confounded its implementation. Louisiana had to revise and clarify its plans for the Road Home program on three occasions between July and November 2006. Then, almost one year into the program after 116,000 applications had been filed, HUD ordered Louisiana to stop the program on March 16, 2007.[114] Louisiana had to change how Road Home payments were made and had to receive HUD approval of an amended Action Plan before the program could resume at the end of May. The timeline for these events, presented in Table 2.3, was taken from a Government Accountability Office report. The source of these problems is a CDBG requirement to conduct site-specific environment reviews when CDBG

Table 2.3. TIMELINE OF EVENTS SURROUNDING THE EVOLUTION
OF LOUISIANA'S ROAD HOME PROGRAM

Date	Event
Phase One[1]	
Feb. 13, 2006	HUD announced Louisiana's first CDBG disaster funding allocation and related waivers.
May 12, 2006	Louisiana submitted action plan to HUD describing Road Home program.
May 30, 2006	HUD approved the Road Home program.
Phase Two	
July 12, 2006	Louisiana re-submitted Road Home program action plan to HUD as a compensation program.
	HUD accepted Road Home as a compensation program.
	Louisiana began pilot of Road Home program.
Aug. 11, 2006	Louisiana submitted clarification and an update to HUD about Road Home.
Aug. 22, 2006	HUD approved the Road Home clarification and update.
	Road Home began accepting homeowner applications.
Nov. 30, 2006	Louisiana submitted further clarifications about the Road Home program.
	HUD accepted Road Home clarifications.
Phase Three	
Mar. 16, 2007	HUD ordered Louisiana to cease and desist Road Home program.
Apr. 9, 2007	Louisiana publicly announced Road Home as lump-sum compensation program.
May 7, 2007	Louisiana submitted Road Home program action plan amendment to HUD; adopted lump-sum compensation model.
May 30, 2007	HUD approved action plan amendment.

Source: Data from HUD and Louisiana's Office of Community Development
[1] This table is reproduced from Table 1 from GAO Report 09–541, Gulf Coast Disaster Recovery; Community Development Block Grant Program Guidance to States Needs to Be Improved, p. 14.

funds are used to rehabilitate a property. Completing environmental reviews for over 100,000 homes to be assisted under Road Home would be prohibitively costly and time-consuming for Louisiana[115] and findings from the reviews posed the risk of imposing environmental compliance costs on homeowners.[116] To avoid this problem, Louisiana (and Mississippi) designed their programs to compensate homeowners for a loss rather than requiring that CDBG funds be used to restore damaged homes. Louisiana officials believed, based on ongoing discussions with HUD and HUD's approval of Road Home Action Plan amendments in August, that the Road Home Program met HUD requirements for a compensation program and no environment reviews were needed. But after HUD officials conducted field monitoring visits, HUD staff concluded that the program was operating as a rehabilitation program and then ordered Louisiana to either cease making grants or conduct individual site environment reviews. State officials ultimately changed the Road Home program to make a single lump sum payment to homeowners that addressed HUD's concerns and allowed Road Home to resume. Louisiana faced still another set of regulatory barriers and conflicting interpretations of federal non-discrimination rules between HUD and FEMA when, at the suggestion of the Office of the Federal Coordinator for Gulf Coast recovery, it tried unsuccessfully to use FEMA Hazard Mitigation Funding in conjunction with the Road Home Program.[117]

New Orleans faced similar problems in implementing recovery programs with CDBG funds. Louisiana, as the grantee for CDBG funds, was responsible for ensuring compliance with HUD rules among cities and other organizations to which it granted CDBG monies.[118] Prior approval by the LRA (later replaced by the state Office of Community Development) was needed for each distinct program or activity that the city sought to undertake with CDBG funds. This approval typically occurred in two stages: first, a short project description was submitted and, if approved, a second detailed application was prepared and sent to the state for approval. Based on their experiences with HUD, state officials carefully scrutinized, and were slow to approve, city proposals. If a program fell outside HUD's normal rules then an additional federal program waiver was required. New Orleans' effort to help moderate-income families buy and repair homes demonstrates the cumbersome, and at times strange, nature of this process.

Many cities and states offer soft second mortgage programs to make home ownership more affordable. A second mortgage loan is provided to cover part of the home purchase price but the homeowner makes no payments on this second mortgage until the new owner sells the property. The share of the second mortgage repaid at this sale declines the longer the buyer lives in the house and often is reduced to zero after many years. This deferral and potential forgiveness of the mortgage is why it is called a "soft" second mortgage. New Orleans had a soft second program for households earning below 80 percent of area median income—the HUD definition of a moderate-income household under CDBG rules—but it wanted to expand the program in two ways. The expanded program would serve families earning up to 120 percent of median income and it would fund not only a straight home purchase (as the existing program did) but also the purchase and rehab of a damaged home and the straight rehab of a home that would otherwise be abandoned. An expanded soft second mortgage program made a lot of sense in post-Katrina New Orleans. It provided an incentive for people to buy and improve some of the city's tens of thousands of abandoned homes, including those acquired by the state via the Road Home Program.[119] With the cost to acquire and rebuild homes close to $200,000, they were not affordable for many low- and moderate-income households, even with a generous soft second mortgage. Extending soft second mortgages to slightly higher-income families helped address this financial gap.

To establish the expanded soft second mortgage program with CDBG disaster recovery funds, New Orleans needed multiple state and federal approvals that, along with capacity issues at the city's initial contractor, delayed the program's implementation for over two and half years.[120] The city submitted its project description for the soft second program on May 21, 2008, which the LRA quickly approved on May 27. In its approval, the LRA indicated that the program would require "special approval and perhaps a waiver from the U.S. Department of Housing and Urban Development."[121] Almost five months passed before HUD issued its waiver in mid-October.[122] With the federal waiver in hand, New Orleans prepared its full program application and received partial state approval on November 17 to use $27 million in recovery CDBG dollars for the soft second mortgage program. The approval allowed the city to move forward with the $10 million part of its program that provided loans for a straight home purchase. More detailed plans, policies, and cost allocations for the other two components still needed state approval. The city planned to use the Finance Authority of New Orleans (FANO) to operate the soft second program since it was already providing soft second loans for home purchases under a separate state program. Since FANO had no experience in or procedures for managing rehabilitation loans, city and FANO officials needed to work out plans and polices for how FANO would implement this new type of soft second mortgage. After several months of working with FANO, the authority informed city officials that it did not want to run the $17 million rehabilitation portion of the program. The city then turned to Neighborhood Housing Services of New Orleans (NHS), a nonprofit organization founded in 1976 that had been providing homeowner assistance and housing rehab loans for several decades.[123] While city employees were working out the details of both programs with the state, FANO, and NHS, HUD officials raised new concerns about two issues during a site visit in fall 2009. One issue raised by HUD was duplication of benefits: they wanted procedures in place to prevent homeowners assisted under the Road Home program from "double dipping" and getting duplicate aid under the soft second program. A second concern was how the program would meet CDBG national objective rules for homeowners with incomes too high to fit the national objective of benefiting low- and moderate-income persons. Over six months passed before the city learned that these issues had been worked out between the HUD staff and the state's Office of Community Development (OCD) in June 2010.[124] With the addition of the NHS as a subcontractor in running the soft second rehab program, New Orleans had to file a program amendment with the state, which was done in July 2010 and approved by OCD in August. Further delays in finalizing and signing contracts with FANO and NHS occurred with the transition to a new mayoral administration and release of a HUD audit in November 2010 that found that FANO had overpaid homeowners and violated federal rules in administering another soft second mortgage program.[125] Mayor Landrieu decided to have FANO fund 62 soft second loans that had already been approved[126] and the city entered into a $10 million contract with NHS to run the soft second rehab program in 2011. Almost three years passed from the time the three-part soft second mortgage program was first proposed and funding was available to homeowners under a scaled-down version of the program.

The combination of delays in completing the city's recovery plan, implementation barriers from the bureaucratic state and federal process, and the city's own capacity constraints meant that most of the federal CDBG funds remained unspent five years after Katrina. Only 23 percent of the CDBG funds obligated to the City of New Orleans for recovery projects had been spent by this date and one-third of all approved projects had no funds spent. When Water and Sewer Board and school projects are included the spending rate increased but was still only 36 percent.[127] Almost two-thirds of the recovery CDBG funds remained unexpended five years after Katrina made landfall and New Orleans flooded.

FEMA PUBLIC ASSISTANCE

Under the Public Assistance (PA) program, FEMA provides recovery aid to governments, Indian tribes, and some nonprofits for emergency work and permanent projects. Emergency work covers short-term activities such as debris removal and steps to protect life and property, while permanent projects address the repair and rebuilding of damaged buildings and infrastructure. PA funds flow to state governments, as FEMA's administrative agent and official grantee, on their way to local governments and other non-state recipients. To receive PA funds, a locality (or other organization) must prepare a project worksheet with supporting evidence that details the scope of work needed and the estimated costs to either repair or replace the eligible facility.[128] Project worksheets are submitted to and reviewed by the state PA agency before submission to FEMA for approval. Similarly, once FEMA approves a project, the PA grant goes to the state, and the state monitors project completion and distributes funds to the local entity. Two layers of government review and action are built into both ends of the process—application and payment—which can slow decisions and disbursements. This description greatly simplifies the process, as a report by the US Government Accountability Office (GAO) identified 18 steps in the PA process.[129]

The many steps and two levels of government decision-making were only part of the difficulties that plagued the PA program.[130] FEMA was overwhelmed by the number of projects seeking PA grants after Katrina and lacked the systems and personnel to effectively manage the explosion in demand for PA grants. No system was established to store and share information on the thousands of projects. FEMA relied heavily on new staff and consultants to manage the workload, but this workforce was poorly trained. In addition, the field staff and consultants working with the state governments and PA applicants changed frequently. This created a situation in which supporting documents were lost, decisions were not well-documented, new employees were unaware of project details and past actions, and past commitments by FEMA were lost or reconsidered. The result was a frustrating process for New Orleans and other local governments, marked by long delays in securing PA funds and a frequent need to appeal FEMA's decisions on both approved projects and their cost.[131] New Orleans officials describe the PA process as a constant battle to get project worksheets approved and funded at an amount that reflected the real cost to repair or rebuild a facility. They report that FEMA rarely put its decisions in writing so when staff or consultants turned over, which happened frequently, decisions changed and prior commitments made to them for either specific funding levels or on how large-scale projects would be funded were not honored. In one case, the city was encouraged to prepare a master plan for rebuilding the criminal justice facilities with the expectation that FEMA would negotiate a PA settlement for the entire system rather than separately review and fund each facility. After the city worked with FEMA assistance to complete a Criminal Justice System Master Plan, FEMA did not agree with the scope of the plan and its estimated $1 billion cost and decided not to fund the plan that it had encouraged the city to prepare.[132] These problems with the PA program were not unique to New Orleans and were documented in a 2009 report by the Government Accountability Office:[133]

> FEMA's approach to making decisions regarding project approvals and appeals also presented challenges to moving forward with rebuilding. For example, in some cases after applicants received approval for their projects from FEMA and had already moved ahead with construction, the agency decided to reconsider and ultimately reverse its decision. As a result of these reversals, some applicants told us that they were hesitant to move forward on other projects.
>
> The lack of continuity in FEMA staffing during project development also hindered rebuilding progress. FEMA's reliance on temporary rotating staff did not provide the level of continuity needed for the complex, long-term demands of Gulf Coast rebuilding. For example, in the absence of reliable electronic access to the case management files, rotating staff did not always document information and decisions about specific projects, which delayed project development because applicants then had to repeat discussions with their new FEMA representatives or provide duplicate documentation.

Disputes over the extent of storm damage, whether it was appropriate to repair or replace damaged facilities, and their true costs tied up some PA projects in multiyear appeals. Without certainty about the final PA grant amount, New Orleans was unable to rebuild many facilities. This problem has been particularly true for large complex projects such as repairing and rebuilding the city's school buildings and major hospitals. For example, FEMA did not reach final agreement on PA funding for the city's schools until August 24, 2010—five years after Katrina.[134] Similarly, a special arbitration panel was needed to settle the PA funding claim for the damaged Charity Hospital, with this decision finalized in January 2010.[135] In both cases, New Orleans received far more funds than FEMA originally awarded but had to wait many years before it could rebuild these critical buildings.

How FEMA funded PA projects created further problems for New Orleans. PA grants for large projects are paid on a reimbursement basis, which required the city to have money to complete the project and then get paid back form FEMA. It also needed money to meet the required 10 percent match. In the aftermath of Katrina, when the city's tax base and revenue was decimated by the twin loss of tourism activities and property destruction, New Orleans was in no financial position to front and match PA funding. Two actions helped New Orleans manage these financial barriers to rebuilding, but not until valuable time had passed. On June 29, 2007, the state of Louisiana signed an agreement to provide a $200 million line of credit to New Orleans to pay costs on construction projects that would be reimbursed by FEMA, using proceeds from a recent bond sale.[136] The city could draw on the line of credit to complete a FEMA-funded PA or Hazard Mitigation project, use the FEMA reimbursements to repay the loan, and then use the line to start another project. The second form of relief came with the federal waiver of the 10 percent match requirement for PA funding, which Congress passed in May 2007.[137] New Orleans no longer had to fund this match, and Congressional action freed up state funds reserved to cover the match to be used for additional recovery monies to local parishes, with New Orleans gaining almost $300 million of these new dollars.

As a result of the FEMA PA process and requirements, there was little progress in rebuilding public facilities in the first two years after Katrina. In January 2007, when the UNOP plan was completed, most of the PA funds paid to New Orleans had been for emergency work. Almost $100 million in obligated PA funds were unpaid as the city sought to raise the funds to complete the projects and then seek reimbursement.[138] As late as 2009, New Orleans city agencies had almost $1.6 billion in unresolved PA claims.[139] This meant that residents had to decide whether to return to their neighborhoods and rebuild before knowing if and when their local school, park, library, or fire station would return. Alternatively, the city government and neighborhood groups could pursue other ways to move these projects forward as they awaited federal assistance.

CITY CAPACITY AND COORDINATION

Completing a recovery plan and securing federal funds were critical hurdles for New Orleans, but they constituted two gears of a three-gear rebuilding machine. The third gear was the city's capacity to implement and coordinate hundreds of recovery projects and programs. The magnitude of this undertaking is reflected in the 1,650[140] projects approved for PA and CDBG funding in August 2010. Any city would find it daunting to implement so many projects at the same time, let alone getting multiple city departments and independent authorities to coordinate their efforts. Coordination was important for two reasons. It would reduce the disruption and waste of resources that would result if, for example, the public works department rebuilt a street only to have the water and sewer board tear up the street the next month to replace damaged water and sewer lines. Coordination also was vital to provide signals and momentum to stimulate private rebuilding investments by residents and businesses. This might involve phasing projects to ensure that essential services were restored to each area of the city before less vital projects were undertaken. It could entail rebuilding facilities and infrastructure on major corridors or in economic centers, as prescribed in the Target Recovery Zone plan, to bring businesses back more quickly. Pursuing any intentional rebuilding strategy would involve coordinating where, when, and how the city's many rebuilding projects and programs were implemented.

New Orleans faced some special challenges in building the structures to implement and coordinate rebuilding projects. Historically, the city was plagued by management problems, nepotism, and corruption, including in the now critical area of administering federal programs. Despite its need for revenue and pressing social and development problems, the city was unable to fully spend its full annual allotment of federal CDBG dollars and had large balances of unspent CDBG funds at the time of Katrina.[141] New Orleans also had been cited in HUD audits for inappropriately spending CDBG funds. At the time of Katrina, HUD had reclaimed $18 million for disallowed costs under the CDBG program from five audits during 2004 and 2005.[142] If New Orleans could not fully deploy $20 million in CDBG funds each year, how would it ramp up to spend over $400 million, and not run afoul of HUD rules?

Problems were not limited to the now crucial CDBG program. Gross mismanagement and poor performance at the housing authority and school department had led to the former being placed in federal receivership in 2002 and the latter being taken over by the state in 2004.[143] The need for this large growth in project management capacity came after extensive layoffs in the city staff with the large revenue losses after Katrina. Although it had retained many of the experienced executive-level staff, New Orleans lost many midlevel employees and support staff who handle the day-to-day work of project and program management.[144] An indication of the extent of the city's budget and staffing problems is that the Office of Recovery Management relied on a large group of interns from MIT and other colleges to provide much of its early staffing and funded several full-time professional staff with foundation grants.[145]

Capacity challenges were not limited to city government. New Orleans also had few nonprofit organizations with a strong track record in developing or rehabbing housing or running community development and economic development programs. Despite the New Orleans Neighborhood Development Collaboration initiative in the 1990s and efforts by the Morial and Nagin

Administrations to strengthen nonprofit community development capacity, this sector was still quite small. In other cities, community-based organizations had developed hundreds or thousands of housing units and had run additional types of programs. Most New Orleans' organizations had only a few staff people and built at most a few dozen housing units each year.[146] Moreover, the precarious state of these organizations before the storm meant that many disappeared after the storm while others took a long time to get reestablished.[147] Thus, the ability of the nonprofit "third sector" to augment the city's rebuilding capacity, especially in the area of housing and community facilities, was quite limited.[148] New Orleans did have stronger capacity in historic preservation[149] and in several small business development organizations that proved helpful in neighborhood rebuilding but were less so in getting federally funded rebuilding projects off the ground.

The responsibility for creating and coordinating New Orleans' rebuilding capacity fell to Ed Blakely as Director of the Office of Recovery Management—a fact emphasized by reference to him as the "Recovery Czar" in the press.[150] Blakely and ORM had a mandate to oversee the city's rebuilding, both in UNOP and in the mayor's appointment of Blakely to "coordinate and direct recovery efforts,"[151] but carrying out this mandate proved difficult in practice. At ORM, Blakely had few staff and resources under his control[152] and was on equal footing with other city executives and mayoral advisors:

> He has no line authority over departments of the city. For example, public works, public facilities are all situated under the CAO's [Chief Administrative Officer's] office. In the hierarchy of the mayor, the CAO, the city attorney, eventually Ed, and the existing housing director are co-equals in city cabinet meetings along with the chief of staff and some policy advisors.[153]

ORM also faced resistance by other agencies that anticipated playing a major role in the rebuilding process. Prior to establishing ORM and appointing Blakely, Nagin had expanded and appointed major civic leaders and political heavyweights to the board of the New Orleans Redevelopment Authority (NORA), positioning it to play a key role in the rebuilding process. NORA had critical powers in property acquisition, development, and disposition for undertaking rebuilding projects and was bound by less bureaucracy than line agencies. Since it viewed itself as one of the lead agencies for rebuilding, it resisted taking direction from Blakely.[154] When the LRA approved New Orleans' Citywide Strategic Recovery and Redevelopment Plan in June 2007, ORM finally gained its first real resources but still lacked the administrative infrastructure to put this money to work.

This situation soon changed when the city's Chief Development Officer, Donna Adkinson, left. Blakely gained control of the city's development agency and consolidated it with ORM to form the Office of Recovery Development and Administration (ORDA).[155] Blakely now ran multiple city offices, including ORM; housing and community development; economic development; and safety, permitting and code enforcement, which together included several hundred employees. Blakely brought in Ezra Rapport, who had worked with him in Oakland, where Rapport had served as deputy city attorney and assistant city manager. As Chief Operating Officer and Chief Development Officer for ORDA, Rapport took on the task of organizing city departments to implement the newly approved recovery plan.

When Rapport arrived, he found that the city departments had not been integrated into the recovery effort. They were operating their normal city functions as they did before Katrina, but had not reoriented their priorities or created new programs to address the city's huge recovery needs. The absence of well-defined recovery programs and an administrative system to implement them was a barrier to receiving federal funds:

> At the time I arrived, the recovery plan had not yet been approved. The administrative units of the city had not been organized to undertake the tasks associated with the proposed recovery plan. And until the city could demonstrate how it would administer a recovery plan to that satisfaction of the state and federal government, the money available for recovery wouldn't flow.[156]

Similarly, the city lacked administrative resources and systems to manage the repair and rebuilding of hundreds of public facilities with FEMA Public Assistance grants. Rapport focused on two critical tasks: (1) establishing a new "superstructure" to manage the large volume of capital projects; and (2) creating new programs to fit the recovery plan priorities and using them to gain and deploy federal recovery dollars that had not been flowing into the city. ORDA scaled up the city's existing capacity to oversee capital projects by creating a new Project Delivery Unit to coordinate and package public facility projects, and it outsourced the project management work to a private engineering firm, MWH.[157] The city also contracted with fifty architectural and engineering firms to create a large pool of firms available to design public building and infrastructure projects.[158] A process was also created to set priorities for rebuilding public facilities whereby a planning team under the CAO's office put together proposals for targeting specific areas for multiple facilities or to aggregate procurements for similar facilities. These proposals went through an internal city review process for approval and, when approved, were sent to the new Project Delivery

Unit (PDU) to initiate a mass procurement rather than individual project design and bidding. One goal of this process was to concentrate public facility investments in the 17 Target Recovery Zones established under the rebuilding plan. ORDA faced considerable obstacles within the city bureaucracy in implementing the centralized project approval and management system under the PDU and MWH. .[159] Multiple city agencies still had authority over capital projects, which slowed down the procurement process, created turf battles,[160] and caused MWH to receive directions from multiple agency heads. Some city employees were also resistant to change or sought to retain their role in the process, and thus preferred to use the former capital projects procurement system even though it could not handle the large volume of projects. By early 2010, under new director Harrison Boyd, contracting responsibility for the city's recovery capital projects and other procurement under the $411million CDBG funding was centralized under PDU. PDU and MWH still had to rely on the cooperation of other city employees and departments for information and other actions, which was not always forthcoming, and were affected by insufficient staffing and outdated systems in these agencies.[161]

To implement new programs and projects required under the recovery plan, ORDA sought alliances with city and regional authorities,[162] which it believed would provide higher-level capacity than city departments, since they were more flexible and operated outside the city civil service salary limits. The primary alliances included:

- working through the New Orleans Redevelopment Authority (NORA) to reuse and redevelop blighted property and undertake some commercial development projects;
- contracting with the Finance Authority of New Orleans (FANO) to provide home ownership financing and subsidies;
- using the New Orleans Regional Planning Commission to advance work on rebuilding the downtown medical district, including engineering work for a new Veterans Administration hospital and plans for land assembly and improvements;
- supporting plans by the New Orleans Building Corporation to improve six miles of the Mississippi Riverfront with a continuous green space, improved public access, and public gathering places;
- working with the Regional Transportation Authority to ensure transit services, especially for Target Recovery Zones; and
- coordinating with the Recovery School District and Water and Sewer Board on repairs, rebuilding priorities, and the completion of FEMA Public Assistance projects.

Rather than using the multiagency Recovery Council to coordinate rebuilding efforts, as anticipated in UNOP, ORDA worked out individual agreements on priorities and recovery funding with each of these organizations. Negotiating these agreements often took many months and in some cases (notably FANO and the Soft Second Mortgage program) they were not implemented.

As ORDA began to implement the Citywide Strategic Recovery and Redevelopment Plan, it also adjusted the plan and some funding priorities. It expanded the original 17 Target Recovery Zones to include a few other neighborhoods and commercial areas with emerging rebuilding activity and added two major projects with large expected economic impacts for the city—a new hospital for the federal Department of Veterans Affairs (VA) and the six-mile riverfront improvement project known as Reinventing the Crescent. Funding for the hospital project resulted from the city's efforts to assemble a large site to prevent the VA hospital from locating outside New Orleans.[163] CDBG funds were shifted to the Reinventing the Crescent project when Mayor Nagin expressed concern about long delays in spending on other projects, and this project was expected to move forward quickly and make a significant impact on the city.[164] These two projects were allocated $75 million and $30 million, respectively, in CDBG recovery funds.[165]

When Mayor Mitch Landrieu took office in May 2010, further changes were made to the city's project implementation capacity and recovery funding priorities. The city let its contract with MWH expire and then hired 30 former MWH employees in city staff positions to manage capital projects, essentially replicating MWH's capacity in-house. This step saved the city considerable money, as the new salaries were less than 60 percent of the fees paid to MWH, and was expected to make the procurement system more effective. With former MWH consultants now working as city employees, PDU leadership believed their new status would reduce mistrust and increase cooperation by other city agencies and employees. Mayor Landrieu also revisited the pipeline of capital projects approved by the Nagin Administration to ensure that it fit current priorities and to scale back $1.5 billion in authorized projects that exceeded the city's available funding. After consulting with each city councillor on his or her priority, Landrieu announced, on August 18, 2010 (his 100th day in office), a list of the top 100 projects that his administration was committed to completing within three years, at a cost of $640 million.[166] The largest amounts were devoted to park and recreation facilities ($163 million); police, fire, emergency medical, and criminal justice projects ($98 million); and road reconstruction and repair ($60 million). Landrieu's priorities included many capital projects initiated under Nagin, but quite a few were omitted for further review or to ensure sufficient funding for their completion.[167]

CONCLUSION

In the first five years after Katrina, New Orleans struggled to address three critical rebuilding needs: creation of a plan to guide its recovery, access to federal rebuilding funds, and creation of the capacity to implement rebuilding projects and programs on a large scale. Despite the initial setbacks in the planning process, the absence of a coherent and realistic recovery plan, and multiple problems with federal recovery funding, important accomplishments and key milestones were attained. Some of the most critical accomplishments addressed funding for rebuilding:

• Substantial federal rebuilding funds were appropriated and then programmed and distributed by Louisiana state government that were particularly important to rebuilding the city's housing stock.
• A key settlement was reached with FEMA that provided $1.8 billion to rebuild New Orleans public schools.
• A state line of credit was established that allowed New Orleans to move forward with projects funded on a reimbursement basis by FEMA.
• $411 million in CDBG funds were in place to fund the city's rebuilding priorities.

Beyond funding, the multiple planning processes engaged thousands of New Orleans residents in rethinking the future of their city and neighborhoods. Although the funding and pathway to implement UNOP did not exist, the process generated and assembled project and policy ideas that entrepreneurial leaders and organizations could pursue. Finally, New Orleans city government expanded its project implementation capacity through a combination of private vendors, partnerships, and nonprofit and quasi-public entities and by creating its own project delivery unit.

However, these accomplishments were accompanied by considerable constraints in how federal recovery funds could be used, as well as large delays, bureaucratic hurdles, and financial burdens in accessing these funds. GO zone tax-incentives that targeted private recovery investment proved very hard to use and were geared toward large projects and businesses. Under state government policy, the bulk of discretionary CDBG funds were allocated to help homeowners rebuild. Nonetheless, homeowners faced long delays in accessing Road Home funds to repair and rebuild properties, worsened by compliance issues with federal regulations. New Orleans made little progress in rebuilding city infrastructure and facilities for several years, faced with mismanagement, long delays and frequent changes in funding awards under FEMA's Public Assistance Program, and financial hardship from policies that required a local government match and advance funding of projects. The City of New Orleans' own lack of project management capacity and limited ability to design and carry out public community development programs also contributed to the confusion and pace at which recovery projects and programs were implemented.

From the vantage point of households, property owners, businesses, and others who needed to make decisions about whether to rebuild and where to invest in New Orleans, there was considerable uncertainty about the timing, scale, and location of public rebuilding investments. Even when clear priorities were established and programs announced, as with the Target Area Plan and Soft Second Mortgage Program, there were long delays or outright failures around their implementation. Consequently, the official citywide rebuilding process did not build strong confidence in New Orleans' recovery, nor provide an effective guide and motivator for private rebuilding decisions and investments. Delays and policies governing federal recovery aid also meant that many residents, businesses, and organizations could neither wait for nor rely on federal assistance to make rebuilding decisions.

With the problems and delays in federal assistance and a weak citywide recovery process, the role of neighborhood-scale rebuilding efforts took on greater importance in New Orleans. Were community-based rebuilding efforts able to fill gaps in the citywide rebuilding system? To what extent did neighborhood-based recovery efforts overcome confusion or problems with the intergovernmental top-down process to build confidence and trigger rebuilding investments by households, businesses, developers, and other organizations? The next three chapters examine these questions by detailing the work and accomplishments of grassroots rebuilding efforts in six New Orleans neighborhoods.

CHAPTER 3

ᴏⅤᴏ

Broadmoor Lives

As they returned to survey the damage in September and October, Broadmoor residents found their neighborhood and the city in a state of devastation. Streets were littered with downed power lines and trees. The doors of homes searched by the National Guard and others were open and possessions were strewn about. A pervasive brown covered the landscape—the brown of dead vegetation and a rank brown film left from the floodwaters. The neighborhood was quiet, devoid even of the sounds of birds and largely absent of people. The primary sounds and presence were those of the National Guard troops who patrolled the city. Hal Roark was one the first residents to return in early September. He was shocked and in a state of disbelief as he contemplated what the storm and flooding meant for him and the city.

> It was horrific; power lines down, trees down everywhere. No one was back. The National Guard had searched all the homes...all the doors were open, all the homes were completely open...It was like a bomb went off. You could walk into anybody's house anywhere in the city...I drove around a bit...power lines were down. All the streets were profoundly littered with downed trees. There was a horrible brown film on everything...everything is dead, there was no sound, no birds...I was thinking about what we would do with our house and our city. I was very concerned about the 250,000 houses damaged, where are we going to get all the sheetrock, all the labor. Just the practicality of it...My business is selling to folks in the middle class, lower middle class, African American first time homebuyers. And that description was exactly who was displaced from the city and wasn't coming back. I could see that the business was gone for at least a year if not two...At an emotional level, just the idea of getting my rentals back in shape after they were in good shape was very traumatic.

Within a few months, Roark's attention would shift to how Broadmoor as a neighborhood could rebuild. Over the next four years, he would emerge as a leader in the neighborhood's efforts to prepare and carry out a plan to rebuild Broadmoor "better than before." There, an existing neighborhood improvement association worked with emerging leaders to undertake a resident-driven planning process, complete a neighborhood rebuilding plan, and create the capacity to implement key rebuilding projects and programs. Along with its successes, Broadmoor has faced challenges in achieving its initial goals for rebuilding housing, creating a high-performing school, and overcoming economic disparities with the neighborhood.

This chapter details the neighborhood's grassroots rebuilding process and concludes with a discussion of its progress, continuing challenges, and the factors that have contributed to its accomplishments.

A LOOK AT BROADMOOR

Not surprisingly, Broadmoor sustained heavy flooding after Katrina. This New Orleans neighborhood is situated in a low-lying basin between the high ground of the Mississippi River's natural levee and the Metairie Ridge (see Figure 3.1). Although close to some of New Orleans' wealthier and older neighborhoods, the Garden District and Uptown, and next to Claiborne Avenue—a major boulevard that connects it to suburban Jefferson Parish and downtown New Orleans, Broadmoor was part of the city's back swamps (with a 12-acre lake in the early nineteenth century[1]) and largely undeveloped until the early twentieth century. Its conversion into habitable land and development was a product of major investments in pumping stations and drainage systems and the introduction of streetcar lines. The initial drainage canals were built in 1885, followed by a pumping station built on the neighborhood boundaries at Broad Street and Washington in 1903.[2] Much more powerful pumps were installed at the Broad Street station in 1915 and in the following years a small population began settling the area.[3]

A housing boom followed in the early 1920s, when over one-third of the neighborhood's homes were built along with its first public school, the Andrew H. Wilson School, which was built in 1922. Broadmoor continued to develop and grow until the late 1950s and 1960s when, like many other New Orleans neighborhoods, it began to lose population to the suburbs of Jefferson Parish and to new development in New Orleans East.[4] Despite the population decline, it remained a fairly stable and

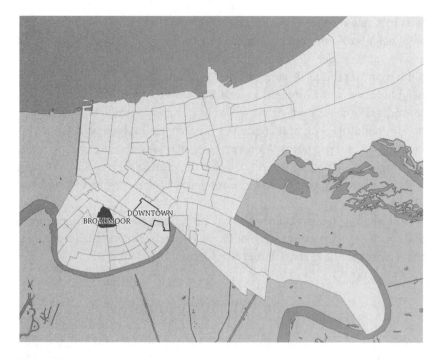

Figure 3.1.
Location of Broadmoor within New Orleans
Source: City of New Orleans GIS Department, New Orleans Neighborhoods, 2007, http://gisweb.cityofno. com/cnogis/dataportal.aspx.

largely residential neighborhood[5] that was a microcosm of New Orleans in many ways. According to the 2000 Census, Broadmoor had 7,232 residents living in 2,915 households, equal to 1.5 percent of New Orleans' population. Its residents closely mirror those of the entire city in their age, race, educational level, and home and car ownership rates (see Table 3.1 and Figure 3.2). Before Katrina, Broadmoor residents were relatively poor within a poor city. Its residents' average income was almost $7,000 below the $43,000 citywide average; at 32 percent, its poverty rate was 4 points above the New Orleans' high 28 percent rate. On the other hand, its residents were more stable—almost 61 percent lived in the same house in 1995 and 2000, and it had a lower incidence of vacant homes than the entire city.

As a neighborhood in a low-lying, heavily flooded part of New Orleans with a population representative of the entire city, Broadmoor faced rebuilding challenges that were common to many neighborhoods: rebuilding the housing stock and getting people of diverse economic means to return, reopening schools and other vital services

Table 3.1. KEY TRAITS FOR BROADMOOR AND NEW
ORLEANS RESIDENTS IN 2000

Population Trait	Broadmoor	New Orleans
Percent black	68.2%	66.6%
Percent white	25.8%	26.6%
Average household income	$36,399	$43,176
Poverty rate	31.8%	27.9%
Percent owner-occupied homes	48.1%	46.5%
Percent vacant housing units	9.5%	12.5%
Percent not completing high school	26.0%	25.4%
Percent with bachelor's degree or higher	23.6%	23.1%
Percent of residents who moved into their house before 1990	38.5%	35.0%
Percent living in same house in 1995	60.7%	56.8%
Percent of households without a car	27.8%	27.3%

Source: 2000 U.S. Census.

for residents, and reducing future flood risks in the rebuilt neighborhood. It also was typical of New Orleans in its social and economic
problems—high poverty, poor-performing schools and widespread
vacant properties. As is often the case in post-disaster planning, its
aspirations included addressing these longstanding problems to rebuild
a better neighborhood.

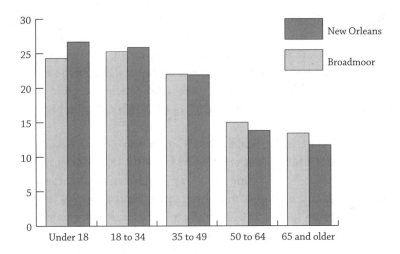

Figure 3.2.
Age distribution of residents, Broadmoor and New Orleans in 2000
Source: 2000 U.S. Census.

ORGANIZING TO REBUILD

Individual homeowners, such as Hal Roark, had started to gut and repair their homes in the fall, but the first community-wide action around rebuilding started months later in response to the January 11, 2006 BNOB Urban Planning Committee report. [6] This report and the ensuing *Times–Picayune* article showed Broadmoor covered with a large green circle labeled "approximate areas of expected to become parks and greenspace [*sic*]." The map sparked residents to act, as reported by one community member:

> I was working at Tulane, and my coworker had a subscription to *The Times–Picayune*. She brought in the article and said, "This looks like exactly where you live," and showed me the BNOB map...We were confronted with the map, and there was a lot of anger and outrage. It spurred a collective will to prevent it from happening. It started with rallies, and built into an effort to build a collective voice.

One resident, Virginia Saussy, began to organize a rally to fight the BNOB plan. She called for a neighborhood rally on January 14 and contacted friends and acquaintances about the rally. Saussy alerted *The Times–Picayune* and a local TV station about the rally and booked a brass band to provide music. She draped a large banner emblazoned with "Broadmoor Lives" on the front of her house, creating what became a defining symbol for the neighborhood's rebuilding. At the same time, LaToya Cantrell, who had evacuated to Houston, was organizing the first post-storm meeting of the Broadmoor Improvement Association (BIA) for the same day. Saussy contacted Cantrell, BIA's President, to get the organization's support for the rally. Cantrell agreed to move the BIA meeting to January 18 to increase attendance and build momentum for a neighborhood meeting and urged BIA board members to join the rally.[7]

The Broadmoor Improvement Association was one of New Orleans' many neighborhood associations known for undertaking minor beautification activities before Katrina.[8] However, unlike many of these associations, the BIA also had a history of organizing and advocacy relating to community issues. In the 1960s and early 1970s, the BIA organized residents to fight block-busting efforts, which involved realtors' and others' efforts to profit by playing on fears of blacks moving into the area—in time, they were able to profit by convincing white families to sell homes at low prices and then reselling them at higher prices to blacks.[9] In the years prior to Katrina, the BIA filed a class action suit on behalf of 125 residents to recover damages to their property from a major drainage project and advocated for the Army Corps of Engineers to restore damaged landscaping and neutral grounds destroyed by the project.[10] More importantly, the BIA had a new leader in LaToya Cantrell, who became president in late 2004. Cantrell had moved to the parkway section of Broadmoor in 2000, where she organized residents into the Louisiana Parkway Area Association to address issues of drug trafficking, slumlords, and speeding traffic. Through this effort, she became more familiar with the neighborhood, built relations with city officials, and developed a reputation for getting things done. This reputation helped convince emerging activists that the BIA could be an effective organization in leading the rebuilding effort. Hal Roark was originally skeptical of the BIA but one of his no-nonsense friends convinced him that the new BIA president "was for real and could get things done." He decided to approach the BIA with his rebuilding idea.

As the Broadmoor rally and BIA meeting approached, Roark crystallized his thinking about how Broadmoor should respond to the BNOB Commission and the notion that it had to "prove its viability." He arrived at the idea that Broadmoor should beat the BNOB at its own game by rebuilding based on the values articulated by the BNOB. He prepared a one-page summary of the BNOB values and proposed that Broadmoor work to defeat the BNOB Plan by presenting its own rebuilding plan as a reflection of those values. When Cantrell met with Roark on January 18, the day of the BIA meeting, she liked his idea and included it in the meeting agenda. Cantrell had her own goals for the meeting. She wanted it to be a well-organized and credible meeting to convince residents that the BIA was an established organization that provided the right auspices under which to undertake rebuilding. She also sought to recruit volunteers at the meeting to join the rebuilding effort, which she proposed to organize in two committees: a revitalization committee to prepare a rebuilding plan and a repopulation committee to help residents return to their homes.

On January 14, several hundred people attended the short forty-five-minute rally[11] to hear speeches and pledge their commitment to rebuild—300 people signed a petition drawn up by the BIA, stating that they were returning to Broadmoor. The rally received local press coverage but was most important in generating residents' commitment to rebuild and in building momentum for taking the next steps. This energy carried over to the BIA meeting, held four days later, which also drew many residents. Cantrell opened the meeting by making the case for her vision of how Broadmoor could rebuild and emphasizing the need for the entire neighborhood to come back, not just better-off residents and homeowners. She proposed the creation of the revitalization and rebuilding committees and asked Roark to present his idea about Broadmoor's creation of its own plan based on the BNOB principles. The BIA also had residents complete a form to indicate their core area of interest and skills for assisting in the planning and rebuilding effort. The names and skill sets of volunteers were then given to each committee chair to help them recruit residents to undertake committee work. The meeting concluded with a vote on what people wanted to do—sell their homes and leave the neighborhood or return and rebuild. The vote was overwhelmingly to return and rebuild.

With the affirmation to rebuild and volunteers recruited from the January 18 meeting, the organizing work began with the formation of the two committees and laying out a process to formulate a rebuilding plan.[12] Virginia Saussy and Kelli Wright, a realtor, served as cochairs of the Repopulation Committee. Wright focused on tracking the status of homes and residents—who was returning and which homes were being put up for sale—by driving around the neighborhood and creating a database and map to monitor repopulation progress. This early work planted the seeds for a repopulation information system that Broadmoor created that included volunteer block captains, a property level database, maps, and an annual neighborhood census. To complement Wright's information system, Saussy tackled marketing the neighborhood to convince residents to return. Her approach was to market the rebuilding effort like a new subdivision and create a Broadmoor brand around the "Broadmoor Lives" slogan. Her first steps were to create a Broadmoor Lives website and to order, with $1,000 provided by the BIA, a few hundred Broadmoor Lives lawn signs for residents to place around the neighborhood. The web-site provided displaced residents with information on plans and efforts to rebuild Broadmoor that might help convince them to return. Homeowners placed lawn signs in front of their houses to show they had decided to return; it was a visible statement of their commitment to rebuild and showed neighbors that they would not be alone if they also rebuilt in Broadmoor.

For the rebuilding committee, the BIA tapped Hal Roark and attorney Mark Morice as cochairs. Working with Cantrell, the cochairs created an organizational plan and process for the challenge of preparing a neighborhood rebuilding plan. Roark wanted to ensure that every meeting held to work on the plan would be a productive one. Cantrell was attentive to

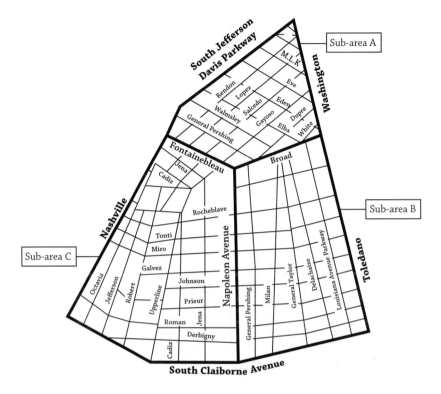

Figure 3.3.
Broadmoor street map and sub-areas
Source: The Redevelopment Plan for Broadmoor. Used by permission, Broadmoor Improvement Association.

creating a community-wide consensus for the plan that would address the entire neighborhood; she was particularly concerned that the plan respond to the concerns of residents from the neighborhood's poorer eastern section. The result was a planning process that divided the neighborhood into three sub-areas, A, B, and C (shown in Figure 3.3), to allow residents in each sub-area to meet in smaller groups with their closest neighbors to identify priorities, develop ideas and proposals, and provide feedback on the rebuilding plan and specific proposals as they emerged.[13] Five subcommittees also were formed to prepare issue-based components of the plan: Urban Planning,[14] Economic Development, Education, Emergency Preparedness, and Transportation, with a sixth committee added to prepare the final plan document. Communitywide meetings were held to review proposals discussed at the subarea meetings and issue subcommittees and to build communitywide consensus for the plan (see Figure 3.4).

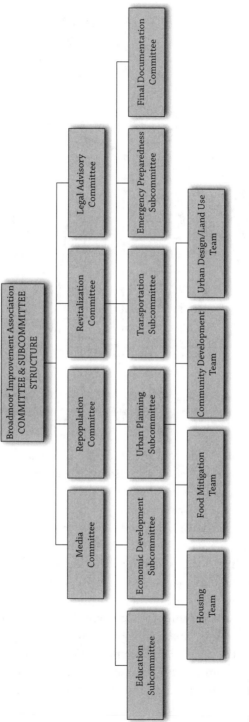

Figure 3.4.
Broadmoor Redevelopment Plan committee structure
Source: The Redevelopment Plan for Broadmoor. Used by permission, Broadmoor Improvement Association.

THE HARVARD PARTNERSHIP

Soon after the planning and repopulation committees were in full swing, Harvard University's Kennedy School of Government (KSG) appeared and ultimately became a valuable partner in the rebuilding process.[15] Doug Ahlers, a senior fellow at the KSG, was asked by the school's dean to organize a service project in New Orleans for students to undertake during the March 2006 spring break. Ahlers owned a home and business in New Orleans. As a member of the BNOB's Economic Development Committee, he recruited Harvard students to help put the committee's final report together. For the spring break project, Ahlers initially considered helping to rebuild a commercial corridor but then decided to pick one neighborhood and work with it on its overall rebuilding needs. After looking at the demographics of the 49 flooded neighborhoods to find ones that closely matched those of the city, Ahlers narrowed the choice down to two neighborhoods unfamiliar to him: Broadmoor and Gentilly. While he considered which neighborhood to approach, Ahlers went to meet with Walter Isaacson,[16] a Harvard alumni and Vice Chair of the Louisiana Recovery Authority, to get his support for the spring break project.[17] Isaacson showed little interest in the project until he learned which neighborhoods Harvard planned to target for its work. When Ahlers mentioned that the choice was between Broadmoor and Gentilly, Isaacson immediately became interested, as he had grown up in Broadmoor and his father still lived there. Isaacson e-mailed his father and put Ahlers in touch with LaToya Cantrell. Ahlers was soon on his way to New Orleans to meet with the BIA board. At this February meeting, Ahlers encountered skepticism from BIA board members about his intentions. Given the history of the ULI recommendations and recent BNOB Urban Planning Committee report, the BIA was understandably wary of outsiders offering to help put a plan together. In his meetings with the BIA board and the chairs of planning committees, Ahlers delivered two messages: "that we did not have any money and that our philosophy was to come in and support them in their efforts and not to tell them what to do."[18] The meetings helped convince Broadmoor's leaders to accept Harvard's offer to assist them over the March 2006 spring break.

In late March, a team of 22 students and three staff traveled to New Orleans and took on two roles in the planning process. One was to help Broadmoor understand what to include in a neighborhood rebuilding plan. Students studied other plans to provide a template for the Broadmoor Plan. Ahlers believed that the Broadmoor Plan would get a lot of scrutiny from politicians and professional planners. Therefore, he advised that it needed to look like and have the content of a professional plan. The template informed the BIA committees about the format and what to include in a professional final plan, e.g., an existing conditions section and implementation plans for its recommendations. In their second role, students were assigned to each committee—repopulation, urban planning, economic development, housing, etc., to conduct research on best practices and compile relevant program and project examples from other communities. This research provided options for the residents and committees to consider in their planning.

After the spring break project, Ahlers continued to serve as an advisor to Broadmoor and created a long-term partnership between Harvard and the BIA. He helped the BIA in setting expectations and thinking through critical strategy issues. For example, Ahlers alerted Broadmoor's leaders that federal aid was unlikely to fund their rebuilding efforts and they would need to secure their own resources to fund implementation. He also pressured the BIA to create realistic plans to implement proposed projects based on neighborhood skills and capacity rather than an expectation that the city or other outside parties would bring their plans to fruition. While advising Broadmoor to focus on internal implementation capacity, Ahlers, through contacts at Harvard, helped to arrange a $1 million grant from Shell Oil to support Harvard's partnership with Broadmoor. Through this partnership, which was still active in 2011, Harvard sent over 100 students to work in Broadmoor on summer internships, short-term projects over January and spring break, and research and course-based student projects. After first focusing on two- to three-week immersion trips in which many students worked intensely on projects, the emphasis shifted to recruiting summer interns for Broadmoor. From 2006 through 2010, between two and eight Harvard students worked as summer interns, providing a source of staff to help implement parts of the plan. Students would take an idea or project in the Broadmoor Plan and work on the detailed steps and tools needed to implement it. For example, one student created a database used by the BDC to track individual families and connect them to assistance needed to return and rebuild their homes. Broadmoor's leadership also visited Harvard for executive training, to recruit students and faculty to work with them, and for short-term consultations with Harvard staff and faculty. In all these efforts, Ahlers approached the partnership with the view that: "Our role is...helping support them, help to build capacities and capabilities within the neighborhood so that they can affect their own recovery."[19] Broadmoor's experience with Harvard demonstrated how Broadmoor could access resources to rebuild by forming partnerships with other organizations. Consequently, partnerships would become central to Broadmoor's approach to implementing its rebuilding plan.

PUTTING THE PLAN TOGETHER

Broadmoor's rebuilding plan was created through a community-driven participatory process.[20] Over six months, more than one hundred meetings were held, involving several hundred residents in discussions about their goals and visions for rebuilding Broadmoor. At these meetings, residents put forward specific ideas and projects to translate their vision into reality, worked out differences and prepared an overall strategy to implement their plan. From January to July 2006, multiple committees and working groups met every week. Initial planning began with the weekly subgroup area meetings held from early February[21] through mid-March with Area C meeting on Wednesday evenings, Area A on Thursdays, and Area B on Fridays. At these meetings, residents focused on what they wanted to see happen in a rebuilt neighborhood—both their main concerns and specific project wish lists. Each week was devoted to a different issue that was discussed at all three subgroup area meetings: overall strategy; how to deal with the BNOB commission; housing; security; and education and cultural activities. Priorities and proposals that emerged from the subgroup committees were then presented at communitywide meetings held monthly from January to July.[22] The community meetings, which Cantrell led, served two functions: (1) to present and acknowledge issues that were raised in each subarea; and (2) to identify and build consensus on the points of agreement. When disagreements occurred between sub-areas, Cantrell would acknowledge them at the community meetings but not try to work them out there. Instead, Cantrell held separate meetings, which she called "shuttle diplomacy," to address the differences—often getting leaders and residents from each group to see their inherent commonalities.[23] One example is a difference over bike paths, which Sub-area C saw as a redevelopment priority but Sub-area B viewed as less important than addressing crime— its priority. In meetings with each group, Cantrell persuaded residents in Sub-area C to agree that they wanted to ride their bikes throughout the entire neighborhood, not just their areas, and thus it was important for Sub-area B to be safe. At the same time, she elicited from area B residents that once their neighborhood was safe, they wanted their kids to be able to ride their bikes and thus bike paths would benefit them. In this manner, both groups acknowledged the value of each others' concern.[24] Once the sub-area meetings (also referred to as subgroup meetings) were completed, the issue committees became more active. The charge for the issue committees was to translate the shared priorities and project proposals that emerged from the sub-area committees into concrete plans and projects for implementation (see Figure 3.5a). Most issue committees worked on their plans in weekly (and sometimes more frequent) meetings from the end of March through late June. A separate Document Writing Committee started work in late March and worked over the next four months to integrate the output of each issue committee (and the entire process) into a final neighborhood rebuilding plan (see Figure 3.5).

Near the end of May, a weeklong deliberation on the draft "urban design plan" took place. The urban design plan was a graphic representation of the vision for Broadmoor that emerged from planning meetings and improvements proposed to actualize this vision.[25] An initial presentation on the plan took place on Monday, with images and maps on display at the BIA offices throughout the week for informal discussion and questions with Urban Design Committee members and residents. A final workshop, with displaced residents participating via conference call, was held on Saturday, May 20, to review, modify, and build consensus on the design plan. The vision presented during this week, and ultimately adopted in the Broadmoor Plan, included an immediate focus on service restoration to enable residents' return and redevelopment of the neighborhood around four nodes—the most important of which was a neighborhood village and educational/cultural corridor intended to provide a vibrant activity center to serve the entire community. The month of June was devoted to drafting sections of the plan, reconciling and incorporating them into a final draft of the entire plan. The Final Plan was completed in July and approved at a communitywide meeting on July 17—six months after the initial rally and BIA meeting first mobilized residents to produce their own neighborhood rebuilding plan.

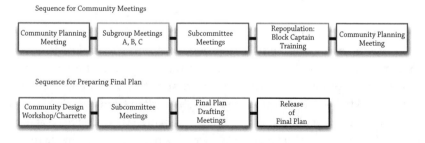

Figure 3.5.
Community meeting and plan preparation phases for Broadmoor's planning process.
Source: The Redevelopment Plan for Broadmoor. Used by permission, Broadmoor Improvement Association.

THE BROADMOOR PLAN

Broadmoor's final plan was a 335-page document organized into nine sections[26] and supported with extensive data, maps, and diagrams. It began with a Goals and Strategy section that presents the plan's vision statement, goals,[27] core values, and a list of the 110 proposed projects according to priority level.[28] The vision was straightforward, as expressed in words:

> The vision for Broadmoor is to fully repopulate the neighborhood, rebuild the infrastructure and the institutions, and develop a safer, stronger community that is committed to providing a better quality of life for all residents.

Yet achieving this vision would be complex and challenging given the multifaceted nature of its goals and the long project list. For example, the goal to Rebuild Housing and Eliminate Blighted Properties sought to return 80 percent of all housing units "back into commerce" by December 2007 through five strategies with 15 discrete projects—all but one of which was high priority. A history of Broadmoor was presented in the second section, followed by two chapters, comprising one-third of the plan, that analyze the neighborhood's conditions before Katrina and in spring 2006 when the plan was prepared. The final five sections presented the Broadmoor Plan, i.e., the specific proposals to rebuild the neighborhood. It was largely organized around a "Future Vision" (the Urban Design Plan presented in late May) that outlined plans for urban development, repopulation, housing, community development, and flood mitigation. Four additional plan components addressed education, economic development, emergency preparedness, and implementation.

The Broadmoor Plan was an ambitious neighborhood rebuilding plan that encompassed 110 projects organized into 16 categories—two-thirds of which were designated as being high priority (see Table 3.2). Despite this broad scope, the plan's core revolved around five main initiatives. The first was an urban development vision aimed at strengthening four neighborhood nodes as centers of community and commercial activity. The plans for three of the nodes, briefly presented in a single page, were not well-developed. For two nodes, only general development concepts were proposed, e.g., mixed-use investment, improved green spaces, a medical district, without any specific projects. The plan for the fourth node was described in far more detail over five pages. It called for a Neighborhood Village Center built around an education corridor that would run from the Wilson School to the Keller Library with two anchor projects—a rebuilt and "high-quality" Wilson School and renovated Keller Library.[29] Ideas

Table 3.2. NUMBER OF BROADMOOR PLAN PROJECTS BY CATEGORY AND PRIORITY LEVEL

Project Category	Number of Projects	High-Priority Projects	Medium-Priority Projects	Low-Priority Projects
Immediate term	8	8		
Housing	15	14	1	
Repopulation	17	15	2	
Flood mitigation	5	5		
Education/ community center	15	4	10	1
Xavier tie-in	3	3		
Free Church of Ann Community Center	6	5	1	
Green space networks	7	2	1	4
Pedestrian enhancements	7	1	3	2
Streets & infrastructure	7	7		
Security	2	2		
Transportation	2	2		
Bike routes	4			4
Economic development	9	6	3	
Neighborhood identification	3			4
Total	110	74	21	15

for programming, implementation steps, and best practices for elementary education at the Wilson School were developed by the Education Committee and presented separately in the plan's education section. The second main initiative was a neighborhood repopulation strategy that was already underway, but the plan proposed expanding the strategy to reach the goal of 80 percent repopulation by former residents by August 2007. To achieve repopulation, the plan envisioned a two-part strategy: (1) marketing the neighborhood and its rebuilding plan to former residents to demonstrate the neighborhood's viability and encourage them to return; and (2) outreach and surveying to identify displaced residents and provide assistance to support their return. Volunteer block captains were the foundation of this outreach effort. They collected information on new returns and still-vacant addresses and served as the first point of contact to welcome people back, provide them with rebuilding information, and connect them to resources. A third set of initiatives, linked to repopulation, focused on rebuilding the housing stock so people would have a place to live. An immediate plan was to secure volunteer labor and donated materials to help homeowners rebuild through partnerships with organizations such as Habitat for Humanity and church and student groups that could bring volunteers to gut and repair homes. The plan provided for creating a dormitory at the Annunciation Mission Church to house and feed volunteers. Another proposed strategy was to acquire and repair abandoned and blighted properties to bring them back into use. Several additional programs were proposed to promote homeownership, attract and assist first-responders to live in Broadmoor, and reduce the number of blighted homes. The fourth core initiative sought to improve neighborhood livability and quality of life through a mix of new projects and activities, such as green space and recreational facilities, better public services (e.g., street repair, trash removal), public safety improvements, and an expanded police presence.

In its fifth key element, the Broadmoor Plan addressed implementation. However, this section did not include specific implementation plans for many of the 110 proposed projects. Rather, the plan's formal implementation section was a chart with a partial list of implementation tasks and very general assignments of responsibility and timing. In place of detailed plans

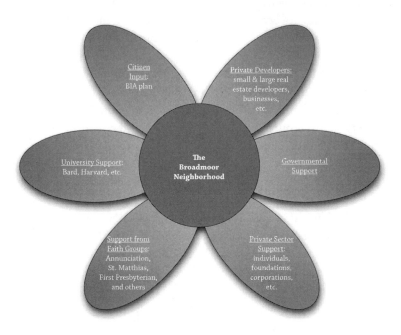

Figure 3.6.
Diagram of Broadmoor's partnership implementation strategy
Source: The Redevelopment Plan for Broadmoor. Used by permission, Broadmoor Improvement Association.

to actualize its many projects, the Broadmoor plan articulated two broad implementation strategies.

The first strategy extended Broadmoor's work with faith-based organizations and universities to proposed partnerships with an array of groups that could offer different implementation capacities. This "Six Point Redevelopment Strategy" was represented by a flower diagram (see Figure 3.6), with the Broadmoor neighborhood as the center and six petals representing the mix of partners or institutions expected to provide the resources to implement the neighborhood plan: citizens; private developers; government; private sector individuals, foundations, and corporations; faith-based groups; and universities. The second implementation strategy was to create the Broadmoor Development Corporation (BDC), a new community development corporation created to secure funding, hire staff, and implement the plan's primary housing and economic development initiatives, including efforts to acquire and repair abandoned properties.

COMMUNITY DEVELOPMENT
CORPORATIONS IN NEW ORLEANS

Community development corporations (CDCs) emerged in the 1960s as part of the war on poverty. They were conceived as a means for local residents and businesses in poor urban and rural areas to direct and undertake efforts to improve their community and especially to expand jobs and economic opportunity. CDCs were originally supported by federal anti-poverty and community development programs, but increasingly became a favored means for corporations and foundations to channel funding and resources to support social, economic, and community development in low-income communities. Several national intermediary organizations were created to assemble private sector dollars and provide financial and technical assistance to support CDCs.[30] The first CDCs sought to address economic development needs of their communities, but by the 1980s the main business of CDCs was building affordable housing fueled by federal policies that stimulated private investment in low-income housing. As CDCs took root and became more successful at housing development and other activities, cities and some states started to rely on CDCs to address their community development goals and allocated more funding to them.

New Orleans was a latecomer to promoting CDCs as a way to stabilize and improve neighborhoods. The first citywide efforts to channel resources to CDCs came in the 1990s when the Marc Morial Administration and Greater New Orleans Foundation (GNOF) established the New Orleans

Neighborhood Development Collaborative (NONDC) to provide operating grants and technical assistance to build the capacity of CDCs in several neighborhoods, primarily to construct affordable rental housing.[31] These efforts, which continued under the Nagin Administration, had limited success. Most of New Orleans' CDCs had only a few staff people and built at most a few dozen housing units each year.[32] Moreover, the precarious state of these organizations before Katrina meant that many CDCs disappeared after the storm and others took a long time to get reestablished.[33] Faced with this situation and the pressing need to rebuild housing, NONDC decided after Katrina to change its focus from being an intermediary that supported other CDCs to a CDC that directly built housing itself. In choosing a CDC as a key implementation strategy, Broadmoor was relying on an established community development model that had a weak track record and little institutional support within New Orleans. Consequently, the BDC's viability and success in advancing Broadmoor's plans would depend on its ability to cultivate its own funding and resources, especially from within the national CDC funding network.

Broadmoor's planning process was effective in several respects but encountered similar problems as the UNOP plan. It succeeded in engaging hundreds of residents in creating a vision for their neighborhood and formulating many proposals to rebuild and improve the neighborhood. The process provided legitimacy for the plan, established a sizable base of resident volunteers to help with implementation, and affirmed residents' commitment to return and rebuild. One of the plan's strengths was the inclusion of initiatives to address the human, social, and organizational aspects of repopulating the neighborhood. It recognized that bringing residents back transcended home repair; it also required fostering confidence that most residents' would return and that essential services would be restored, and it aimed to work with individual households to overcome barriers to returning. The planning process helped create confidence but the plan also focused on creating the day-to-day system needed to identify households, track their progress, and connect them to resources to help them rebuild. A second strength of the plan was its attempt to coordinate plans to restore critical services in both the short and long term. This included proposals for temporary health, education, and other community services along with longer-term plans to rebuild the Wilson School, Keller Library, a police substation, and cultural and adult education activities. Finally, the Broadmoor Plan proposed six strategies to mitigate future flood risks, the most elaborate of which involved buying out existing raised basements and seeking FEMA funds to add raised basements to single-story homes.

Like UNOP, the Broadmoor Plan did not do a good job of setting priorities and linking its proposals to feasible funding and specific implementation plans. With 110 total projects and 74 high-priority ones, the plan did not directly address the inevitable trade-offs that would be faced during implementation. Participatory planning can result in adding proposals together rather than setting priorities and making choices, since it is easier to reach consensus by incorporating proposals favored by different people or groups than by making choices among them based on resource constraints. Broadmoor's process may have contributed to this challenge by dividing the planning work into three neighborhood sub-areas and separate issue committees. This meant priorities and proposals had to be reconciled first across the three geographies and then among multiple issue areas. As shown in the case when Area B and Area C had different priorities over public safety and bike paths, consensus can be reached by acknowledging the value of both concerns and including both in the final plan. Despite its 74 high-priority projects, the Broadmoor Plan implicitly pointed to repopulation, housing, and education as the neighborhood's greatest concerns and as the areas that warranted the most action. These areas each had fifteen or more projects (the next highest area had nine). Moreover, among the fourteen categories (omitting immediate-term projects), these three areas accounted for 48 percent of high-priority projects. As noted in the earlier discussion, the Broadmoor Plan did not include project-specific implementation plans. It also largely ignored the question of how to fund implementation beyond an overall strategy of relying on partnerships, as most project proposals did not identify funding sources. Even its key implementation recommendation, establishing the Broadmoor Development Corporation, included little discussion of how to finance this new organization. Neighborhood leaders would be forced to address the critical tasks of setting priorities and securing funding as they moved forward to implement their rebuilding plans.

BROADMOOR AND THE CITYWIDE PLANNING PROCESS

With their plan completed in July 2006, Broadmoor was ready to undertake rebuilding projects when the Lambert Plan was still in process and the agreement for UNOP had just been signed. Yet Broadmoor's leaders monitored and engaged with these planning efforts to ensure that the Broadmoor Plan was incorporated into these later plans and to prevent new proposals that might undermine or conflict with what residents had already decided. Participation was also a way to learn what residents in other neighborhoods were planning and find good ideas for adoption in Broadmoor. Finally, Broadmoor's leaders participated as citizens of New Orleans to advance the city's overall rebuilding efforts, which was part of Broadmoor's values and reflected in the final goal in the Broadmoor Plan: "to become a partner in city revitalization."

When the Lambert process got underway, consultants contacted Broadmoor about participating in their process to prepare a neighborhood plan. With Broadmoor's plan close to completion, BIA leaders suggested that the Lambert team's resources would be better used working with other neighborhoods. They shared their current plan drafts and received an agreement from the consultants that the final Lambert plan would incorporate the final Broadmoor Plan as approved by the neighborhood's residents. But when the Lambert Plan was presented to the city council for approval on October 27, 2006, the Broadmoor Plan was not included. The BIA leadership mobilized several hundred residents to attend the next city council in protest and, as a result, the City Council amended their prior vote to include Broadmoor's Plan in the New Orleans Neighborhood Plan.[34] The UNOP process went more smoothly with the Broadmoor Cultural and Commercial Corridor included as one of the twenty high-value projects in the District 3 Plan. This "project" was an amalgamation of several Broadmoor priorities, including the education corridor anchored by the Keller Library and Wilson School, revitalization of the Washington Street and Broad Street intersection, support of residential reinvestment and housing repair, and an interpretive center at the Broad Street pumping station.

BRINGING BACK BROADMOOR RESIDENTS

From the start of its rebuilding efforts, Broadmoor took the task of repopulating the neighborhood very seriously. [35] It created a Repopulation Committee that focused exclusively on bringing back residents concurrent with the neighborhood planning process. The Repopulation Committee was initially motivated by an expectation that the city would require neighborhoods to demonstrate their viability, which the BNOB Urban Planning Committee considered a 50 percent return rate. However, it took on a life of its own, well after the BNOB expired, to become a central part of Broadmoor's rebuilding strategy.

Broadmoor was better positioned than other flooded neighborhoods to attract residents back to the area.[36] It is centrally located in New Orleans and was close to the nonflooded Garden District and Uptown neighborhoods, which gave residents better access to stores and services. Broadmoor also had many homes with raised basements and two stories, which lessened the impact of flooding on living spaces and made it possible to start repair work on these homes more quickly. Along with these conditions, the determined work of the Repopulation Committee, led by Kelli Wright and Virginia Saussy, helped to spur the neighborhood's repopulation. These efforts enlisted volunteers to reach displaced residents, identify and address their barriers to rebuilding, market the neighborhood to convince residents that returning and rebuilding was a good decision, and track repopulation progress. Under the leadership of these two businesswomen, the Repopulation Committee also applied a marketing and public relations orientation to its task.

Repopulation efforts focused first on homeowners, as they were believed to be the easiest to locate and bring back quickly given their financial stake in rebuilding and ability to make the decision themselves. Renters, on the other hand, had to wait for landlords to rebuild before they could come back. The committee first conducted outreach and surveys to learn about residents' plans to return and rebuild. The BIA obtained assessor records and purchased forwarding addresses for all Broadmoor properties to provide a baseline of information for contacting residents and property owners. Several methods were used to get this information, including an online form on the BIA web site, tables at polling places during the April 2006 mayoral election and a direct mail survey prepared with pro bono help from Digitas, a Boston-based marketing firm. Survey information was used to track repopulation on a parcel by parcel basis. This information ultimately formed the basis for a detailed census and database of properties that was used to connect returning residents to assistance needed to support their return, including volunteer labor to gut and repair their homes. With the help of Harvard and Bard students, Broadmoor also developed its own forms and system to conduct a property census to track and document repopulation. One of the most important tools in tracking resident plans was a Broadmoor map of every property, which was prepared by Kelli Wright and posted on a large tri-panel board. Wright brought the map to community meetings and events and asked residents to mark their parcel if they planned to return and gathered information on other residents. Wright intentionally left out information for some properties to motivate residents to track down information on their neighbors. The map provided a picture of repopulation that informed residents about their neighbor's intentions and was a public way for residents to demonstrate their commitment to rebuilding.

Surveys were supplemented by a BIA block captain system that provided regular information on rebuilding plans and progress on a block-by-block basis. Volunteer block captains kept track of the status of each property on their block and collected information on their neighbors' plans and any rebuilding problems that they were encountering. Block captains operated as a two-way information source that supported repopulation in several ways. They supplied information and connected residents to resources to help them overcome barriers to returning; which included distributing a rebuilding guide entitled "I'm Back Now What" prepared by the BIA. If a resident had a special need, such as locating a trusted contractor or finding a doctor to address a health problem, the block captain worked with the BIA to address that need. When there was a recurring need among many residents, the BIA attempted to create a more systematic way to address it. For example, the frequent request for legal advice led to establishing a free legal clinic with Tulane University Law School. Through block captains, the BIA hoped to influence residents who were undecided about returning. Block captains reported information on the recent activities and decisions of others on their block, which helped reassure people that they would not be returning to a largely vacant block, and provided subtle pressure to join the rebuilding wave.[37]

Saussy and Wright also ran a marketing campaign to convince residents to return, viewing their efforts as akin to selling a new residential subdivision.[38] First, they applied their marketing skills to the first direct mail survey by creating a four-color mailer that featured a sign reading "Broadmoor: Population 0." Their goal was to motivate people to answer the survey.[39] Second, they used a brand marketing approach, coining "Broadmoor Lives" as the rebuilding slogan and putting it on bumper stickers, lamppost banners, lawn signs, and other materials. Broadmoor Lives served to build neighborhood pride but more importantly it communicated to residents and others that the neighborhood was rebuilding. Every resident who decided to rebuild put a Broadmoor Lives lawn sign on their property, providing visual evidence of how many residents were returning. As the signs spread across the neighborhood in the summer and fall of 2006, they provided a vivid picture of rebuilding progress. Doug Ahlers explains the effect of a simple sign in the rebuilding process:

> My future is also dependent on what you decide to do. If I move back and you do not, then I am in trouble. You are fine in Atlanta but I am left sitting with a blighted house next door . . . . You need simultaneous decisions to rebuild a neighborhood, which is a cooperation game. . . . .Broadmoor understood this intuitively and used lawn signs to signal cooperation. The lawn signs signal to everyone else that I am coming back, especially at a time when you are not living in the neighborhood. You might only come back on weekends and see the vacant

houses next door or down the block. You have no way of knowing whether all of your neighbors are coming back...But the "Broadmoor Lives" lawn signs signaled who was coming and the overwhelming reaction to them was wow!, this neighborhood is coming back, so if I move back, I will not be the only one on my block.

FROM PLAN TO IMPLEMENTATION

As the Broadmoor Plan neared completion and rebuilding priorities came into focus, the BIA and residents began to tackle implementation. [40] One of the first steps was to organize and fund the Broadmoor Development Corporation. Its board was formed and the organization incorporated in June 2006 but it needed to attract a full-time Executive Director to build and manage the new organization. Although the BDC board began advertising for the position, there was a lot of support for hiring Hal Roark based on his role in preparing the plan and his experience as a housing developer. Cantrell suggested to Roark that he was the best person to run the BDC, but he initially resisted the idea. Roark viewed his role as ensuring that the rebuilding plan was "teed up to succeed," but he never expected to be responsible for its implementation. After working full-time on the plan for six months, he wanted to turn his attention to rebuilding his home construction business. After Doug Ahlers urged Roark to take the position, upon further reflection he decided to become BDC's first Executive Director, starting in September 2006. At that time, the BDC had no funds; Roark worked with the expectation that his salary would be reimbursed after initial grants were raised. With a legal structure and a full-time director in place, the BDC was in a position to seek grants from foundations and other sources. By early 2007, the BDC had succeeded in raising $250,000 for its operations. A private individual donated $50,000; Mercy Corps and the Surdna Foundation[41] each made $50,000 grants. NeighborWorks, a federal intermediary that funds community-based home ownership and community development programs, provided the largest grant of $100,000 to fund the Executive Director's salary.

The first task for the BDC, like New Orleans after UNOP, was to set priorities. Since all 74 high priority projects could not be implemented at once, decisions had to be made about which ones to tackle first. A critical criterion for selecting the initial projects was the likelihood that they would succeed, and thus build momentum and establish credibility for the rebuilding effort. Broadmoor's leaders were aware of New Orleans' reputation for ineffectiveness and corruption and felt it was critical to be transparent and successful to change this perception. As Roark noted, the "first generation of success leads to the second generation of success." Broadmoor's leadership also wanted its first projects to have the greatest impact on rebuilding—to convince residents to return, improve the neighborhood and attract partners to support its efforts. After discussions within the planning committees and among BIA's leadership, Broadmoor settled on the Keller Library as its first rebuilding project, as recounted by Roark:

> First off, we'll go after Keller, we'll go after funding for the Library because it's a community center and it's a children's library. The internal phrase we had for it was 'the big warm fuzzy bunny'. Who doesn't want to pet the big warm fuzzy bunny. Who is against a children's library? Okay, we have to go after that.[42]

A second focus was the Wilson School and creating the education corridor as the heart of the rebuilding plan. Bringing an improved school back to the neighborhood served two goals. It would convince more residents with young children to return and would provide access to good education and thereby help address poverty among families in Broadmoor. Working to secure a school charter and funding to rebuild the Wilson School become the second priority project during the summer and fall of 2006.

The BDC was a fledging organization but had volunteers to help move projects forward and assist in securing funding. Several issue committees had completed research and planning to formulate their proposals, and they became a platform for implementation. The Education Committee, in particular, took on establishing a new charter elementary school at the rebuilt Wilson School. It continued working on this project through summer 2006 as other committees took August off and others were disbanded with the plan's completion. Similarly, the Repopulation Committee relied on volunteer block captains and others for its outreach, resident assistance, and marketing activities. This work laid the foundation for case management and housing programs later implemented by the BDC. A new Library Committee also was formed during summer 2006 to begin work on restoring the Keller Library. Broadmoor used the talents, skills, and time of its residents to advance projects before any paid staff was in place and, once hired, to augment staff expertise and capacity. Widespread resident participation in creating the plan and their resulting sense of ownership in its implementation helped Broadmoor to apply a common and appealing notion in community development: that every community has assets and should identify and use these local assets as the foundation for development.[43]

If the BDC and resident volunteers were the first two legs of the Broadmoor implementation strategy, the third was forming partnerships with other organizations. Partnerships represented four of the six petals on Broadmoor's strategy flower and were important in providing expertise, resources, and capacity to implement its ambitious rebuilding plan. The faith-based community emerged as Broadmoor's first partner via a local Episcopal church, the Free Church of the Annunciation. At the initial January 12 rally, the church's priest, Father Jerry Kramer, recognized the need to merge the church's efforts with those of the BIA. That night, he offered to share the church's two recently acquired trailers with the BIA for community meetings and office space.[44] In the early months of 2006, it provided cash, office supplies, and the use of its equipment to the BIA, which, although small, were vital resources for the fledgling rebuilding effort. A much larger request came a few months later when Broadmoor looked for a way to tap into the large pool of national volunteers who were coming to New Orleans to help with rebuilding. Roark realized that Broadmoor needed to recruit hundreds of these volunteers to make a dent in repairing and rebuilding damaged properties, and this necessitated having a place to house and feed them. He approached Father Kramer to ask him to devote significant space in the church's buildings to volunteer housing for the foreseeable future. Kramer agreed and began to raise funds to renovate one of the church buildings into a dormitory for volunteers.[45] The dormitory opened in spring 2007 and operated as the Annunciation Mission to support and house volunteers who came to New Orleans to assist in rebuilding efforts.[46]

Universities were a second logical partner, given the large contribution made by Harvard to the Broadmoor plan. The BIA and BDC cultivated relationships with other colleges and universities, including Bard College, MIT, and Notre Dame. Bard students were particularly vital to conducting a regular census of neighborhood homes and residents. Bard College also worked with the Wilson School to place college students in the school's classrooms to provide tutoring and serve as classroom aides. Several MIT students helped prepare grant applications, drafted implementation plans for early projects, and assisted with planning and design for its housing and home ownership programs. Multiple schools provided winter and summer interns who added capacity to the BDC staff.

One of the most valuable early partnerships, brokered by Harvard's Doug Ahlers, was a September 2006 commitment by the Clinton Global Initiative (CGI) to provide $5 million in aid to Broadmoor.[47] Along with funding to implement the Broadmoor Plan, CGI provided a high-profile endorsement of the neighborhood by the former President's foundation and other prominent business and political leaders. It added credibility to Broadmoor's efforts and opened doors to potential partners and financial supporters. One of the early fruits of the CGI commitment was a large grant by the Carnegie Corporation to fund rebuilding the Keller Library.

Partnerships became key to Broadmoor's rebuilding strategy, as they attracted resources and brought other organizations into the work of implementing an ambitious plan. Although a partnership model was central to Broadmoor's early thinking about how to approach implementation, the specific partnerships emerged organically in response to necessity and opportunity, as noted by Cantrell:

> The strategy revealed itself to us. I say that from how groups and residents and people in general came to our aid based on how we were organized or what they saw in us. It started with the residents, we started it and then it lead to the faith-based community with the Free Church of the Annunciation, that partnership was providing us office space and general operating support. So that was faith-based community. Then we had Harvard...Then Bard College. So, these are the universities. Then, of course, private foundations and corporations. That was easy, because we knew we had to go get money. We knew government had to be a player, and also developers. So the strategy became very clear and revealed itself to us, but we embraced it. We saw it, we embraced it and we said this was going to be the way that we will rebuild because, organically, this is how it's happening.

TACKLING THE FIRST PROJECTS

Keller Library

To advance plans for the Keller Library, a small Library Committee began work on a vision for the building and fundraising for its renovation. The committee members, all volunteers, included three librarians, an architect, and the head of a green development firm. Two milestones were reached in June 2007 when a community vision for the Rosa F. Keller Library and Community Center was adopted and, through work with the Clinton Global Initiative, a $2 million grant was secured from the Carnegie Corporation.[48] With a vision and funding in hand, Broadmoor sought to move forward quickly with the project's design and construction, but it met resistance from the city's Library Board, which owned and controlled the building. When the Broadmoor Library Committee sought the board's approval to release the building for renovation under its initial plan, they learned that the Library Board had a different vision for the building. Broadmoor planned to repair the existing building while the Library Board wanted to construct a new building using FEMA public assistance funds. Resolving these different visions and securing FEMA funding delayed the project for over two years. After FEMA allocated $300,000 for the Keller Library, the city appealed the decision and then completed three building assessments to convince FEMA that new construction was warranted.[49] The FEMA appeals process continued until September 2009 when a $3.4 million grant was awarded. With sufficient funds available to build a new library, Broadmoor's leadership decided to work with the Library Board and use the funds that it had raised to enhance the building's design as a green building and to equip it with computers, books, and other resources. The new library's design was completed and construction was underway in July 2010. Although resolving differences with the Library Board delayed implementation of its lead rebuilding project for close to three years, Broadmoor ultimately succeeded in getting the library built. Cantrell recognized the need to work through the city bureaucracy to achieve its goals:

> It was unfortunate. I understand the city wanting to get more money for the library so FEMA could pay the cost. I got that. As a result of all of that Broadmoor is going to get a new library that it designed. And it is going to be better than even what we planned ourselves.

Despite the deviation from its original plans, Broadmoor assembled an array of partners to help design and equip the library and establish a temporary modular library until the new library was complete. In addition

Table 3.3. PARTNERS FOR THE ROSA F. KELLER LIBRARY
AND COMMUNITY CENTER

Partner	Funds of Resources Provided
New Orleans Library Board/FEMA Public Assistance Grant	$3,400,000
Carnegie Corporation	$2,000,000
AT&T Foundation	$50,000 grant for telecommunications services and equipment
CH2MHill	Volunteer full-time project manager and $50,000
RosaMary Foundation	$100,000
Dr. Joey and Walter Isaacson	Private donation
Gates Foundation	Funds for temporary modular building
University of Utah	Plans and conceptual designs for initial renovation project
Powell's Books, Mercy Corps, Flight of Friendship, National Cathedral School (DC)	Book donations

to FEMA and the Carnegie Corporation, ten organizations contributed money, goods, or services to enhance the final library building, equipment, and collection (see Table 3.3) and expand the number of learning resources available to community members.

Grassroots Educational Reform in New Orleans

Well before Katrina, New Orleans' public schools were in crisis. Over half of public school students did not meet basic reading and basic proficiency standards in 2005 and a large achievement gap existed between white students and black students—twice the average differential statewide.[50] These conditions reflect Louisiana's legacy of racial segregation[51] and underinvestment in education, while mismanagement and corruption in the school system worsened the situation and made internal education reform implausible. Federal investigations into corruption in the Orleans Parish School Board in 2004 led to criminal charges against eleven employees[52]; further charges resulted in 20 school board employees pleading guilty to activities including theft, fraud, conflict of interest, and kickbacks in 2006.[53]

Prior to Katrina, the state asserted increasing control over New Orleans schools. To implement the federal No Child Left Behind law, the Louisiana legislature passed the Recovery School District Act (RSDA) in 2003, which created the statewide Recovery School District (RSD) to take over schools that failed to make adequate progress in education outcomes for four consecutive years.[54] In 2004, the state declared New Orleans public schools in academic crisis and the Louisiana Recovery School District began taking more responsibility over public schools in the city.[55] With limited capacity to manage individual schools, the state government often relied on charter schools as the means to bring in new school management and reform educational practices. Charter schools are publicly funded schools that are given the freedom to operate outside of the normal bureaucratic rules, student assignment processes, and collective bargaining contracts that govern schools run by local school boards, with the goal of promoting educational excellence,[56] A local neighborhood or community group applies for a charter to operate a school that reflects its preferences in educational approach, curricula emphasis, and attention to cultural and social needs, and creates its own board to ensure accountability and education quality. Since charter schools are established via local initiative and overseen by community-based boards, they were an appealing option for New Orleans' neighborhoods to accelerate rebuilding their schools while gaining more local control over them. Reliance on locally driven charter schools also was an attractive way for the state Recovery School District to seed many new schools (to replace those previously run by the Orleans Parish School Board) without having to create and operate them itself.

State takeover was accelerated after Hurricane Katrina when the Orleans Parish School board, with over 100 schools in need of significant repairs and a budget deficit of over $25 million,[57] announced that it was unable to operate schools in the 2005–2006 academic year. In response to this decision, Governor Blanco announced that the state would reopen the public schools. To authorize a state takeover, the legislature amended the RSDA in November 2005 by expanding the definition of a failing school[58] and directing the state Recovery School District to oversee these failing schools for at least five years. Many in the state government saw the takeover of New Orleans schools as an opportunity to remake the New Orleans public school system. RSD Superintendent Robin Jarvis announced that RSD would operate as many schools as charters as possible.[59] This set the stage for neighborhood groups, parents, and community activists to form charter schools, seeking to gain more control of the quality of local schools. Broadmoor is one example of how grassroots neighborhood rebuilding sought to combine efforts to reopen schools with broader goals of education reform. It also shows how physical rebuilding goals have proven easier to attain than sustained advances in educational quality.

Moving the Wilson School from Plan to Reality

Plans for the Wilson School progressed more readily than those for the Keller Library,[60] with a school charter secured in 2007 and a newly constructed school open at the beginning of 2010. Since creating a high-quality school was a priority in the Broadmoor Plan, the Education Committee had already researched school options and educational best practices during the planning process. After the plan's approval, the Education Committee moved quickly to gain a state charter to open a new school. Residents voted unanimously to establish Wilson as an open-enrollment charter school at a BIA meeting in August 2006. The education committee, which had researched charter operators with the help of Harvard KSG interns, selected Edison Learning to run the charter school that same month. Finally, the Broadmoor Charter School Board (BCSB) was created as a separate organization to prepare a state charter school application and oversee the new school. Before the end of 2006, the charter application was completed and submitted to the Louisiana Board of Elementary and Secondary Education. In February 2007, these efforts were rewarded when the state awarded the Broadmoor Charter School Board a charter to operate a new neighborhood-run school.

With a charter in hand, the BCSB focused on the next task—establishing the new school in the Wilson School building. They had an initial setback when the RSD found that the Wilson School building was too heavily damaged to be used. Unable to find an alternative building within Broadmoor, the Wilson Charter School began its first school year in fall 2007 at a building in a different neighborhood[61] two miles from Broadmoor. As work began to open the school at its temporary location, an opportunity arose to reclaim the Wilson School site. In late July, the Louisiana Board of Elementary & Secondary Education and the Recovery School District announced a plan to rebuild and reopen five schools by fall 2009. Called the Quick Start Initiative, it would select five schools—one in each city council district—to be constructed before other New Orleans public schools, which depended on completing an overall school master plan and resolving FEMA Public Assistance funding.[62] Broadmoor mobilized to prepare a proposal within the tight three-week deadline and to secure political support. These efforts succeeded and Wilson was chosen among 18 proposals to be a Quick Start school. The Quick Start designation came with $25 million to build a new school building; the Broadmoor Charter School Board seized this opportunity to design a green school with facilities to accommodate new teaching methods. The BIA also raised $1 million to equip the school with state-of-the-art equipment that was not covered by Quick Start funding. School construction began in June 2008 and the new campus for the Andrew H. Wilson Charter School opened in January 2010. The new school provided Broadmoor with an anchor for its Educational and Cultural Corridor and what it expected to be a key asset in reducing neighborhood poverty.[63]

The Andrew H. Wilson School, shown in Figure 3.7, provides a much improved facility and innovative design for the New Orleans school children served there. The new school includes: 26 classrooms, a cafeteria, a gymnasium, an art studio, a music room, a computer lab, a library, and administration facilities. Its design incorporates the old and new (see Figure 3.8):

> They left an historic exterior [of the old building] on the interior of the new building and put a history of the neighborhood on an open wall that is one of the main corridors that students go through on their way to class. So you can read the neighborhood history on the wall of your school.[64]

As a green building that received a LEED Gold designation from the US Green Building Council, it incorporates many features to reduce energy

Figure 3.7.
New Andrew H. Wilson Charter School
Source: photo by author.

Figure 3.8.
Inside of Wilson School with section of former school wall
Source: photo by author.

and water usage and contains recycled materials from the original school building.[65] The school's design maximizes daylight, has an energy-efficient building envelope, and uses both a solar hot water system and photovoltaic cells to generate up to five kilowatts of electricity. The new building uses the concrete and gym floor from the former building and all construction debris from the demolition of the old school was recycled. A series of rain gardens, rainwater tanks, permeable surfaces, and underground retention systems reduce runoff and potential flooding from stormwater—an important issue for this low-lying part of New Orleans. Several learning tools use the school's environmental design for experiential learning.[66]

The Wilson School serves 540 students ranging from prekindergarten to eighth grade. The philosophy behind the Wilson School is to serve as a community learning center for students and all Broadmoor residents. The core kindergarten to eighth-grade school seeks to incorporate strong parent involvement, student learning, and educational enrichment. An extended school day and year, state-of-the-art facilities, tutoring and enrichment programs[67] are all deployed to improve student learning. For community residents, the Wilson School offers classes and workshops on adult health issues, sports, and family services; it also houses the Next Level Institute to provide job training, job placement, and career coaching services.[68]

Despite the innovative new facility and efforts to incorporate effective education approaches, the Wilson School has not reached the goal of providing a high-quality education for neighborhood residents. After some early progress in educational outcomes in which Wilson School students tested higher in math and reading than students in other schools within New Orleans,[69] the school received an academically unacceptable state school performance rating for 2009 to 2010.[70] Its performance score improved by almost 30 percent the following year, when it ranked thirteenth statewide, but its overall grade was a D+.[71] Moreover, since Wilson School students are 96 percent black and largely from low-income families (93 percent receive free or reduced price lunches), the school has attracted few students from Broadmoor's higher-income and white households. This suggests that the Wilson School is not viewed as a school of choice among many white and higher income families. However, this situation is not unique to Broadmoor but reflects the composition of the city's public school system, including new charter schools created after Katrina. New Orleans' public school enrollment in February 2011 was 89 percent black, with the percentage at RSD charter schools even higher at 95 percent. Similarly, the share of students receiving free or reduced price lunches was 87 percent and 94 percent at all New Orleans public schools and RSD charter schools, respectively.[72]

BUILDING CAPACITY AT THE BDC AND BIA

Volunteer committees helped move initial projects forward, but the scope of the Broadmoor Plan called for a dedicated full-time staff and greater implementation capacity through the BDC. To secure the human and financial resources to build this capacity, the BDC looked to foundation grants to raise funds and used student interns and the service-based AmeriCorps program for much of its staffing. Most of the BDC's initial funds came from private foundations and corporations with one main quasi-governmental grant from NeighborWorks (see Table 3.4). In the early years after Katrina, there was considerable philanthropic interest in funding rebuilding efforts undertaken by community-based organizations. Broadmoor was well-positioned to secure grants with its detailed plan and newly formed CDC. Nonetheless, the BDC still needed to discover which foundations fit its priorities and rebuilding approach and to increase its capacity to prepare proposals.[73] Its partners and other New Orleans CDCs helped connect Broadmoor to potential funders but the process resembled a "two-way smorgasbord" in which foundations traveled to New Orleans to survey and

Table 3.4. BROADMOOR DEVELOPMENT CORPORATION FUNDING IN FIRST THREE YEARS[1]

Funding Sources	Amount	Uses
Surdna Foundation	$175,000	General operating funds; case management staff
NeighborWorks	$100,000	Staff and operating costs
Mercy Corps	$76,100	Executive Director salary, initial operating costs
Private Donor	$50,000	Executive Director salary, initial operating costs
Louisiana Disaster Recovery Fund	$250,000	Community outreach, case management
Deutsche Bank	$50,000	Grant writer's salary
Motorola Foundation	$50,000	Operating expenses
Shell Oil[2]	Specific amount unknown	Student interns, board and staff training through grant to Harvard
Blue Moon Fund	$100,000	Administrative staff
Total	$851,100	

[1] This information was assembled from interviews, BDC minutes, and other documents.
[2] This represents part of Shell's $1 million grant to Harvard University to support its partnership with Broadmoor. Part of these funds paid for Harvard student interns for Broadmoor and funded executive training for the BDC board and staff members, although the exact amounts used for these purposes were not available.

select which organizations and initiatives to fund while local organizations looked for good partners to fund their work.[74]

BDC raised enough grant funds to support a $250,000–$300,000 annual budget. But this was still a modest figure given that the staff had to implement its priority projects and activities. If the BDC chose to rely solely on professional staff, it had funds to hire two to three people beyond its executive director—a small staff to tackle the scope and scale of its agenda. Instead, the BDC board decided to hire AmeriCorps participants[75] as its primary staff and supplemented them with a full-time office manager,[76] and an active internship program. Since 2007, a dozen AmeriCorps members have worked for the BDC on case management, coordinating volunteers for home rebuilding, tracking properties and securing resources for blight remediation efforts, planning for new programs, serving as community and school liaisons, and implementing community programs.[77] As noted by one BDC staff member, the value of AmeriCorps members transcended their formal staff roles:

> They are young, energetic, and have new approaches. Without the AmeriCorps positions, I'm not sure where we would be. People come in and immerse themselves in Broadmoor. They are flexible, and you have to be flexible, nothing here is ever static, and you have to do what has to be done. The AmeriCorps understand that. They have intelligence and capacity for flexibility and change, and that might be hard with a salaried staff.

Student interns also provided a boost to BDC's capacity. They conducted research, collected data, and worked on short-term organizational and project needs. Bard College interns have been central to Broadmoor's system, which tracks the status of every property by providing the field staff needed to survey every neighborhood property. Student interns peaked in summer 2009, when more than twenty college and graduate students worked at the BDC.

AmeriCorps employees and student interns were a great boon to the BDC, but they also presented challenges to its Executive Director, who had to supervise a large number of relatively inexperienced people. Moreover, as BDC activities expanded into housing program management and development, which required administering state and federal grants, the need for more stable and experienced staff emerged. The BDC Board of Directors looked to add this expertise when it hired a new executive to replace Hal Roark, who resigned in August 2010 to attend the Yale Divinity School. They chose Santiago Buros, a community development practitioner from Philadelphia who had considerable experience in local government and in managing programs that relied on federal funding.

The BIA also acted to enhance its capacity and role in the neighborhood. In 2010, as LaToya Cantrell sought to strengthen and sustain the organization, she approached State Senator Karen Carter about the possibility of creating the Broadmoor Improvement District to provide a regular source of revenue. An improvement district is authorized by state law to allow property owners in a specific area to pay a special property assessment toward services or projects that benefit them. Carter encouraged Cantrell to act on the idea quickly and agreed to sponsor and help secure passage of the legislation. Senate Bill 703 was passed by the legislature and signed into law by Governor Jindal as Act 554 on June 25, 2010. It provided for a new Broadmoor Neighborhood Improvement District that could levy a $100 per-year parcel fee on each property owner. A governing board elected by voters within Broadmoor would decide how to spend the funds raised by the fee, which was expected to total $220,000 per year. To be established, the district and the parcel fee had to be approved by Broadmoor votes in the 2010 general election held on November 2, 2010. On that day, the district was approved by 69 percent of voters, with a large yes vote across all parts of Broadmoor. The BIA would now operate with a stable funding and as an elected governmental body.

AN EVOLVING PATH TO REBUILD HOUSING

As Broadmoor worked to repopulate the neighborhood, how to rebuild damaged homes became an increasingly pressing and challenging issue. Two problems confronted Broadmoor and the BDC as they worked to craft viable home rebuilding programs. One problem was overcoming the barriers that homeowners faced in restoring their property. The second problem, discussed later, was how to convert blighted and abandoned properties into new housing. A key barrier for returning homeowners was the financial gap between the cost to repair their home and the funding available through insurance, the Road Home Program, and FEMA. Beyond money, homeowners also needed assistance in applying for aid under these programs and finding trusted contractors to undertake repairs, as contractor fraud was commonplace.[78] By summer 2007, as repopulation began to plateau, BDC staff recognized that more intensive assistance was needed to get the remaining 25 percent to 30 percent of residents to return.[79] To address these harder cases, the BDC charged a Harvard summer intern with creating a database to keep track of the needs and status of individual homeowners.[80] BDC then hired three case managers in early 2008 to work with residents to get them financial assistance and volunteer crews to help rebuild their homes[81] and assist with other issues.

Along with the case management system, the BDC formed partnerships to provide homeowners with home repair resources. Two of these partnerships were most fruitful.[82] The first, with the Annunciation Mission, recruited volunteer crews from congregations and organizations across the country, primarily to gut Broadmoor residents' homes, and used the Mission's newly renovated dormitory to house and feed them. According to BDC records, the Annunciation Mission recruited over 9,600 volunteers who gutted 895 homes and helped repair another 75 through mid-2010.[83] Rebuilding Together—a volunteer-based home repair program established by New Orleans' Preservation Resource Center (PRC)—was the second key partnership.

The PRC worked to preserve New Orleans' historic housing stock in the face of declining population and disinvestment in the 1970s and 1980s.[84] As part of its efforts, it created Christmas in October in 1988 in an effort to use volunteer labor during October to repair the homes of the disabled, elderly, low-income, or single-parent households and first responders. This program was a New Orleans affiliate of the national organization Rebuilding Together.[85] After Katrina, Rebuilding Together recognized the need to greatly expand the scale and scope of its activities to complete more substantial repairs to hundreds of homes.[86] Through expanded funding and staff, Rebuilding Together transformed itself into a mission-oriented construction firm that combined paid staff and volunteer labor to increase its capacity to rebuild homes. With this greater capacity, it sought neighborhood-based partners to focus its impact.[87] Hal Roark first approached Rebuilding Together in 2007 to form a partnership around rebuilding homes. BDC was an attractive partner because it had good information on and contacts with residents, and could readily identify properties for Rebuilding Together's efforts.[88] Through its partnership with Rebuilding Together, the BDC provided volunteers to gut and repair homes owned by the elderly, disabled, and first responders. Over 4,200 Rebuilding Together volunteers repaired 65 Broadmoor homes through mid-2010.[89]

By summer 2010, virtually all Broadmoor homes had been gutted and resources were needed to undertake more advanced repair work than volunteers could do. BDC secured an $896,000 grant from the Louisiana Housing Finance Authority (LHFA) in late 2009 to address this need by providing funds to hire contractors for more extensive home repair projects.[90]

Through these multiple home rebuilding efforts, the BDC helped reduce rebuilding costs for hundreds of Broadmoor houses and assisted more homeowners than the state Road Home program. Volunteer gutting reduced rebuilding costs for 28 percent of the neighborhood's homes and made a far greater contribution to the rebuilding of another 170 housing units, or

5.3 percent of Broadmoor's pre-Katrina housing stock.[91] The contribution of Broadmoor's volunteer-based partnerships to rebuild homes is demonstrated by the figures in Table 3.5. Volunteer and local partnership efforts assisted 960 housing units—86 more than were assisted by either the Road Home program or state Small Rental Assistance Program. The monetary value of this assistance was much lower than the state aid—9.3 percent of the total provided by the two state programs—but it was an important resource in the scope of residents reached. In effect, the BDC used these two partnerships, its case management system, and a large volunteer network to overcome the delays and funding shortfalls under the Road Home Program that posed rebuilding barriers to many homeowners. In this manner, it helped to accelerate the neighborhood's repopulation.

Broadmoor's second housing challenge was to address the many abandoned and blighted properties concentrated in the historically poorer section of the neighborhood. Converting these properties back into housing has been a major challenge for the BDC, as it required rethinking the aggressive home-building strategy envisioned in the Broadmoor Plan. Based on its property census, 21 percent of Broadmoor properties were neither rebuilt nor in the process of being rebuilt in mid-2010.[92] Among these 477 buildings, Broadmoor considered 170 to be blighted and presenting safety and nuisance problems, which made them the highest priority. The BDC's first strategy in addressing blighted properties was to acquire them, then to either repair them or demolish them to build new homes on their lots, and finally to sell the new or repaired homes to displaced residents or to police, firefighters, or teachers seeking to live in the neighborhood. The BDC spent over two years working to acquire properties and secure funds to complete

Table 3.5. NUMBER OF BROADMOOR HOUSING UNITS ASSISTED AND VALUE OF ASSISTANCE UNDER STATE AND VOLUNTEER-BASED HOME REBUILDING PROGRAMS

	Road Home and Small Rental Assistance Programs	Volunteer Labor and Partnerships	Volunteer as % of State Programs
Number of units assisted	874	960[1]	109.8%
Value of assistance	$81,576,345[2]	$7,584,275[3]	9.3%

Source: Louisiana Office of Community Development and Broadmoor Development Corporation

[1] Includes 895 units gutted by Annunciation Mission plus 65 units repaired by Rebuilding Together. The 75 units repaired by the Annunciation Mission are assumed to be among the 895 gutted units.

[2] Road Home figure is only for grants to rebuild an original home. Another $4.5 million was provided to 39 Broadmoor homeowners to rebuild at another location.

[3] Figure is based on 371,000 hours of volunteer labor valued at $18.75 per hour plus construction costs of RBT.

Table 3.6. FUNDING GAP FOR NEW HOME CONSTRUCTION

Cost to develop a home	$244,000
Mortgage that target buyers could afford	$80,000–$140,000
Financial gap	$104,000–$164,000

a first building phase to repair and build 35 homes. By bidding on city-owned properties and directly purchasing other houses offered for sale, the BDC gained site control of over two dozen properties. However, it needed substantial subsidies to cover a gap of over $100,000 between the cost of constructing new homes and a sales price that was affordable to targeted buyers—moderate income families working as teachers, police, and other first responders (see Table 3.6). Broadmoor planned to use the soft second mortgage program that the city sought to expand with federal CDBG funds to fill part of the gap, but the long delays in implementing the soft second program, detailed in chapter 2, made this infeasible. Instead, the BDC secured funds from two sources to fill the gap: (1) a new green housing program developed by the Salvation Army (Environew); and (2) funds from a grant that the New Orleans Redevelopment Authority received under the federal Neighborhood Stabilization Program.

In late 2010, after the BDC had resolved how to combine funds from these two sources to meet each program's requirements and was ready to start construction to complete 35 homes in two years, it decided to revamp its housing development strategy. During that fall, a team of Harvard students prepared an analysis of real estate sales in Broadmoor over the prior ten years. This study revealed that the market for homes in the BDC's targeted area for new housing development, the poorer and more heavily blighted "Sub-area B," was quite small. Home sales in the five years before and after Katrina averaged six per year. Moreover, longer sales periods and a widening gap between the asking and sales prices also suggested that demand for homes in the area had weakened over the prior year.[93] With this new information, the BDC questioned the feasibility of building and selling so many new homes in a two-year period and decided to rethink its strategy to address blighted properties. Another change that contributed to the strategy shift was the tightening of financial markets after the 2008 financial crisis. Reduced credit hindered the BDC's ability to secure construction loans needed to rehab and build homes while making it harder for potential homeowners to obtain mortgages to buy the completed properties.[94] Over the next few months, the BDC board and staff decided on a new approach that balanced limited new home construction with greater emphasis on repairing heavily blighted properties that existing homeowners sought to rebuild and demolishing some heavily blighted homes to convert them to green space, such as small parks, playgrounds, or side yards for adjacent properties.[95] Furthermore, the BDC sought to concentrate these improvements in several small sections of Sub-area B with the expectation that focusing investments would have a greater impact. This would allow the removal and reuse of most blighted properties in several blocks, which had more potential to change market perceptions and demand in that area and hopefully spill over into surrounding areas. To implement this new approach, Broadmoor sought approval from its key funders in early 2011 to reprogram some grant money from new housing construction to rehabbing existing owner-occupied houses and converting blighted properties into green space.

BROADMOOR AT YEAR FIVE

More than five years after Katrina, Broadmoor showed considerable rebuilding progress and had become a stronger and better neighborhood in several ways. Many homes and properties had been rebuilt and its repopulation rate exceeded the citywide average. Several new community facilities (a school, library, and arts and wellness center) were completed or under construction to expand services for residents. Significant physical improvements to the neighborhood's infrastructure had occurred. Beyond physical rebuilding, Broadmoor had become a more cohesive community with a shared vision for its future and greater capacity to advance this vision and improve the entire neighborhood over time. This combination of physical improvement and stronger community cohesion were highlighted by Broadmoor's leaders:

> The neighborhood looks great. It looks better than it did before because everybody has renovated and repainted. We also have the BIA running roughshod on people who don't take care of their property, which is great. We now have a resource to help you in all that kind of stuff. There is a stronger sense of community. I for one know a lot more of my neighbors.[96]

> Better attitude, better sense of hope. Profound sense of community and community involvement. The irony is that the trauma of the storm ... gave us a common experience to bond around, even if we were people that were different races, or ages or classes or political affiliation, or whatever. And that was very real, profoundly real. People were side by side. A lot of pride in the neighborhood ... We never were on maps before, never. When the city, [or] *The Times–Picayune* came

out with a map, they would have Uptown, French Quarter, and all the rest. They always now have Broadmoor. They may only have four or five different neighborhoods highlighted, but always Broadmoor.[97]

Along with these accomplishments, the neighborhood still faced significant rebuilding challenges and difficulties in realizing elements of the Broadmoor Plan. Residential restoration and repopulation remained slow in the neighborhood's eastern Sub-area B, which contained numerous vacant and blighted properties. After its plans to develop and sell 35 homes proved too aggressive, the BDC had to revamp its housing development agenda following several years of work. The vision for high-quality education at the Wilson School was not yet fulfilled despite the success in quickly building a new innovatively designed school and efforts to improve education practices. Given the city's legacy of poor education and continued poverty among much of the school's population, it is not surprising that the achievement of strong educational outcomes was not readily accomplished. Similarly, pre-Katrina conditions in Broadmoor's eastern section, with higher poverty rates, lower home ownership, and more vacant properties, contributed to its slower repopulation and recovery progress, detailed below.

Repopulation Progress

Repopulation and housing occupancy rates are key indicators of Broadmoor's rebuilding progress. Based on US Census of Population and Housing data presented in Table 3.7, Broadmoor's 2010 population was 5,381, or 74 percent of the 2000 count.[98] At 74 percent, the neighborhood's repopulation rate was above the city's overall rate of 71 percent. Despite its high level of flooding and lower average income, Broadmoor repopulated at

Table 3.7. CHANGE IN BROADMOOR POPULATION AND HOUSING UNITS, 2000–2010

	2000	2010	Total Change 2000–2010	Percent Change 2000–2010
Population	7,232	5,381	−1,851	−25.6%
Total housing units	3,222	3,183	−39	−1.2%
Occupied housing units	2,915	2,203	−712	−24.4%
Vacant housing units	307	980	673	+219.2%

Source: 2000 and 2010 U.S. Census.

Table 3.8. BROADMOOR POPULATION BY RACE, 2000–2010

Race/Ethnicity	Percent 2000	Percent 2010	Total Change 2000–2010	Percent Change 2000–2010
White	25.8%	32.5%	−259	−12.9%
Black	68.2%	61.4%	−1,627	−33.0%
American Indian and Native Alaskan	0.2%	0.4%	8	57.1%
Asian	0.6%	1.1%	12	25.5%
Hispanic	3.7%	6.7%	93	35.0%

Source: 2000 and 2010 U.S. Census.

a faster rate than New Orleans. However, repopulation was uneven racially and spatially. White residents were more likely to return than black residents. In 2010, the white population was 87 percent of its 2000 level while the black population had declined by 33 percent (see Table 3.8). In fact, the vast majority (88 percent) of Broadmoor's population decline from 2000 to 2010 was among black residents. White repopulation rates exceed those of blacks in all three Broadmoor census tracts (see Figure 3.9), with the disparity greatest in the eastern census tract 103. Although this eastern section of Broadmoor gained white residents between 2000 and 2010, it experienced the largest overall population loss, at three to five times that of the other two census tracts, as shown in Table 3.9. Over 75 percent of the decline in Broadmoor's black population also occurred in this eastern section. On the other hand, there was parity in repopulation between homeowners and renters. Data in Table 3.10 show that homeowners and renters constituted almost the same share of Broadmoor's population in 2000 and 2010, and the population decline for both groups was comparable at slightly above 900.

It is more difficult to evaluate Broadmoor's progress in rebuilding properties due to discrepancies between Broadmoor's data and US Census figures. Broadmoor's property census reported that 83.6 percent of damaged properties were fully recovered by January 2010.[99] However, the 2010 Census reported a 31 percent housing vacancy rate, which suggests that a lower share of units were rebuilt. In contrast to its repopulation rate, Broadmoor's 2010 residential vacancy rate (as measured by the US Census) was above the citywide level (24 percent). When the US Census figure is adjusted for vacant units that probably had been rebuilt (e.g., units for rent, units rented or sold but not yet occupied, etc.), the vacancy rate drops to under 25 percent, which is still considerably higher than the 16 percent figure from Broadmoor's data. This difference likely reflects discrepancies

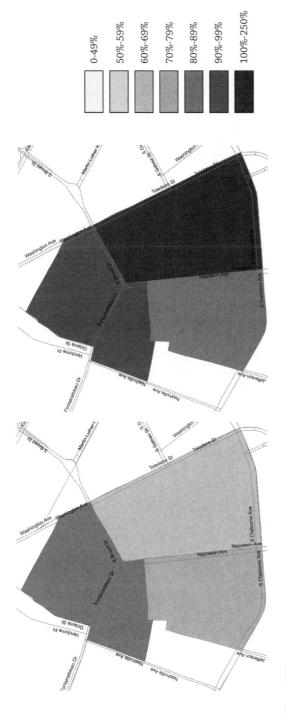

Figure 3.9.
Broadmoor African American (left) and white (right) repopulation rates by Census tract
Source: 2000 and 2010 U.S. Census.

Table 3.9. BROADMOOR POPULATION CHANGE
BY CENSUS TRACT 2000–2010[1]

	Tract 103	Tract 112	Tract 123
Total population	–1,225	–251	–375
White	45	–102	–59
Black	–1,262	–115	–250
Homeowners	–487	–197	–232
Renters	–718	–63	–147

Source: 2000 and 2010 US Census.
[1] The census data has a slight difference between total population
change and sum of changes between renters and owners.

in what was counted in each census: Broadmoor's figures are for residential and nonresidential buildings while the census counted housing units, not buildings. If far more vacant units are in multiunit rental buildings than in single-family homes, then the vacancy rate for housing units would be higher than the percentage of nonrestored buildings.

Both the census and Broadmoor data confirm the neighborhood's uneven geography of rebuilding: rebuilt properties and resident occupancy rates were much greater in the higher-income area west of Napoleon Avenue (Tract 112) than in the eastern section (Tract 103). Virtually all of the blocks in Broadmoor's western section had at least 80 percent of their properties fully repaired or under renovations in January 2010 and the US Census occupancy rate was 77 percent. In contrast, most blocks in the eastern section had completed or started renovations for less than 80 percent of their properties; for almost one-fifth of the blocks, the share was 60 percent or less. With this lower level of rebuilding, only 61 percent of housing units in Tract 103 were occupied in 2010. Consequently, its vacancy rate was almost twice that of the western section.

One way to measure Broadmoor's repopulation progress is by comparing it to the nearby Hollygrove neighborhood. Hollygrove is a neighborhood on the northwestern edge of District Three, the same planning district in which

Table 3.10. SHARE AND CHANGES IN BROADMOOR
HOMEOWNERS AND RENTERS, 2000 AND 2010

	Percent 2000	Percent 2010	Total Change 2000–2010	Percent Change 2000–2010
Homeowners	47.7%	47.0%	–916	–26.7%
Renters	52.3%	53.0%	–928	–24.6%

Source: 2000 and 2010 U.S. Census.

Table 3.11 COMPARISON OF BROADMOOR AND
HOLLYGROVE NEIGHBORHOODS

	Broadmoor	Hollygrove
2000 homeownership rate	48.1%	54.2%
2000 poverty rate	31.8%	28.4%
2000 percent living in same house in 1995	60.7%	68.5%
Population change, 2000–2010	–1,851	–2542
% change	–26%	–37%
Repopulation rate	74%	63%
Change in housing units	–39	–355
Change in vacant housing units	673	539

Broadmoor is located. Both neighborhoods are in the lowest elevation sections of the district and experienced the greatest flooding, with over six feet of water throughout.[100] They are similarly sized neighborhoods that had populations close to 7,000 and 3,000 housing units in 2000.[101] Hollygrove had slightly better social indicators for rebuilding than Broadmoor, with a higher homeownership rate, a lower poverty rate and greater residential stability, as measured by the percentage of residents living in the same house from 1995 to 2000 (see Table 3.11). Yet, Broadmoor achieved a 74 percent repopulation rate in 2010 compared to 63 percent in Hollygrove. While Broadmoor had a larger increase in vacant housing, Hollygrove lost 355 housing units. Combining lost and vacant units, occupied housing units dropped by 182 fewer units in Broadmoor (712) than in Hollygrove (894). This provides evidence that Broadmoor's organized community-wide repopulation efforts helped accelerate the neighborhoood's recovery.

Progress with its Rebuilding Vision

A second accomplishment after repopulation was implementing its vision for the education corridor, the core of its plan to improve the neighborhood with expanded services and a more diverse and vibrant community center. Key anchors of the corridor—the Wilson School and Keller Library—were funded and either completed or under construction in mid-2010. A pedestrian walkway, new landscaping, and new lighting connected the three buildings. The three institutions expanded the neighborhood's learning and personal development resources and the potential for a new neighborhood center as a space for community gatherings and celebrations. They also symbolized the neighborhood's aspirations and its capacity to complete priority rebuilding projects. Getting all three projects funded and underway in five years—a total investment of more than $40 million—was a significant accomplishment, especially in light of the long delays in federal recovery funding.

Broadmoor's ability to secure funds outside federal recovery programs was an important factor in the timely completion of these projects and contributed to repopulation through funding the large home gutting and repair program. For every dollar of FEMA PA and Recovery CDBG funds invested in Broadmoor projects (excluding the Road Home funds), Broadmoor raised almost $4 in additional funds (see Table 3.12). The $30 million Quick Start award for the Wilson School represented the bulk of these funds, but the BIA and BDC also raised another $8.5 million from six other sources. Even including Road Home grants, Broadmoor raised 43 cents for every dollar of federal disaster recovery funds invested in the neighborhood through August 2010.

Table 3.12. FUNDING FOR BROADMOOR'S REBUILDING: NONFEDERAL AND FEDERAL FUNDS, THROUGH MID-2010[1]

Funding Source	Amount
LHFA Home Repair	$897,000
Salvation Army Environew	$1,820,000
Neighborhood Stabilization Program	$1,700,000
Rebuilding Together Home Repair	$715,000
Keller Library Grants	$2,300,000
Kennedy School/Shell Grant	$1,000,000
Wilson School	$30,000,000
Total Non-Federal Disaster Recovery Funds	*$38,432,000*
FEMA Public Assistance Funds	$4,365,321
Recovery CDBG Infrastructure	$3,200,000
Small Business Loans and Grants	$113,135
Small Rental Assistance Program	$2,649,001
Subtotal, Federal Disaster Recovery Fund without Road Home Program	*$10,327,457*
Road Home Program, Option 1[2]	$78,927,344
Total Federal Disaster Recovery Funds	$89,254,801
Total Funding. All Sources	$127,686,801

[1] Table lists major grants and funding contributions and is not a comprehensive list of all sources. Figures on nonfederal recovery funds are from Broadmoor Development Corporation. Data for federal recovery funding were provided by the Louisiana Office of Community Development and represented obligated funds as of August 2010.
[2] Option 1 required the homeowner to rebuild their original home. Since the other options involved rebuilding at another location, either within or outside Louisiana, funds awarded under these options were not invested in Broadmoor and were not counted.

This fundraising capacity made Broadmoor less dependent on the federal recovery funding process; it was able to move some rebuilding projects forward at a faster pace than could occur when using federal recovery dollars only. It also helped the BDC and BIA pursue goals and undertake activities that were not supported by federal programs, such as case management, community education services, and more environmentally sustainable rebuilding.

Expanded Civic Capacity

Broadmoor's physical rebuilding accomplishments reflect the neighborhood's social and organizational development. Through the rebuilding process, Broadmoor, as a community, gained tangible and intangible capacities to shape its future and to respond to new problems and disasters that may arise. Four new tangible capacities were created through the rebuilding process:

- A new community development corporation to undertake projects and programs that further the neighborhood's goals and vision and respond to new problems or concerns that arise. The BDC also is a vehicle to assemble money and other resources to implement the neighborhood's agenda beyond what is allowed by city or state priorities and funding.
- A stronger Broadmoor Improvement Association linked to the Broadmoor Neighborhood Improvement District. With the Broadmoor Plan and its implementation progress, the BIA emerged as a stronger organization with greater resident support and engagement, and more political capital. It also spurred the creation of an improvement district that provides an institutionalized source of funding for its activities. Under this new quasi-governmental entity, residents collectively supply funds that are administered by a representative elected body in pursuit of their shared goals for a better community.
- A better understanding of individual residents' expertise and skills, and experience tapping this resource to implement local projects and programs. This allows Broadmoor institutions, such as the BDC, BIA and the Charter School Board, to more readily use volunteerism to advance key organizational and neighborhood agendas.
- More diverse and stronger partnerships with a range of organizations. Broadmoor's focus on this arena, as a cornerstone of its rebuilding strategy, yielded the BIA and BDC strong relationships and programmatic partnerships with universities, local and national non-profit organizations, foundations, developers and government agencies.

The intangible capacity is a stronger community identity and the presence of a shared vision and confidence in the neighborhood's capacity to advance that vision. These shared goals and values and the ability to work collectively to solve problems, what social scientists call "civic capacity," are critical resources that allow communities to establish and achieve shared goals, mobilize political and financial capital, and adapt to change. As the core of community resilience, this is critical not only to recovery from disasters but in responding to the ongoing economic, political, and social changes faced by cities and neighborhoods.[102]

Remaining Challenges

Despite these accomplishments, Broadmoor faced important gaps and challenges in advancing its rebuilding vision in late 2010. The neighborhood aspires to rebuild 100 percent of its homes, which will require addressing several hundred blighted properties. Based on its initial experience working to restore and redevelop abandoned properties and market realities, this goal may not be feasible for quite some time. BDC's revised housing strategy for the neighborhood's eastern section retreats from the 100 percent goal, at least in the short- to medium-term, but includes the demolition of some blighted homes for parks, playgrounds, and side yards. A related challenge is returning rental units to the market and full occupancy. Broadmoor has seen progress in restoring owner-occupied rental units—the double shotgun homes and other two-family homes common to New Orleans. These properties benefited from resources targeted to homeowners—both the Road Home grants and the volunteer-based help. Investor-owned rental properties have been harder to rebuild.[103] The state program to assist small rental properties has not been well used and often provided too little funding to restore properties; only 54 apartments in Broadmoor received funds to rebuild from this program.[104] Moreover, no rental housing projects have been built in Broadmoor with the GO Zone Low-Income Housing Tax Credits. Despite these challenges, census figures indicate that, by 2010, rental units returned to occupancy at almost the same rate as owner-occupied homes by 76 percent and 75 percent, respectively. However, rental housing was far more likely to be vacant, as there were four times as many unoccupied units for rent in 2010 than empty houses for sale.

Few business and economic development initiatives were pursued during the first five years of rebuilding. The Broadmoor Plan focused on the neighborhood's commercial nodes as locations for new commercial development and businesses. It also proposed establishing workforce training partnerships for residents and using several tools to promote small business development.[105] With the exception of work on a new development at Broad and Washington Streets, none of these economic development initiatives were implemented. As noted by Cantrell, this was partly by design as Broadmoor focused on repopulation, housing, and public facilities, but it remains part of the BIA's long-term agenda and vision for reducing the neighborhood's economic disparities:

> Economic development is a part of our plan. That is one area that we are the weakest. It wasn't the top priority. With the future of the organization, that is a part of the vision...that is the commercial corridors...workforce development, training, helping to establish more businesses. Wilson School is an economic development opportunity for this community. We're looking at ways to create those opportunities for residents in Broadmoor ....do things in house and employ Broadmoor residents to run it...You have to be thinking of how you are going to build people up in your community. Wealth creation has to be a part of the vision.

Broadmoor was also in a period of transition in fall 2010. The BDC was undergoing a change in leadership, with Hal Roark's departure to attend the Yale Divinity School and the hiring of a new Executive Director, Santiago Burgos, a community development professional from Philadelphia.

The second transition involved implementation of the Broadmoor Improvement District, which provided the benefits of new funding, but now introduced a new structure and an electoral process into the selection of its leadership. In one sense, these changes exemplify Broadmoor's success—a move to institutionalize and professionalize its newly built capacity and funding. At the same time, these changes bring a new challenge—how to sustain residents' ownership and engagement as the process becomes more formal and professional. It is this grassroots activism that provided the drive, legitimacy, and local expertise essential to Broadmoor's successful first five years of rebuilding, and that will remain vital to progress over the next five years.

CHAPTER 4

༚

A Village Rebuilds

At the far eastern edge of New Orleans is a neighborhood known as Village de L'Est (see Figure 4.1). It belongs to New Orleans East—the last frontier of the city's growth that began development in the 1960s on drained marshland that sits between Lake Pontchartrain and the Intercoastal Waterway. New interstate highways made this distant part of New Orleans more accessible and feasible for residential development. A single company, the Wynne-Murchison Interests of Dallas, Texas, acquired most of the area's property, incorporated it as New Orleans East, and planned to build housing for 250,000 people on its 32,000 acres. The company went bankrupt and New Orleans East was developed into smaller subdivisions of primarily ranch-style homes that attracted many middle-class black home owners.[1] Village de L'Est is one of these subdivisions: a 600-acre section that opened in 1964 and, from the 1970s through the 1990s, developed into a neighborhood of mostly single- and two-family homes with several large apartment complexes and a mix of small businesses and other commercial uses along Chef Menteur Highway (the main street that traverses New Orleans East). Across Chef Menteur is New Orleans' largest business and industrial park, which includes NASA's Michoud Assembly Facility (used to manufacture large aerospace structures)[2] and a Folgers coffee roasting plant that permeates the neighborhood with a persistent aroma of percolating coffee.

Village de L'Est includes a large Vietnamese American community that first settled there in the 1970s under the US refugee resettlement program and grew to nearly 5,000 people by 1990.[3] Initially, 1,000 refugees were resettled in the area through the Associated Catholic Charities of New

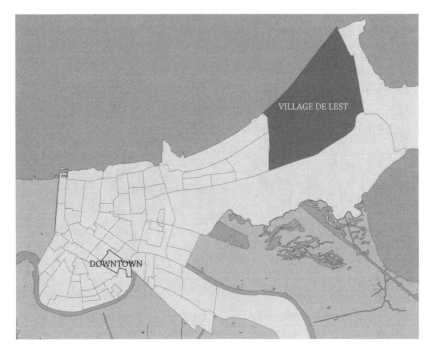

Figure 4.1.
Location of Village de L'Est within New Orleans.
Source: City of New Orleans GIS Department, New Orleans Neighborhoods, 2007, http://gisweb.cityofno.com/cnogis/dataportal.aspx

Orleans, which found them housing in a subsidized apartment complex called Versailles Arms. Thus, the neighborhood is also known as Versailles.[4] Although the largest number of Vietnamese refugees settled in Village de L'Est in the late 1970s following the end of the Vietnam War, immigration into the neighborhood continued through 2000 (see Figure 4.2).

The Vietnamese immigrants who arrived in Village de L'Est had a unique history of repeated relocation associated with their pursuit of religious freedom as Catholics. Many community members had originally lived in the Catholic diocese of Bui Chu Phat Diem in North Vietnam. Following the partition of Vietnam under the 1954 Geneva Convention and increasing differences between the Catholic church and the North Vietnamese government, several thousand largely Catholic residents fled to South Vietnam, settling in several areas about 70 miles southeast of Saigon.[5] After the fall of Saigon in 1975, many of these same people fled communist rule again and ended up in refugee camps. At these refugee camps, New Orleans Archbishop Phillip Hannan invited priests to bring their refugee communities to New Orleans and recruited Catholic Charities to assist in this effort,[6]

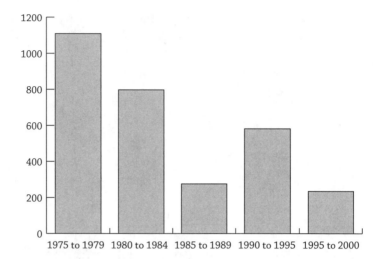

Figure 4.2.
Number of Village de L'Est residents who emigrated to the United States, 1975 to 2000.
Source: 2000 US Census.

facilitating a third shared migration for Village de L'Est's first Vietnamese American residents. Throughout these three migrations, ending in New Orleans East, the Catholic Church was central in the decisions to migrate and in providing the social support to reestablish a community:

> In 1985, the community founded its own ethnic parish, centered on Mary Queen of Vietnam Church. The religious faith, church leadership and social organization that informed the migration decisions of these Vietnamese refugees and immigrants have contributed to a strong community identity.[7]

In its first decades, Mary Queen of Vietnam (MQVN) Church focused on religious and spiritual aspects of the community and building a new church complex and was not active in either social services or community development activities.[8] Through MQVN Church and its new pastor, Father Vien The Nguyen, who arrived in 2003, the Catholic Church again played a pivotal role in determining the future of this Vietnamese American community as it struggled to rebuild after Hurricane Katrina.

Village de L'Est was unique in New Orleans for its large Vietnamese American population but was also representative of New Orleans in some ways. Its homeownership rate was close to the citywide level, as was its residential stability based on two measures: share of residents in 2000 who first moved to the neighborhood before 1990 and percentage who lived in the same house from 1995–2000 (see Table 4.1). The neighborhood also

Table 4.1. KEY TRAITS FOR VILLAGE DE L'EST AND
NEW ORLEANS' RESIDENTS

Population Trait	Village de L'Est	New Orleans
Percent black	55.4%	66.6%
Percent white	3.6%	26.6%
Percent foreign-born	24.3%	4.2%
Percent Asian	37.1%	2.3%
Average household income	$36,856	$43,176
Poverty rate	29.9%	27.9%
Percent owner-occupied homes	47.1%	46.5%
Percent vacant housing units	4.6%	12.5%
Percent not completing high school	35.5%	25.4%
Percent with bachelor's degree or higher	13.0%	23.1%
Percent of residents who moved into their house before 1990	33.2%	35.0%
Percent who live in same house in 1995	57.7%	56.8%
Percent of households without a car	20.3%	27.3%

Source: 2000 US Census as compiled by Greater New Orleans Community Data Center.

was a relatively poor section of New Orleans. Its poverty rate was above that of New Orleans in 2000 (30 percent versus 28 percent), and its average household income of $36,856 was 15 percent lower than all of New Orleans. A concentration of subsidized apartments and immigrant residents with low incomes contributed to the high poverty and low household income rates, despite the neighborhood's location within a middle-class enclave of single-family homes.[9] (See Figure 4.3 for a photograph of a typical residential street in Village de L'Est.) In one respect, Village de L'Est was in better shape than many other New Orleans neighborhoods before Katrina; its level of vacant housing units, at 4.6 percent, was about one-third of the citywide vacancy rate.

Since Village de L'Est was a majority black neighborhood prior to Katrina, its recovery depended on rebuilding both the Vietnamese American and African American communities. Thus, in looking at rebuilding efforts within the Vietnamese American community, this chapter addresses one part of the neighborhood's recovery. Nonetheless, there is still much to be learned by documenting the extensive community-based recovery work within the Vietnamese American portion of the neighborhood and what it was and was not able to accomplish. The process, successes, and failures within Village de L'Est's Vietnamese American enclave informs how grassroots rebuilding efforts can contribute to a city's recovery from large-scale

Figure 4.3.
A typical street in Village de L'Est
Source: Photo by author.

disasters. While focusing on rebuilding within the Vietnamese American community, the narrative highlights cases of cooperation between the two communities and instances in which specific services or projects undertaken through the MQVN Church affected the larger neighborhood. This chapter's conclusion also compares differences in repopulation across the two racial groups in 2010.

A FLOODED NEIGHBORHOOD

Situated closer to the storm surge that approached New Orleans from the east, with large water bodies to its north and south, Village de L'Est experienced widespread flooding when the levee system failed after Katrina. All residential areas had at least 4 feet of flooding, with the area between Michoud Boulevard and Palace Street inundated with 6 to 8 feet of water.[10] Most buildings also had considerable wind damage, with many roofs fully or partially torn off. For most homes, structural damage affected less than 50 percent of the house, although some pockets had more extensive wreckage. As with the entire city, widespread downed trees and storm debris remained for some time.[11] Fallen trees made travel on streets difficult for weeks after the flood waters receded. Similar to Broadmoor, the returning residents and volunteers who arrived in September and October found a foul odor, a brown film covering the ground, and little evidence of plant and animal life.[12] Schools, hospitals, parks, and open space were heavily damaged.[13] Memorial Methodist Hospital, New Orleans East's major health care facility, was in need of substantial repairs after receiving 10 feet of water. Consequently, through 2006 the entire New Orleans East area was served by a single temporary health clinic housed in a mobile home on Read Road.[14] On the other hand, the neighborhood's commercial areas, located on higher ground near a ridge that runs along Chef Menteur highway, had minimal flooding and property damage.

THE DECISION TO REBUILD

Two weeks after Katrina made landfall, Father Vien The Nguyen returned to Village de L'Est.[15] He had been traveling to evacuation locations in other cities in search of a missing elderly community member whom he sadly discovered had passed away in her home on September 29. Water had receded from most of the neighborhood, leaving a film of dirt everywhere and watermarks on all buildings. In touring the area, Father Vien found pervasive damage, many homes with roofs caved in or completely peeled off, and other homes sitting beneath fallen trees. One part of the neighborhood was still flooded and remained so for another month. The roof of the Mary Queen of Vietnam Church was badly damaged and part of the northwest wall of the religious school building, in which the Father and some residents rode out the storm, had collapsed and its bathrooms had flooded. Despite the wreckage and some congregants' belief that the church should relocate, Father Vien was committed to rebuilding his community:

> In my mind, there was never a doubt that we would rebuild and I operated out of that mode of thought. A few people spoke with me. I remember one man in particular. He was the leader of one of the choirs. He met with me and said he had spoken with members of the choir and that at least 60 percent of them have made the determination not to return. Maybe I should consider that. I said that sounds strange, it is not my estimation...Another priest suggested that maybe we should move all of the people over to the north side of the lake and do a wholesale migration. My response to him was that to find enough land to accommodate that many people, we would have to go 60 or 70 miles north of here. The next question is what kind of jobs are they going to have? Are they

going to have to travel 60 to 70 miles one way each day to work? So I tried to squelch all of that. The rest of the people, the older people were very determined to return. They had invested all of their lives in their homes and there wasn't any way they could begin again.[16]

Determined to rebuild, Father Vien worked with two other priests and a few volunteers to repair the church complex and provide supplies and support to residents who were returning to clean out their homes and begin repair work. Since all of the church buildings were damaged and uninhabitable,[17] the three priests and other volunteers stayed in a church on the west bank of the Mississippi River and, once repair work began, traveled to Village de L'Est every day. Relief efforts started in early October, once the city was reopened, and were centered at the Mary Queen of Vietnam Church (see Figure 4.4). Supplies needed to clean homes were collected and distributed by church leaders and volunteers. Three meals a day were cooked at the church so people could stay all day to work on their homes. Water and ice were trucked in, first by volunteer groups and then by FEMA, as neither potable water nor electricity were available. Two generators at the church allowed food to be stored and cell phone batteries to be charged,

Figure 4.4.
Mary Queen of Vietnam Church
Source: Photo by author.

which enabled residents to communicate with church leaders. Father Vien also organized small teams to help residents move refrigerators and other heavy items from their homes. Work to repair the church buildings continued throughout October and the three priests were able to move back into the rectory in early November.

Weekly mass served as a focal point for residents as they worked to clean, gut, and rebuild their homes. In the early days when residents returned, a man approached Father Vien about holding a Vietnamese mass and suggested holding it on the coming Sunday. Although uncertain about the number of people who would attend, Father Vien decided to proceed and organized the first mass for that Sunday, October 9. To publicize the mass, two large plywood boards spray-painted with "Mass 10am Sunday" were attached to the fence around the church. On Saturday night before the mass, church leaders and volunteers had to decide how many lunches to prepare. Were fifty enough? Would they need 100? Father Vien decided to prepare lunch for 150 people. When 300 people arrived for mass the next day, they quickly ran out of food.[18] Word spread quickly and on the next Sunday, 800 people attended mass. Residents who had evacuated to the west bank, Houston, and other areas returned on Sunday for mass and then stayed to clean and gut their homes. The church coordinated donations of supplies and food to aid residents in these efforts. As residents spent more time in Village de L'Est rebuilding their homes, the demand for mass grew. By mid-November, the MQVN Church was holding two daily masses. In early November, church leaders invited residents from throughout New Orleans East to a "Mass of the Resurrection," as an affirmation of the larger community's commitment to return and rebuild.

TAPPING THE NATIONAL VIETNAMESE AMERICAN COMMUNITY

Just as Broadmoor drew on external partners to aid in rebuilding, Village de L'Est mobilized a resource network beyond its borders to support rebuilding: the Vietnamese American community across the United States. Along with New Orleans, Vietnamese American communities were located in other cities and regions, including Houston, San Jose, Orange County (California), Seattle, and Boston. Father Vien recruited people from these cities to come to New Orleans to help with rebuilding efforts. One of the first volunteers was Trang Tu, a city planner from Seattle who had prepared plans for Seattle's Chinatown/International District, led planning for new development around several new light rail stations, and served as an advisor to Mayor Paul Schell on housing, community development, and urban design policies. Soon after Katrina, Trang travelled to Houston to help with emergency assistance for evacuees. While traveling back to Seattle, she received a call from Father Vien asking her to come to Village de L'Est for a year to assist with rebuilding. She made arrangements to volunteer for four months and arrived on October 15 to join an emerging leadership group. During this same period, Long Nguyen, the founder and former executive director of Viet-AID in Boston—the first Vietnamese American community development corporation—had been working to create a national community service program called the Dan Than Fellows Program to place recent college graduates with community development and social service organizations in Vietnamese American communities. In the aftermath of hurricanes Katrina and Rita, the National Association of Vietnamese American Service Agencies (NAVASA), the fellowship programs' administrator, and Long Nguyen decided to focus the Dan Than Fellows Program on relief and building efforts along the Gulf Coast in Biloxi, Houston, and New Orleans. Soon after arriving in Village de L'Est, Trang received a call from Long Nguyen and Huy Bui, NAVASA's Executive Director, asking her to serve as NAVASA's Gulf Coast regional coordinator for the Dan Than Fellows program. One of the first Dan Than Fellows was Mary Tran, a Village de L'Est resident and volunteer teacher in the church's religious school, who had recently moved to Houston to continue her studies. Father Vien convinced Tran to return and help with the rebuilding effort. She arrived in mid-November 2005 and worked on the recovery of Village de L'Est through summer 2009. Along with Mary Tran, the Dan Than Fellows program brought a half-dozen young people to Village de L'Est. They became the core day-to-day staff, coordinating many of the early planning and rebuilding efforts and working closely with resident volunteers.

EARLY ACTIVISM AND ORGANIZATION

> Even early on in the immediate rebuilding, it became clear that being so far from the urban center, the community had to start engaging in community organizing and advocacy to fight for some of the things they needed.[19]

In November, the Vietnamese American community transitioned from focusing on individual rebuilding—getting aid and supplies to help homeowners—to organizing as a community to advance their shared rebuilding needs and goals.[20] The first effort involved getting Entergy, the electric utility for New Orleans, to restore power to the neighborhood. As with many matters, Father Vien took the lead. He contacted Entergy and arranged a meeting in Baton Rouge with Rod West, the company's Director of New Orleans Metro Electric Distribution Operations, who was responsible for restoring power after Hurricanes Katrina and Rita. West explained to Father Vien that only eleven of Entergy's 23 power stations in New Orleans were working, with just two restored to full power. As a result, Entergy's priority was to supply power to the Central Business District. When Father Vien asked how he could bring electric power back to Village de L'Est, West said that power could only be restored if he could justify the load, which meant showing that a large number of paying customers had returned and wanted their electric service back. West resisted giving Father Vien a specific number but when pressed he replied that, hypothetically, if 100 people signed up, then the two of them could go before the Entergy board to make a case that sufficient load existed to restore power. With so many people returning for Sunday mass, church volunteers quickly collected the names, addresses, and flood depths[21] for 500 residents who requested the restoration of electric power, which Father Vien passed on to Entergy. Within two weeks, on November 10, homes and businesses in Village de L'Est started receiving electricity. Water service also was restored during this time. With both electricity and water, people could do far more work on their homes: power wash them, make repairs with power tools, and stay and work for longer periods of time.

A second project involved securing FEMA trailers to house residents as they worked to repair their homes.[22] In this case, it was a Pyrrhic victory. During a visit to Baton Rouge in October, Father Vien met with a FEMA official and offered a site owned by the church located on Dwyer Road across from its main building (see Figure 4.5) as a location to place trailers. He agreed that the church would lease the land at no cost to FEMA in return for providing community residents a preference in receiving a trailer. A formal agreement was reached to lease the church land to FEMA to locate 199 trailers; the lease agreement cited the purpose of the trailers "to provide temporary shelter on the premises in order that the Lessor may assist in providing housing to Mary Queen of Vietnam Parishioners and other New Orleans Vietnamese American community members as determined by Mary Queen of Vietnam Parish as disaster assistance recipients granted occupancy of housing units established within the emergency housing facility."[23] Before the trailers could be installed, a city permit was needed. When the permit was requested but not received, church leaders and volunteers organized to pressure the city council and mayor. After establishing a "tent city" on the trailer site, residents slept there to dramatize the need for trailers. They also demonstrated at the city council to push for the permit. A national news story by CNN reporter John King helped publicize the issue, and a turning point occurred the following week when Senators Mary Landrieu and Hillary Clinton attended mass and agreed to speak with Mayor Nagin on the need for a permit. The next week, right before Thanksgiving, the mayor's office contacted the church to report that the permit had been issued. Construction to prepare the site began in January and the trailers were ready for occupancy six months later in July 2006. During this time, the church identified over 300 residents who were interested in a FEMA trailer and expected many of them to move in once the trailers were ready.

The church's goal to use the trailers as temporary shelter for local residents was set back when FEMA began to place nonparishioners in the trailers. Many who received the trailers were neither on the church's waiting list, nor Village de L'Est residents. Father Vien contacted FEMA and was told that (1) it was illegal to give preference in assigning trailers—even though FEMA had earlier agreed to this arrangement; (2) many Village de L'Est residents were no longer eligible for the trailers; and (3) FEMA could not dedicate the trailers for the exclusive use of Catholic parishioners.[24] The priest contacted the offices of Senators Landrieu and Vitter about the problem and invited them to attend an upcoming meeting with FEMA representatives to attempt a resolution of the issue. At this meeting, FEMA did not change its policy on resident preference, but did agree to look into reimbursing the church for the $80,000 it had paid for liability insurance as the landowner for the trailer site (these funds were eventually received) and to remove the trailers within one year so that the site could be used for a senior housing project.[25] Mary Tran spent considerable time helping community members apply for the trailers and advocating for them with FEMA to get members into the trailers (see discussion below). These efforts succeeded in getting around 50 Vietnamese American residents into the trailers—of some value but far short of providing temporary housing for several hundred residents as originally envisioned and provided for under the FEMA lease.

This episode not only demonstrates how bureaucratic delays and shifting FEMA commitments made the implementation of recovery projects more difficult, but also reveals the tensions between a neighborhood's priorities and citywide rebuilding needs. While the church had a clear need to secure trailers for its parishioners and nearby residents, there was also a shortage of temporary housing for residents of New Orleans East and the entire city. Trailers were one of the solutions at the time and there were not enough of them to fill residents' needs. Engaging in a practice of linking

Figure 4.5.
Site used for FEMA trailer park and proposed for senior housing project
Source: Photo by author.

trailer sites to specific congregations or immediate neighborhoods would make addressing the larger citywide need for trailers more difficult (and raise issues of equitable access to temporary housing). Conflicts between neighborhood priorities and citywide rebuilding goals are part and parcel of the recovery process, and thus need effective and equitable mechanisms for their resolution.

ORGANIZING AND PLANNING FOR REBUILDING

Trang Tu proved an important asset to the recovery effort, providing ideas to improve short-term effectiveness while facilitating work on long-term rebuilding goals. When relief and recovery efforts began in October, Father Vien held almost daily meetings with the church priests, pastoral council leaders, and volunteers to address immediate issues such as securing supplies and following up on offers of help. With her experience as a project manager and planner, Tu observed the types of work that needed to be done and the variety of talents among members of the leadership group. Based on these observations, she prepared an organizational structure to present to Father Vien that involved four functions and one person assigned to lead each function:[26]

1. An executive and administration function that also handled external and media relations;
2. A resource procurement function to coordinate obtaining supplies, receiving donations and working with volunteers;
3. An operations function to distribute supplies, coordinate assistance for house cleanup and repair, and set up the Sunday mass; and
4. A long-term planning and development function to work on a redevelopment plan to address long-term needs for employment, senior housing, and the like.

Despite her concerns about presenting these ideas as an outsider, Tu decided to share her plan with Father Vien after discussing it with another volunteer. On November 3, they took Father Vien to lunch outside the neighborhood and presented the organization plan. Father Vien liked the proposed structure, which was then presented to and adopted by the church leadership group. It remained in place when Trang Tu returned to Seattle in February. Tu was also instrumental in advancing two pillars of Village de L'Est long-term rebuilding: holding a design charrette to create a long-term community vision, and creating a community development corporation to implement the vision.

DESIGN CHARRETTE AND COMMUNITY VISION

The impetus for creating a community rebuilding vision emerged from interest in building a senior housing project and was spurred by plans presented by the BNOB Commission. [27] Housing for seniors had been an aspiration of the MQVN Church before Katrina. The death of an elder resident who was unable to evacuate heightened Father Vien's interest in the project; he asked Trang Tu to initiate plans to develop it. Tu completed an initial feasibility analysis and introduced Father Vien to Doris Koo, her mentor and a top executive at Enterprise Community Partners—a national intermediary that finances and assists with affordable housing development. As her work on the senior housing project progressed, Tu saw the need for wider community input into its design. At the same time, the Urban Land Institute's report to the BNOB raised concerns about the neighborhood's future and whether resettlement of Village de L'Est would be part of the city's rebuilding plans. Tu believed having its own rebuilding vision and plan would provide the Vietnamese American community with a stronger voice and more credibility in decisions about the neighborhood's future. Tu met with Father Vien in early December to share the results of her analysis on the senior housing project and proposed holding a community design charrette. A charrette is a collaborative process that involves designers and community members in a discussion about solutions to design problems. These discussions often occur in multiple sessions in which separate groups work on a specific problem and then present their ideas to all participants for discussion and refinement. In this manner, a charrette combines many people's skills and ideas in producing a design solution fairly quickly. Tu recognized that a full planning process would take many months, but thought the simpler charrette approach might work and could be organized within one or two months. With Father Vien's support, Tu worked with Mary Tran to organize the charrette. They contacted and invited professional planners and architects from around the United States. Two architects from Vietnam also attended to add cultural authenticity in the design process. In preparation for the charrette, two meetings were held with community members in early January to better understand their needs and elicit goals and ideas. One meeting included elderly residents in a discussion of the senior housing project; the second engaged business owners in plans for the commercial district.[28]

The charrette occurred from February 1–3, 2006 with close to 35 professionals and a dozen community members. Four teams that mixed professional designers with local residents were formed; two teams worked on plans for the senior housing project while the other teams prepared plans for the neighborhood's business district along Alcee Fortier Boulevard and Chef Menteur Highway. Each team presented its plans, which were reviewed and refined at the charrette and led to a final design vision that was presented at the annual Tet New Year Festival on February 4. These were conceptual plans for the senior housing site along with building façade and design ideas for the business district organized around specific blocks. The plans for the senior housing project envisioned a combination of independent living apartments, assisted living units, and a skilled nursing facility that would provide housing and services with Vietnamese language capacity in a culturally-appropriate setting. Improvements to the business district were linked to a plan to make it a regional ethnic tourist destination. An additional idea from the charrette was to create a green space with pedestrian and bike trails along the Maxent Canal that traverses the neighborhood. Although the plans were conceptual, they were well-received by community members and established a development agenda for the church leadership and Vietnamese American community. This process marked an important transition as aspirations now moved beyond rebuilding the preexisting neighborhood to plans for an improved community with new assets.

Although the charrette process succeeded in setting several development priorities for the Village de L'Est Vietnamese American community, it was neither as comprehensive nor as participatory as a standard neighborhood planning process. A relatively small number of residents were involved, and the process lacked background information and analysis on existing conditions that would help to inform decisions on future priorities. Moreover, it focused on physical development and improvements and did not address important community needs such as schools, recreation and health care. Consequently, the charrette did not provide Village de L'Est with a complete neighborhood plan like the one created by Broadmoor residents. This had the advantage of providing a less ambitious and more focused agenda for the church and neighborhood leaders. However, this agenda proved incomplete and additional projects were added as additional neighborhood needs were identified. Within a few months, a major shift in community priorities came in response to the city's decision to open a new landfill at the edge of Village de L'Est.

COMMUNITY MOBILIZATION AND
THE LANDFILL CAMPAIGN

As residents actively rebuilt their homes, the Vietnamese American community and all of New Orleans East learned, in April 2006, that a new landfill for construction and demolition debris had opened nearby on Chef Menteur Highway. The cleanup of damage from the two hurricanes and extensive flooding after the levee system failures had generated a huge volume of waste, estimated at that time at 7.2 million tons.[29] Federal, state, and city officials sought new landfill sites to receive this debris and accelerate the cleanup.[30] The need for additional landfills was heightened by a lawsuit against another landfill in New Orleans' Gentilly neighborhood, which resulted in a legal settlement that limited the amount of waste deposited there while its impact was being studied.[31] A large site at 16600 Chef Menteur Highway had been used as a waste transfer facility but twice previously had been denied a city permit to serve as a construction waste landfill.[32] The site's owner approached the city of New Orleans and the Louisiana Department of Environmental Quality (LDEQ) about using the site as a landfill for construction and demolition waste.[33] On February 14, 2006, Mayor Nagin signed an agreement with the site owner and Waste Management, Inc., the proposed operator of the landfill, which allowed them to operate the site as a landfill for construction debris. The mayor then sent a letter to the LDEQ asking it to approve the landfill for "the duration of hurricane Katrina disaster cleanup efforts, at this time estimated to be 12 months."[34] The prior week, Nagin had signed an executive order suspending a requirement, under the city's zoning laws, for a conditional use permit to open the landfill. Two months later, the LDEQ authorized the landfill to accept construction and demolition debris; the Army Corps of Engineers quickly gave approval for the landfill to begin operations while its permit application was being reviewed.[35] The Chef Menteur landfill opened on April 26 and was soon accepting truckloads of waste.

Church leaders immediately began organizing to stop the landfill, which risked exposing the community to soil and water contamination since no linings or other barriers were installed to prevent leakage of toxic materials into the marshy land and waterways near the landfill site. The Maxent Canal, next to the landfill site, traverses Village de L'Est and is a source of water for many backyard gardens. Any toxic chemicals that leached into the canal threatened to pollute home sites that bordered the canal and, moreover, to contaminate residents' gardens—an important community food source. With its proximity to the Bayou Sauvage National Wildlife Refuge, the landfill also risked polluting this sensitive habitat and environmental resource, a situation that heightened environmental organizations' interest in the issue. Two of these groups, the Louisiana Environmental Network (LEAN) and the Sierra Club, played important roles in the campaign to close the landfill. Health and environmental risks from the landfill increased when the LDEQ expanded the types of debris that could be accepted at the landfill to include treated wood, asbestos-containing materials, and drywall wallboards, which raised the possibility of hydrogen sulfide, arsenic, and asbestos leaching into ground water and offsite.[36]

Several community meetings were held to inform residents and business owners about the landfill and involve them in working to shut it down. Additional community outreach and organizing for the campaign was conducted by a core staff that included the NAVASA Dan Than Fellows, people assembled by the church to assist with rebuilding and staff from the newly formed Mary Queen of Vietnam Community Development Corporation (MQVN CDC) (described below).[37] An important part of this work was keeping abreast of the health risks associated with the landfill and ongoing legal and political developments, and translating this information into Vietnamese and nontechnical language to keep residents well-informed.

MQVN church leaders reached out to other neighborhood associations and faith-based groups in New Orleans East and formed a coalition, Citizens for a Strong New Orleans East, to fight the landfill. This was the first issue to politically unite leaders within the Vietnamese American community and the New Orleans East black community but followed earlier actions by Father Vien to invite black Catholics to mass and open up the MQVN church for use by black leaders and organizations.[38] The landfill campaign established a foundation of biracial cooperation that carried over to other activities:

> In the years since the landfill struggle, political alliances between Vietnamese Americans and black residents have persisted through various channels. The two communities worked closely together in influencing the so-called master plan for New Orleans, ensuring that the area be recognized as an important cultural heritage district. Young activists from both communities have also been jointly active in struggles to reopen area schools.[39]

Community leaders first worked with their City Councilor, Cynthia Willard-Lewis, to set up a meeting with LDEQ and Waste Management Incorporated (WMI). At that meeting, they asked WMI to install a liner and monitoring system to reduce the risk of leaching and to take other steps to reduce the amount of material dumped in the landfill.[40] After state officials and WMI rejected these requests, arguing that the landfill was safe, LEAN and Citizens for a Strong New Orleans East filed suit in federal court seeking an injunction against the US Army Corps of Engineers' approval of the landfill. This suit was not successful and the campaign against the landfill shifted to the political arena.

Campaign leaders sought and obtained a unanimous city council resolution calling upon Mayor Nagin to rescind his executive order that allowed the landfill to operate without a permit. A demonstration at City Hall was organized in early May, two weeks before the mayoral election, at which several hundred New Orleans East residents called for the closing of the landfill (see Figure 4.6). During the demonstration, the mayor met with several community representatives and then announced to the demonstrators that he would stop dumping at the landfill for 72 hours to allow testing of materials there.[41]

He also pledged to terminate his executive order if any toxic waste was found.[42] LDEQ, WMI, and community activists could not reach agreement on a testing protocol. WMI proposed testing trucks with debris prelandfill entry, while community leaders and LEAN proposed testing and full characterization of materials already present in the landfill. The landfill was reopened after testing conducted under the WMI protocol did not reveal hazardous materials. Community residents, however, did not view the testing as comprehensive or legitimate, as it only tested new incoming

Figure 4.6.
City hall demonstration against the Chef Menteur landfill
Source: Courtesy of James Bui.

waste and not the full complement of materials in the landfill.[43] After this setback, the campaign shifted to the state legislature. New Orleans' legislators introduced resolutions in both the State Senate and House of Representatives calling for complete testing of the Chef Menteur landfill. Local organizers generated over 500 calls to state legislators and the resolution passed both houses unanimously. An effort to mediate the testing dispute between WMI and community leaders ensued but, in spite of the legislature's action, WMI would not agree to a testing protocol that community leaders felt would provide an accurate assessment of landfill waste.[44]

As residents became frustrated with their inability to get landfill contents tested and convince regulators to address their concerns, some segments of the Vietnamese American community began to consider other tactics to close the landfill.[45] It was increasingly believed that public officials and Waste Management held the same views and would not negotiate either an alternative to the landfill or ways to reduce its health risks. The idea of taking direct action by engaging in civil disobedience to block trucks' entry into the landfill emerged; by late July efforts were underway to organize this protest for mid-August.[46] Elderly residents and teenagers, who had become active in the landfill campaign in prior months, were especially active in preparing for the August protest.

During this period, LEAN and Citizens for a Strong New Orleans East continued to pressure Mayor Nagin to rescind his executive order and close the landfill. They filed a second lawsuit in state court, arguing that the mayor had exceeded his authority in using emergency powers to suspend the zoning law and allow the landfill to open without a permit.[47] Under increased pressure, Nagin announced that he would not extend the landfill's exemption from the city permit requirement, which would expire on August 14.[48] Nagin's action led the state to withdraw its authorization for the landfill. WMI then filed its own lawsuit against LDEQ, seeking to keep the landfill open. The legal battles and drama continued when LQED reversed itself at an August 11 hearing on the WMI lawsuit and stated that it would allow the landfill to remain in operation. The next day, Nagin reiterated his decision not to extend the waiver and indicated a plan to issue a cease-and-desist order at midnight on August 14 if the landfill was still operating. WMI was defiant—it would seek a court injunction to keep the landfill open. Empowered by their recent victories and committed to preventing the landfill from remaining open, organizers moved forward with plans to engage in civil disobedience and block trucks from entering the site at the landfill on August 15. Close to eighty people volunteered for the protest and were trained in preparation for undertaking a civil disobedience action. This large group of protesters were divided between the landfill site and the courthouse, where the Waste Management injunction was being heard.[49] On the morning of August 15, scores of people gathered in front of the landfill gates with signs and placards and formed a human chain to block the entrance. This intergenerational act of resistance involved both teenagers and the elderly. During the protest, demonstrators received word that a federal judge had denied WMI's injunction request and the order to close the landfill would stand.

The landfill campaign changed the internal and external relationships in the Village de L'Est and especially in the Vietnamese American community, as each gained a new sense of political empowerment. The campaign became a cross-generational effort—elders saw the importance of protecting the health of their community for their children, and their teenage grandchildren became politically active. When organizers sought volunteers for the human chain to blockade the landfill entrance, the majority were senior citizens. James Bui, NAVASA's Gulf Coast Regional Director at the time, recounts the involvement of the community's elders and the political significance of this decision for one senior:

> When we decided to do the direct action in August...the majority of people
> who responded were seniors. In the Vietnamese-American community context,

typically their civic engagement is around homeland politics. It is not around landfill issues, rebuilding and those types of things. They are the ones who took environmental justice to a new level and brought environmental justice semantics into everyday Vietnamese-American language... One thing that hit me the most was when I was with some students from UMASS and they asked one senior... "Why are you doing this campaign, why are you volunteering to be arrested, to be in this direct action?" Her response was: "The very reason why I became a US citizen is so I can get arrested." She said that, time and time again... For Vietnamese-Americans, particularly the older generation has seen the United States as like a second home. But now, she is saying that to become a US citizen is so I can get arrested and understand that [the] constitution protects me.[50]

The commitment of seniors sparked greater youth involvement in the fight against the landfill, including their desire to have a greater role in planning the campaign.[51] Youth activism on the landfill issue was a catalyst for the creation of a new youth organization, the Vietnamese American Young Leaders of New Orleans (VAYLA-NO), and ongoing attention to civic engagement and leadership development among youth in Village de L'Est. Another outcome was recognition of shared interests and a political coalition between New Orleans East's African American and Vietnamese American communities, who had rarely worked together on issues before Katrina.[52] The shared agenda carried over into the UNOP process, when both communities sought to include common priorities in the plan around restoring education and health services and revitalization of the Chef Menteur Highway.[53]

Perhaps of greater significance, the campaign awakened political awareness and activism. Village de L'Est, under Father Vien and the MQVN church leadership, had already asserted itself politically by demonstrating at a BNOB commission meeting and advocating for utility service and FEMA trailers, but the landfill campaign was more transformative. It involved far more people in a longer and more complex process. Community residents, leaders, and staff learned about and interacted with different government institutions at the city, state, and federal levels. The campaign involved meetings with Mayor Nagin and state environmental regulators, the securing of city council and state legislative resolutions, testimony before a congressional committee, and multiple lawsuits. Furthermore, their political activism succeeded in getting Mayor Nagin and a federal court to take action to close the landfill. With this level of activism and political victory, Village de L'Est not only formed new alliances and learned how to use the political process to achieve its goals, but became a recognized political constituency and force in New Orleans.

New attention to environmental issues and environmental justice also emerged from the fight against the Chef Menteur landfill. The new MQVN CDC, established to implement the community's rebuilding agenda (discussed below), continued to work on environmental justice and health matters.[54] One focus was monitoring the lawsuits and status of the Chef Menteur and Gentilly landfills to prevent them from either reopening or becoming a further source of contamination through poor management. The CDC expanded beyond Village de L'Est and worked with other groups to clean up and stop illegal waste-dumping at 30 sites in the New Orleans East and Gentilly neighborhoods. Since lax monitoring and enforcement enabled illegal dumping, these advocacy efforts focused on getting state and federal regulators to step up enforcement efforts. As a result, the state LDEQ and US Environmental Protection Agency (EPA) increased monitoring and enforcement activities, including setting up cameras at several sites.[55]

BUILDING IMPLEMENTATION CAPACITY: MARY QUEEN OF VIETNAM COMMUNITY DEVELOPMENT CORPORATION

Newfound political influence did not directly translate into expanded rebuilding capacity. Village de L'Est leaders still needed the organization and resources to undertake projects and pursue the rebuilding vision that emerged from the February charrette, especially the senior housing project and revitalized business district.[56] As with Broadmoor, Father Vien and the MQVN church leaders chose a community development corporation as the means to undertake these projects. The idea of creating a CDC was suggested first by Doris Koo of Enterprise Community Partners, whom Trang Tu had introduced to Father Vien.[57] Koo met with Father Vien and Mary Tran in spring 2006 to discuss the senior housing project and recommended forming a CDC to build the project. Father Vien gave Mary Tran and another volunteer, Kim Nguyen, the task of researching and forming a CDC. A team of MIT graduate students also recommended forming a CDC to create a business development program to address the needs of Village de L'Est businesses.[58] Mary Tran spoke to staff at the Ujama CDC in New Orleans' Tremé neighborhood, who referred her to an attorney, Kelly Longwell, who prepared the articles of incorporation, bylaws and application for 501(c)(3) tax-exempt status.[59] MQVN CDC was incorporated in May 2006 as a nonprofit Louisiana corporation with a seven-person board that included Father Vien, members of the MQVN Church Parish Council, and other community leaders who had worked with the church on rebuilding efforts[60]. Although the CDC was intended to be a locally based organization focused on improving the Village de L'Est neighborhood, its governing documents were not aligned with this mission. Its Articles of Incorporation did not target or limit the CDC to the Village de L'Est neighborhood and listed its purposes as improving conditions for residents in Orleans Parish and the state of Louisiana. Under the CDC's bylaws, there was no provision for either membership in or governance of the CDC by neighborhood residents or businesses.[61]

Mary Tran was appointed the first Executive Director during her tenure as a NAVASA Dan Than fellow. She planned to serve temporarily but ended up staying for three years—until the summer of 2009. Her first tasks were to raise funds for the organization so that it could hire more staff and to begin work on two priorities that emerged from the community charrette: the senior housing development and strengthening the local business district. With resources from several sources, MQVN CDC quickly assembled a relatively large staff for a startup CDC. The CDC's initial funding included $10,000 from the MQVN Church, $40,000 from a local foundation, and several other small grants.[62] With these funds, the MQVN CDC hired a Business Development Director, May Nguyen, in June 2006. Catholic Charities also placed two of its staff at the CDC through early 2007 to help residents secure resources to return and rebuild. The CDC also benefited from the Dan Than Fellows, who transitioned to working for the CDC upon its establishment. Furthermore, James Bui, who had replaced Trang Tu as NAVASA's Gulf Coast Regional Director in March 2006, was an active consultant to the CDC. He helped supervise the fellows, advised Father Vien and Mary Tran, and provided access to a larger network of NAVASA consultants. By October 2006, one year after Village de L'Est residents began returning, MQVN CDC had five full-time staff augmented with another five Dan Than Fellows. Many staff received modest pay or were compensated by other organizations (NAVASA and Catholic Charities)—in all, this large team allowed the CDC to undertake several initiatives. With 10 people, the CDC had outgrown its initial space at MQVN Church and moved into its own offices just off Alcee Fortier Boulevard.

In its first months, MQVN CDC was active in three areas: (1) advancing the senior housing project; (2) assisting residents in gaining access to FEMA trailers and other recovery resources; and (3) organizing and providing assistance to local businesses. The initial motivation to create the CDC was to build senior housing so this naturally became an early priority. As a new organization with young staff, the CDC lacked the capacity to undertake a multimillion dollar housing development. To address this problem, MQVN CDC formed a partnership with Providence Community Housing—a new nonprofit housing developer formed after Hurricane Katrina with support from Catholic Charities of New Orleans and other community-based organizations to bring over 18,000 displaced residents back to New Orleans through the restoration, repair, and new development of 7,000 housing units.[63] Since MQVN CDC's senior housing project fit Providence's mission and goals, a partnership agreement between Providence and MQVN CDC was negotiated with the CDC as the lead development partner. A more detailed development program and cost estimates for the project were formulated next. This development plan was for 84 affordable independent apartment units, a 500-person community meeting hall, two physician exam rooms, an exercise room, a computer lab, and a commercial kitchen and dining area. Development costs were estimated to be $13 million.[64] For the project to be feasible and serve the community's low-income elderly residents, the CDC needed an allocation of federal low-income housing tax credits (LIHTC) to subsidize the project's cost.[65] MQVN CDC and Providence prepared the long and detailed application to the Louisiana Housing Finance Authority for a 2007 allocation of tax credits—a task that took up much of Mary Tran's time in her first months as executive director.

Another early CDC focus was assisting residents in gaining access to recovery and rebuilding resources—institutionalizing a role first undertaken by church leaders and volunteers. Since aid agencies rarely had staff who spoke Vietnamese, the CDC staff filled this void by helping residents to prepare applications and to communicate with FEMA, the Small Business Administration (SBA), and other agencies on behalf of residents to follow up on applications. In 2006, the most time-consuming part of this effort involved working to place residents into the 199 FEMA trailers installed near the MQVN church, as recounted by Mary Tran:

> I was working for FEMA but not getting paid by them. They had no one who
> spoke Vietnamese working for them so when people called up to request a trailer
> who did they go to? I ended up being the person that people went to when they
> needed a trailer. I would have at least twenty people a day come in asking for a
> FEMA trailer...A lot of them were in really sad situations with people living in
> their cars....I would get their FEMA number and then I would call FEMA and
> ask to put them in their files and see whether or not they can be approved for
> a FEMA trailer. That process took about a week and then I would have to call
> every week to follow up on each FEMA number. Initially, I gave them 300 FEMA
> numbers...It took months for FEMA to approve most applications. By the time
> they were approved, they were done moving into their homes. In the end, out of
> 199 trailers, maybe 50 of them were community members.

As recovery CDBG funds became available for the Road Home program and small business assistance, CDC staff helped community residents prepare the paperwork to apply for these funds. CDC staff also functioned as trouble shooters for the many rebuilding and resettlement challenges faced by returning residents—the same role played by case managers at the Broadmoor Development Corporation. A typical problem addressed by CDC staff involved working out school transportation for parents during the 2006–2007 school year. With limited space in the one neighborhood school that reopened by fall 2006, most Village de L'Est children attended schools across New Orleans, which often entailed a bus ride of 30 minutes or longer. Bus transportation was erratic during this first year as schools reopened; parents relied on the CDC to notify the Recovery School District when buses did not arrive and to push for reliable student transportation.[66] These efforts established the CDC as the neighborhood hub for information and assistance on issues; in addition the CDC worked to secure rebuilding resources for black and other New Orleans East residents outside the Vietnamese American community, as recounted by former city councilor aide Mimi Nguyen:[67]

> The CDC has become a one-stop shop for all kinds of stuff: social services, any assistance, even legal assistance. With all this, the CDC has become the hub. It also created an entity that the outside community can use rather than just Vietnamese [residents] ....They have space for various organizations [to provide services], Catholic Charities and the credit union...The CDC served as a safe haven in a way. Any information you needed came from the CDC. At the same time, the CDC started to go out to other neighborhoods to let them know there is a Vietnamese community and that we have the CDC. Information can be like two-way traffic. They went to different neighborhood meetings. If the neighborhood needs information on certain things, they can come to the CDC. So it served a wide range of populations in New Orleans East.

CDC advocacy and resident services paid off for Village de L'Est by helping the community access considerable rebuilding aid. This is evident in the level of Road Home assistance received by the neighborhood, despite its language and cultural barriers. Almost 1,900 families received Road Home grants totaling $161 million (see Table 4.2), which represents virtually 100 percent of the neighborhood's owner-occupied homes, based on the 2000 Census.[68] As a point of comparison, 849 properties in Broadmoor received Road Home Grants, or 61 percent of the neighborhood owner-occupied homes in 2000. The high level of Road Home grants may reflect more extensive damage and lower levels of insurance among Village de L'Est homes.

Table 4.2. ROAD HOME AND SMALL RENTAL PROPERTY HOUSING
ASSISTANCE TO VILLAGE DE L'EST

Program	Total Assisted Units/Homes[1]	Total Amount of Assistance
Road Home	1,899	$160,997,507
Small rental	31	$1,888,350
Total	1,930	$162,885,857

Source: Louisiana Department of Community Development.
[1] The 1,889 units includes 1,812 homeowners who received aid under Option One to rebuild the original home and 87 who received grants to buy a home at another site.

Still, it indicates that MQVN CDC assistance was effective in helping this community, with many Vietnamese immigrants extensively utilizing the complex and bureaucratic Road Home program.

BUSINESS DEVELOPMENT AND COMMERCIAL DISTRICT MARKETING

One of MQVN CDC's earliest successes involved its support for local businesses at two nodes on the Chef Menteur Highway at Michoud Boulevard and Alcee Fortier Boulevard. Historically, these entrepreneurs had financed their businesses with their own savings and loans from other family and community members. The extensive damage and financial losses throughout the community after Hurricane Katrina caused business owners to quickly exhaust their savings and those of family and friends.[69] At the same time, many businesses had returned and reopened by spring 2006.[70] The earliest stores to open in New Orleans East attracted customers from outside the community and saw expansion potential. With limited funds and expansion opportunities, business owners sought financing from outside Village de L'Est and approached the CDC for assistance—a role that the CDC embraced. Beyond helping businesses to access resources, the CDC worked to advance its new vision of an ethnic business district that attracted shoppers from throughout metro New Orleans.

As the new Business Development Director, May Nguyen quickly established programs to address both goals.[71] Her family's long history in Village de L'Est proved valuable in her new position, as did her creativity and ability to build partnerships and a professional network. Nguyen's parents and grandparents were among the original migrants from North to South Vietnam in 1954 who later evacuated from South Vietnam as boat people, settling in Village de L'Est. Her parents had helped build the current

MQVN church building and her grandmother started the Saturday morning market still held on Alcee Fortier Boulevard. When her father lost his job in the late 1980s, her family moved to California but her grandparents and several aunts remained and still live in Village de L'Est.

Nguyen enlisted her relatives to tackle one of her first tasks—organizing a business association. The association's purpose was to organize business owners to address issues of common concern and collaborate on marketing and improvement of the two business centers. Nguyen initially recruited her family members to form an association and then moved the association's meetings around to different businesses to gain their participation. Business owners' greatest concern was public safety, which affected their ability to stay open at night. To address this concern, Nguyen worked with business owners to locate a police substation in the neighborhood, ensuring an expanded and more visible police presence. They targeted a vacant space at the former church building on Alcee Fortier Boulevard, just past the business district. To entice the police to locate there, the association worked with a youth group to clean out the space and provided funds to purchase furniture and office equipment. Their work convinced the police department to move some administrative activities to the building and demonstrated the effectiveness of the business association. Over the next year, May Nguyen worked with the business association to implement a marketing campaign and to connect business owners to small business recovery grants and loans.

To expand the marketing of the Vietnamese American business community, Nguyen raised over $200,000 in grants, including $3,000 from Lockheed Martin Corporation (a contractor at the nearby NASA Michoud Facility), $50,000 from the Louisiana Disaster Recovery Foundation, and $150,000 from the Louisiana Economic Development, the state economic development agency.[72] The CDC used these funds to create a branding identity for the Vietnamese American business district that was reinforced with banners, business signs, and a marketing brochure. Nguyen convinced the CDC to hold a competition among neighborhood youth for the branding name and logo and provided a $1,000 prize for the winner. She saw the competition as a way to excite youth about the community's economic development and avoid relying on the more common "Little Saigon" to brand the area. The winning logo design was announced at the February 2007 Tet Festival, with the $1,000 check awarded to the winning teenager, who promptly gave the money to her family to help rebuild their house. The winning "Viet Village" name and design were incorporated in a business directory brochure (see Figure 4.7) and banners installed on light poles.

Figure 4.7.
"Viet Village" logo from business directory cover
Source: Use by permission, Mary Queen of Vietnam Community Development Corporation.

Although state funds were tied to visitor marketing, business owners wanted to attract workers from the nearby industrial area to shop at their stores. The business association created a committee to build relationships with firms in the industrial park and market the district to their employees. Several meetings were held with the industrial park association to discuss plans to improve Village de L'Est, distribute the business directory, and encourage their workers to patronize Village de L'Est businesses.

A third part of the business development program entailed helping business owners to access financing. Under the state Action Plan for recovery CDBG funds, Louisiana allocated $138 million for a Small Business Recovery Grant and Loan program that provided grants and no-interest loans to small businesses that had suffered losses from hurricanes Katrina and Rita. Both programs were administered locally by designated community-based financial institutions. Although MQVN CDC was not designated to process recovery grant applications, it informed local businesses about the program and helped them prepare application materials. For the Small Business Recovery Loan Program, which awarded funds under a separate request for proposals, Nguyen created a partnership between MQVN CDC and ASI Federal Credit Union. Under the partnership, the CDC conducted outreach and packaged loan applications for businesses while ASI was responsible for underwriting, closing, and servicing the loans.

Through this collaboration, ASI opened a credit union branch in Village de L'Est, originally in part of the CDC's office space and later at offices next to a grocery store on Michoud Boulevard. Thus, this CDC helped attract a new financial institution to serve community credit needs. MQVN CDC worked with other organizations to help local enterprises get technical assistance and loans. These included the Small Business Development Center, which had a Vietnamese American business counselor, and SEEDCO Financial Services, a nonprofit lender that financed several shrimp and fishing businesses owned by Village de L'Est residents.

Through May Nguyen's initiative and ongoing outreach, assistance, and partnerships, MQVN CDC helped over one hundred local businesses access the state business recovery programs. Table 4.3 shows the number and amount of business recovery grants and loans received by Village de L'Est businesses. Almost $3.9 million was provided to 131 businesses—an average of nearly $30,000 per firm. This was a significant investment in a community that was short of capital, and one that benefited a large share of the neighborhood's businesses. MQVN CDC demonstrates the value of community organizations as a bridge to federal and state recovery aid. By helping business owners overcome language and other barriers, the CDC helped to effectively deploy this resource to rebuild the neighborhoood's small business base.

When May Nguyen left the CDC in July 2007 to attend law school, she recruited Tuan Nguyen, Mary Tran's husband, to replace her. Tuan continued to help firms apply for business loans, and implemented new programs. He established a façade improvement program with a $105,000 grant from Louisiana Disaster Recovery Foundation. Tuan worked with a team of MIT students in fall 2008 to design the façade program and ultimately targeted the funds to businesses on Alcee Fortier Boulevard. By June 2010, new

Table 4.3. STATE COMMUNITY DEVELOPMENT BLOCK GRANT (CDBG) RECOVERY ASSISTANCE TO VILLAGE DE L'EST BUSINESSES

Program	Number of Assisted Businesses	Amount of Funding
Small Business Recovery Grants and Loan Program	131	$ 3,882,144
Small Business Technical Assistance	117	$ 141,525
Bridge Loan Program	0	0
Total		$4,023,669

Source: Louisiana Office of Community Development.

façades for 15 businesses in the Alcee Fortier commercial node were completed, partially funded by the façade program.[73] (See Figure 4.8 for a photograph of several new façades.)

In fall 2007, NAVASA received a three-year federal Job Opportunities for Low Income Individuals (JOLI) grant for a Gulf Coast business development program in Biloxi, Houston, and New Orleans, named Access to Equity (A2E). MQVN CDC was a partner in the program and received funds to provide training and technical assistance to support both the creation of new businesses and the expansion of existing businesses in Village de L'Est. The program was short-lived and never reached its potential—the MQVN CDC withdrew after new leadership at NAVASA changed the A2E strategy and management in 2008. However, the CDC has continued to assist local entrepreneurs with business planning and securing financing, reportedly helping local businesses obtain $12 million in financing—$8 million above that provided under Louisiana's business recovery programs.[74]

Under the 2007 Target Recovery Area Plan, Alcee Fortier was designated as one of the 17 target zones and slated to receive $400,000 for streetscape improvements. Several community meetings were held to provide input on the streetscape design and this project was included in the

Figure 4.8.
New business façades on Alcee Fortier Boulevard
Source: Photo by author.

Landrieu Administration's list of 100 priority projects released in fall 2010. However, construction had not yet begun when 2010 ended. MQVN CDC also gained Viet Village's designation as a state cultural products district in 2008. This designation exempts works of art sold in the district from the state sales tax and provides state tax incentives for new commercial and business investment within the district.

A CATALYST FOR CIVIC PARTICIPATION

After the community mobilization to oppose the Chef Menteur Landfill, MQVN CDC began several initiatives to sustain and strengthen civic participation. It organized a Language Access Coalition with other immigrant organizations to secure resources to train interpreters and advocate for translation services at public meetings.[75] The coalition convinced the city council to pass a resolution recognizing the need for translation services and bilingual information for public meetings. With funding from the Louisiana Disaster Recovery Foundation, the CDC purchased 50 translation headsets that could provide simultaneous translation at public meetings for up to 100 people (with splitters that divide the audio signal for two listeners). MQVN CDC used the headsets in the UNOP planning meetings and other community meetings and shared them with other organizations. In 2010, the Language Access Campaign reemerged to advocate for translation services at meetings related to the BP oil spill.

The CDC also monitored and participated in the UNOP process to ensure that community members were aware of and had access to all planning documents and meetings. This involved translating UNOP documents into Vietnamese, ensuring that the CDC was informed of and invited to all neighborhood and district planning meetings, publicizing meetings within Village de L'Est and to Vietnamese Americans in other parts of the city, and advocating to include neighborhood priorities in the final UNOP plan. These efforts resulted in two community goals being included as priority projects in the UNOP district plan:[76] (1) establishing Village de L'Est as an ethnic tourist destination; and (2) developing Chef Menteur Highway as a commercial "Main Street." The Vietnamese American community's expanded civic and political involvement, catalyzed by the work of MQVN CDC, brought about internal and external changes, as noted by community organizer Mai Dang:[77]

> Internally, [as a result of] the Chef Menteur landfill organizing...coupled with folks going to all the UNOP meetings and understanding how these community

processes worked, our community became more comfortable going to these type of meetings and speaking out at public meetings instead of just relying on us younger folks to do it.

From folks outside the community looking at Village de L'Est, it was the first time that many people knew there was such a large Vietnamese community in the East and one that was rebuilding and wanted change in the neighborhood. To the point that people asked where are the Vietnamese folks, why aren't they at the table, have we spoken to anyone from the Vietnamese Community to make sure they are there?

Another MQVN CDC priority was to expand the voice and involvement of all segments of the Vietnamese American community, especially teenagers and women. The initial work with young people began in early 2006 when a series of workshops were held with neighborhood youth to develop their ideas and priorities for the neighborhood's future. When many teenagers became involved in the landfill campaign, the CDC staff ensured that the teens had a distinct role that included holding their own meeting with city councillors and conducting outreach to elders.[78] As noted earlier, youth activism against the landfill campaign spawned VAYLA-NO, a youth leadership group that runs programs and events with its own board, staff, and funding.[79] When CDC staff observed that men were far more active in attending and speaking at meetings, they worked to give women a voice in planning for their community. A leadership campaign for young women was conducted with VAYLA-NO that evolved into an ongoing women's leadership development program and a door-to-door outreach project to speak with middle-aged working women. This outreach identified health issues as a key concern for women, laying the foundation for the CDC's community health outreach and education program around cervical cancer and diabetes discussed later in the chapter.[80]

THE CHALLENGE OF COMPLETING DEVELOPMENT PROJECTS

The MQVN CDC's agenda quickly expanded from its early focus on case management, connecting residents and businesses to resources, and community organizing, to a broader emphasis that encompassed multiple development projects. Some projects addressed neighborhood recovery by ensuring basic services, e.g., organizing a charter school, while others, notably the senior housing project, reflected a vision for an improved Village de L'Est with expanded services, amenities, and new development. This expanded community development agenda had its roots in the initial community charrette but grew with additional community planning and the influence of new advisors and partners. It motivated the CDC to initiate four development projects from 2006–2007: (1) a senior housing and retirement development; (2) a charter elementary school; (3) a community health center; and (4) a 20-acre urban farm. This development agenda was ambitious, especially for a new organization. With a young staff and novice board of directors, MQVN CDC encountered its share of setbacks as it worked to complete these projects, but succeeded in establishing a new charter school and health center in a temporary space while it worked to secure long-term real estate for both facilities.

Senior Housing Development

MQVN CDC overcame its first financing hurdle for the senior housing project in early 2007, when it received a LIHTC award after being on a waiting list for several months. With these tax credits in hand, MQVN CDC and Providence Community Housing began predevelopment work to finalize the project's design and financing plan, and even purchased $1 million in steel for the building. But the tax credits proved insufficient to ensure the project's financial feasibility. Since the expected tenants would have very low incomes, and their rents would be set at 30 percent of income under tax credit rules, the rental income would be too low to cover operating costs and repay the loans needed to supplement the tax credits. To address this problem, Providence Community Housing and the CDC worked with HUD and the Housing Authority of New Orleans to gain a contract that provided rental subsidies and additional income for the project.[81] By the time this occurred and the project was ready to move forward in fall 2009, financial markets had collapsed and the country was in a steep recession. The market collapse eliminated two of the largest investors in LIHTC—Fannie Mae and Freddie Mac—as they were taken over by the federal government. It also wiped out profits, and thus the need for tax credits, among many banks and corporations that purchased the housing tax credits. With little investor demand, the amount of capital that could be raised from the tax credits plummeted and MQVN CDC faced a $2 million funding gap for the senior housing project.[82] Since the project was no longer viable and faced a December 31, 2010 completion deadline,[83] the CDC returned the tax credits to state. This project exemplifies how the problems faced in utilizing Gulf Opportunity (GO) Zone tax incentives to fund projects delayed the implementation of neighborhood recovery plans.

MQVN CDC and Providence Housing Corporation then pursued another option to build senior housing at the site that involved Christopher Homes, a housing developer with the Archdiocese of New Orleans. The plan was to build senior housing at the MQVN church site by transferring FEMA funds awarded to rebuild a senior housing project in the lower Ninth Ward. By late 2010, this option disappeared once the FEMA funds were transferred to another site, in Slidell,[84] and MQVN CDC ended its efforts to develop the senior housing project. The collapse of the senior housing project after more than four years of work was a major setback for MQVN CDC. The project was central to the early community rebuilding vision and was the primary impetus for the CDC's own creation. It also left the Village de L'Est Vietnamese American community without an asset designed to protect the health, safety, and welfare of its elders.

One factor in the CDC's decision to end work on the project appears to have been a leadership change at MQVN church. New pastor Reverend Nghiem Van Nguyen replaced Father Vien in June 2010, who took a new position with a church tribunal at the New Orleans Archdiocese.[85] Informants indicated that Reverend Nghiem did not support developing senior housing on the church-owned land. While information on the decision-making process is not available, the fact that a key community priority was so readily reversed suggests some limitations to the community activism and engagement that accompanied the rebuilding effort. One possibility is that the senior housing project was the vision of the CDC leadership rather than a strongly supported goal within the community, and thus the new pastor was able to change course without much community opposition. If this was the case, it may reflect how the project emerged from Father Vien's vision and a charrette that included limited community involvement, rather than through a more extensive resident-based planning process. Another possible explanation is that centralized church leadership allowed the new pastor to abort the project despite community support. In this case, the expanded civic activism within the Vietnamese American community after Katrina did not extend to changing hierarchical power within the church or allowing parishioners to influence some key leadership decisions.

Intercultural Charter School

With many families rebuilding their homes by early 2006, the question of where and when schools would open to educate returning children became increasingly important.[86] Seeking an answer, Cam Tran (a CDC staff person at the time) and Father Vien met with Recovery School District (RSD) Superintendent Robin Jarvis in early 2006. The RSD was just beginning to assess schools and develop plans for which schools to open, so the superintendent was unable to provide a clear answer. In August 2006, the church and CDC were informed that the RSD would open one school in Village de L'Est, but a single school was insufficient to meet the community's need. It quickly filled up, leaving many children with a commute of at least thirty minutes and sometimes more to reach downtown and uptown neighborhoods to attend school.

During this same period, Cam Tran and Father Vien learned at a meeting with Tulane University President Scott Cowan about the possibility of opening a charter school. Since it was too late to meet the 2006 application deadline, MQVN CDC prepared and submitted an application in winter 2007 to open a new Intercultural Charter School for the 2007–2008 school year. The Recovery School District rejected the application, primarily because the CDC board of directors would also serve as the charter school board. The RSD wanted a separate board to oversee the charter school. In October 2007, MQVN CDC filed a second application, this time with a separate school board and the Edison Learning Corporation as the school operator. Ten months after the RSD approved this application, the Intercultural School (ICS) opened on August 18, 2008, with students from kindergarten through fifth grade. One new grade was added in each of the next two years. During the 2010–2011 school year, 218 students were educated from kindergarten through grade 7.

ICS's goal is to be an "excellent school for our community with academic rigor, great pride in diverse cultures, and a passion for learning throughout life."[87] The school offers Vietnamese as a foreign language to all students and plans to offer more languages, including Spanish, in the future. The Recovery School District has not provided a permanent building for the school, which opened in the MQVN church's catechism school and then moved into modular buildings on the campus of the Sarah T. Reed High School in New Orleans East, where it remained in the 2010–2011 school year. MQVN CDC is looking for a site for a new permanent building for the school and potentially a companion high school.[88]

The school is an example of a MQVN CDC-initiated project that serves the larger neighborhood, not just the Vietnamese American community. Among the 366 students enrolled in February 2011, 66 percent were black, 27 percent were Asian, and 7 percent were Hispanic. Despite the racial and ethnic diversity, almost all students were from households with modest incomes, since 93 percent of the students were eligible for free or reduced lunches. The ICS also has struggled to achieve strong academic results. Its school performance rating improved from 65.8 in 2009 to 75.4 in 2011, but this score resulted in a barely passing grade of D.

Community Health Center

Health care was one of the most severely impacted sectors after Hurricane Katrina. Many hospitals were badly flooded and unable to reopen for some time as they assessed the costs of rebuilding and future service needs and negotiated for public assistance funds with FEMA. Only three of the region's sixteen hospitals were in operation in the aftermath of the storm, with all three located outside of New Orleans.[89] Prior to Katrina, the city's health care system was highly centralized and emphasized specialized clinic and hospital-based treatment without widespread primary and preventive care. This situation was especially true for poor and uninsured city residents who often received their medical services at Charity Hospital in downtown New Orleans. Large racial and income-based disparities in health conditions and care also existed. Poor New Orleanians were more likely to have serious chronic illnesses. State rules that limited Medicaid to the extremely poor and a paucity of federally funded community health care centers—an important provider of primary care to low-income families elsewhere in the United States—contributed to inequitable health care access and outcomes.[90] As with public education, New Orleans' health care system was in dire need of reform; the extreme breakdown in health care delivery after Katrina presented an opportunity to rethink the delivery of health care services.

Discussions about reconfiguring the city's health care system around a stronger neighborhood-based preventive and primary care network started almost immediately in September and October 2005, as the city's health care providers examined patients and struggled to reestablish basic health services. In October 2006, these discussions generated recommendations for a new state health policy framework, prepared by the Louisiana Healthcare Redesign Collaborative[91]. In parallel with the state health policy proposals, dozens of new health care sites flourished across New Orleans, initiated by varied groups in response to the immediate need for health care. Many of these sites evolved into clinics that practice preventive and team-based health care, combining primary care with mental health services. Their growth and semipermanence were made possible by special federal appropriations and state decisions on the allocation of federal funds.[92] Consequently, a large network of decentralized community-based health care clinics created in New Orleans has improved both access to health services and its delivery. Despite this huge accomplishment, long-term funding and stability for this nascent network are uncertain.[93]

Village de L'Est exemplifies these changes to New Orleans' health care system and shows how grassroots rebuilding efforts facilitated them. New Orleans East was served by three hospitals before Katrina: Methodist Memorial in New Orleans East and Lakeland and Chalmette Hospitals in neighboring St. Bernard parish. All three closed after Katrina and their reopening was still in question more than three years later.[94] Residents in New Orleans East had to travel well beyond their neighborhood to obtain care. Despite this situation, restoring local health services was not an early priority for the MQVN church and CDC, since residents first focused on rebuilding their homes. However, restoration emerged as a vital need when a detailed community survey conducted in fall 2006 revealed that many residents had serious health problems but lacked access to regular health care.[95] This discovery led MQVN CDC to partner with two large New Orleans medical institutions—Tulane Medical School and Children's Hospital—to establish small health clinics in Village de L'Est.

Children's Hospital provided the impetus to establish a children's clinic. Hospital staff reached out to Father Vien and MQVN CDC in October 2007 on ways to provide health care to the area's children. At this meeting, Dr. Parin expressed the hospital's desire to set up pediatric services in the community. Since the lack of health care for children prevented some families from returning, the CDC acted quickly to locate space for a children's clinic. A building owner who had available space was willing to fund the improvements needed for the clinic. After an eight-month construction period that started in January 2008, the children's health clinic opened its doors in early August. This clinic provides services to 300 children each month and is staffed by a physician bilingual in Spanish and English, an office manager who speaks English and Vietnamese, and a nurse.

To address the need for adult and geriatric health care, MQVN CDC contacted Touro Hospital/Infirmary about opening a health clinic in Village de L'Est. After these discussions continued for several months without progress, Diem Nguyen, the MQVN CDC staff person charged with bringing health services to Village de L'Est, searched for other options. On September 3,2006, right after the first anniversary of Hurricane Katrina, *The Times–Picayune* ran a feature entitled "Heroes of the Storm." Among those profiled were Father Vien, as well as Karen DeSalvo, Tulane University's Chief of General Internal Medicine and Geriatrics, who had started a new community health clinic at Covenant House in New Orleans' Tremé neighborhood. Upon discovering the article, Diem Nguyen scheduled a meeting with Dr. DeSalvo. This meeting fell through and several months passed when, in late 2007, Dr. DeSalvo and the new Dean of Tulane Medical School, Ben Sachs, traveled to Village de L'Est to meet with Father Vien about opening up a health center.[96] After investigating the idea for several more months and gauging community support, Tulane Medical School decided in early 2008 to partner with MQVN CDC to open a new health clinic. Tulane Medical School recognized the enormous need for health services in New Orleans East and the university already had a good working relationship with MQVN CDC through the School of Architecture's work on an urban farm project (discussed below) and surveys by the School of Public Health.[97] After spending six months raising funds, assembling the clinicians and finding space, the clinic opened in August 2008 in a small office on Alcee Fortier Boulevard.

Tulane's health center has provided vital health services while incubating new community-based health care methods with MQVN CDC. The clinic sees, on average, 250 patients each month, provides services in three languages (English, Spanish, and Vietnamese) and focuses on primary and preventive care. The clinic's small size has allowed Tulane to test new clinical approaches before replicating them in larger health centers.[98] For example, the Diabetes Education in Vietnamese Americans (DEVA) uses bilingual residents trained as local health workers (LHW) to help diabetes patients control their diabetes and receive proper medical care. LHWs communicate regularly with Vietnamese American patients, conduct home visits to help patients self-manage their condition, and work with physicians and medical assistants to address patients' health care needs.[99] The clinic's value includes serving as a test bed to improve health care practices among Tulane's community health sites, as explained by DeSalvo:

> [The] clinic is really fun because we get to experiment with things that are on a small scale. I want to do this community health worker program at Covenant House but I don't have the same community relationships and it's just a much bigger clinic. I see four times as many patients at Covenant House as I do in the East. So I can try out this, work out the communications tools, the web site...We did that with the pharmacy. We introduced Xavier Pharmacy out there and the faculty goes there with students. They're part of the medical home team. Now we've taken what we've learned there and imported it to Covenant. It used to be that what we did at Covenant we exported to MQVN but now we find that it's such a more controlled environment we can try out stuff. It's controlled but messy. In this little 1,000 square foot space, you've got three languages and I don't know how many cultures. If you can make it work there, you can make it work anywhere is what I think .... all the way to stuff like sliding scale, and using credit cards at the front desk, our business stuff too we pilot out there.... It's

been a great project. Great for informing the rest of our practice, [the clinic is] well used, needed and expanding.

The two clinics met an immediate need for medical services but fell short of providing a permanent solution to the community's health care delivery problems. Both clinics were in cramped temporary spaces that were too small for a full-service clinic and without long-term funding. MQVN CDC found a permanent location for a larger clinic on a site west of Michoud Boulevard—a vacant 5,000 square-foot former post office building that the owner was willing to sell for $200,000 (see Figure 4.9). This site also provided an option to expand the clinic in the future, as it was bordered by two sites with vacant buildings.[100] During fall 2008, a MIT student team worked with the CDC to prepare plans to finance the health center's development under several scenarios.[101] From this analysis, MQVN decided on a phased plan to develop a new independent federally qualified health center (FQHC). The first phase entailed renovating the former post office into a 5,000 square-foot clinic. In the second phase, the two adjacent buildings would be demolished and a new 7,000 square-foot addition would be built with a pharmacy, eye care center, additional exam rooms and clinician offices, and community space. The FQHC option allowed MQVN CDC to create a community-controlled health clinic that would receive ongoing federal operating grants to serve low-income and uninsured patients. In 2009, the CDC secured a $1.1 million commitment of New Orleans recovery CDBG funds to make the first phase feasible and obtained federal FQHC "look-alike" status—the first step toward being a full federally qualified community health center—in the following year.[102] At the end of

Figure 4.9.
Tulane's clinic (left) and the new community health center site (right)
Source: Photo by author.

2010, design work for the health center's first phase was underway, with construction scheduled to begin in summer 2011and the new permanent clinic to open in 2012.

Urban Farm

Family garden plots were an established tradition among Village de L'Est's Vietnamese American families. These plots preserved a rural tradition and supplied traditional Vietnamese vegetables. In addition to growing their own food, families sold produce at a community market held on Saturday mornings in a parking lot on Alcee Fortier. Many garden plots abutted the Maxent canal and sat on land envisioned as a future public greenway under the plan developed at the January 2006 charrette.[103] Furthermore, with increased awareness of environmental conditions after the landfill campaign, community members were concerned about the health of produce grown adjacent to an unsafe water supply. An urban farm project was conceived to provide new safe plots for the community's largely elderly gardeners. A privately owned ten-acre site near the MQVN church was targeted for this project and Peter Nguyen, a Vietnamese American farmer from Florida, was hired to manage the urban farm project. Although Peter was an experienced farmer, he was unfamiliar with how to undertake a land development or public improvement project. NAVASA's regional coordinator and consultants advised him on the steps needed to implement the project, including preparing a professional site plan, developing design and improvement cost estimates, creating a financing plan, and determining what permits and public approvals were needed to create an urban farm.[104] NAVASA referred Peter Nguyen to Tulane University's City Center to access professional design assistance to prepare a site plan. The City Center, a community outreach project of the Tulane School of Architecture, connected community organizations in need of professional designers with university architecture programs. City Center first connected MQVN to faculty at the University of Montana. Later, the farm's design team was expanded to include the LSU Urban Landscape Lab and the private design firm of Spackman Mossop + Michaels.

Through this process, the concept of creating community garden plots was transformed into plans for a much larger project with four components: (1) an area for small garden plots; (2) a commercial produce farm; (3) a commercial poultry farm; and (4) a new site and building for the Saturday community market (see Figure 4.10). The new plan was ambitious—implementation would require several million dollars in funding.

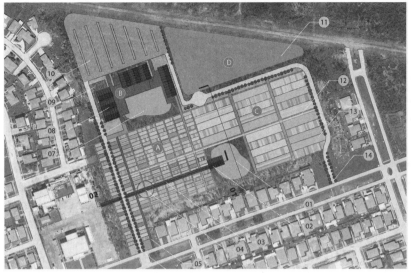

VIET VILLAGE SITE PLAN
SCALE | 1" = 200'

1 CENTRAL RESERVOIR | 2 COMMUNITY PAVILION | 3 CENTRAL BOARDWALK + LINEAR MARKET | 4 CHILDREN'S PLAY AREA | 5 PEDESTRAIN ENTRANCE | 6 VEHICULAR ENTRANCE | 7 SECONDARY RESERVOIR + MARKET POND | 8 MARKET BUILDINGS | 9 RAIN GARDENS | 10 GRASSPAVE EVENT PARKING + BIOSWALES | 11 LIVESTOCK FARM OPERATION |12 CENTRAL BIO FILTRATION CANAL | 13 COMMERCIAL LOTS | 14 SERVICE ENTRANCE

Figure 4.10.
Site plan for expanded urban farm project. Section A encompasses the small garden plots. Section B is the new Saturday market site with a market building, parking lot, rain gardens, and secondary reservoir. Section C includes the large commercial farm plots, the primary reservoir, and a community pavilion. Section D is a livestock farm.
Source: Copyright Spackman Mossop + Michaels

However, its compelling vision and receipt of a major design award led the CDC to adopt it as its development concept. Before a viable financing and development plan was in place, the CDC, through Father Vien, negotiated a purchase and sale agreement for the site and gained the property owner's permission to begin clearing the site to prepare it for use as a farm. Work to clear and prepare the site began before the CDC either researched permitting requirements or surveyed the site for wetlands or other critical environmental conditions. Site clearing led to the discovery of wetlands; the CDC then learned that the area was under the jurisdiction of the Army Corps of Engineers. To resolve the wetlands issue and obtain an Army Corps of Engineers permit for the project, the CDC needed to replace the wetlands that would be lost through the farms project. This required the CDC to purchase and preserve another wetlands site of equal size, at a cost of several hundred thousand dollars. This immediate funding issue stalled the project, but wetlands replacement represented the first part of a much larger financing challenge. While the project's cost was estimated at over $7 million, the proposed uses would generate only a fraction of the revenue needed to support this scale of investment. Given these costs, MQVN CDC decided to seek an alternative site for the urban farm project that would not require wetlands replication and would provide a lower-cost option for the farm plan.[105]

VILLAGE DE L'EST FIVE YEARS AFTER KATRINA

By fall 2010, large sections of the Vietnamese American community in Village de L'Est had been rebuilt. Community leaders viewed the neighborhood as having transcended recovery into improvement and development. Most single-family homes had been repaired and occupied. Businesses were back and filled the commercial nodes at Michoud and Alcee Fortier Boulevards along with some new enterprises. Alcee Fortier Boulevard sported recently improved signs and facades. Expanded health and education services existed with two new clinics, some new community-based health programs, and a new charter school. Among the community leaders, CDC staff, and consultants interviewed for this book, all agreed that Village de L'Est had been rebuilt into a stronger community with improved services after Katrina. Father Vien cited the transition from recovery to development, marking August 2008 as its starting point:

> It's a strange situation at this point. Recovery, I believe, for our community ended in August, 2008 because at that point we had a new charter school, we opened two clinics. None of those had been there before. At that point we were really on development rather than recovery. We were done with recovery.

These accomplishments occurred via rebuilding and community development, yet some needs remained unfulfilled at the five-year mark. Bearing witness to unfinished rebuilding are the deteriorated and abandoned properties along Chef Menteur Highway between the Michoud and Alcee Fortier nodes, many of which appear untouched since 2005. Some commercial development has occurred and the new community health center will reuse at least one vacant property, but large sections of Chef Menteur are marked by vacant properties in poor condition. One of the largest blighted sites is an apartment complex, shown in Figure 4.11, which remains in a severely damaged state, its roofs and facades destroyed. The Versailles Apartments, in which the Vietnamese American community first settled in the 1970s, also is vacant and boarded up, behind barbed wire fences a few blocks from the stores on Alcee Fortier Boulevard (see Figure 4.12). These vacant and damaged housing complexes provide vivid evidence of the disparate nature

Figure 4.11.
Blighted apartment complex on Chef Menteur Highway in November 2010
Source: Photo by author.

of the neighborhood's recovery: homeowners have rebuilt most single-family residences but the majority of rental apartments in Village de L'Est remain in disrepair.

US census data confirm the differential in rebuilding efforts for homeowners and renters. In 2010, Village de L'Est's population stood at 62 percent of the 2000 level—below New Orleans' 71 percent repopulation rate. However, 85 percent of the neighborhood's owner-occupied homes were inhabited in 2010 compared to only 44 percent of rental units (see Table 4.4). With far less rental housing today than before Katrina, Village de L'Est has changed from a neighborhood with a majority of renters to one that is almost two-thirds homeowners (see Table 4.5). This change likely has altered the income mix for households living in Village de L'Est, and, as discussed below, contributed to uneven repopulation across racial groups. Addressing this loss of rental housing is not a priority for MQVN CDC, which has expressed little support for rebuilding apartment complexes—the shared belief is that New Orleans East already has a large concentration of low-income housing. While this view is supported by data that indicate that the number of housing units with low-income rental vouchers doubled in New Orleans East after Katrina,[106] questions remain about what

Figure 4.12.
Vacant and fenced Versailles Arms apartment complex in November 2010
Source: Photo by author.

will happen to vacant apartment complexes and about housing opportunities for renters of all incomes in Village de L'Est.

Recovery also was quite different for Asian (Vietnamese American) and black residents, the neighborhood's two major population groups before Katrina. Although the populations in both communities declined significantly, repopulation among Asians was 75 percent while the 2010

Table 4.4. CHANGE IN VILLAGE DE L'EST POPULATION
AND HOUSING UNITS, 2000–2010

	2000	2010	Total Change 2000–2010	Percent Change 2000–2010	Ratio of 2010/20000
Population	12,912	8,008	−4904	−38%	62%
Total housing units	3,999	2,836	−1163	71%	71%
Occupied housing units	3,817	2,414	−1403	63%	63%
Owner-occupied	1,779	1,536	−263	−15%	85%
Renter-occupied	2,018	878	−1,140	−56%	44%
Vacant housing units	182	422	240	132%	232%

Source: 2000 and 2010 US Census.

Table 4.5. CHANGE IN VILLAGE DE L'EST HOUSING TENURE, 2000–2010

Housing Tenure	Percent 2000	Percent 2010	Total Change 2000–2010
Homeowner units	47%	64%	−263
Rental units	53%	36%	−1,140

Source: 2000 and 2010 US Census.

black population was still below half of its 2000 level (see Table 4.6). Part of this difference is due to the higher homeownership rate within the Vietnamese American community, which was 62 percent in 2000 compared to 46 percent for blacks. However, the repopulation rate in the Vietnamese American community exceeded its level of homeownership by 13 percentage points while the 48 percent black repopulation rate closely matches the black homeownership rate. The organized rebuilding effort and the associated social and material support provided by the MQVN church and CDC likely contributed to the higher repopulation rate for Vietnamese American residents. Additional evidence of this impact is provided in Table 4.7, which compares repopulation rates and pre-Katrina home ownership rates for seven neighborhoods in New Orleans East. Although Village de L'Est ranked fifth in repopulation among the seven neighborhoods, it is one of three neighborhoods for which the repopulation rate exceeded the home ownership rate by double digits. Moreover, Village de L'Est was one of two neighborhoods in which this occurred despite a large decline in total housing units that constrained repopulation capacity.

The development vision created at the initial charrette and expanded through the CDC's planning needs assessment work was incomplete

Table 4.6. CHANGE IN VILLAGE DE L'EST POPULATION BY RACE, 2000–2010

Race/Ethnicity	2000	2010	Total Change 2000–2010	Percent Change 2000–2010	Ratio of 2010/20000
White	504	320	−184	−37%	63%
Black	7,308	3,526	−3,782	−52%	48%
American Indian and Native Alaskan	13	19	6	+46%	146%
Asian	4,802	3,589	−1213	−25%	75%
Hispanic	304	712	408	+134%	234%

Source: 2000 and 2010 US Census.

Table 4.7. REPOPULATION AND HOMEOWNERSHIP RATES, NEW ORLEANS
EAST NEIGHBORHOODS

New Orleans East Neighborhood	2000 Population	2010 Population	2010 Repopulation Rate	2000 Home Ownership Rate	Percent Change in Housing Units, 2000–2010
Little Woods	44,311	31,698	72%	51%	–8%
Pines Village	5,092	3,410	67%	64%	–14%
Plum Orchard	7,005	3,951	56%	57%	–29%
Read Blvd East	8,240	7,283	88%	89%	–3%
Read Blvd West	5,564	4,213	76%	85%	–2%
West Lake Forest	9,596	4,015	42%	24%	–50%
Village de L'Est	12,912	8,008	62%	47%	–29%

Source: 2000 and 2010 U.S. Census, GNOCDC, *Population Loss and Vacant Housing in New Orleans Neighborhoods Data Tables,* compiled from US Census Data.

five years after Katrina, with several components unlikely to be built. The health center and Intercultural Charter School were established but awaited permanent facilities. MQVN CDC had abandoned the senior housing development and faced major hurdles to the urban farm project. Other parts of the vision—a new pedestrian greenway along the Maxent Canal and new commercial development to make Chef Menteur highway a vibrant commercial corridor—represented long-term community goals that were infeasible without a much-improved economy and stronger city finances to supply the required investments. CDC leaders also expressed a desire to address the limited number of stores and services, which forced residents to travel some distance to suburban Jefferson Parish for many shopping needs. This retail gap could be addressed by the community's vision for new development along Chef Menteur Highway but such development will be hard to achieve without an improved national economy, a larger New Orleans East population, and stronger real estate development capacity. Although several factors affected the limited progress on its development agenda, MQVN CDC's own lack of real estate expertise contributed to this outcome. It relied on a young staff without real estate development experience, which may have led to the new CDC's ambitious undertaking of four new projects at the same time. It certainly led to missteps on some projects and ultimately proved the CDC was unable to manage and utilize its partners effectively to move projects into development. Consequently, the rebuilding of homes and small businesses within the Village de L'Est Vietnamese American community has proven more readily attainable than the new development projects and investments designed to realize the expanded vision for the community that emerged after Katrina.

Village de L'Est's recovery and MQVN CDC's difficulties in completing development projects reflect the nature of federal recovery aid and limited coordination of recovery investments. Recovery CDBG dollars, accessed with strong church and CDC assistance, helped homeowners and businesses rebuild. GO tax incentives, on the other hand, failed to contribute to any new investments; they proved infeasible for the senior housing project and did not fund the new charter school, health clinics, or farm and did not address the blighted and abandoned properties on Chef Menteur highway. Moreover, the CDC had to develop each recovery project individually by finding a separate site and assembling the funding on a case-by-case basis. No process existed to link recovery funds to support a combination of these projects or to combine them into a larger multiservice facility, perhaps linked to adjacent neighborhoods. Better city-level leadership and more coordination between MQVN CDC's grassroots plans and city recovery investments could have accelerated completion of these projects, perhaps with better facilities, aiding the rebuilding and improvement of Village de L'Est and nearby neighborhoods.

Beyond the rebuilt homes and restored businesses, there is a less observable but still critical change in the Vietnamese American community's political and civic culture in Village de L'Est. As noted by scholars and residents, the Village de L'Est Vietnamese American community is tight-knit, communitarian, and well-organized within its church—qualities that facilitated its repeated migrations and fast recovery after Katrina. Before 2005, the community was focused inward without either a strong political voice or a shared agenda for its improvement and development. In 2010, this was no longer true. The Vietnamese American community had become well-informed and active in the political and governmental processes of New Orleans. It had aspirations and specific plans for its future improvement. It had a new organization, MQVN CDC, which worked to improve the well-being of residents and the entire neighborhood in several ways: through direct services to residents; by providing information and technical assistance to access government and philanthropic resources; by organizing the neighborhood to speak out on public policy, planning, and development issues; and by implementing projects and programs to address local needs and goals.

This new awareness and civic engagement extend beyond the church and CDC to other parts of the community. Business owners are a case in point.

They are now better informed about how to finance their enterprises and gain access to resources and information and are pursuing new markets outside their ethnic community. According to local leaders, community residents of all ages are more engaged in the political process and more likely to volunteer for community service activities.[107] Father Vien noted this increase in community engagement in Village de L'Est after Hurricane Katrina and how it is especially strong among the neighborhood's youth:

> There is a certain direction in the community. There are certain things that we are aiming for. Prior to that [Hurricane Katrina], we were not aiming for the social structure of work. It was more just parish. It was church. Now it is more comprehensive. It is really interesting, young people were making a living before but now they are doing it building their own community. They are very excited about that, very dedicated.

This shift in how young adults view their future and that of Village de L'Est is borne out in the experience of Tuan Nguyen, Deputy Director of MQVN CDC:

> In this community, every parent wants their child to be some kind of doctor, or priest or nun. That's just the way it is in this community. So for myself, for Diem, for Tap, people who were born and raised in this community or been here for a very long time, working in a non-profit, doing development work is unheard of, they really don't understand it...So for us as community members, it has really taught us that you can have a career to do really good work for the community outside of the medical field.

Like Broadmoor, Village de L'Est emerged from rebuilding with a stronger political voice and more institutional capacity to tackle problems and community development needs. Although the Vietnamese American community had strong social ties and trust before Katrina, and Broadmoor built its social capital through the recovery process, both neighborhoods had broadened their perspectives on how to deploy this social capital to improve their communities.

The rebuilding process was driven by three similar features in both the Vietnamese American community and Broadmoor: a focus on bringing back homeowners, the ability to leverage partners and outside resources to accelerate recovery, and strong leadership. Yet these features worked differently in Village de L'Est given its distinct history and culture. Village de L'Est did not need the marketing campaign, property database, and hundreds of volunteers that Broadmoor used to bring residents back and help repair their homes. In this tight-knit community with a history of self-help, the mutual aid organized and supported by MQVN Church and strong family networks provided the confidence to rebuild (and augmented it with crucial social and material support). After Katrina, an important change to this mutual aid network occurred: MQVN CDC provided a new capacity as an advocate and case manager for residents in navigating the complex and forbidding system of federal, state, and private recovery aid.

Partnerships and external resources were vital to Village de L'Est's recovery but they operated on a smaller scale than was the case in Broadmoor. Universities provided valuable technical assistance to Village de L'Est but with small student teams and faculty from MIT, Tulane and UNO that worked on a few projects, including business development, the urban farm and the health center. Broadmoor, on the other hand, had scores of students from a half dozen schools who supported its neighborhood planning process, conducted a neighborhood property census, created a property-mapping system and worked on multiple projects. Most notably, the national Vietnamese American community provided financial and material donations, volunteer expertise, and many young staff to support rebuilding efforts in Village de L'Est. Broadmoor had considerable breadth of professional expertise within its own neighborhood; Village de L'Est used a national co-ethnic network to compensate for its less diverse human capital. Political coalitions also played an important role in advancing the Vietnamese American's community's agenda for environmental justice and language access issues, but also to expand education, health care, and other investment in New Orleans East. Broadmoor, on the other hand, largely relied on its own political capital. It was a neighborhood with influential corporate and political leaders among its current and former residents and a central location that made it difficult to ignore. The Vietnamese American community, remote physically and in the mental maps of New Orleans' leaders, needed the added visibility and influence to be gained through building political alliances.

Strong leadership was a defining feature and driver for rebuilding in both Broadmoor and Village de L'Est. Broadmoor's leadership was secular and multifaceted. LaToya Cantrell was arguably the neighborhood's pivotal leader, but her inclusive style allowed Hal Roark, Virginia Saussy, Kelli Wright, and others to take on critical leadership and decision-making roles. At the five-year mark, Broadmoor looked to broaden and legitimize its leadership with a new publicly elected board for the Broadmoor Improvement District. In Village de L'Est, leadership was more centralized in Father Vien and connected to the church's position within the community. His leadership authority also came by virtue of his position as church pastor, which commanded considerable support and deference within the Vietnamese American Catholic community.[108] It also relied on the church's large cultural and historic role within this community and a network of lay church leaders organized under the pastoral council.[109] But Father Vien's vision and forceful leadership style were also critical to his impact. Father Vien committed early to rebuilding and sought out the resources and decision-makers needed to realize this goal. He was a tireless advocate for Village de L'Est and its Vietnamese American community and was open to bringing in outside experts and to embracing a broader community development mission for himself and for MQVN church. His willingness to serve as both spiritual and political leader for his community and his skill in this newly assumed role were vital to the rebirth of Village de L'Est.

Some problems accompanied the heavy reliance on a determined leader. For example, it contributed to MQVN CDC's pursuit of an ambitious development agenda beyond its capacity as a new organization. It also posed a barrier to attracting an experienced director for the CDC and cultivating strong leadership within the CDC, as final decisions and key relationship building often rested with Father Vien. With such a strong and paramount leader, the Village de L'Est Vietnamese American community faced a challenging transition when Father Vien's tenure as MQVN's priest ended in June 2010, as few experienced civic leaders could fill Father Vien's shoes. The change in church leadership was followed by a decline in political power when Representative Joseph Cao, the nation's first Vietnamese American member of congress, was not reelected in November. As the Vietnamese American community looked to fill these leadership voids, there was an opportunity for the young professionals who embraced a career in community development to assume more leadership and to foster new paths and sources of legitimacy for future community leaders.

In the summer and fall of 2010, the newfound political and civic capacity in the Vietnamese American community and its emerging young leaders were put to the test by a new crisis: the British Petroleum (BP) oil spill. Many Village de L'Est residents and the larger Gulf Coast Vietnamese American community owned businesses and worked in the seafood industry, particularly shrimping. As the prolonged oil spill stopped shrimp harvesting for months and threatened its long-term economic viability, the Vietnamese American community suffered—many families lost all or a large part of their livelihood. MQVN CDC responded to the crisis in a number of ways: it transformed its office into an information and service center for shrimp harvesters and their families, organized a multistate coalition to advocate for policies to address the economic impacts on the shrimp industry, and began research on new employment and business ownership opportunities for displaced shrimpers. This was a clear sign that Village de L'Est had transitioned from rebuilding to new challenges. But it was tackling these challenges with its legacy from the rebuilding process—new civic and political capacity and an emerging young leadership.

CHAPTER 5

c\\o

A Tale of Four Neighborhoods

Broad Street[1] is a wide thoroughfare that runs through the center of New Orleans, parallel to the French Quarter and the downtown business district, connecting the lakeside Gentilly neighborhood to Broadmoor. It is the shortest route from the city's lakeside and central neighborhoods to uptown New Orleans. Along its path, Broad Street bisects four neighborhoods. Faubourg St. John and Mid-City lie on the street's northwest side toward City Park and Lake Ponchartrain; Tremé, and Lower Mid-City fall on the southeast river side of Broad Street, bounded by the French Quarter and New Orleans' medical district (see Figure 5.1). The fate of these four neighborhoods after Katrina provides a rich and varied canvas of the city's rebuilding. As discussed in chapters 3 and 4, the residents of Broadmoor and Village de L'Est banded together within each of these communities, marshaling their own and external resources to rebuild based on their own vision. But the neighborhoods around Broad Street typify the different fortunes of New Orleans' residents and neighborhoods after Katrina. They demonstrate how conditions before the storm, resident income and poverty, neighborhood geography, and large-scale rebuilding plans combined to shape rebuilding results in different neighborhoods. Those neighborhoods with a sizable base of homeowners with the resources to return and who were able to organize and mobilize around shared neighborhood goals realized faster and more extensive neighborhood recovery. But three of the four neighborhoods also were targeted for major new development interest after Katrina. The nature of this development and the ability of each neighborhood to negotiate around and shape these development plans was a major factor in how their rebuilding unfolded.

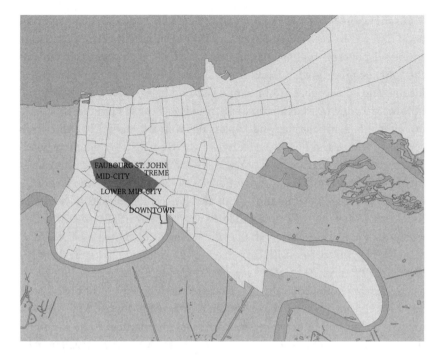

Figure 5.1.
Location of Broad Street neighborhoods within New Orleans.
Source: City of New Orleans GIS Department, New Orleans Neighborhoods, 2007, http://gisweb.cityofno.
com/cnogis/dataportal.aspx

A SNAPSHOT OF THE NEIGHBORHOODS

Despite their proximity, these four neighborhoods differ in important ways.
Faubourg St. John and Tremé are older neighborhoods built on higher
ground. Tremé lies next to the French Quarter and was settled early in the
city's history, having been subdivided for development in 1810[2]. Tremé
and Faubourg St. John also sit along Esplanade Ridge—a higher elevation
formation that connects the Mississippi River to the Bayou St. John, which
is a waterway that extends to Lake Pontchartrain. Esplanade Ridge's elevation and significance in the city's early transportation—it was the portage
route used by Native Americans to move goods between Lake Ponchartrain
and the Mississippi River[3]—allowed earlier settlement of these neighborhoods and meant they received minimal flooding from the levee breaches
after Katrina. Lower Mid-City and Mid-City, on the other hand, sit on lower
ground and were developed later, once the area was drained to become feasible for settlement. Consequently, these two neighborhoods had more
extensive flooding.

As shown in Table 5.1, the population characteristics of each neighborhood differed in 2000. Faubourg St. John resembled the entire city in its extent of poverty, homeownership rate, and racial composition. Among the four neighborhoods, it was the most prosperous—it had the highest income and educational attainment levels and had the lowest poverty and housing vacancy rates. Not apparent from these census figures, its northern side between Ursilines and Esplanade Avenues was fairly affluent. In contrast, Tremé and Lower Mid-City were extremely poor neighborhoods with much larger black populations, lower levels of homeownership, and a majority of households that did not own a car. Families in these neighborhoods had average incomes under half of the citywide average. Poverty was the norm: 57 percent of Tremé residents and 56 percent of Lower Mid-City residents had incomes below the poverty level. Despite its poverty, Tremé had a stable population, with 61 percent of its residents living in the same house in 1995 and 2000. Mid-City was similar to Faubourg St. John in its average income, poverty rate, and share of the population that was black, but it had lower education levels and home ownership rates. Mid-City was unique in that one in ten of its residents were Hispanic—a rate far above the other three neighborhoods and three times New Orleans' level. Its residents also were less stable as 59 percent moved between 1995 and 2000.

Table 5.1. KEY TRAITS FOR FOUR NEIGHBORHOODS AND NEW ORLEANS, 2000

Population Trait	Faubourg St. John	Lower Mid-City	Mid-City[1]	Tremé	New Orleans
Population	4,861	4,234	19,909	8,853	484,674
Percent black	68%	78%	64%	92%	67%
Percent white	27%	14%	23%	5%	27%
Percent Hispanic	3%	3%	10%	2%	3%
Average household income	36,311	16,569	31,442	19,564	43,176
Poverty rate	32%	56%	32%	57%	28%
Percent owner-occupied homes	35%	19%	28%	22%	47%
Percent not completing high school	28%	38%	45%	40%	25%
Percent who live in same house in 1995	53%	46%	41%	61%	59%
Percent of households with no vehicles	29%	50%	36%	56%	27%

[1] The population figures for Mid-City included a prison population over 6,078, 87% of whom were black.

FAUBOURG ST. JOHN: HOMEOWNER-LED RECOVERY

Named for the adjacent Bayou St. John, Faubourg St. John is a neighborhood that combines tree-lined streets with large well-kept homes with streets of densely packed shotgun cottages, some in poor repair. [4] The larger homes and more affluent residents are found in the blocks close to Esplanade Avenue and near the Bayou. The poorer and denser areas with more traditional shotgun homes are between Ursilines and Orleans Avenue, and closer to Broad Street. Figure 5.2 shows examples of the neighborhood's varied housing stock. Faubourg St. John is also next to the fairgrounds racetrack, which hosts the annual JazzFest music festival—a major local event that attracts thousands of music fans from around the nation. A distinct feature of Faubourg St. John is a small park and collection of small businesses located around Esplanade Avenue and Ponce de Leon Street that serve as gathering places and community centers for the neighborhood (see Figure 5.3). These local stores include several restaurants, two grocery stores, a coffee house, spa, pharmacy, and laundry.

Rebuilding in Faubourg St. John progressed fairly quickly and smoothly. As a largely residential neighborhood with limited flooding and a sizable well-off population, its recovery was driven by homeowners who were able to return quickly, repair their homes, and restore valued local amenities. Through their neighborhood association, residents undertook early planning that established a vision for their community and spawned several new resident-led initiatives to improve Faubourg St. John and its surrounding neighborhoods. However, disparities in recovery occurred spatially and by race and housing tenure. White residents and homeowners were far more likely to return than black neighbors and renters, and the poorer section had a lower rate of repopulation and more vacant properties in 2010.

Figure 5.2.
Diversity of housing in Faubourg St. John
Source: Photo by author.

Figure 5.3.
Faubourg St. John businesses on Ponce de Leon Street
Source: Photo by author.

With its higher elevation, Faubourg St. John experienced modest flood-ing. Large portions of the neighborhood—close to the Bayou and Esplanade Avenue—had less than 2 feet of flooding. Flood depths increased moving southeast toward Broad Street and Lafitte Street, where they reached 4 to 6 feet.[5] Building damage was contained due to the low flood levels and the fact that many older homes were elevated several feet on pillars. Many homes in Faubourg St. John had structural damage below 25 percent and the vast majority had less than 50 percent damage. In the southern part of the neighborhood, structural damage above 50 percent was more com-mon, with properties in a four-square-block section around Broad Street and Orleans Avenue suffering almost complete structural damage.[6] Not surprisingly, these more heavily flooded areas, which were also poorer and had more rental housing, have been slower to rebuild.

Residents first returned to Faubourg St. John in October and November 2005. With electric power restored in October, homeowners could move into their homes and begin needed repairs. Most people were not back yet, but those who had returned by fall quickly connected with their neighbors to help out with rebuilding tasks—removing refrigerators, clearing away fallen tree limbs and the like. Since there were no city services at this time, residents took on simple public maintenance tasks like cutting the grass on street medians and parks and picking up street trash.[7] Expanding on these volunteer efforts, a group of friends organized a day-long cleanup of the green space along Bayou St. John, which was traditionally a popular place for dog walking, evening strolls, and picnics, but had become a dumping ground for trash, discarded appliances, and fallen tree limbs as people cleaned up from the storm and citywide flooding. The organizers advertised the cleanup day, assembled tools and supplies, and arranged with another group cleaning up the nearby City Park to pick up their collected trash. For over six hours, volunteers removed garbage, raked, mowed, and collected appliances, restoring Bayou St. John to a state close to its prehurricane condition.[8] This neighbor-to-neighbor cooperation laid the foundation for expanded volunteerism, since it led to a larger and more diverse group of residents becoming involved in the neighborhood association and undertaking new volunteer-initiated improvement projects.[9]

Business owners also returned to rebuild and reopen their stores, which added momentum to resident rebuilding.[10] Stores provided basic goods and services that were hard to come by in the first months after Katrina. Businesses, especially coffee houses and restaurants, also provided a place to gather, share information, and find community and support during an extremely difficult time. Fair Grinds Coffee House on Ponce de Leon was emblematic of the connection between residents and businesses (see Figure 5.4). Although its owner, Robert Thompson, did not fully rebuild and reopen the coffee house until June 2007, in fall 2005 he started brewing coffee and providing it free, on the shop's patio, to residents and construction crews[11]. He also allowed people to use showers on the building's second floor, which was not damaged. The Fair Grinds quickly become a makeshift community center where people exchanged information, obtained ice and water, and used the free Wi-Fi service. Thompson was a regular presence in front of the coffee house along with musicians; donated materials were left on a set of shelves there for people who lost everything after Katrina.

Planning and Projects

The Faubourg St. John Neighborhood Association (FSJNA) was formed in 1977 as a benevolent association to undertake neighborhood improvement projects. In the years before Katrina, the association completed projects, such as park improvements and an annual cleanup to beautify and better the area, and hosted several social events.[12] After the storm and flooding, it attracted more residents concerned about the future of their city, who

Figure 5.4.
Fair Grinds Coffee House
Source: Photo by author.

wanted Faubourg St. John to rebuild and remain an attractive place to live. FSJNA became a focal point for two types of activities: (1) efforts to shape rebuilding plans for the neighborhood; and (2) volunteer-led recovery and improvement projects.

During March and April 2006, the neighborhood association organized three planning meetings to identify priorities and develop proposals to rebuild and upgrade Faubourg St. John. A March 25 meeting engaged residents in small-group discussions to complete a SWOT[13] analysis that defined what people liked and wanted to change in the neighborhood, and created a list of priorities for future action.[14] Five task forces were formed, and each met in April to create proposals around housing, parks and green space, transportation, schools and community facilities, and the Broad Street/Lafitte corridor. These meetings produced the Faubourg St. John Vision Plan (see Figure 5.5), with goals and desired uses for different parts of the neighborhood and surrounding sites.[15] Each task force created a more detailed three-year vision and one-year goals for their area, along with potential resources and next steps, and continued to meet to advance implementation of their ideas.[16] Although this process did not lead to a detailed neighborhood plan or organized rebuilding

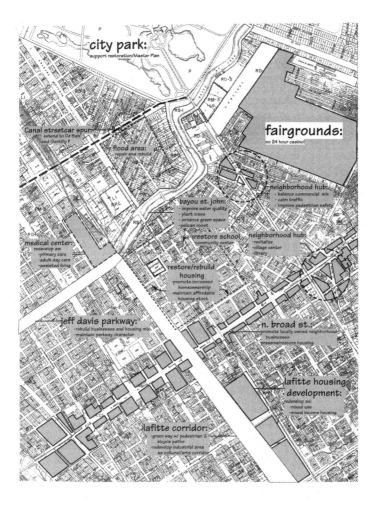

FAUBOURG ST. JOHN VISION PLAN

APRIL 8, 2006

Figure 5.5.
Vision Plan created by the Faubourg St. John Neighborhood Association
Source: Daniel R. Samuels, Architect.

effort, as in Broadmoor and Village de L'Est, it planted the seeds for several long-term rebuilding initiatives that linked Faubourg St. John with its adjoining neighborhoods.

Lisa Amoss, a long-time resident and FSJNA activist, focused on the revitalization of Broad Street. According to Amoss, "the neighborhoods that lined the corridor never interacted before the storm and that bothered me. Broad Street seemed like a way to overcome that." Broad Street was included in the Faubourg St. John Vision Plan with the goal of establishing the corridor "as a uniting commercial/gathering area with small, locally-owned businesses."[17] Amoss and FSJNA were not sure how to undertake or fund this type of project. An opportunity arose in the summer of 2006 when the New Orleans Regional Planning Commission sought applications to establish and fund four urban Main Street districts.[18] A team of residents and businesses from Mid-City and FSJNA prepared an application for Broad Street that was unsuccessful but led to the formation of a core group committed to improving Broad Street and introduced them to the Main Street program.

A second opportunity arose in November, during the search for a client and site for students in an MIT graduate city planning course on urban main streets. After a meeting to learn about the class, Amoss assembled a committee that worked with MIT's Revitalizing Urban Main Streets class in spring 2007 to prepare a plan for the Broad Street corridor. Later that year, Broad Community Connections (BCC) was created as a new nonprofit organization to focus on improving Broad Street; its board members were drawn from the surrounding neighborhoods. BCC was designated a state Main Street organization in 2008 and hired Jeff Schwartz, a student from the MIT Main Streets class and lifelong New Orleans resident, as its Executive Director. In its first two years, BCC established a monthly bazaar and annual festival on Broad Street, funded and implemented an iconic sign program, worked to shape the nature and design of new development, and celebrated the history and culture of Broad Street and its surrounding neighborhoods.

A second long-term effort sparked by post-Katrina planning in Faubourg St. John and other neighborhoods is the Lafitte Greenway. A largely abandoned Norfolk Southern rail line cuts a three-mile path through New Orleans from the edge of the French Quarter to the far end of Mid-City near Delgado Community College. Planners had long proposed converting this rail line into a linear park but little action was taken. As residents in Faubourg St. John, Mid-City, and other neighborhoods gathered to formulate plans for rebuilding their neighborhoods, the proposal for a new park along the Lafitte Greenway gained support. A new organization, Friends of the Lafitte Corridor, was incorporated in November 2006 to advocate and plan for creating a new greenway along the rail line.[19] This group commissioned a Master Plan for the greenway that was completed in December 2007 and ultimately succeeded in gaining city support and an allocation of $11.6 million in Community Development Block Grant (CDBG) funding.[20] Implementation was advanced in 2010 when Mayor Landrieu included it on his list of 100 priority projects. By August 2010, the city had purchased a 16.5-acre portion of the proposed greenway, and Design Workshop was selected to complete detailed plans for the project.[21]

Figure 5.6.
Alcee Fortier Park
Source: Photo by author.

These long-term projects were complemented by several volunteer-led improvement projects that produced more visible and immediate impacts on Faubourg St. John and restored valued neighborhood amenities. Alcee Fortier Park, on Esplanade Avenue across from the neighborhood's commercial node, was a spot to relax and meet, as well as to hold community events (see Figure 5.6). The park was damaged by the storm and prospects for city action to repair it were poor given the slow pace of rebuilding plans and funding. Faubourg St. John residents organized to restore the park and approached FSJNA about organizing work crews.[22] FSJNA worked with neighborhood residents, set up work days, and recruited residents to clean up and restore the park's green space and furniture. By December 2006, Alcee Fortier Park was in good shape and once again providing residents with a shaded space to read, gather, or play a game of chess.

Volunteers also helped build neighborhood playgrounds in partnership with KaBoom!, a national nonprofit organization that established Operation Playground in December 2005 to rebuild 100 playgrounds in Gulf Coast communities.[23] FSJNA recruited volunteers and raised funds to build a new play area and basketball court at the abandoned Olive Stallings playground. Over two hundred volunteers from the surrounding neighborhoods and as far away as California, New Jersey, and Minnesota[24] showed up to create this new playground on a single day in January 2008. KaBoom! and the neighborhood association collaborated again in November 2010 to build a new playground at the McDonough City Park Academy.

Homeowners Rebuild

Homeowners were the main rebuilders of Faubourg St. John. The neighborhood association strengthened connections among neighbors and catalyzed some visible improvement projects, but the decision made by hundreds of individual homeowners to return and rebuild secured the neighborhood's future. With limited flooding and the financial resources to rebuild, most residents who owned a home chose to return and reclaim the neighborhood that they valued:

> It's one of the most affluent neighborhoods in the city so most of the rebuilding in the core of the neighborhood has been done by individuals. People just came back. It has a very high return level compared to other neighborhoods. People love living in this neighborhood. Most of them came back and invested in their houses. It wasn't terribly flooded so it was easier to do.[25]

Homeowners in Faubourg St. John decided to rebuild on their own, without the extensive campaigns and organized rebuilding efforts in Broadmoor and Village de L'Est. With less extensive flooding and damage than other neighborhoods, most homeowners relied on insurance settlements and their own resources to repair their homes without aid from the state's Road Home program. Only 277 homeowners in Faubourg St. John received Road Home grants through August 2010, equal to 39 percent of the owner-occupied homes counted in the 2010 Census.[26] In other neighborhoods, over 50 percent of owner-occupied homes received Road Home grants: 61 percent in Broadmoor and 53 percent in neighboring Mid-City.

In the poorer sections near Broad Street and Orleans Avenue, where renters prevailed and property owners had fewer resources, original residents were less likely to return and so the pace of home repairs was slower.[27] By 2010, just over 75 percent of the housing units in this area were occupied compared to 89 percent in the more affluent section near Esplanade. Clearly, homeowners were critical to rebuilding in both sections of the neighborhood. The recovery rate for owner-occupied homes was above 90 percent and well above that for rental units in both areas, as shown in Figure 5.7,

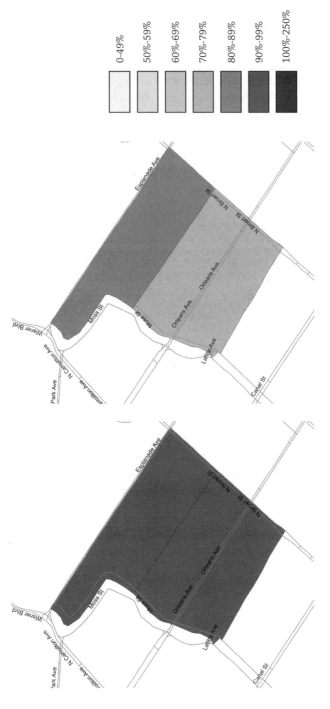

Figure 5.7.
Faubourg St. John 2010 homeowner (left) and renter (right) repopulation rates by Census tract *Source:* 2000 and 2010 US Census.

which compares these recovery rates[28] for Faubourg St. John's two census tracts, corresponding to these two sections of the neighborhood.

In this poorer section (Census Tract 45), long-term residents saw evidence of change with the influx of higher-income residents and homeowners:

> The part between Ursilines and Orleans is a much less affluent part of the neighborhood, but after Katrina what happened is that a lot of people who lived in that part of the neighborhood didn't come back... they didn't have the financial wherewithal and it was a higher renter percentage. So people started buying up those properties and the level of affluence has spread back into that neighborhood. People started buying up and fixing them up. Now it's a very mixed neighborhood, it used to be very poor.[29]

Census figures support these perceptions of changed population by documenting a higher concentration of homeowners and more white residents. The homeownership rate grew from 28 percent in 2000 to 35 percent in 2010, and the number of white residents increased by 203, or 40 percent. Less reliable data covering the 2005 to 2009 period also show a 37 percent rise in the average household income for Census Tract 45.[30]

Five Years Later

Despite a fairly rapid recovery that outpaced the evolution of the entire city, Faubourg St. John still experienced the type of uneven racial and geographic rebuilding that occurred in Broadmoor and Village de L'Est. Based on data in the 2010 Census, five years post-Katrina, Faubourg St. John had restored 81 percent of its occupied housing units and regained 73 percent of its population (see Table 5.2), exceeding 76 percent and 71 percent rates,

Table 5.2. CHANGE IN FAUBOURG ST. JOHN POPULATION AND HOUSING UNITS, 2000–2010

	2000	2010	Total Change 2000–2010	Percent Change 2000–2010	2010 Recovery Rate
Population	4,861	3,529	–1,332	–27.4%	73%
Total housing units	2,352	2,284	–68	–2.9%	97%
Occupied housing units	2,113	2,203	–394	–18.6%	81%
Vacant housing units	239	565	326	+236.4%	NA

Source: 2000 and 2010 US Census

Table 5.3. CHANGE IN FAUBOURG ST. JOHN POPULATION
BY RACE, 2000–2010

Race or Ethnicity	Percent 2000	Percent 2010	Total Change 2000–2010	Percent Change 2000–2010
White	26.7%	44.6%	225	16.7%
Black	67.8%	49.9%	−1,562	−47.0%
American Indian and Native Alaskan	0.4%	0.1%	−22	−81.5%
Asian	0.9%	0.9%	−11	−25.6%
Hispanic	3.2%	6.3%	68	44.2%

Source: 2000 and 2010 US Census

respectively, for New Orleans. However, the neighborhood's repopulation was markedly different for white and black residents. While the white population increased by almost 17 percent from 2000 to 2010, Faubourg St. John lost 1,562 black residents, a decline of 47 percent (see Table 5.3). Most of this change occurred in Census Tract 45, which accounted for 90 percent of the growth in white residents and two-thirds of the drop in black population (see Table 5.4 and Figure 5.8). The loss of black residents along with a doubling of the neighborhood's small Hispanic population meant that Faubourg St. John was no longer a majority black neighborhood in 2010.

Coinciding with the disparity in recovery by race and geography, renters were far less likely to return to the neighborhood than were homeowners. Almost all homeowner units (96 percent) were reoccupied by 2010 compared to fewer than 75 percent of rental units (see Table 5.5). This disparity was greatest in Census Tract 45, where only 70 percent of the rented apartments in 2000 had returned to occupancy by 2010—a recovery rate far below the 94 percent level for homeowners.

Table 5.4. FAUBOURG ST. JOHN POPULATION AND
HOUSING CHANGE BY CENSUS TRACT, 2000–2010

	Tract 41	Tract 45
Total population[1]	−295	−1,037
White	22	203
Black	−287	−1,275

Source: 2000 and 2010 US Census
[1] The Census data have a slight difference between total population change and sum of changes between renters and owners.

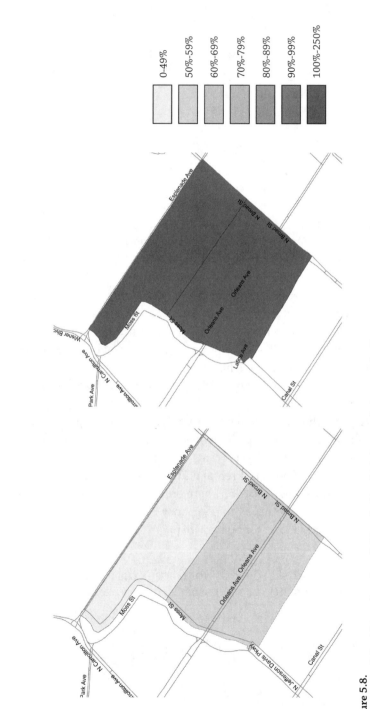

Figure 5.8.
Faubourg St. John African American (left) and white (right) repopulation rates by Census tract
Source: 2000 and 2010 US Census

0–49%
50%–59%
60%–69%
70%–79%
80%–89%
90%–99%
100%–250%

Table 5.5. SHARE AND CHANGES IN FAUBOURG ST. JOHN HOMEOWNER- AND
RENTER-OCCUPIED HOUSING UNITS, 2000 AND 2010

	Percent 2000	Percent 2010	Total Change 2000–2010	2010 Recovery Rate
Owner-occupied	35.0%	41.4%	−28	96.2%
Renter-occupied	65.0%	58.6%	−366	73.3%

Source: 2000 and 2010 US Census

In late 2010, Faubourg St. John was a diverse and attractive neighborhood that had retained and improved on its prestorm assets but that had
undergone considerable demographic change. The vast majority of homes
were repaired, parks and playgrounds were rebuilt, and its commercial center was active with businesses—some new and many that returned after
Katrina. Its residents were racially diverse, with an increased number of
Hispanic and white households, but the neighborhood lost almost half of its
black residents and over a quarter of its rental households. Rebuilding progress was evident in Faubourg St. John's physical environment, but also in
the priorities of its neighborhood association. In 2010, FSJNA was focused
on enhancements to the physical landscape and quality of life rather than
basic recovery and reconstruction problems, such as restoring key services
and eliminating large areas of blighted properties. Its newest initiative was
to raise $1.1 million to repair and spruce up two bridges across Bayou St.
John.[31] Neighborhood activists describe a community that has improved
physically but for which civic and social changes have been most profound:

> There's been a very strongly renewed sense of neighborhood here...people who
> before just lived their quiet lives and didn't really engage so much got engaged.
> The volunteer activities that the neighborhood association has put on have had
> far greater participation. People didn't just fix the damage to their houses, they
> spruced them up. They planted more gardens. To me, the neighborhood looks
> better than it did before the storm, again with the exception of the occasional
> house. People are more appreciative than ever of the neighborhood.[32]

> You realize that everybody who is living in the city made an intentional decision
> to live in the city. No other city in the world could say that...Because it was
> so hard to get back, residents are now highly motivated and highly dedicated.
> There is greater involvement in neighborhood associations. There is greater vol-
> unteerism. There is greater pride and concern about the simple things that go
> to quality of life.[33]

While the homeowner-led recovery resulted in widespread physical improvements and greater civic participation, it did not address disparities in rebuilding that left renters and poorer, largely black residents with fewer resources to return and rebuild in their former neighborhood.[34]

CITIZEN-LED PLANNING MEETS DEVELOPMENT IN MID-CITY

So named because it sits midway between the Mississippi River and Lake Ponchartrain, Mid-City is a large historic neighborhood developed in the late nineteenth and early twentieth centuries, when major drainage improvements made its swampy land inhabitable.[35] Since its early development was largely residential, the neighborhood includes many examples of historic New Orleans architecture, such as shotgun homes and Creole cottages. With major boulevards and good rail and water transportation, Mid-City also attracted industry and commercial businesses as it developed during the twentieth century. Its industrial businesses, such as the American Can Company, have left, but many office buildings, shopping centers, and restaurants remain, especially along Canal Street and Carrolton Avenue. These include some landmark New Orleans businesses, such as Mandina's, Brocato's ice cream store, and Rock' N Bowl—a combination bowling alley and music stage. It is also home to the city's criminal court complex and the Lindy Boggs Medical Center (which closed after Hurricane Katrina) and borders New Orleans' large City Park and Xavier University.

Before Hurricane Katrina, Mid-City was home to a diverse population of homeowners and renters with mixed incomes. In 2000, 64 percent of its residents were black; the neighborhood also housed sizable white and Hispanic populations. Among the four Broad Streets neighborhoods, it ranked second in key economic indicators, including household income, homeownership rate, and car ownership. With many affordable historic homes (as shown in Figure 5.9), and spurred by the return of the Canal Street streetcar line, Mid-City was experiencing renewed investment and homeownership in the years before Katrina.[36] Its reputation as a welcoming and easygoing neighborhood was a draw for many residents:

> People in Mid-City don't have any pretenses. They're just people. You might have a well-known defense lawyer who lives next door to a line cook in a restaurant who lives next door to somebody from a long line of a wealthy family. People live side by side with very different white collar, blue collar, no collar lives and we just get along.... One of my cooks at the restaurant [in Mid-City]...didn't have

Figure 5.9.
Mid-City historic houses on South Clark Street
Source: Photo by author.

a car...so when he got the job with us he decided to move to a[n] apartment close enough so that he could to walk to work...I talked to him the weekend after he moved in to the apartment...and he said, "I found my people. I live on a street where I sit on my porch and I talk to my neighbor sitting on his porch and you get off the porch and go over to your neighbor's house and say 'hi.'" People walk around the block and visit with each other. To me, that's one of the defining cultural aspects of Mid-City[37].

Along with historic homes and friendly neighbors, Mid-City also faced the poverty and crime problems commonly found in many New Orleans' neighborhoods. One-third of its residents lived in poverty; the average Mid-City household income was almost $12,000 below the citywide level. There was regular drug activity, small crimes and robberies,[38] and several neighborhood crime watches had been created to reduce and control these incidents.[39]

Mid-City residents led a more extensive and organized rebuilding process than that found in Faubourg St. John. Through the Mid-City Neighborhood Organization (MCNO), they completed a detailed neighborhood plan and formed multiple committees to advocate for its implementation. These efforts, in combination with other grassroots initiatives, succeeded in establishing a new library, charter schools, and community gardens. Mid-City also attracted considerable investment in new real estate projects after Katrina. This development brought new businesses and multifamily housing to the neighborhood and helped the city address its need for rental housing. It also meant that proposed development projects were an important part of the neighborhood's rebuilding process—shaping the nature of these projects became an important focus for MCNO and its leaders.

Flooding and Damage

As a low-elevation section of New Orleans that largely sits at or below sea level, Mid-City endured considerable flooding. The entire neighborhood took in water, with an estimated 90 percent of homes and businesses experiencing at least 4 feet of flooding.[40] Elevated homes and buildings in higher-ground sections needed minimal repairs, but the vast majority of buildings were at least 40 percent damaged, with many suffering losses well above 50 percent.[41] The extent of flooding and damage slowed the revival of businesses and public facilities. Only one of the neighborhood's seven schools had reopened by fall 2006 and one of the area's major employers, Lindy Boggs Medical Center, closed permanently. With over 70 percent of its housing in rental units, restoring Mid-City's apartments was both a critical rebuilding need and a barrier. as many apartments were owned by small landlords who did not have the financial resources to repair multiple heavily damaged buildings.[42] Parts of Mid-City were without electricity for almost four months until it was restored on December 21, the winter solstice.[43] The absence of utilities posed a deterrent to residents returning and rebuilding, even when flood damage was not a barrier, as recounted by Bart Everson:

> I moved down here before Thanksgiving...we were staying on our friend's couch. We still didn't have electricity or gas. We weren't quite ready to move in. It wasn't until the end of November when we had our gas turned on, and thus heat and hot water, that we felt comfortable moving back in...We had the good fortune of having a raised basement style house. The lower floor of the house had six feet of water but the main floor of the house is the upper floor [which didn't flood] so we were able to move right back in to the upstairs...Nobody else was living on the block. Nobody else was living on the surrounding blocks, and there was no electricity. So when the sun would go down, it was really dark and really quiet, and kind of eerie for an urban area to be so deserted.

Creating the Mid-City Neighborhood Plan

Residents returned to Mid-City at a slow pace, hampered by the late restoration of electric service and sluggish reopening of businesses and availability of mass transit service. Slow repopulation also reflected Mid-City's lower incidence of homeowners—the people who could most readily return to their homes and who had a financial incentive to rebuild. A critical mass of homeowners returned by early 2006, either living in their homes' upper floors or elsewhere in the region as they worked to gut and repair damaged homes. Neighbors began to communicate and connect through a Yahoo group started by Bart Everson, a resident and computer-savvy media artist at Xavier University, and started meeting under the aegis of MCNO.

As in Faubourg St. John, a neighborhood association emerged as the platform for Mid-City's initial rebuilding efforts. MCNO was formed in 1990 from the merger of two neighborhood improvement associations. Similar to many New Orleans' neighborhood associations,[44] MCNO focused on beautification and physical improvement projects in its first fifteen years, but after Katrina it became a magnet for returning residents who were committed to rebuilding their neighborhood. In early 2006, MCNO called its first meeting following the city's flooding and evacuation, which attracted around 100 people to the Parkway Bakery, a local po'boy restaurant just off Bayou St. John. Everson left the meeting inspired and hopeful that MCNO could become a more inclusive organization that would work to rebuild Mid-City for everyone and not just homeowners. He volunteered to be the group's webmaster, established a Yahoo group that grew to include 500 members, and later helped rewrite the organization's bylaws.

By March, information on the city's effort to create neighborhood plans bubbled up and several residents pushed for Mid-City to create its own plan based on the neighborhood's priorities rather than relying on the city and its consultants. Everson took the lead in drafting an initial vision statement for a neighborhood plan and shared it with MCNO members and the Urban Conservancy, on whose board he served. Everson then posted on his blog, b.rox, on May 31, 2006 under the title, "Mid-City Needs a Plan":

> Vision: As Mid-City recovers from the devastation of Katrina, we envision a neighborhood where people of all races and economic backgrounds can find and enjoy a high quality of life together and find opportunities for meaningful employment and home ownership. We want a walkable (and bikeable) neighborhood with plenty of green space. We want mixed-use, with appropriate locally-owned businesses interspersed intelligently with private residences. We want an increasing number of owner-occupied homes. We want to preserve the historic

character of our neighborhood while expanding modern amenities. The recovery of Mid-City should be just, humane and democratically controlled by the people of Mid-City.

The posting continued with his ideas and proposals in several realms, such as housing, green space, education, transportation, and the like. Everson's vision statement was well-received and provided a starting point and guide for the ensuing work on the Mid-City plan.[45] Sparked by this vision statement and a desire to craft their rebuilding plan, Mid-City residents began meeting weekly on Monday nights at the Grace Episcopal Church on Canal Street. These weekly meetings continued for six months, evolving into 12 committees through which over 80 members worked on different rebuilding issues.[46] When the Lambert Advisory & SHEDO consultants arrived to start the official city council planning process, they adopted the existing Mid-City initiative and used its committees' work for much of their plan's content.[47]

The Mid-City Neighborhood Rebuilding Plan, released under the Lambert process in October 2006, emphasized rebuilding and improvement projects organized into three phases: (1) critical early action recovery initiatives; (2) needed mid-term initiatives; and (3) desired long-term projects.[48] Early action priorities included the repair and restoration of utilities, infrastructure, and schools; a new neighborhood public library; a cleanup of the neighborhood; better basic city services; and the rehabilitation of blighted properties to provide expanded housing options for returning residents. Most medium-term projects sought to expand and improve green space and recreation facilities, including a new linear park along the Lafitte Corridor.[49] A second emphasis was on improving public safety through increased funding and efforts around youth outreach, vocational training, and crime prevention. A diverse long-term agenda was proposed that included a new recreation and community center at Comiskey Park and the YMCA, new community centers around schools, expanded transportation options, full funding of City Park and several studies of development options for major commercial corridors and intersections.

After the consultants distributed a draft of the Mid-City plan, the MCNO resident committees sought several changes and additions to the plan but were unable to get Lambert Associates to include them. Instead, they issued a 12-page addendum to explain their concerns and make corrections.[50] In contrast with the Lambert Plan, they proposed greater local control over the rebuilding process and city zoning decisions, proposed a major effort under a neighborhood controlled corporation to increase homeownership and to preserve historic homes, supported a different site for a new library, and sought to maintain the Lindy Boggs site as a medical complex. The addendum also noted proposals in the Lambert Plan that did not have community support[51] and detailed updates to the Economic Development Committee's plan that were absent from the Lambert Plan.

Mid-City's Recovery Plan was the product of thousands of hours of work by scores of local citizens. In this respect, it paralleled the Broadmoor Plan as a grassroots resident-driven planning effort to define how the neighborhood should be rebuilt and improved. Without the considerable student research and advice that Harvard provided to Broadmoor, Mid-City's Recovery Plan was less detailed and comprehensive than the Broadmoor Plan, but it reached the same level of neighborhood legitimacy:

> It was like some micro version of 1776. We thought this was The Document. Whenever we had a question we would go back to that original document and we still do with different issues because it clearly was a neighborhood generated plan. There must have been more than 100 people who had direct input in it...had a hand in writing it. Lots of other people through surveys and just walking around and talking to people had input in it as well. It was difficult to get that many people to agree on various things. I think it really did speak well for the people who were living in Mid-City at that time.[52]

Mid-City's plan shared similar goals with those derived for Broadmoor, Village de L'Est, and Faubourg St. John. They all pursued what might be called a "complete neighborhood"—one in which essential, good-quality services for individuals and families are available within the neighborhood. The desired services for this complete neighborhood included schools; health care; a library; parks and recreation; and businesses—such as grocery stores, pharmacies, and restaurants—that meet residents' daily needs. "Completeness" also entailed ways for residents to connect physically via new pedestrian pathways, and socially through centers of community activity—such as the learning corridor in Broadmoor, the expanded community market included in plans for the Village de L'Est urban farm, and the new community center proposed for Comiskey Park in Mid-City.

Unlike the Broadmoor Plan, which was intended to provide a blueprint for the neighborhood's own actions, the Mid-City plan emphasized the community's priorities for investments and activities to be undertaken by the city government and other parties. Consequently, Mid-City's leaders, unlike those in Broadmoor and Village de L'Est, did not form an organization to implement their plan and its proposed projects.[53] They also did not view MCNO as the primary plan implementer. Instead, they expected their plan to be implemented by New Orleans city government with the "spigot of federal funds" that presumably would flow to the city. As a result, MCNO focused on advocating for the plan and working with city councilors and city agencies to implement projects in accordance with their vision. MCNO restructured its board into new committees that matched the plan's main sections and worked to advance the plan's implementation. These committees' priorities included establishing a permanent library branch in Mid-City, working to create a new charter school and reopen local schools, and fighting to ensure that proposed development projects fit the neighborhood plan.

Pursuing a Complete Neighborhood: Libraries, Schools, and Parks

One of MCNO's most successful advocacy efforts created a permanent neighborhood library. Mid-City had been without a library since 1958, when an earlier branch on Canal Street was closed, so establishing a new library was a short-term priority under its recovery plan. This goal was pursued by the MCNO Education Committee and Jeanette Thompson, a 25-year Mid-City resident and a librarian at Tulane University. Thompson met with the Library Board Chair Tania Tetlow to present the proposal and to get her advice on next steps to take toward convincing the Library Board of Directors to open a Mid-City branch. Tetlow suggested that MCNO submit a letter with its request to the Library Board. The Education Committee put together a brief proposal to the Public Library Board of Directors that explained why a Mid-City library branch was needed and offered the neighborhood's assistance in "planning, fund-raising efforts and continuing involvement over the years and decades to come."[54] Within a few days, the library staff responded that they were interested in proceeding, as they had been looking into opening a Mid-City branch before Katrina.[55] With grant funds received from the Southeastern Library Network Gulf Coast Libraries Project[56] to reopen public libraries, the New Orleans Public Library developed plans to open six temporary library sites, including one in Mid-City.[57] With the grant funds and temporary library plans in place, Thompson and Education Committee Chair Michael Holman searched for possible locations for the temporary library; their goal was to locate space in an existing building on a streetcar line that had expansion potential so that it could transition into a permanent library. They found an ideal site on Carrolton Street and approached the building owner, who was initially resistant but then changed his mind and agreed to lease his space for the temporary library.[58] A temporary 3,500-square-foot branch library opened

on June 11, 2007 at 330 N. Carrollton Avenue—the first of the six temporary libraries to open. Mid-City had its first library in almost fifty years and
MCNO achieved one of its short-term recovery priorities.

The new Mid-City library served several recovering neighborhoods and
quickly became heavily used, with the second highest circulation behind
the main downtown branch. MCNO publicized the new library and organized fundraisers to generate money for library needs, especially furniture,
since the branch was twice the size called for in the library's initial plan and
budget. These MCNO events included a gala ball and an online campaign
in which residents voted via donations on whether MCNO members Bart
Everson and Michael Holman would stop drinking for a year. The events
raised money that paid for the circulation desk, children's room fixtures,
and other items.[59] In mid-2010, after the grant funds ended and the lease
for the temporary branch was expiring, Mid-City's long-term aspiration was
fulfilled when the New Orleans Public Library chose a permanent home for
the Mid-City branch at the American Can Company complex—a large project from 2000 that converted a former can factory into housing, offices,
and retail space[60] (see Figure 5.10). After a four-month hiatus, when the
temporary branch closed in October, the new library opened in February

Figure 5.10.
American Can Company: Site of the permanent Mid-City library branch
Source: Photo by author.

2011 to positive reviews. In an online review, one resident complimented its many desktop and laptop computers, and a book and music collection that catered to New Orleans residents.[61]

In contrast to the quick establishment of a new library, Mid-City residents faced a longer and more challenging struggle to rebuild neighborhood schools. While MCNO worked collaboratively with the city Library Board, it had a rockier relationship with the state-run education system. It participated in a neighborhood advocacy campaign to make changes in the Recovery School District's initial plans for schools in Mid-City while the State Board of Elementary and Secondary Education (BESE) repeatedly rejected plans for a new charter school developed under the MCNO Education Committee. On the other hand, parents in Faubourg St. John and Mid-City organized a successful grassroots effort to create a new Morris Jeff charter school.

In early 2008, when the RSD was holding community meetings around its school facilities master plan, a group of Faubourg St. John and Mid-City residents began to meet and discuss reopening the Morris X. F. Jeff school building as a neighborhood elementary school. Mid-City residents Broderick and Jenny Bagert, along with several relatives and neighbors, began organizing residents regarding reopening the closed school. Through a neighborhood walk, they went door-to-door to talk to residents and found strong support and enthusiasm for reopening the school. Next, they held a community meeting on a Saturday morning in March 2008 to create plans for the school, and then formed Neighbors for Morris X. F. Jeff School. Over fifty members worked on these plans and brought them to fruition.[62] In one of their first actions, Neighbors for Morris X. F. Jeff School organized residents to show up dressed in special tee-shirts at a planning meeting for the Recovery School District Master Plan to make a strong unified stand to reopen the school.[63]

When the RSD released its draft Master Plan in August 2008, Mid-City residents were surprised to learn that the plan called for closing and land-banking three elementary school buildings, including the Morris X. F. Jeff School, and postponed the construction of most new replacement schools until Phase 2.[64] To challenge these plans, Neighbors for Morris X. F. Jeff School completed their own analysis of Mid-City's K–8 education needs, using RSD and state board of education data on the projected student population.[65] They found that Mid-City had a current shortage of 698 seats for K–8 students under the proposed RSD Master Plan and this shortage would grow to over 1,300 seats after Phase 1 and 1,500 after Phase 2.[66] The group held a press conference on August 22 to release their analysis and call for reopening the Morris X. F. Jeff School, and later presented their case at public hearings on the RSD Master Plan.[67] MCNO's education committee also prepared its own letter of protest to the RSD.[68]

Through these protests and negotiations with the RSD and its new superintendent Paul Vallas, substantial changes were made to the Master Plan for Mid-City schools. The final plan called for three elementary schools in Mid-City, but Vallas and the RSD insisted on closing the original Morris X.F. Jeff School building. They argued that the renovation costs were too high and that a larger school could be built on an alternative site for the same amount. Ultimately, the RSD worked out a plan with Neighbors for Morris X. F. Jeff School to fund a new building for a reopened Morris X.F. Jeff School under community control whereby local residents would select the principal and control the school's revenues and curriculum.[69]

With this agreement in place, Neighbors for Morris X.F. Jeff School worked to establish the new school. After some debate, they decided to apply for a state charter as a community-based school. A Board of Directors was elected to oversee the new school, and it undertook a national search to hire a principal. A daylong interview process involving over twenty community residents was used to select the new principal from among five finalists. A small committee then worked with the principal to prepare a state charter application, which was submitted in August 2009 and approved in January 2010. The Morris Jeff Community School opened in August 2010 with grades K–2 at a temporary building at 2239 Poydras Street (see Figure 5.11). The school is committed to open access (not using testing as a basis for admission) and having a diverse student body reflective of New Orleans. Its pedagogy is based on the International Baccalaureate Program that focuses on teaching basic skills as tools in inquiry. Morris Jeff also strives to stay close to its grassroots origin and commitment to community control; it returned to door-to-door canvassing to inform residents about its opening and recruit its first class. This class is largely drawn from the 70119 zip code, which encompasses Mid-City and Faubourg St. John, and matches the city's racial and ethnic makeup.[70] In spring 2011, planning was underway for a new permanent school building at a more central Mid-City location that would accommodate students from kindergarten through eighth grade with the goal of a fall 2013 opening.

MCNO's Education Committee also worked to establish a community-run charter school with strong resident and parent involvement.[71] It submitted its first charter application in spring 2006 before Mid-City schools had reopened, but this application and two subsequent ones, submitted in 2007 and 2008, were rejected. According to Education Committee

Figure 5.11.
Morris Jeff Community School temporary site on Poydras Street
Source: Photo by author.

Chair Michael Holman, the state Board of Elementary and Secondary Education said that their applications were among the best submitted, but BESE was apprehensive about issuing a charter to a startup community-run school that was not using an established charter school operator. By 2009, with changes in state and city education leadership, MCNO might have succeeded with a fourth application, but it was no longer a priority since several Mid-City schools had reopened.

After MCNO ended its own charter school effort, it was approached to help convert an existing school into a community-based charter school. The RSD was encouraging the John Dibert School, which it operated, to become a charter school. The principal contacted MCNO and other residents about the idea and they formed a group to work with the principal to select a school operator and apply for a school charter. After several months of investigation, the group chose First Line Schools as the school operator and worked with First Line to complete a charter application. This application was approved and the school began operating as John Dibert Community School at the end of 2009.

A strange and frustrating saga unfolded regarding the rebuilding of Comiskey Park that reveals how some private investors sought to profit from New Orleans' rebuilding efforts to the detriment of the city and neighborhood. This experience emphasizes the importance of choosing partners carefully with appropriate background research and not being swayed by celebrity status. In their plan, Mid-City residents proposed a long-term project to renovate Comiskey Park and the YMCA into a recreation and community center with "indoor tracks, pools, basketball courts, fitness center, and meeting the intergenerational elements that serve the needs of both the youth and elderly." Soon after the plan's completion, a promising way to accelerate the project surfaced in late 2006 when California movie producer Damon Harman and his company DNA Creative Media proposed to finance park improvements and a new community center at Comiskey Park as part of filming a seven-part television documentary.[72] Harman planned to complete the project in 14 weeks while filming it as a makeover and renewal story entitled ReNewOrleans. Investors would pay for the new center as part of the film's production costs—and gain the benefits of Louisiana's 25 percent tax credit on film production costs. The project had some high-profile participants, including the actor Lou Gossett, Jr., and retailer Brand Source, and quickly gained the support of city officials and the Mid-City Neighborhood Organization. Initial state tax credits to help fund the project were approved in April 2007, and the prime contractor, Paul Davis National, began drilling piles for the center that spring.[73] At a bricklaying event in August, Mayor Nagin, Gossett, and Harman celebrated and publicized the project, but the excitement soon faded as construction slowed and the number of episodes to be filmed was reduced to three. By the end of 2007, the entire enterprise had collapsed. Two of Harman's companies were dissolved, which left the site with a collection of wooden piles sticking up and the contractor with $680,000 in unpaid bills.[74] To add insult to injury, a federal appeals court found the City of New Orleans liable for these unpaid bills and ordered it to pay the contractor the full amount.[75] In the end, taxpayers were left with a $1.9 million price tag (when the $1.2 million in state film production tax credits are added to the city's $680,000 payments to the contractor) and a site that could not be used. The park remained empty and fenced in November 2010 (see Figure 5.12). While taxpayers, the City, and Mid-City residents were all losers under the scheme, the producers and promoters for the show gained over one million dollars in fees.[76] Comiskey Park is in line to be repaired and reopened as part of Mayor Landrieu's 100 priority projects at a projected cost of $400,000 to $500,000, but without the neighborhood's vision for a new community center.

In contrast to this flawed business scheme, the grassroots effort to build the new Lafitte Greenway linear park, discussed as part of Faubourg

Figure 5.12.
Comiskey Park, fenced and still closed in late 2010
Source: Photo by author.

St. John's rebuilding plans, has progressed. Planning and implementation of this park project has been based on resident leadership, partnerships with universities to advance planning and design, local government support and funding, and sustained grassroots engagement to design and promote the project. A local organization, Friends of Lafitte Corridor (FOLC), was created in 2006 to plan and advocate for the project. FOLC completed a Master Plan for the corridor in December 2007 that drew on the work of students and faculty at several universities, including Louisiana State University, Tulane, and the University of Missouri-Kansas City.[77] FOLC holds an annual Lafitte corridor hike to raise awareness, funds, and support for the project, and has undertaken additional efforts to engage residents in planning for the greenway. For example, two MIT graduate planning students prepared a community engagement toolkit to support resident and business owner participation in the final plans for the greenway being prepared by the Design Workshop under contract with the City of New Orleans. Although the project has faced its share of delays, as have many CDBG-funded recovery projects, with strong support across several neighborhoods, well-developed plans, and city funding, construction of the Lafitte Greenway seems likely to move forward.

Individual Initiative

Along with MCNO and its committees, individual homeowners and businesses were critical agents in rebuilding Mid-City, just as they were in Faubourg St. John and other neighborhoods. In his book *A Season of Night,* Ian McNulty details the trials, tribulations and triumphs that he faced in returning and rebuilding his home on South Scott Street in Mid-City during the first 18 months after the flooding—a trial repeated by thousands of Mid-City residents. Entrepreneurs risked reopening their businesses and even starting new ones, as Jennifer Weisshaupt did with The Ruby Slipper restaurant, at a time of great uncertainty about how many residents would return and how large a market would materialize. When bars and restaurants reopened, they took on importance as symbols of rebuilding and reminded residents that what they valued most about New Orleans— drinking with friends, live music, and good food—could and would return. Ian McNulty recounts the sentiments evoked at the reopening of Lola's restaurant in Faubourg St. John in November 2005:

> ...when the paella, and the garlic shrimp and snapper ceviche were set down on the table, our tears showed up too. It wasn't a big, demonstrative group sob, but all over the room people quietly wiped back tears with the napkins and loudly toasted each other around the table in voices rattled and shaken by emotion. There were pledges to never leave, or to come back soon, or to keep on fighting the forces we could feel lining up to take turns on us now that we were brought low, the politicians and insurance men and clucking pundits.[78]

In these challenging conditions, some Mid-City residents took even greater steps to rebuild their city through initiating civic rebuilding projects, as illustrated by Joseph Brock's work to turn abandoned lots into community gardens.[79] Brock grew up in New Orleans and moved to Mid-City around 1990. After returning and rebuilding his home over a two-year period, he was concerned that only a few people on his block had returned. The many vacant and blighted properties discouraged people from returning and made it difficult to attract businesses to the area. Brock began pressuring property owners to repair abandoned property and then decided to convert an abandoned parking lot next to one building into a garden. After approaching the owner with a proposal to convert the site into a garden, he signed a lease for the lot on South Salcedo Street and began working with several volunteers to build the garden in September 2008. After three months, the garden and a chicken coop were completed. The garden provides fresh produce and eggs and hosts barbecues, community gatherings, and gardening classes. According to Brock, the garden also served to bring activity and interest back to a largely vacant section of Mid-City:

> [The garden] serve[s] as a strategic method of bringing folks back into the neighborhood...when we built this, there were only four people in my block, we couldn't get people into the neighborhood. Once the garden was built, landlords and homeowners started pointing toward the community garden—showing potential tenants the benefits of having this garden, that they would have lettuce and tomatoes. That made people interested in moving to Mid-City. Several portions of Mid-City that didn't know about this side of the city, I wanted to bring them together.

After this first project, an opportunity arose for Brock to build a second, larger Mid-City garden. Domain Company partner Matt Schwartz, who was developing a large apartment complex in Mid-City, approached Brock about building a garden on two lots that the firm owned on South Hennessy Street across from its Preserve apartment project.[80] Brock saw the potential for this larger site and created a plan for a second garden that incorporated space for artists to show their work and paths with pavers that display words of wisdom (the reason it is named Wise Words Community Garden), along with sites to grow vegetables that include lettuce, tomatoes, bell peppers, corn, okra, broccoli, eggplant, spinach, celery, potatoes, and herbs. After Domain donated the land in November 2009, over 250 volunteers worked for seven months to build the new garden, which opened in May 2010[81] (see Figure 5.13). From these two projects, Brock established NOLA Green Roots as a nonprofit organization to design, build, and manage community gardens across New Orleans and to conduct workshops and classes to teach gardening skills to residents. NOLA Green Roots built a third garden in the Lower Ninth Ward, and supplies fresh produce and eggs to several hundred households through these three gardens.

Mid-City Attracts Development

Soon after the Mid-City plan was completed, private developer interest emerged in undertaking a range of projects in Mid-City. The neighborhood's central location, access to highways and amenities, and proximity to the medical district attracted proposals for new housing, retail development, and reuse of the Lindy Boggs hospital site. Consequently, an important part of MCNO's work involved responding to these proposals—opposing some and working with developers to refine others to fit their vision for Mid-City.

Figure 5.13.
Wise Words Community Garden
Source: Joseph Brock.

The first project that sparked MCNO into action was a large retail project proposed by Georgia-based Victory Real Estate Investments. In early 2007, Victory started assembling 20 acres of property to build a new 1.2 million-square-foot primarily retail development that included demolishing the Lindy Boggs complex.[82] At meetings with the area's city councillor in April, residents opposed the project due to its size and big-box suburban character.[83] MCNO, which had earlier opposed Victory's plan to develop a Walmart in the area, met with the developer to review the project plans after it had applied for a demolition permit in late 2007[84]. The neighborhood association saw some positive aspects to the project but felt that Victory was unwilling to work with them to reduce the development's impact and address their concerns about its design, relationship to the Lafitte Greenway, and other issues.[85] Neighborhood concerns and opposition slowed the project, which soon became infeasible after the 2008 financial market crisis and recession.

As Victory sold its properties, new proposals were better aligned with MCNO's vision. St. Margaret Daughters, a Catholic nonprofit health care

Figure 5.14.
Lindy Boggs Medical Center complex
Source: Photo by author.

provider, acquired the Lindy Boggs hospital complex (see Figure 5.14) and planned to convert the site into a nursing home and small hospital.[86] These uses were close to what the Mid-City plan proposed for the site—either a "multi-use community healthcare clinic" or a "senior housing and medical facility" and the project received MCNO's support. At another property controlled by Victory, developer Green Coast Enterprises proposed a project called Building Blocks that would provide offices and retail space to a dozen or so "green" businesses.[87] MCNO supported this project but the developer's option on the site expired and it was never built. A new retail center was then proposed in 2011 with a Winn Dixie supermarket as its primary tenant.[88] Given the project's scale and location next to the Lafitte greenway, MCNO took a strong interest in the project and approved a formal position that addressed aspects of the project's design, operations, and tenants. Key items in the 15-point statement included opposition to having an entrance to the retail center that would cut across the greenway, several design proposals to "reflect the industrial history of the site and the urban ambiance of Mid-City," including adding 100 bike parking spaces and seeking local businesses and national stores as retail center tenants.[89]

Figure 5.15.
Crescent Club Apartments on Tulane Avenue
Source: Photo by author.

Mid-City was also the chosen neighborhood for new housing development, often financed with Gulf Opportunity (GO) Zone tax incentives.
Domain Companies, a developer owned by two Tulane University graduates
that provided the site for Joseph Brock's second garden, completed three
housing developments in Mid-City, along or near Tulane Avenue. In addition to the Preserve, which converted a former hot sauce factory into 183
apartments, they converted the International School of Louisiana, whose
buildings were badly damaged by Katrina, into the Meridian development
with 75 apartments and turned an abandoned car dealership into 225 new
apartments, named the Crescent Club[90] (see Figure 5.15). These three projects, all financed with federal low-income housing tax credits, added 489
new apartments to Mid-City housing stock after Katrina, which offset the
loss of damaged housing units and helped Mid-City regain population lost
when the neighborhood flooded. Although MCNO had a good relationship with the Domain Companies, the fast growth in apartments has made
Mid-City resistant to further higher-density housing development. They
opposed proposals in the New Orleans Master Plan, prepared in 2009 and
2010, for more mixed-income apartment development in Mid-City and
even spoke out against some smaller projects, such as the conversion of a

vacant apartment building into 25 condominiums, arguing that "Mid-City already has enough high-density housing."[91]

Mid-City at Year Five

As one of New Orleans' largest and most diverse neighborhoods, it is not surprising that rebuilding results in Mid-City were quite mixed. Mid-City has undergone far more extensive changes than Faubourg St. John— consequently, the neighborhood has more varied conditions and differing views about the state of rebuilding. In terms of population, Mid-City had regained almost 84 percent of its 2000 population by 2010—well above the 71 percent citywide rate (see Table 5.6). Its housing recovery was even greater with a 5 percent increase total housing units between 2000 and 2010 and a return of occupied housing units to 90 percent of the 2000 level. In contrast, New Orleans had a 12 percent decline in total housing units over the decade while occupied housing units were at 76 percent of the number in 2000. Despite the progress in restoring housing, there was still a significant vacancy problem. One in four Mid-City housing units were vacant in 2010, as the number of vacant homes doubled.

Mid-City, like other neighborhoods, experienced disparities in repopulation by race, geography, and housing tenure. The number of white and black residents declined, but the black population loss was over ten times that of white residents (see Table 5.7). Hispanic residents increased by 238, or almost 13 percent. With these racial differences in repopulation, Mid-City was no longer a majority black neighborhood (excluding the prison

Table 5.6. CHANGE IN MID-CITY POPULATION AND HOUSING UNITS, 2000–2010

	2000	2010	Total Change 2000–2010	Percent Change 2000–2010	2010 Recovery Rate
Population[1]	13,831	11,574	–2,257	–16.3%	83.7%
Total housing units	6,728	7,079	351	5.2%	105.2%
Occupied housing units	5,830	5.248	–572	–9.8%	90.2%
Vacant housing units	898	1,821	923	102.8%	NA

Source: 2000 and 2010 US Census
[1] The population figures in these tables exclude the institutionalized prison population in the criminal justice complex located on the downtown edge of the neighborhood near Broad Street.

Table 5.7. CHANGE IN MID-CITY POPULATION BY RACE,
2000 AND 2010

Race/Ethnicity	Percent 2000	Percent 2010	Total Change 2000–2010	Percent Change 2000–2010
White	35.2%	40.3%	−197	−4.1%
Black	55.2%	48.1%	−2,058	−27.0%
American Indian and Native Alaskan	.7%	.9%	−68	−60.2%
Asian	1.3%	.2%	−58	−39.3%
Hispanic	13.4%	18.1%	238	12.8%

Source: 2000 and 2010 US Census

population). In 2010, it was more racially balanced with more parity in the number of white and black residents and a sizable Hispanic population. Repopulation also varied across Mid-City's six census tracts (see Table 5.8). Population declined in four census tracts but increased for all racial groups in two census tracts at the edges of the neighborhood. Tract 54 is adjacent to City Park at Mid-City's western edge while Tract 71.01 is closest to downtown New Orleans and where several of the new apartment projects were built. Repopulation rates were highest for black and white residents at the neighborhood's edges, but in Mid-City's central census tracts, black repopulation was lowest and below that for white residents (see Figure 5.16).

Mid-City is noteworthy in the higher repopulation rates for rental households compared to homeowners. Rental households had returned to 95 percent of their 2000 level by 2010 while the rate for homeowners was much lower at 77.6 percent (see Table 5.9). This pattern is quite different than that found in Village de L'Est and Faubourg St. John, where homeowner

Table 5.8. CHANGE IN MID-CITY POPULATION BY CENSUS
TRACT, 2000–2010[1]

	Tract 50	Tract 54	Tract 63	Tract 64	Tract 65	Tract 71.01
Total Population	−419	273	−733	−689	−931	242
White	−34	163	−103	−54	−275	106
Black	−366	82	−648	−629	−555	58
Hispanic	59	45	136	94	−188	92

Source: 2000 and 2010 US Census
[1] The census data have a slight difference between total population change and sum of changes between renters and owners.

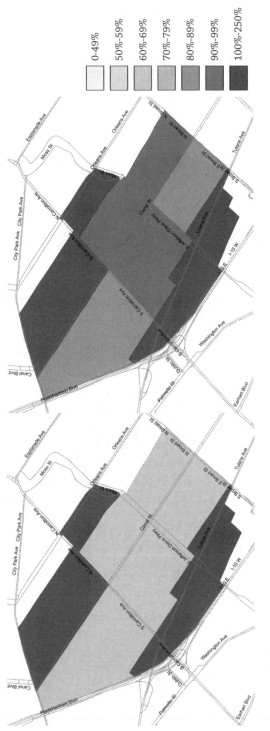

Figure 5.16.
Mid-City African American (left) and white (right) repopulation rates by Census tract
Source: 2000 and 2010 US Census.

Table 5.9. SHARE AND CHANGES IN MID-CITY HOMEOWNER- AND
RENTER-OCCUPIED HOUSING UNITS, 2000 AND 2010

	Percent 2000	Percent 2010	Total Change 2000–2010	2010 Recovery Rate
Owner-occupied	27.9%	24.0%	–363	77.6%
Renter-occupied	72.1%	76.0%	–209	95.0%

Source: 2000 and 2010 US Census

recovery was at much higher rates than that for renters. The new apartment developments, which added almost 500 rental units, clearly contributed to this pattern, in which Mid-City retained a large base of renter households. Consequently, Mid-City is a neighborhood for which federal Low Income Housing Tax Credits (LIHTCs) made an important contribution to housing recovery and helped achieve a greater balance in rebuilding for homeowner and renter households.

Neighborhood leaders noted these changes in Mid-City's population, especially a decline in older residents and African Americans and the arrival of many new residents and what appeared to be a more transient population. One person moved to live in a more stable part of the neighborhood and another reported a need to adjust to new residents and businesses:

> It's different because before you knew everybody. Now you don't. So you are relearning. It's a whole new New Orleans. You've got to give me a chance to see what this is about. They've got to give you a chance to see what it's about. It's a new New Orleans. There are new things in neighborhood that you didn't have before. It's a new segment of stuff. We need to sit back and watch this one.[92]

The sense that Mid-City's population was changing and more transient was accompanied by the seemingly paradoxical view that people knew more of their immediate neighbors and knew them better—the result of their common struggle to repair their homes and rebuild their neighborhood.

> People in our neighborhood know each other so much better now. Not just these meetings, but helping each other out with rebuilding projects or, recommending a plumber. I think people pay more attention to trying to buy locally.[93]

> We are more of a community. We all know our direct neighbors. We all reach out to neighbors. We meet new neighbors. Things that maybe you might have done

---

Table 5.10. FEDERAL FINANCIAL ASSISTANCE TO MID-CITY

Program/Type of Assistance	Number	Total Amount of Assistance	Average Grant
Road Home[1]	864 households	$83,761,644	$96,946
Small rental	129 units	$4,660,850	$36,131
Small business technical assistance, loans, and grants[2]	83 businesses	$2,964,768	$35,720

Source: Louisiana Office of Community Development, August 2010
[1] This includes 811 households that received $78.5 million to rebuild their pre-Katrina home and 53 that received $5.3 million to rebuild at other locations.
[2] These are combined figures for three programs: Small Firm Loan & Grant Program, Small Firm Technical Assistance Program, and Louisiana Bridge Loan Program.

[before] with the two or three people that immediately surrounded you...now I know my neighbors in the two to three blocks that immediately surround me very well.[94]

Federal recovery funds aided Mid-City's rebuilding and contributed to a more diverse range of projects than in other neighborhoods. Over half of Mid-City's pre-Katrina homeowners received Road Home grants totaling $84 million to rebuild their homes.[95] CDBG-funded loans and grants also helped 83 businesses to rebuild (see Table 5.10). Since Mid-City is home to several major public facilities, over $382 million in FEMA PA and CDBG funds were committed to restoring these building and services (See Appendix table A.7). The vast majority of funds were for two projects with a citywide scope: rebuilding the Orleans Parish Sheriff's Office's multifaceted criminal justice complex; and restoring and replacing public transportation equipment, along with restoring infrastructure for the Regional Transportation Authority. Approximately 5 percent of these funds were obligated for neighborhood-oriented projects such as parks, schools, and libraries, with $19 million devoted to public schools. These figures do not include the GO Zone tax credits used to finance the new apartment complexes in Mid-City.

These large federal recovery investments, however, did not overcome the uneven rebuilding in Mid-City that is evident in the coexistence of new improvements and projects with many abandoned and blighted properties. A new library, rebuilt schools, more restaurants and businesses, and new gardens are post-Katrina improvements to Mid-City that are valued by the neighborhood's leaders and help to create a complete neighborhood. At the same time, these activists noted the disparate nature of recovery and widespread blight across Mid-City: many homes are still in poor shape, pockets within the neighborhood are not rebuilt, and empty commercial buildings mark the neighborhood's main corridors. Housing vacancy rates are high throughout Mid-City: five census tracts have rates above 24 percent, with the lowest rate at 18 percent in Tract 54. Although MCNO functioned as a coordinating force to shape school, library, and private investments, its impact was constrained by aspects of federal assistance and limited city capacity to coordinate both public and private projects. LIHTCs made larger apartment projects possible but did not address vacancies in small rental properties. As in Village de L'Est, MCNO worked separately with different public agencies to advance key projects without mechanisms to link related projects, expand their scope to address key neighborhood priorities, or target multiple investments to heavily blighted areas.

Mid-City gained greater civic capacity along with its physical improvements, services, and expanded amenities. Like Broadmoor, Village de L'Est, and Faubourg St. John, Mid-City emerged from the rebuilding process with a stronger neighborhood association, a more influential voice in city policies, and a better informed and more engaged community. MCNO is recognized by city officials as having an influential voice in city zoning and development permitting decisions and as willing to engage with city agencies to create solutions to issues in their neighborhood.[96] Its activism and engagement with city and state agencies to establish a new library and schools is evidence of Mid-City's civic engagement and effectiveness. According to Jennifer Weisshaupt, this newfound civic engagement marks a changed understanding among residents that is likely to endure:

> We are educated and we know our government and we fight for what we think is right in our government...We learned that these decisions have long-lasting effects...and when we're interested in a cause we have to stand up for it...As a community, we have become much more engaged. It doesn't mean that we always agree. We certainly have quite a lot of issues that we have debates on but it's better for us to be out in the open and debate things than to not care about them and just let the will of the government become the will of the people.

TREMÉ: CONFLICTING VALUES AND VISION

Across Rampart Street from the French Quarter is Tremé, one of New Orleans' oldest neighborhoods and home to some of the city's most important cultural traditions. Tremé was developed on land acquired by Claude Tremé, a French plantation owner, in the late eighteenth century. After Tremé started to sell off portions of his property, it was officially subdivided into lots and streets and established as the city's first suburb—Faubourg

Figure 5.17.
Tremé's historic architecture: Shotgun homes on Governor Nichols Street (left) and a large
home on tree-lined Esplanade Avenue (right)
Source: Photos by author.

Tremé—in 1810.[97] This new neighborhood was settled by a diverse population that included former slaves, recent Haitian and Cuban immigrants,
and free people of color[98] who purchased and built homes on its subdivided
lots. Due to its early settlement by a large free black and mixed-race population, Tremé is often referred to as America's oldest black neighborhood.[99]
Tremé was largely developed by the late nineteenth century, with modest
shotgun houses and Creole cottages, often designed and built by the neighborhood's many skilled craftsmen that created an essential element of New
Orleans' unique architecture (see Figure 5.17). Tremé also became home to
wealthier Europeans and Creoles who built grand homes along Esplanade
Avenue, small stores and businesses, and, in 1841, St. Augustine's, the
city's third Catholic church.[100]

Tremé also occupies a special place in the musical and cultural history
of New Orleans, as it nurtured the birth of jazz and is central to the second line and Mardi Gras Indian traditions. At the root of Tremé's cultural
history is Congo Square, located at the historic slave market, where slaves
gathered to dance and drum on Sundays. Since laws passed in the early
nineteenth century restricted slave dancing to Sundays and at designated
areas,[101] Congo Square helped to sustain African musical traditions in New
Orleans that contributed to the birth of jazz.[102] New Orleans jazz emerged
from the influence and melding of several New Orleans activities—benevolent and social aid societies, parades and funerals featuring brass bands,
and the proliferation of music halls and clubs, often linked to the social
aid societies.[103] The social aid societies, of which some 300 existed in New
Orleans in the early twentieth century, sponsored parades with brass bands
for funerals and to celebrate their anniversaries. Musical parades happened
throughout New Orleans, but Tremé is closely linked to the development

of jazz, as it housed several musical halls where early jazz musicians, such as Kid Ory and Louis Armstrong, regularly played and developed their music. Through its tradition of brass band parades and live jazz played in private clubs, bars, and music halls, Tremé was an important place for sustaining these parts of New Orleans' musical culture throughout the twentieth century.

Scars of Redevelopment

Tremé's history and rich culture was often ignored by the city leaders and planners who viewed the neighborhood as a place to advance their development priorities. Beginning in the 1920s, they pursued a series of projects that demolished homes and businesses, displaced hundreds of residents, removed cultural and entertainment venues and undermined a vibrant commercial corridor, and left Tremé with the scars of many ill-conceived and poorly designed projects. The first project was a municipal auditorium constructed to replace the French Opera House destroyed in a fire in 1919.[104] Rather than rebuild at the original opera house site, city leaders chose to demolish a large section of Tremé to accommodate the new auditorium as part of their plan for a larger civic center. The civic center project replaced an entire square block in Tremé that housed a public market,[105] Globe Hall (an important dance hall), and numerous homes. In 1937, less than a decade after the municipal auditorium was completed in 1930, the Housing Authority of New Orleans (HANO) was formed to build housing for working-class families. It soon undertook an expansive building program that demolished large sections of six historic neighborhoods to create new public housing developments.[106] Tremé was the site of one such project, the Lafitte complex, which was completed in 1941 with 896 apartments. Under New Orleans' segregation policies, Laffite housed black families while the nearby Iberville project, developed on the site of New Orleans' famous Storyville[107] red light and jazz district, was built for white families.[108]

Another round of government redevelopment projects from the 1960s through the 1990s further reshaped Tremé. Following the passage of the Federal-Aid Highway Act in 1956, the city and state governments selected a section of Claiborne Avenue that ran through Tremé for part of New Orleans' new I-10 elevated interstate highway. Claiborne Avenue had a large grass median (or neutral ground in New Orleans parlance) lined with oak trees. This wide neutral ground was of interest to highway engineers. They could build the new elevated highway on its existing public right-of-way to

Figure 5.18.
Interstate 10 bisecting Tremé along Claiborne Avenue
Source: Photo by author.

reduce the required land takings, and continue to use Claiborne Avenue as a surface road.[109] Claiborne Avenue was Tremé's main commercial center and the neutral ground served as a recreation area for local children, a family picnic site, and the place for Mardi-Gras celebrations and other cultural events within the black community.[110] After two public hearings at which no protests from Tremé residents or businesses were recorded,[111] the highway project went forward and was constructed from 1961–1969. Interstate 10 eliminated the neutral ground and several hundred oak trees, created a large hulking structure over its main boulevard (see Figure 5.18), and, to build three sets of ramps, destroyed 125 buildings with 170 residences and 50 businesses.[112] With these changes, Tremé's commercial district along North Claiborne Avenue suffered and the number of businesses declined rapidly from 115 in 1965 to 64 in 1971. With continued disinvestment over the next three decades, only 35 remained in 2000.[113]

In the 1960s, New Orleans also moved forward with earlier plans to create a large cultural center adjacent to its Municipal Auditorium. The grandiose plan called for a new opera house, concert hall, theater, museum, and outdoor areas for exhibits and concerts, along with parking, shops, and restaurants.[114] With new urban renewal powers and funding created in 1964,

Figure 5.19.
Main entrance to Louis Armstrong Park under repair in 2010
Source: Photo by author.

the city began to relocate residents and clear the land for the cultural center. After the land was cleared and families removed, the site sat vacant for years as plans for the complex were reconsidered and funding assembled. Almost a decade later in 1973, the Center for the Performing Arts was built while the rest of the site remained fallow for years until it was chosen to house the memorial Louis Armstrong Park, which opened in 1980.[115] Building Louis Armstrong Park (see Figure 5.19) cleared another large part of Tremé and displaced several hundred residents.[116] As happened with the cultural center, much of the cleared land remained vacant and fenced for many years as a series of ambitious plans for the park failed to materialize.

This long history of public redevelopment projects, combined with suburbanization and New Orleans' economic stagnation, resulted in significant disinvestment and growing poverty in Tremé. By the 1950s, the clearing of homes, businesses, and community cultural venues had taken its toll on Tremé. More prosperous families began to leave, large homes were converted to apartments, and the neighborhood became more concentrated with poorer black residents.[117] This process continued over the ensuing decades until, in the years before Katrina, Tremé had become a very poor neighborhood, with over half its residents living in poverty.

Tremé was also changing prior to Katrina, as it attracted new residents and investment. With many historic homes and proximity to the French Quarter, individuals and investors were drawn to Tremé to restore historic properties either for their own homes or to rent and sell to others. Developers also pursued plans for larger-scale condominium development.[118] Many new residents attracted to Tremé had a different vision for their neighborhood and did not welcome Tremé's culture of loud music, street life, parades, and bars, which was a source of conflict within the neighborhood.[119]

These two dynamics—competing views over Tremé's future, character, cultural activities, and large-scale urban redevelopment, continued to influence the neighborhood and shape its recovery after the storm. Rebuilding efforts were fragmented among multiple community organizations with different priorities and contrasting views of what constituted the Tremé neighborhood. Alongside the work of grassroots organizations, and overshadowing them in its impact, was a plan for Tremé's latest urban renewal project: the demolition and redevelopment of the Lafitte public housing project—the product of an urban renewal initiative completed over sixty years earlier.

Tremé Organizations before Katrina

Tremé's history includes a prominent role in the abolitionist and early civil rights movement. Tremé activists organized the Citizens' Committee (Comite des Citoyens), which spearheaded the landmark *Plessy v. Ferguson* supreme court case that, contrary to their goals, established "separate but equal" as the legal basis for segregation for over fifty years.[120] This activism continued during the civil rights movement in the 1950s and 1960s, when several community organizations were established that remained active in Tremé prior to Katrina. An early community organizer was James Hayes, who cofounded the Tremé Community Improvement Association with Ron Chisom to fight the impact of urban renewal projects.[121] Hayes later formed the Greater Tremé Consortium in 1993 to address the growing problems of blighted properties and a lack of jobs for Tremé residents by repairing homes for sale to local residents and advocating for jobs for Tremé residents at a temporary casino planned for the Municipal Auditorium in Louis Armstrong Park.[122] Over the next dozen years, the Greater Tremé Consortium (GTC) repaired over 100 homes to rent or sell to low-income and moderate-income residents, including nine rental units that it owned in August 2005. Tambourine and Fan, another Tremé organization with roots in the civil rights movement, was founded in 1980 by civil rights activist Jerome Smith. This organization has worked with neighborhood youth to pass on African American culture and heritage, including the second line and Mardi Gras Indian traditions, for over thirty years.[123] Smith is also the volunteer director of the Tremé Community Center, a neighborhood recreation center built in the early 1970s in conjunction with the initial planning for Armstrong Park.

Organizations with roots in other segments of the community also worked to improve Tremé in the decade before Katrina. Saint Peter Claver Church, a large Catholic congregation, formed the Ujamaa Community Development Corporation to build affordable housing and community facilities. It completed the 44-unit St. Ann Apartments in 2001 and had just opened the Sankofa-McKinley Wellness Center to provide social services to Tremé youth and elders a few months before Katrina hit.[124] Another organization, the Esplanade Ridge-Tremé Civic Association (ERTCA), was formed as a neighborhood association in 1996 but undertook limited activities until 2002, when its membership grew. This association focused on neighborhood watches to reduce crime, securing computers for a local high school, and helping secure free home repairs for elderly residents through the Preservation Resource Center's Christmas in October program.[125] ERTCA's members tended to be white homeowners who lived across Claiborne Avenue and the I-10 corridor from the section of Tremé next to the French Quarter. In 2003, several Esplanade Ridge-Tremé Civic Association members left to form a new organization named Downtown Neighborhoods Improvement Association (DNIA).[126] DNIA's founders viewed ERTCA as a "Not in My Back-Yard" organization that sought to stop changes to the neighborhood. They formed a new organization to bridge different parts of the community and, unlike most neighborhood associations, aimed to address the neighborhood's social and economic conditions.[127] Since DNIA was organizing and developing its agenda in 2004 and 2005, it did not become an active force in Tremé until after Katrina.

A Slow and Fragmented Recovery

Despite its geography and limited flooding, Tremé recovered at a slower pace than Mid-City and Faubourg St. John, impaired by a fragmented recovery effort and its dependence on the return of rental housing, notably the Lafitte public housing development. As one of New Orleans' oldest neighborhoods settled on high ground near the Mississippi River and Esplanade Ridge, Tremé had less flooding and building damage than many other neighborhoods. Flood depths were less than four feet throughout Tremé and below two feet in large sections of the neighborhood. Some streets close to the French Quarter did not flood at all[128]. Consequently, building damage was less severe than in many parts of the city, with structural damage in most Tremé properties less than 50 percent. The section between Claiborne Avenue and Rampart Street was the least damaged: FEMA's assessment found most buildings with structural damage between zero and twenty-five percent.[129] Still, many buildings were damaged and the neighborhood was quite a mess, as one resident found when returning to visit on September 18:

> We were affected by the storm. Our properties that are in Tremé, even the new construction that we did, received flood water. Our downstairs office had at least three to four feet of flood water in it. There were broken lines and poles . . . There were boats throughout the neighborhood and of course a lot of abandoned cars. More importantly, there were no people.

Although the storm and flood damage to Tremé's housing stock was less severe than in many other neighborhoods, two factors slowed its rebuilding. First, Tremé had considerable vacant housing before Katrina and its housing stock needed more extensive repairs due to its age and deferred repairs prior to the storm.[130] Storm and flood damage exacerbated these problems so that property owners often faced significant costs to make their buildings habitable again. Second, the vast majority of Tremé's housing was in rental properties, which received less financial assistance and returned to the market at a slower pace than owner-occupied homes. This situation was exacerbated by the closure of the Laffite public housing development, which accounted for one-third of Tremé's rental apartments.

Another disadvantage for Tremé was the fractured nature of grassroots rebuilding efforts. Unlike Broadmoor, Mid-City, and Village de L'Est, no one organization or leader emerged to unify local residents, businesses, and groups around a coordinated rebuilding agenda. Instead, multiple organizations each undertook separate initiatives in pursuit of their own goals within varied geographic boundaries. The Greater Tremé Consortium worked to help homeowners in its immediate area return and restore its damaged housing units. ERTCA devoted its limited resources to opposing a plan to reuse a closed nursing home for transitional housing. DNIA concentrated on improving schools and economic development. Along with these efforts, a new organization, Historic Faubourg Tremé Association (HFTA), was formed to repair homes, address crime, and otherwise improve the smaller Historic Tremé neighborhood between Claiborne Avenue and the

French Quarter. Without a unified approach to rebuilding their neighborhood or creating their own plan, Tremé organizations neither pooled their resources to address shared priorities nor formed an alliance to exert greater political pressure on how public and private rebuilding resources would be invested. Along with these splintered grassroots efforts, Tremé was the focus for several external recovery initiatives by parties as diverse as the Qatar Katrina Fund and the AFL-CIO Building Trust. While these external resources contributed to rebuilding, they were neither coordinated with other community-based rebuilding efforts nor invested to advance resident-driven rebuilding plans.

In the first months after Katrina, GTC provided support and assistance to residents seeking to return to Tremé, but it never gained the resources to undertake a large scale repopulation effort. In fall 2005, when a resident, Ms. Olivia, returned and opened up her house to help other residents who needed shelter, GTC worked with her to use her house as a resource center.[131] They put a copy machine inside to help distribute information, cooked meals, and formed a "listening circle" where residents could share personal stories about their experiences during Katrina and their efforts to rebuild. This home became a place for residents to share and seek information about missing friends and relatives, and learn about assistance available from FEMA, the Red Cross, and other aid agencies. This work continued for several months until financial pressures forced GTC to focus on securing funding to repair its damaged buildings. Through a project with Fannie Mae, it also counseled 50 residents to help them buy new homes in New Orleans, but none were successful due to personal credit problems that prevented them from qualifying for a mortgage.[132]

Esplanade Ridge-Tremé Civic Association also played a limited role in neighborhood rebuilding.[133] At first, association members stayed in touch, shared information, and helped each other clean up and repair their homes. Later, as they became concerned about the number of blighted properties in their area, they notified city agencies and the Preservation Resource Center about problem properties that they identified. ERTCA's most visible and vocal effort has been a two-year campaign to stop plans to convert the closed Bethany nursing home on Esplanade Avenue into 40 apartments for low-income households, including 20 for homeless persons.[134]

In contrast to the Greater Tremé Consortium and the Esplanade Ridge Tremé Civic Association, DNIA became more active following Katrina, with an agenda that focused on education and economic development. The largest and longest-standing initiative has been to improve public education in New Orleans and Tremé. In early 2006, as a critical mass of its membership returned, the DNIA Education Committee developed several projects in response to concerns about how the state Recovery School District take-over of most New Orleans schools would affect the community's voice in local schools and the poor conditions under which schools were likely to reopen.[135] First, it aimed to empower young people to shape their own education by holding several youth forums in June and July 2006. From these forums, the Fyre Youth Squad was established as a youth advisory body to DNIA. A second project sought to make the local John McDonough High School a community center school with strong connections to local parents, residents, and businesses. The Education Committee drafted and proposed an agreement with the Recovery School District to establish a community partnership around the McDonough High School. Although this agreement was not signed, DNIA continued to work with the RSD to improve conditions and inform educational polices and curricula, including a 2008 plan to establish specific career specialties within each high school.[136] These efforts led to a new Enrichment and Entrepreneurial Academy Program that works with businesses to provide internships, teach students about careers in different industries, and introduce students to the option of becoming an entrepreneur. Under this program, DNIA is working to add a culinary program to train students to work in the restaurant industry.[137]

In addition to its education work, DNIA has promoted cultural heritage as a way to expand business and economic development building on a recovery project undertaken by several business owners. In late 2006, four African American women entrepreneurs worked with a local property owner to open several contiguous businesses on Bayou Road near Broad Street.[138] Two of the entrepreneurs, Vera Warren-Williams and Pam Thompson, were already located there before Katrina. Warren-Williams owned her own building, in which she ran the Community Book Center—a combination bookstore, community space, and education center dedicated to promoting knowledge of African American history and culture. Thompson operated CocoHut, a popular Caribbean restaurant, in a block of storefronts owned by publisher Beverly McKenna. Just prior to Katrina, McKenna was fixing another space to rent to Dwana Makeba for a beauty salon. The storm delayed Makeba's plans but she renewed her efforts and opened in fall 2006. In the meantime, McKenna found Yashika Jordan, who wanted to open a daycare center in the last vacant space. Securing resources to repair properties and reopen businesses in the year after Katrina was quite difficult and it took several months for all the pieces to come together.

During this time, these women entrepreneurs shared resources, installed a single phone line and Internet access, and provided mutual support and encouragement to reopen while McKenna and Williams repaired their properties. McKenna also convinced a local business assistance organization, The

Figure 5.20.
Belles of the Bayou businesses on Bayou Road
Source: Photos by author.

Idea Village, to provide grants and technical assistance to the four business owners. All four businesses opened with a grand opening on December 11, 2006, promoted as "The Belles of Bayou Road" in a cover story published by McKenna's *Tribune* newspaper. Figure 5.20 shows the repaired properties and four businesses in operation almost four years later.

The Belles of the Bayou opening garnered considerable attention and catalyzed new economic development initiatives. It came a little more than a year after Katrina, when many businesses still had not reopened and neighborhoods lacked basic goods and services. Moreover, as a recovery project driven by African American women of modest means (at a time when race and income influenced the demographics of returning populations to New Orleans), and on a historically significant street, it elevated Bayou Road as a focus for further revitalization in this part of Tremé. When DNIA leaders and other community activists learned of the Belles of the Bayou business cluster, they sought to support it and build upon it. They advocated making Bayou Road a priority for investment in the Lambert Plan and including it as one of the 17 target areas established by the Office of Recovery Management.[139] DNIA also helped prepare an application to designate Bayou Road as a Cultural District under a new state program created in 2007. The area was designated as the Bayou Road African American Cultural Heritage Corridor in 2008, which exempts original works of art sold in the district from the state sales taxes and provides tax credits for the rehabilitation of historic structures.[140]

In 2010, DNIA initiated a project to convert vacant properties at the St. Rose of Lima church complex next to the Community Book Center on Bayou Road into a community arts and education center. Their plan for the four-building complex includes a new charter school, a cultural business incubator, and a community center. In June 2010, they gained development rights to the property when the Archdiocese of New Orleans agreed to lease DNIA the site for 45 years. DNIA assembled several partners and tenants for the project, including NewCorp, the Creative Alliance of New Orleans, and a startup charter school, the Lagniappe Academy.[141]

Through the initiative and dedication of the five women entrepreneurs, Bayou Road attracted further businesses as well as public and civic investment. Since the Belles opened, a half dozen other businesses started nearby on Bayou Road, including a record store, two shops selling clothing and beauty supplies, a barber shop, and a restaurant. Merchants successfully advocated for the street to be repaved with historic red bricks after the Sewer and Water Board tore up the road to repair a broken water line. NewCorp, a nonprofit agency that provides technical and financial assistance to small businesses, opened a contractor assistance center at the Community Book Center. As noted above, DNIA and other organizations are focused on strengthening the area as a commercial node and developing community-based arts and education there.

Along with these preexisting groups, a new neighborhood association emerged soon after Katrina with a strong focus on physical improvements in Tremé. The Historic Faubourg Tremé Association (HFTA) was founded in spring 2006 by several historic preservationists seeking to preserve historic architecture and reduce blight and crime in Tremé.[142] Its focus was on the section of Tremé between Claiborne Avenue and the French Quarter (referred to as Historic Tremé) rather than the larger "Greater Tremé" area that extends past Claiborne Avenue to Broad Street, which is served by the other organizations. HFTA's founding leaders were Naydja and Adolph Bynum, who had purchased and restored a number of historic homes in Tremé. Their first initiative targeted several blocks along North Robertson Street for cleanups and crime watch activities. During 2007, they continued to focus on eliminating blight, restoring vacant homes, and reducing crime. Close to 80 trees were planted along and near the street. Several association members also acquired and restored homes and other historic properties on North Robertson, including Joe's Cozy Corner property, a long-standing bar, jazz club, and community gathering place that closed in 2004 after a violent confrontation involving its owner[143]. The various restorations brought these homes and buildings back into productive use and helped to preserve the neighborhood's architecture. Naydja Bynum cited major improvements to North Robertson from their efforts, especially in the 1000 block,

> We could stand in the middle of the street and hold a meeting... The block looks
> much much better. All the blighted properties are gone in that block... There are

trees and they're growing. The houses are painted and repaired. The bar, there was a main bar in that area called Joe's Cozy Corner which was popular but still had elements of crime. It was purchased by one of the members of our group. She took the bar and converted it into two efficiency apartments. We're talking about at least an 80 percent improvement.

More recently, the Historic Faubourg Tremé Association has become active in zoning and development issues, playing a similar role as the Mid-City Neighborhood Organization in shaping the type and design of new development in the neighborhood. According to Bynum, HFTA expects developers to come to its Land Use Committee to share their development plans, answer questions, and address requested changes. HFTA has also influenced development plans by voicing opinions with the Historic District Landmark Commission, which regulates the design of new projects within Tremé's designated historic district. One of their actions was securing Zoning Commission and City Council approval of a zoning change to allow commercial uses in spaces that formerly housed businesses but had reverted to residential zoning after being vacant for six months.[144] HFTA made the proposal to help attract stores, such as grocery stores, coffee shops, and bakeries, back to Tremé to provide needed goods and services. Although it passed the City Council on a 6–0 vote in August 2010, some residents and groups initially opposed the zoning provision because they wanted it to allow for bars and businesses that offered live music.[145] In another instance, HFTA opposed a 70-unit mixed-income apartment project but then helped broker a compromise plan approved by the City Council that reduced the project to 49 units and increased its share of market-rate apartments (versus units subsidized for low-income households).[146]

Outside Support and Aid

In Tremé, like many New Orleans neighborhoods, rebuilding was aided by labor and funding from outside the neighborhood. Rebuilding Together, the national organization that had long partnered with New Orleans' Preservation Resource Center to repair homes, chose Tremé as one of seven target neighborhoods. Through several community organizations, it identified homeowners who needed help to gut and rebuild their properties and had completed 50 projects through 2009.[147] Another source of aid was the Nation of Qatar. Right after Katrina, the Amir of Qatar, Sheik Hamad bin Khalifa al-Thani, pledged $100 million from his nation to help New Orleans and on September 18, 2005, the Qatar Katrina Fund (QKF) was created to deliver that aid.[148] Funds were distributed to local organizations for projects related to education, health care, and housing. With a $2.5 million grant from the fund, Covenant House, a Tremé-based organization that provides shelter and services to the homeless and youth, established Qatar Tremé/Lafitte Renewal Project as a separate organization to repair homes for people of modest means.[149] The project moved quickly to rebuild homes: Cathy Puett was hired as project manager in May 2007, construction on the first homes began in July, and work on 28 homes was at or near completion by the end of the year.[150] Covenant House originally planned to repair 100 homes with the QKF grant, but higher than expected repair costs lowered the number of projects to 60, or 8 percent of Tremé's owner-occupied homes before the storm.[151]

A third rebuilding project in Tremé involved a collaboration among Providence Community Housing, the AFL-CIO Building Trust, and MIT. In June 2006, the AFL-CIO Building Investment Trust announced a $1 billion initiative to finance housing and economic development projects related to Gulf Coast recovery and began seeking partners to assist in this effort. They connected with MIT Professor J. Phillip Thompson, who had been teaching a spring practicum class that focused on Tremé, and Providence Community Housing, a new Catholic housing developer formed by several organizations in March 2006. With assistance from two MIT Ph.D. students, Providence put together a proposal to acquire and build housing on 192 city-owned properties in Tremé and Lower Mid-City in response to a city government effort to redevelop 2,000 city-owned properties.[152] There were long delays in acquiring these properties, but over 60 units were ultimately secured by Providence and became part of its larger-scale effort to redevelop the Lafitte public housing project elaborated upon later in this chapter[153].

These resources helped rebuild housing and allowed more homeowners to return to Tremé, but they were not integrated with a larger neighborhood rebuilding effort. When the 110 homes assisted by Rebuilding Together and the Qatar Katrina Fund are combined with 391 homeowners that received $36 million in Road Home grants to rebuild their pre-Katrina home, they account for two-thirds of Tremé's owner-occupied homes in 2000. As a result, Tremé reached an 88 percent recovery rate for owner-occupied housing in 2010—the second highest level behind Faubourg St. John. However, unlike Broadmoor and Village de L'Est, these homeowner grants were not part of an overall neighborhood plan and were not coordinated with work to bring back and improve other neighborhood services, such as schools, day care, grocery stores, and health services. They also were not connected to sustained services to help people rebuild their lives and return. Since none of the Tremé neighborhood organizations recruited staff or volunteers to create a resident-focused case management system, there was no organized project to locate displaced residents and assist them to address their barriers and secure resources to return, if they so desired. Although Tremé realized a high rebuilding rate for owner-occupied housing without these case management services, their absence likely affected the income level of homeowners who rebuilt and the capacity of tenants to return and small landlords to rebuild.

A critical gap in the private rebuilding resources provided to Tremé was the focus on homeowners. Since over three-quarters of Tremé residents were renters, any successful rebuilding plan had to restore a large number of rental houses and apartments. This was especially true if residents who lived in Tremé before Katrina were to have an option to return. At the center of any plan to restore Tremé's rental housing was the Lafitte public housing development. Restoring Laffite's 896 units, one-third of Tremé's rental housing, would go a long way toward making more apartments available to repopulate the neighborhood. It was shuttered after Katrina and remained closed for years, entangled in the federal Department of Housing and Urban Development plans for the 7,000 units of public housing under its control.

Public Housing in New Orleans

The future of Lafitte was critical to Tremé, but it was also part of a larger attempt to reform New Orleans' severely troubled public housing. Distressed public housing was a serious problem in many cities and the subject of a new federal policy initiative in 1992 entitled HOPE VI. Congress created the National Commission on Severely Distressed Public Housing in 1989 to study the problem and develop an action plan. The Commission found that the plight of these distressed projects transcended physical deterioration to include extreme poverty and social and economic isolation among residents and an environment plagued with crime and disorder.[154] In response, they proposed transforming distressed projects into new mixed income housing developments to reduce the concentration of poverty that contributed to crime and social isolation and to combine housing improvements with supportive services and community building efforts to promote economic self-sufficiency.[155] To implement this policy, Congress enacted the HOPE VI program, which provided large grants to cities to undertake the transformation of troubled public housing developments. Cities competed for grants in response to periodic funding notices issued by HUD. The federal program emphasized proposals that linked public housing improvements to larger neighborhood revitalization efforts and involved public-private partnerships that promised to improve housing management and supplement HOPE VI grants with other funding.[156] New Orleans participated in the HOPE VI program well before Katrina through grants to redevelop the Fischer and St. Thomas complexes. The latter was quite controversial due to the inclusion of a Walmart store and its plan to replace 1,500 apartments for low-income residents with 1,142 new units for households with mixed incomes, of which only 337 would be low-income.[157] Low-income residents were promised the right to return and vouchers to rent apartments elsewhere, but the large loss of a permanent housing stock for low-income families generated opposition from residents and affordable housing advocates. It also contributed to a growing belief that the intent of Hope VI projects was to displace poor residents, enrich developers, and promote gentrification rather than to improve the well-being of public housing tenants and residents in surrounding neighborhoods.[158]

In New Orleans, addressing troubled housing projects was intertwined with decades of mismanagement and corruption at the city's housing authority. HUD first found the Housing Authority of New Orleans (HANO) to be troubled in 1979 when it began rating local housing authorities.[159] After two reports found extensive management and maintenance problems at HANO, HUD completed a 1988 agreement with HANO that required it to contract with a private firm to manage its operations. Over the ensuing years, as HANO's problems continued, HUD took a series of actions seeking to improve HANO management and eliminate Board interference with day-to-day operations. By 1995, it was clear that these efforts had failed to improve living conditions in HANO units when inspections found that 93 percent of randomly selected units failed to meet HUD quality standards. Many units were in such poor condition that inspectors described them as "deplorable, unsafe, and in many instances unfit for human habitation."[160] HUD's Secretary then declared HANO in breach of its contract and entered into a cooperative endeavor agreement with New Orleans Mayor Marc Morial that made HUD and the city jointly responsible for administrative oversight of HANO.

The agreement eliminated HANO's board and transferred oversight to HUD's Assistant Secretary of Public and Indian Housing. However, this arrangement also proved futile as housing conditions remained deplorable and HANO operations continued to be marked by incompetence and corruption. At a 2001 congressional subcommittee hearing in New Orleans, HUD Inspector General Michael Beard testified that despite spending $139 million in HUD modernization funds, HANO had failed to rehabilitate a single one of its ten housing complexes.[161] HUD audits revealed a seriously corrupt and dysfunctional organization: contracts were awarded based on favoritism; contractors were paid for work that wasn't performed; buildings were not maintained; funds were unaccounted for; and employees were assigning Section 8 vouchers to themselves to pay their own rent.[162] In January 2002, after a court challenge by Mayor Morial who sought judicial oversight rather than a federal takeover, HUD assumed full control of HANO and continues to operate it in receivership. Consequently, the decisions about what to do with Lafitte (and other New Orleans public housing projects) after Katrina rested with HUD.

Rebuilding Lafitte

During the evacuation of New Orleans, HANO closed all of the city's public housing projects. At the time, HANO owned approximately 7,379 apartments—5,147 or 70 percent were occupied.[163] Most complexes remained closed well into 2006. Residents had returned to about 1,100 units by June 2006 when HUD announced plans to clean up and reopen another 1,000 units within 60 days and to demolish 5,000 units in four public housing developments—C.J. Peete, B. W. Cooper, St. Bernard, and Lafitte.[164] The demolished units would be converted into mixed-income housing similar to the Hope VI approach. Since the residents of these four projects could not return to their apartments, they would receive rental vouchers to find replacement housing while the projects underwent redevelopment. To address higher rents that accompanied the housing shortage after Katrina, HUD raised voucher amounts by 35 percent.[165] Critics pointed out the limited value of vouchers, even at the higher level, with many rental properties still damaged and few apartments available to rent.[166]

HUD moved forward with its plans to redevelop Lafitte in August when it selected a partnership between Providence Community Housing, a nonprofit Catholic housing developer formed after Katrina to help bring 20,000 people back to New Orleans,[167] and Enterprise Community Partners, a large national funder of affordable housing created in 1982 by developer James Rouse. Enterprise had helped form Providence after its president Doris Koo met Jim Kelly of Catholic Charities at a December 2005 meeting in Baton Rouge,[168] and was a natural partner for the Lafitte project. It provided Providence with greater capacity to raise financing and experience with large scale and HOPE VI housing projects. Providence's interest in redeveloping Laffite emerged from a post-Katrina shift in focus that increased Tremé's importance for Catholic Charities. Catholic Charities had been more active in other New Orleans neighborhoods before Katrina, especially Central City and the Lower Ninth Ward, but Providence chose Tremé and Lower Mid-City as a priority for its post-Katrina rebuilding:

> We decided that Lower Mid-City and the Tremé neighborhood were two criti-
> cal neighborhoods to the community... These two neighborhoods, we believed
> because of the way they abutted the medical district, the business district and
> the French Quarter, were going to be critical to the future New Orleans. So we
> decided, in addition to all we were doing in other places, that we would one,
> work on those properties we had a relationship with... and we would focus in
> on this particular neighborhood... We had in fact been awarded by the city 192
> adjudicated properties prior to being asked by HUD to do Lafitte.

This decision clearly made Lafitte, the largest concentration of housing in these neighborhoods, a critical project to undertake. As Providence and Enterprise started to move forward on planning for Laffite, the project was stalled as the wisdom of demolishing the city's large public housing projects was challenged.

The Demolition Controversy. The plan to demolish four New Orleans public housing projects and rebuild them as lower-density, mixed-income housing was quite controversial, with Lafitte at the center of this controversy. The closure of most of New Orleans' public housing units meant that several thousand of the city's poorest and largely black residents were unable to return. Demolition clearly prevented the projects' reopening and would further delay the return of former residents (and others) to these projects for several years, given the time required to demolish buildings and construct new housing. Moreover, with the limited supply of rental apartments and increasing rents in the first year after the storm, the standard housing market was not a feasible alternative for public housing residents, even with their replacement housing vouchers.[169] Several groups advocated for reopening the closed public housing complexes, some of which had sustained limited damage from Katrina, to help residents return to the city. In June 2006, several local attorneys, along with the Advancement Project (a national social justice organization) and a Chicago law firm, filed a class-action lawsuit on behalf of displaced New Orleans public housing residents, seeking court action to block demolition and allow residents to return to their units. The suit claimed that the closure and planned demolition violated fair housing laws by discriminating against black residents.[170]

Laffite generated the greatest opposition to demolition among the four projects for several reasons. First, it was located on high ground and sustained little flooding. Providence Community Housing's own investigations found that most buildings at Lafitte did not flood, and those that did flood had less than 12 inches of water.[171] This meant that less extensive cleaning and repairs were needed to prepare Lafitte's apartments for occupancy. Second, historic preservationists and planners viewed Lafitte as one of the best designed and well-built public housing projects in the city. Its design was based on the Pontalba apartments along Jackson Square in the French Quarter.[172] Constructed by local craftsmen, it had withstood two major hurricanes largely unscathed. There were also concerns that many of the demolished units would not be replaced, as occurred with the St. Thomas Hope VI project, leaving many former residents without the option of returning to their neighborhood or without access to other affordable apartments. Finally, some former residents wanted to return to Lafitte, which they remembered as a tight knit community in which people looked after each other, as shown in this quote from Katy Reckdahl's article "Razing a Community"[173]:

> "Everybody knew everybody," says Lois Nelson Andrews, whose musical children include James "Twelve" Andrews and Troy "Trombone Shorty" Andrews. She and her kids were living in the St. Bernard project, but her children and their cousins "were practically raised in the Lafitte" in the apartment of her mother, Miss Dorothy Hill, she says. "My mother had 12 children herself; all of us have children and we all brought them to my mama, because she was the one doing the cooking. In the summer, she would cook five-dozen eggs every morning and feed everyone. People would come in, 'Grandma, you got an egg?'"

The desire to save Laffite buildings was not shared by all residents. Others preferred to see it demolished and replaced with new units rather than return to conditions in the prior development. Emelda Paul, President of the Lafitte Resident Council, testified before Congress that "People want to come home, but we can't have people living in the same conditions they were living in before Katrina. We need and want up-to-date kitchens and bathrooms. We're tired of the patch jobs on buildings from the 1940s." [174]

With protests, law suits, and mixed opinions on the wisdom of demolition, the plans for Lafitte were stalled for some time. A federal judge ruled that HANO could proceed with demolition in February 2007,[175] but the project still needed city approval for the demolition. Under a 2002 law passed during the conflict over the St. Thomas project, all properties controlled by HANO or HUD required a city demolition permit. When the city's Housing Conservation District Review Commission considered the demolition requests in early December 2007, it approved permits for three projects but was deadlocked over Lafitte. HANO appealed the decision to the city council, which approved demolition subject to several conditions: that financing plans were in place, that the master-development agreement and agreements with all resident councils were signed, that the documentation that sufficient affordable housing units existed for returning public-housing residents was in place, and that HANO's board be expanded to increase local participation. Several months of negotiations between the city government, HANO, and HUD ensued before Mayor Nagin signed the Lafitte demolition permit on March 24, 2008,[176] which allowed demolition of the project's 76 buildings to begin in April. Sixteen months later, and almost four years to the day after Hurricane Katrina struck, Providence Community Housing broke ground on the new Lafitte housing development, named Faubourg Lafitte, on August 27, 2009.

Faubourg Lafitte. Providence and Enterprise created an ambitious plan for the Lafitte redevelopment. Faubourg Lafitte envisions 1,500 units of new housing: 900 subsidized rental apartments to fully replace the original units at Lafitte and 600 new homes to sell to homeowners. A little more than one-third (517 units) of the new housing will be at the former Lafitte site, with the balance to be built as in-fill housing on lots throughout the surrounding neighborhoods.[177] Density at the Laffite site will decrease with 376 apartments and 141 homeownership units replacing the 896 pre-Katrina apartments. Restoring the historic street grid to connect the site with the surrounding neighborhood and using historic architectural styles are two important elements of the new design. These design changes are illustrated in the site plans in Figure 5.21 and photos in Figure 5.22. Initial plans also envisioned a phased redevelopment in which several hundred families would be moved back into refurbished apartments in existing buildings as other properties were demolished and rebuilt. Providence and Enterprise originally sought to repair 200 to 300 units under this phased approach but only 94 units were restored at a cost of $2.7 million.[178] Since these apartments did not open until August 2008, the 42 households that eventually moved into the repaired units lived there for seven months before their leases ended and they had to move to make way for demolition[179].

Redesigning Lafitte was considered a central part of making it a safer and better place to live. When Laffite was built, public housing was designed to be insulated from its surrounding neighborhood with large public courtyards intended to promote peace and quiet. Instead, the design contributed to social isolation and exacerbated crime problems.[180] By integrating the new housing into the neighborhood and creating smaller buildings that face the street with front porches, the design seeks to encourage more activity and "eyes on the street" to help reduce crime. Under this theory,

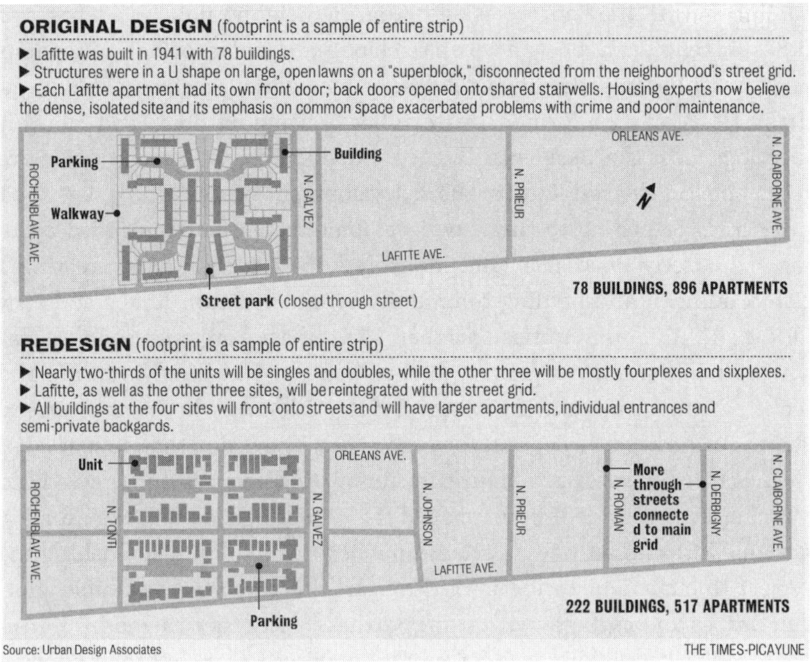

ORIGINAL DESIGN (footprint is a sample of entire strip)

▶ Lafitte was built in 1941 with 78 buildings.
▶ Structures were in a U shape on large, open lawns on a "superblock," disconnected from the neighborhood's street grid.
▶ Each Lafitte apartment had its own front door; back doors opened onto shared stairwells. Housing experts now believe the dense, isolated site and its emphasis on common space exacerbated problems with crime and poor maintenance.

Parking — Building
ROCHENBLAVE AVE.   N. GALVEZ   N. PRIEUR   N. CLAIBORNE AVE.
ORLEANS AVE.
Walkway —
LAFITTE AVE.

Street park (closed through street)

78 BUILDINGS, 896 APARTMENTS

REDESIGN (footprint is a sample of entire strip)

▶ Nearly two-thirds of the units will be singles and doubles, while the other three will be mostly fourplexes and sixplexes.
▶ Lafitte, as well as the other three sites, will be reintegrated with the street grid.
▶ All buildings at the four sites will front onto streets and will have larger apartments, individual entrances and semi-private backgards.

Unit — ORLEANS AVE.
ROCHENBLAVE AVE.   N. TONTI   N. GALVEZ   N. JOHNSON   N. PRIEUR   N. ROMAN   N. DERBIGNY   N. CLAIBORNE AVE.
More through streets connected to main grid
LAFITTE AVE.

Parking

222 BUILDINGS, 517 APARTMENTS

Source: Urban Design Associates   THE TIMES-PICAYUNE

Figure 5.21.
Comparison of original Lafitte design with the plan for its redevelopment
Source: The Times–Picayune.

the opportunities for criminal activity are reduced since residents will be able to watch the street from their front porches and yards and more pedestrians will pass by with the new street grid.

The new design and larger Faubourg Lafitte neighborhood plan emerged from a fifteen month planning process that Providence and Enterprise

Figure 5.22.
Faubourg Lafitte under construction along Orleans Avenue in November 2010
Source: Photos by author.

conducted with the Lafitte Resident Council, neighborhood residents, and other stakeholders. It began with a weeklong series of information sessions and workshops in early October 2006 and included a December 2006 meeting in Houston with former Lafitte public housing residents and monthly meetings with the Residents Council. Providence used several means to reach and engage residents in the redevelopment process and gauge their interest in returning to the new development. Outreach included sending a quarterly newsletter and monthly letters to residents, creating a call-in number, and holding community events in Baton Rouge and New Orleans.[181] All Communities Together, a faith-based organization that was active in community organizing before Katrina, was hired to locate and make personal contact with former Lafitte residents who lived in several states. An early survey of 400 former residents revealed that almost all of them wanted to return to Lafitte, including 90 percent of those who lived out of state.[182] Resident input shaped the new design, at times reinforcing national ideas about how to rebuild public housing, but also pushing the project to include historic New Orleans architecture such as double shotgun homes and cottages with front porches.[183] Another theme from resident feedback was their need for support services to sort out their housing situation and to access transportation, health services, elder services, child care, and jobs that were critical to returning and rebuilding their lives.[184]

In response to residents' needs after Katrina and established HOPE VI policy, Providence and Enterprise incorporated social services and economic development components into the Faubourg Lafitte Plan. They raised $5 million to make case management and counseling services available to former residents living in New Orleans, Baton Rouge, and Houston, partly addressing the previously noted gap in rebuilding efforts among Tremé neighborhood organizations.

At the renovated Sojourner Truth Neighborhood Center, a range of social services are provided that include youth and elder programs, recreational activities, personal finance classes, and job search and readiness workshops. It also houses a community technology center with a computer lab and classes. Under HUD's Section 3 program regulations, contractors that receive HUD funding must hire low-income residents for a portion of the jobs created with HUD funds, and HANO committed to hire low-income city residents for 30 percent of these jobs.[185] One strategy that Providence used to achieve this goal was contracting with minority-owned firms and smaller contractors that were expected to employ more local residents and would need to hire employees when they received new contracts. As part of this strategy, they worked to break down contracts into smaller subcontracts for which minority-owned and small firms were better able to win bids. Data provided by HANO indicates that this approach likely helped Providence and Enterprise to advance low-income hiring goals. One-third of the $59 million in construction contracts awarded through fall 2011went to New Orleans-based contractors and 30 percent went to firms owned by minority, women, or low-income entrepreneurs. Moreover, half of the 283 people hired to work on the Lafitte development were city residents and 36 percent were identified as low-income. Six of the new hires were former Lafitte residents. The bulk of low-income workers were in the laborer and carpenter trades with hourly wages between $9.50 and $16.00.[186]

By early 2011, the first phase on the redevelopment was nearing completion and the first group of former residents, eight families, had moved into new homes built on the former Lafitte site. At a February 4 event, US Secretary of Housing and Urban Development Shaun Donovan announced that the first 50 homes were ready to be occupied and that another 80 units would be completed that spring.[187] In his comments at the event, Secretary Donovan emphasized the importance of bringing former residents back to live in the redeveloped public housing projects: "We are going to help the thousands of families that were displaced from the 'big four' to get back home." Through its first phase, Faubourg Lafitte made progress toward this goal with 94 (70 percent) of the first 134 apartments rented to people who were residents of Lafitte at the time of Katrina.[188] New Orleans Mayor Mitch Landrieu highlighted the broader vision for Lafitte in creating a stronger community: "We're not just building buildings, we're building communities, we're building soul, and we're re-grabbing what is important to us."[189]

Faubourg Lafitte promises to be the defining project in rebuilding Tremé. As the neighborhood's largest project, it will have the greatest impact on who lives in Tremé and the neighborhood's physical character. If all 1,500 units are built, rented, and sold, they will account for 44 percent of Tremé's occupied housing stock in the year 2000. In addition, its successful completion will remove many blighted and vacant properties and restore the traditional street layout and associated neighborhood character to an eight-square-block area along Orleans Avenue, one of the neighborhood's major streets. In one sense, Lafitte repeats Tremé's 80-year history of being reshaped by large urban redevelopment projects conceived by political leaders outside the neighborhood. In another sense, it is a break from past urban renewal projects in terms of neighborhood residents' involvement in designing the project and the attention to local architecture and reintegration with the neighborhood form. Moreover, Lafitte's focus on building housing and a healthy place for neighborhood residents to live contrasts with past urban renewal projects conceived to serve city and regional economic development interests.

Tremé at Year Five

In late 2010, five years after Katrina, Tremé was in the paradoxical situation of rebuilding more slowly than other neighborhoods and facing major changes. With the slow rebuilding of its large rental housing stock, occupied housing units in 2010 were just 54 percent of the 2000 level, and its population had reached only 47 percent of the pre-Katrina population in 2000 (see Table 5.11). Despite its higher elevation and less flooding than much of New Orleans, Tremé lost half of its pre-Katrina population. This telling outcome reflects how the supply of rental housing and residents' low incomes affected their ability to return. Poorer residents needed money to return and rent an apartment, likely at a higher rent than before the storm, and they depended on landlords to fix up apartments and rent them to former neighborhood residents. The low repopulation rate also reflects HUD and HANO—Tremé's largest landlord—decision to demolish and redevelop the Lafitte project. Lafitte was still under development in 2010, and the 600 families who lived there before Katrina were without these apartments in June 2010. If these units had been open and occupied in June 2010, then Tremé's occupied housing rate would have stood at 73 percent, just below the citywide level (76 percent). Moreover, it would have restored tenants to 69 percent of its pre-Katrina occupied rental housing and achieved more balanced rebuilding between homeowners and renters. Instead, Tremé experienced the greatest disparity in recovery rates between homeowners and renters among the four neighborhoods, and on par with the large difference seen in Village de L'Est. As shown in Table 5.12, 88 percent of owner-occupied units had returned by 2010, while occupied rental units had only reached 47 percent of the 2000 level (matching the total repopulation rate).

Table 5.11. CHANGE IN TREMÉ POPULATION AND HOUSING UNITS, 2000–2010

	2000	2010	Total Change 2000–2010	Percent Change 2000–2010	2010 Recovery Rate
Population	8,853	4,155	−4,698	−53.1%	47%
Total housing units	4,254	3,037	−1,217	−28.6%	71%
Occupied housing units	3,429	1,913	−1,516	−44.2%	56%
Vacant housing units	825	1,123	298	36.1%	NA

Table 5.12. SHARE AND CHANGES IN TREMÉ OWNER- AND
RENTER-OCCUPIED HOUSING UNITS, 2000 AND 2010

	Percent 2000	Percent 2010	Total Change 2000–2010	2010 Recovery Rate
Owner-occupied	21.8%	34.3%	−90	88%
Renter-occupied	78.2%	65.6%	−1,425	47%

Source: 2000 and 2010 US Census

Along with slow repopulation, Tremé had not fully recovered key businesses and services that provided for a "complete neighborhood." Some
landmark Tremé businesses had returned, such as Dooky Chase, a restaurant across from the Lafitte development where President Obama had
picked up a takeout lunch during his first trip to New Orleans in October
2009, but many stores had not reopened. Two supermarkets just outside
Tremé closed after Katrina, as did a third smaller grocery store within its
borders.[190] This left the neighborhood without access to a grocery store and
fresh food. Four of seven schools were reopened, including the newly renovated Craig Elementary School, but several neighborhood activists pointed
to the absence of a library, few neighborhood parks, and reduced access to
health and day care services. As noted below, several projects to provide for
day care, health services, and parks were in the planning stages in 2010.

Five years after Katrina, Tremé had changed across several dimensions.
There was widespread agreement that demographic changes that had begun
before the storm were continuing. Tremé was attracting new residents with
higher incomes who were more likely to be white or Hispanic, as well as
younger adults without children. These observed changes are confirmed by
US Census data. Tremé's white and Hispanic population increased almost
75 percent between 2000 and 2010, with the former growing by 343 and
the latter by 94. These changes were accompanied by the loss of over 5,000
black residents, a 62 percent decline[191] (see Table 5.13). Although the growth
in white residents was largest in areas adjacent to the French Quarter, the
2010 white population exceeded its 2000 level in every census tract except
the one with Lafitte. Black residents, on the other hand, declined by at least
35 percent and 500 in each tract (see Table 5.14 and Figure 5.23). Two to
three thousand black residents may repopulate Tremé as Faubourg Lafitte
is completed and occupied, but the neighborhood is likely to permanently
lose a large share of its black population. It is also positioned to gain more
middle-income residents since the new Lafitte development is designed
as a mixed-income project. Gentrification through investment by new

Table 5.13. CHANGE IN TREMÉ POPULATION BY RACE, 2000 AND 2010

Race/Ethnicity	Percent 2000	Percent 2010	Total Change 2000–2010	Percent Change 2000–2010
White	5.3%	19.6%	343	72.8%
Black	93.1%	75.3%	-5,113	-62.0%
American Indian and Native Alaskan	.3%	.4%	-14	-45.1%
Asian	.1%	.4%	11	220.0%
Hispanic	1.5%	5.4%	94	71.2%

Source: 2000 and 2010 US Census

homeowners and real estate developers seems likely to continue given the strong interest in the neighborhood's historic homes and culture, heightened by the HBO *Tremé* television series, the neighborhood's proximity to the city's downtown and medical district, and several planned park and transportation improvements discussed below. Another result of rising rents and displacement after Katrina has been a decline in the number of musicians living in Tremé, who have long been vital to the neighborhood's way of life and cultural traditions. One news article reported that only five jazz musicians still lived in Tremé's historic core in spring 2010.[192]

Neighborhood leaders expressed mixed opinions about the desirability and impact of these changes. Some feared that gentrification was transforming Tremé into a neighborhood of younger and higher-income residents with the risk, stated by one activist, that "lower income folks probably over time will relocate elsewhere." Another recognized that the sense of community and social connections was being lost but expressed acceptance of new residents:

> We don't have the same people here, and that may not be a bad thing that they're all not here ... But it's not like you can walk out at ten, eleven o'clock at night and

Table 5.14. TREMÉ POPULATION CHANGE BY CENSUS TRACT, 2000–2010

	Tract 39	Tract 40	Tract 44.01	Tract 44.02*
Total population	-252	-722	-1,220	-2,504
White	242	79	27	-5
Black	-539	-831	-1,252	-2,491
Hispanic	81	13	12	-12

Source: 2000 and 2010 US Census *Contained the Lafitte public housing development.

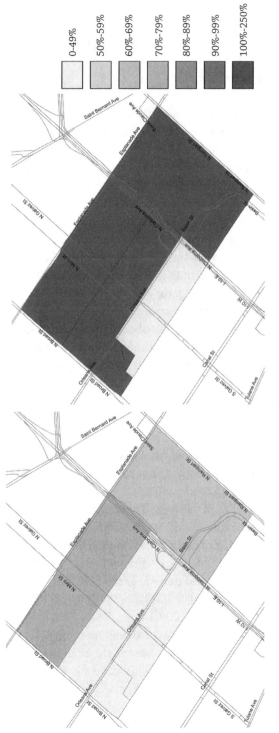

Figure 5.23.
Tremé African American (left) and white (right) repopulation rates by Census tract
Source: 2000 and 2010 US Census.

know that you may pass someone you know. You have to be more mindful of where you are going and who you may encounter. Our community is stable with people in houses but they're not the people we're accustomed to seeing or knowing. Is that good or bad? Personally, it doesn't really make a difference. . . . I haven't had any problems with people.

A second change was a wave of new investments planned for Tremé and its environs. Although many of these investments promise to add vital services and amenities and improve the neighborhood's quality of life, they are largely being undertaken by different nonprofit organizations and city agencies without an organizing plan and coordinated recovery strategy. These "community-oriented" projects include the Lafitte Greenway, a new community health center operated by Tulane University; a Head Start preschool at the former Lafitte public housing administration building; repairs to the gym and pool at the Tremé Community Center; and a new school at the St. Rose of Lima church complex.[193] With $90 million in federal stimulus funding, a new street car line long Rampart Street on Tremé's riverside boundary was moving forward.[194] One potentially transformative project that did emerge from a collaborative of grassroots leaders and community-based organizations was a proposal to remove the section of I-10 that bisects Tremé. The outlook for this initiative was uncertain since it had just begun with a planning grant to study the option obtained in late 2010.[195] Many of these projects were in the planning or design phase in late 2011, but several seemed likely to be completed since the required funding was committed.

Renewed investment included projects to recognize and preserve Tremé's history and culture. In addition to the designation of the Bayou Road Cultural Products District and private efforts to preserve historic homes, a major expansion of the New Orleans African American Museum was planned. The museum, one of several initiatives to revitalize Tremé under the Marc Morial Administration, restored a historic Creole mansion built from 1828 to 1829 to house exhibits on the city's African American history and provide a public and tourism gateway to Tremé.[196] After opening in 2000, the museum closed in 2003 when the city cut off financial support[197] and did not reopen until 2008. Under the leadership of a new board and Executive Director John Hankins, a $6 million campaign was launched to address damage from Katrina and expand the museum's buildings and exhibits. with the city of New Orleans committing $3 million in recovery CDBG funds to the project. Hankin's vision is to "restore this entire neighborhood to look like it did in the 1840s. It was the heyday of Tremé. That was when this was the richest and most sophisticated neighborhood of people of color in America, and this was one of the premier squares in that era."[198] The centerpiece of this expansion is restoration of the severely blighted Passebon Cottage, built in 1848 by Tremé builder and free person of color Pierre Passebon, to house an exhibit on Tremé's history.[199] Although abated by the loss of musicians and closing of live music spots, Tremé retains its musical traditions with periodic second lines and jazz at several reopened bars. The Back Street Cultural Museum, reopened for the 2006 Mardi Gras, remains a center for the preservation of and education about African American cultural traditions rooted in Tremé: Mardi Gras Indians, social aid and pleasure clubs, and second lines.

Although fragmented among organizations with different priorities, after Katrina Tremé experienced a similar surge in civic activities as that of Faubourg St. John and Mid-City. A new active neighborhood association, the Historic Faubourg Tremé Association, was created that established a new voice around planned development projects and mobilized engagement in several improvement efforts. DNIA was strengthened after Katrina, with expanded membership and leaders and a newfound agenda to improve schools, support businesses, and catalyze cultural development. Perhaps most importantly, Tremé's civic and political activities after Katrina became less insulated as organizations connected to larger initiatives to rebuild and improve several neighborhoods. The rebirth of civic activism after Katrina nurtured new collaboration across the four Broad Street neighborhoods—a development explored further at the end of the chapter.

As with many things in Tremé, the neighborhood's condition in 2010 was a contested issue and refracted through the lens of one's economic status. Some believed Tremé had improved and its future looked bright.

> It's improved significantly, it's improving, and it stills has a ways to go. We've done renovations, the neighborhood is cleaner in general...I think crime has decreased. The community's involvement, I mean the neighborhood association's involvement with everything in the neighborhood is a big accomplishment. Our relationship with the city, it's more of that than anything. I mean Craig School, every little bit, every tree...There is discussion about removing I-10 on Claiborne, another hope; and streetcar on North Rampart street—all of it is exciting, even though we might not be able to see it all.

Others saw a fundamentally different place in which many poorer people were displaced and those that had returned were not better off.

> What we have to realize is that there's a large segment of population that did not and will not return. People just stayed where they were, resources were available

to them that, as much as they longed to be home, they could not receive when they return home: health care, quality schools, affordable housing. I think that has had a tremendous impact. With the lack of public housing, you lost a lot in terms of the workers of the city, who in turn are the consumers who do business locally, they don't exist anymore. I think that there's a more transient community now where people are here for short time and they're moving from place to place, so they don't really ground themselves in a particular neighborhood or community.

A FORGOTTEN NEIGHBORHOOD

Leaving downtown New Orleans on Canal Street, you discover Lower Mid-City, the fourth neighborhood bordering Broad Street. It begins at Claiborne Avenue and extends for ten blocks until Broad Street, bordered on the riverside by the I-10 Pontchartrain Expressway and lakeside by St. Louis Street. Lower Mid-City, long known as the Tulane-Gravier neighborhood,[200] is densely developed with industry, medical institutions, and streets packed with single and double shotgun homes (see Figure 5.24).

Figure 5.24.
Residential street in Lower Mid-City
Source: Photo by author.

After passing between a series of property owners, the area was first developed in the nineteenth century by industry drawn to the nearby Carondelet and Basin Canals that connected Lake Pontchartrain and the Mississippi River. It was home to New Orleans' brewery district, which is still evident, as the vacant Dixie Brewery building remains as a neighborhood landmark. Residences were built in the late 1800s and early 1900s, followed by commercial investment along the major streets. Health care uses in Lower Mid-City date back to 1859, when the Daughters of Charity founded the Hotel Dieu, but the main expansion of medical institutions occurred in the 1970s and 1980s when a new hospital and the Louisiana State University (LSU) Schools of Nursing and Allied Health Professionals[201] were built. After Katrina, hospital development again became a major force in the neighborhood's evolution.

Residents in Lower Mid-City, like those in Tremé, were quite poor in the years before Katrina. Based on the 2000 Census, 56 percent of the neighborhood lived below the poverty line. Its average household income, at $16,569, was the lowest of the four neighborhoods and below two-fifths of the city's average income. Four out of five residents rented their homes and, similar to Mid-City residents, they moved fairly often, as less than half remained in the same home from 1995 to 2000. While it shared some socioeconomic conditions with Tremé, Lower Mid-City lacked Tremé's historic and cultural identity within New Orleans and its political organization. As a result, Lower Mid-City had not gained the attention of city political or civic leaders and was never a priority under neighborhood improvement or community development initiatives.[202] According to one activist, it "had been forgotten for years" with its lack of a recognized name and fluid boundaries indicative of its invisible status within New Orleans.[203] Lower Mid-City did not possess the type of community organization found in the three other neighborhoods; it had neither the established neighborhood associations found in Mid-City and Faubourg St. John nor the civil rights, historic preservation, and cultural activism present in Tremé. These conditions left Lower Mid-City without a strong grassroots organization, a large homeowner base, or political leadership that galvanized community-based rebuilding effort in other neighborhoods.

One institution that had worked to improve Lower Mid-City was St Joseph's Church, a Catholic parish dating back to 1844 that moved into its current building on Tulane Avenue in 1893.[204] Sister Vera Butler, Director of Outreach Ministries for St. Joseph's Church, spearheaded efforts to organize residents to improve their neighborhood in the late 1990s, which led to the formation of the Tulane/Canal Neighborhood Development Corporation (TCNDC). Sister Vera organized an 18-month planning process among 30 neighborhood residents and businesses from 1999 to 2000 that identified homeownership as a critical neighborhood improvement need. TCNDC was created in 2001 to foster home ownership for low-income residents with Sister Vera serving as its Executive Director.[205] TCNDC first worked with Rebuilding Together to repair existing homes and then focused on building new houses for first-time home-buyers on blighted empty lots in the neighborhood. It took the TCNDC several years to get connected to affordable housing networks, gain control over city-owned vacant lots, and raise funds to build new houses. Through its persistence, the TCNDC gained ownership of several lots and began construction of five new homes prior to Katrina. One home was completed and sold, while four others had just started construction when the hurricane struck.[206]

In addition to the challenge of rebuilding with limited community organization and political influence, Lower Mid-City had considerable flooding and building damage. Situated in a low-lying area between Esplanade Ridge and the Mississippi River, the failures of the 17th Street and London Avenue Canals left water throughout the neighborhood. Although not as badly flooded as Mid-City, water depths across Lower Mid-City were above two feet; large sections close to the medical area received 5 to 6 feet of water. As a result, FEMA classified most buildings as having structural damage in the 25 percent to 75 percent range, with the area furthest from downtown between Galvez and Broad streets suffering the greatest damage. With extensive building damage, limited owner-occupied housing, and largely low-income residents, Lower Mid-City faced a particularly challenging road to repopulation and rebuilding. Among the four neighborhoods, it had the least extensive community-based recovery effort and its recovery progress was severely set back by plans to build two new large hospitals in Lower Mid-City.

Early Rebuilding Efforts

Hampered by the slow return of residents and weak community organization, no grassroots neighborhood-wide planning or rebuilding effort took root in Lower Mid-City. Instead, two groups concentrated on aiding returning homeowners to repair their properties and renovating and building homes to repopulate the neighborhood. St. Joseph's Church helped returning homeowners apply for FEMA financial assistance and trailers and also hosted visiting volunteers, who provided free labor to gut homes.[207] Since senior homeowners found it difficult to stay outside the city and commute to work on their homes, the church sought to house FEMA trailers in its parking lot to provide the neighborhood's many elderly residents with temporary housing near their properties. After 12 months of meetings and conversations, FEMA agreed to their proposal but required St. Joseph's Church to provide insurance to cover damages and injuries while the trailers were on its site.[208] Due to the delays and insurance cost, the church decided not to proceed with hosting the FEMA trailers. Another church project championed by Sister Vera was the creation of the Rebuild Center as a site to provide rest, daytime meals, health care, and social services to New Orleans' homeless and transient residents. The Rebuild Center, completed in 2007, was not focused on Lower Mid-City, but it provided vital services to a poor and often neglected part of New Orleans' population.

Tulane/Canal NDC also worked to revive its home-building program after Katrina. It had to determine the cost to finish the four homes under development, in light of new damage and higher construction costs after Katrina, and had to raise additional funds to complete construction. TCNDC also found it challenging to find low-income buyers targeted to buy its homes since low-income workers were slow to return to New Orleans. Through the perseverance of Sister Vera and other board members and with financial support from the city, foundations, and other religious congregations, Tulane Canal NDC built 11 new homes through fall 2011 and began offering classes to prepare prospective home-buyers for homeownership and help them qualify for mortgages.

Soon after Katrina, another organization was formed by Tulane University medical student Paul Ikemire to support rebuilding in Lower Mid-City. Ikemire was new to Lower Mid-City; he had purchased and moved into a house there one month before the city flooded. When he came to New Orleans, Ikemire did not plan to form a nonprofit organization, start a housing repair operation, or support neighborhood organizing, but he assumed these roles in the wake of Hurricane Katrina. With previous disaster recovery experience in Indonesia after the 2004 Tsunami, Ikemire saw parallels between his past work and the challenges facing Lower Mid-City:

> When I came back after the storm, my house was damaged and the neighborhood was pretty much empty...I had experience with recovery disaster work since Indonesia and I found myself in a place where I had learned the skills and had some sense of how to organize and get resources for this neighborhood. It has a similarity to a small village in Indonesia. It was in the middle of the city but the neighborhood was poorly maintained and had poor access to resources that were flying all around New Orleans. For a little effort, I thought you could organize whoever was coming back and try to get resources.[209]

He decided to create a new organization and named it Phoenix of New Orleans (PNOLA) to provide a strong identity and the image of rebirth, seeking to counter his neighborhood's often invisible status. Ikemire then created a website with pictures of houses in Lower Mid-City and asked for sponsorships and contributions to rebuild them. After incorporating as a nonprofit and gaining tax-exempt status in early 2006, PNOLA secured larger donations and support from organizations such as the Red Cross and the Salvation Army. It also hired several staff people through the AmeriCorps youth service program.[210] In its first year, PNOLA focused on attracting and supervising volunteers to help Lower Mid-City homeowners gut, repair, and rebuild their homes and return. By the end of 2006, it had worked on more than 50 homes[211].

PNOLA has continued to recruit volunteers and secure resources to gut and repair homes for homeowners without the financial resources to rebuild. As it gained more experienced staff and secured a general contractor's license, PNOLA expanded its services to include directly undertaking home repair projects at little or no cost to homeowners without financial means and serving as a trusted contractor for owners who have funds to rebuild but want to avoid the risks of contractor fraud or poor quality work.[212] By 2010, PNOLA also sought to help residents to transition into home ownership as well as to build assets by owning small rental properties. It initiated a pilot program to build several rental housing units and began to help residents become first-time home-buyers. PNOLA has been able to reduce homeowners' rebuilding costs through both volunteer labor and fundraising. It has repaired over 200 properties during its first five years, which, according to PNOLA estimates, saved property owners over $2 million in labor costs.[213]

PNOLA's success has made it the most visible and active organization in Lower Mid-City but it neither assumed a leadership role in the neighborhood's rebuilding nor formed a larger recovery effort with Tulane Canal NDC. Beyond repairing and building homes, PNOLA has participated in the planning processes and improvement efforts that affected the neighborhood, filling a void in the neighborhood's weak community organization. PNOLA also worked with Tulane Canal CDC to engage residents in the Lambert neighborhood planning process. They organized a group of 10 to 15 residents and business owners who met biweekly during summer 2006 to help prepare the Tulane-Gravier Neighborhood Plan. PNOLA also sought to connect residents to each other and to public officials, developers, and planners who could support rebuilding. Yet PNOLA's mission is to provide resources and connections for local residents to take action themselves, as opposed to playing a leadership or advocacy role itself, as Paul Ikemire explained in his description of PNOLA's role in Lower Mid-City:

A community resource organization has been our on-the-fence statement about who we are. We are not a neighborhood association. We are not a development corporation....We are not completely without opinion but we try to keep a pretty neutral resource-based approach.

In the first two years after Katrina, Lower Mid-City had two organizations helping homeowners rebuild, working to repopulate the neighborhood and representing the neighborhood in the ongoing planning process. But it lacked the level of neighborhood activism and organization found in other neighborhoods in which a large base of residents participated in planning and rebuilding efforts and provided a strong neighborhood political voice. This lack of political organization and influence was noteworthy as Lower Mid-City confronted new proposals to redevelop a large part of the neighborhood.

Old Style Urban Renewal in Lower Mid-City

After some rebuilding progress in 2006 and 2007, Lower Mid-City's future was put into question in late 2007 when plans were finalized to build two hospital complexes. These two new hospitals were proposed to replace the federal Veterans Affairs medical complex and state-run LSU/Charity Hospital, both of which were heavily damaged by flooding after Katrina, on a 70-acre site in the middle of Lower Mid-City. This site ran almost the entire length of the neighborhood, extending from Claiborne Avenue to Rocheblave Avenue—a distance that covers eight blocks of Lower Mid-City's ten-block footprint (see Figure 5.25). Along its other axis, the site occupied the heart of the neighborhood between Tulane Avenue and Canal Street, its two major commercial corridors. In total, the proposed hospitals encompassed 25 full city blocks and would demolish dozens of homes and commercial buildings.

Plans for the twin LSU/VA hospital development were reminiscent of the urban renewal projects undertaken in Tremé during much of the twentieth century. They involved the large-scale displacement of residents and businesses, in which decisions were made by government officials with little or no consultation with the impacted neighborhood or larger public. Together, the two hospital projects would displace over 500 Lower Mid-City residents and 56 businesses and nonprofit organizations (see Table 5.15). Since the hospital site was in a historic district, the redevelopment threatened to demolish many historic homes, as well as the Deutsches House German Cultural Center and a historic 1879 school building.[214] Although

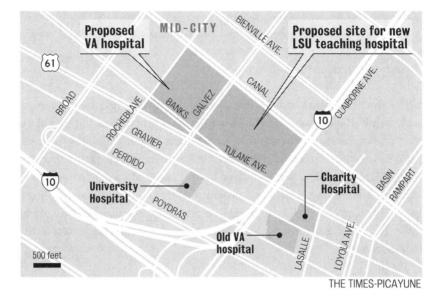

THE TIMES-PICAYUNE

Figure 5.25.
Sites for Veterans Affairs and LSU hospitals
Source: The Times–Picayune.

the Environmental Assessment for the VA project concluded that "given the small number of residents on the site in comparison with the total population of the City of New Orleans, the potential impacts to population would be minor,"[215] its effect on Lower-Mid-City would be large. The displaced residents represented 14 percent of the neighborhood's 2010 population and 28 percent of those living in the section between Tulane and St. Louis Avenues.

A top-down process was used to select the sites for the new medical centers, with little involvement of Lower Mid-City residents, especially in the

Table 5.15. DISPLACEMENT IMPACTS OF THE LSU/VA HOSPITALS

Type of Displacement	LSU University Medical Center	Veteran's Affairs Medical Center	Total
Housing units	125	140	265
Residents	176	331	507
Businesses and nonprofit groups	32	24	56

Source: Site-Specific Environmental Assessments for Veterans Affairs Medical Center (April 2010) and University Medical Center (July 2010)
[1] These figures are estimates presented in the two environmental assessment reports. The VA report counted commercial parcels while the LSU report listed displaced businesses. The stated number of parcels owned by businesses (24) was used as the estimate of displaced businesses for the VA project.

case of the VA Hospital. LSU started planning to replace Charity Hospital, which it viewed as an outdated facility, before Hurricane Katrina. A consultant had identified the 37 acres between Claiborne Avenue and Galvez Street as the recommended site for a new teaching hospital in 2005.[216] This location for the new LSU hospital was acknowledged in both the Lambert and UNOP plans, although it was not supported by neighborhood residents. The Tulane-Gravier Neighborhood Rebuilding Plan cited neighborhood opposition to the proposed LSU site "since it requires the wholesale removal of homes in the area."[217] It offered an alternative location, just southwest of LSU's proposed site, between Tulane and Poydras Streets, that the neighborhood preferred since it did not displace any residences[218] (see Figure 5.26). During summer 2006, several neighborhood residents met with the LSU Vice Chancellor to discuss alternative hospitals sites but left with the impression that the university was committed to the original site despite the required displacement of homes and businesses.[219]

While the LSU hospital site was the subject of public discussion as plans were finalized, the new site for the VA medical center was determined in private negotiations between the City of New Orleans and the federal government. After its medical center flooded, the federal Department of Veterans Affairs searched for a site to build a new hospital. Before Katrina, the VA and Charity hospitals were located next to each other and they sought to replicate this arrangement. In February 2006, the VA entered into an agreement with LSU to build a joint teaching hospital and trauma center in downtown New Orleans and began working with LSU with the intent of building both hospitals on the 37-acre site that LSU had identified.[220] This site was expected to house both hospitals in early 2007, when the UNOP plan was adopted, and the final District 4 UNOP Plan included it as the location for the joint LSU/VA Regional Medical Center.[221] Another UNOP recovery project listed in the District 4 Plan was revitalizing the Galvez commercial corridor as "the western face of the proposed LSU / VA Medical Center,"[222] which is further evidence that there was no discussion of locating the VA hospital on a new site across Galvez Street. However, the Department of Veterans Affairs (DVA) later decided that this site was too small to accommodate plans for both hospitals and announced that it would seek a new site in either New Orleans or neighboring Jefferson Parish.[223] Seeking to retain the VA hospital in New Orleans, city officials began negotiations with the DVA and offered to acquire 34 acres next to the LSU site to accommodate plans for the VA hospital. City officials had chosen the site by spring 2007 and entered into a cooperative endeavor agreement with the state of Louisiana on April 30 to acquire and prepare the site for the VA hospital.[224] As reported in *The Times–Picayune*, Recovery

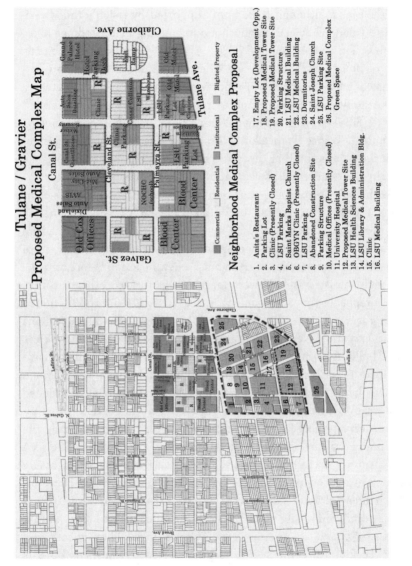

Tulane / Gravier
Proposed Medical Complex Map

Canal St.

Galvez St.

Claiborne Ave.

Tulane Ave.

Old Cox Offices | Dixieland Auto Sales | Mid-City Auto Sales | Water Board | Auto Sales Building | Grand Palace Hotel

Hotel | Parking Deck

R | NOCHC (school) | R | Canal St. Courthouse | Clinic Parking | Clinic | R | Soft Ramp

Blood Center | Blood Center | R | Palmyra St. | Cleveland St. | Caesar Collision | R | LSU Warehouse | Old Motel

R | R | Southern Recreation | LSU Parking Lot | LSU Electronics Clinic | LSU Parking Old Motel | Old Motel

Neighborhood Medical Complex Proposal

1. Anita's Restaurant
2. Parking Lot
3. Clinic (Presently Closed)
4. LSU Parking
5. Saint Marks Baptist Church
6. OBGYN Clinic (Presently Closed)
7. LSU Parking
8. Abandoned Construction Site
9. Parking Structure
10. Medical Offices (Presently Closed)
11. University Hospital
12. Proposed Medical Tower Site
13. LSU Health Sciences Building
14. LSU Library & Administration Bldg.
15. Clinic
16. LSU Medical Building

17. Empty Lot (Development Opp.)
18. Proposed Medical Tower Site
19. Proposed Medical Tower Site
20. Parking Structure
21. LSU Medical Building
22. LSU Medical Building
23. Dormitories
24. Saint Joseph Church
25. LSU Parking Site
26. Proposed Medical Complex
    Green Space

Commercial Residential Institutional Blighted Property

Figure 5.26.
Sites for new LSU teaching hospital from Tulane-Gravier Neighborhood Rebuilding Plan. Area outlined with a dashed line is the alternative site.
Source: Tulane / Gravier Neighborhood, Planning District 4 Rebuilding Plan.

Czar Ed Blakely indicated that "he, the mayor, City Council members and others unapologetically scrambled to offer the VA whatever was necessary for the agency to stay and build a new hospital."[225] City officials made their formal offer to Veterans Affairs in August 2007 and worked out a detailed Memorandum of Understanding, signed on November 19, 2007, in which the City agreed to acquire the entire 34-acre site, demolish all buildings and some water and sewer lines, and provide a construction-ready site to DVA.[226] To fund its commitment to prepare the VA site, New Orleans allocated over $75 million of federal recovery CDBG funds to the project[227]; the city was using almost 20 percent of this key federal recovery resource to retain a federal facility and, in effect, subsidize part of its replacement cost.

Lower Mid-City residents and businesses did not seem to factor into these negotiations and were not consulted during this process. They first learned that their neighborhood was the chosen site for the VA hospital when it was announced to the media,[228] as explained by former Lower Mid-City resident Bobbi Rogers:

We woke up one morning...opened the paper, read an article and found out that our neighborhood was slotted to be demolished for a hospital. That's exactly how everyone in the neighborhood found out. I remember looking at it thinking no, because we knew across Galvez they were talking about rebuilding Charity. I thought that was what they were talking about and was confused. They had a little map. I looked at the map and said "no that is wrong" and then I looked at the map again and thought wait a minute my house is right in the middle of this map. Then it all started sinking in.[229]

Despite their anger over the VA hospital announcement, sparked by the prospect of losing their homes and the disregard that public officials had shown by ignoring them as the decisions were made, Lower Mid-City residents did not organize the neighborhood to stop the project. Their first opportunity to discuss the project with city officials came in November 2007, the month when the city and DVA signed a Memorandum of Understanding setting out the terms for the land assembly and transfer, including a requirement for the city to pay penalties if it was late in preparing and transferring the site to the DVA.[230] Approximately twenty Lower Mid-City residents and business owners began to meet monthly to learn how the hospital development process would work and figure out how to respond. Opinions within the group, known as Lower Mid-City Residents and Businesses, were mixed, and they decided not to oppose the VA project but rather to work to ensure that the city, state, and DVA adhered to legal requirements and treated residents and property owners fairly.[231] During 2008, this group and others pushed for the city and DVA to consider an alternative site at the closed Lindy Boggs Medical Center, after Victory Real Estate withdrew its plans for a big box retail development. The Lindy Boggs site was rejected, as the DVA wanted to locate next to the LSU teaching hospital where it expected to gain financial savings and medical synergies.[232]

Two lawsuits challenged the legality of the process under which the hospital development occurred. The National Trust for Historic Preservation filed suit in May 2009 against the DVA and FEMA, seeking to stop the planned land acquisition and construction. The suit argued that the federal agencies were mistaken in finding that the project would produce "no significant impact" on the neighborhood, and should have ruled that a significant impact existed and undertaken more significant analysis of alternatives and options to reduce the impact.[233] US District Judge Eldon Fallon decided in March 2010 against the National Trust and allowed the project to proceed. He concluded that federal and state agencies had conducted sufficient environmental reviews and had taken appropriate action to reduce impacts on historic buildings.[234] A second lawsuit was filed in state court by four city residents, two of whom owned property within the hospital's footprint, arguing that the mayor violated the city charter and exceeded his authority by entering into the agreement with the VA without public notice and without City Council and City Planning Commission approval.[235] This lawsuit also failed to stop or alter the VA hospital project.

One outcome of the hospital projects was the slowing of rebuilding investments in Lower Mid-City. With the likelihood that their properties would soon be taken, businesses and property owners in the hospitals' footprint had no incentive to invest. For those near the site, the prospect of a long disruptive construction period was another disincentive for near-term reinvestment. Property owners in adjacent areas had reason to rethink their rebuilding plans since now they would be next to an institutional district with two large hospitals. They had an incentive for land speculation rather than rebuilding, since land values might rise as a result of further institutional expansion or businesses seeking to locate near the hospitals. Moreover, economic barriers to rebuilding were reinforced by city action to stop investment in the hospital footprint. On December 6, 2007, the city council passed a moratorium on new building, repair, or demolition permits within the 70-acre area that was now slated for government land-taking and demolition.[236] In addition to slowing rebuilding activity, the hospital projects eradicated private and public recovery investments made within the site during the two years after Katrina. These included over $3 million in Road Home grants provided to 41 homeowners to repair their properties.[237]

Once the federally mandated environmental and historic preservation review processes were completed, the legal challenges dismissed, and the public taking of properties well underway, construction to clear the VA hospital site was launched on June 25, 2010, with a groundbreaking attended by Veterans Affairs Secretary Eric Shinseki, Louisiana Governor Jindal, and the new mayor, Mitch Landrieu. At the event, Landrieu announced that the city would reallocate $3.2 million of the federal CDBG recovery funds budgeted to prepare the site to move and preserve historic homes in the hospital footprint. As part of the project's historic preservation review, a program was created to allow homeowners to elect to have their homes moved rather than demolished. Few homeowners elected this option and historic preservationists criticized the program as failing to preserve the large number of historic homes in Lower Mid-City.[238] Mayor Landrieu and several city councillors worked with the DVA and other organizations to find a way to move more historic homes to vacant lots owned by non-profit organizations elsewhere in Lower Mid-City and Tremé for restoration and sale to new buyers. Providence Community Housing identified a contractor that was experienced in moving historic homes—Builders of Hope—to complete this part of the project.[239] The additional CDBG funds were expected to permit 100 historic homes to be moved and avoid demolition. By fall 2010 the demolition and moving of buildings was in full swing (see Figure 5.27), and by March 2011 the first phase of the VA hospital urban renewal project was complete. A large vacant land site, shown in Figure 5.28, was all that remained of this section of Lower Mid-City.

The setbacks to Lower Mid-City that resulted from the LSU/VA hospital development are exemplified in the story of Bobbi Rogers and Kevin Krause. This couple came to New Orleans to volunteer in the rebuilding effort, bought and restored a home in Lower Mid-City, and then had their newly rebuilt home taken and demolished for the VA hospital site.[240] Rogers and Krause had sold their home in Phoenix to travel and change careers. In early 2006, they looked for volunteer opportunities in New Orleans and found information on PNOLA. After meeting with Paul Ikemire in Houston, they moved to New Orleans in early March and began volunteering with PNOLA to gut and repair homes. Their original plan was to stay for two months, but after six weeks, they decided to stay and buy a house, and then signed up for one-year AmeriCorps positions with PNOLA. Rogers and Krause were motivated by PNOLA's public service mission and the opportunity to build up its logistical capacity to manage volunteers and assist homeowners to gut their homes and move forward with home repairs. After the one-year

Figure 5.27.
Historic home on VA hospital site being prepared for relocation
Source: Photo by author.

stint with PNOLA working to rebuild homes and improve conditions in Lower Mid-City, Rogers and Krause left to focus on repairing the house they bought at 2316 Palmyra Street. They had been able to gut their home during the first year but found little time to repair it while working 60 to 80 hours per week at PNOLA. In the next year, with funds from a state historic preservation grant and a construction loan, Rogers and Krause began to restore their home. Midway through the process, they learned of the VA hospital plans. Since the work was well underway, they decided to complete the restoration and moved into their carefully restored home in March 2008. Over the next two years, they were in limbo waiting to find out what would happen to their home, while working with their neighbors to monitor the environmental and historical preservation review processes that preceded the land-taking and site preparation. Frequent news articles created the impression that the land-takings were imminent, but it was not until November 2009 when Rogers received the first official notice that her house would be acquired. Although she expected the process to move quickly at that point, nothing happened for almost six months; then she was contacted to have the appraisals done that would set the amount to be offered for her home. Rogers and Krauss received this offer in September

Figure 5.28.
Cleared VA hospital site viewed from Tulane Avenue facing Galvez Street and the LSU hospital site
Source: Photo by author.

2010. After waiting for close to two years, they were given 90 days to vacate their home. Unable to find a new home in such short notice, they prepared to leave New Orleans and move to Michigan. At the last minute, they found a house on South Clark Street in Mid-City, which allowed them to stay in New Orleans.

Lower Mid-City as Economic Development District

Lower Mid-City also fell within a state and regional economic development initiative, the Greater New Orleans Biosciences Economic Development District (GNOBEDD), which raised the prospect that another city and state initiative would take precedent over residents' goals in shaping the neighborhood's future. GNOBEDD, however, unfolded slowly and in a much different manner and with different goals than the hospital developments. Its mission extended beyond biomedical development projects to encompass "place-based development" aimed at improving the physical conditions and quality of life within its boundaries, while its CEO sought to involve local residents, businesses, and community-based organizations in formulating its plans. Although the district was in a planning phase during late 2010 with its agenda, funding, and capacity still up in the air, GNOBEDD was an emerging institution with the potential to link some of the city's major medical and educational institutions to the rebuilding and improvement of some of New Orleans poorest neighborhoods.

GNOBEDD was the latest iteration in a twenty-year project to use New Orleans' medical schools and hospitals to drive economic development in the biotechnology and health-related industries. These efforts began in 1991 when the legislature established the Louisiana Biomedical Research and Development Park to spur development of a research park to attract investment, businesses, jobs in medical research, and products and services. A comprehensive plan was completed and a nonprofit corporation formed to oversee the park, but these plans were never implemented.[241] Ten years later, new legislation reauthorized the research and development park and prompted a second comprehensive plan. No research park resulted from this second attempt, but it did contribute, along with other state initiatives, to establishing a Gene Therapy Research Consortium and a BioInnovation Center to incubate new biotechnology businesses.[242] In 2004, city and regional economic development leaders began working with local universities to create a new Biosciences District to supersede the earlier research park organization. These discussions generated the proposal to form GNOBEDD, with a far larger 2.4-square-mile geography that extended from downtown New Orleans to Xavier University, and with expanded powers to achieve its economic development goals. Legislation to create GNOBEDD was signed into law on July 12, 2005, seven weeks before Hurricane Katrina struck.[243]

In the aftermath of Katrina, GNOBEDD remained dormant for several years until a former real estate developer took up its cause. Two studies related to GNOBEDD were undertaken by the Regional Planning Commission in 2006 and 2008, but the district itself did not hold its first meeting until April 2008 and was without funding until 2009.[244] GNOBEDD has moved forward, in large part, through the efforts of its CEO James McNamara. McNamara, a former real estate developer, devoted himself to starting GNOBEDD with the goal of making it a vehicle to transform the city's economy from its dependence on low-paying jobs. He has served as GNOBEDD's first CEO, without pay, since 2008, and helped secure its first funding through a $2.4 million grant from the LRA. With the LRA grant, GNOBEDD hired consultants to prepare a master plan, a baseline economic analysis, and a study to recommend permanent revenue sources for the district. The master planning process started in 2010, and in contrast to the VA and LSU hospital projects, GNOBEDD has solicited community

participation to gain strong public and political support for the plan and
its initiatives:

> A good master plan is one that actually brings people together. A good master
> plan is one where citizens own the plan because if you do it from on high, then
> the next administration comes in before it is fully implemented, decides to put
> its imprimatur on it, it gets tossed out and nothing ever happens. If it is citi-
> zen- owned and community-owned, then it is more likely to be adhered to and
> transfer from one political term to another.[245]

Community participation in GNOBEDD's planning began by conducting
interviews with civic, neighborhood, and community leaders on a range
of issues. Next, it held a series of workshops for a larger group to provide
input on initial plans and findings from prior data analysis. Finally, five
design charrettes were held to address urban design and physical planning
issues, including where to locate additional green space,[246] preferred areas
for institutional expansion, and key community uses to preserve. This process revealed resident concerns about the extent of blighted properties and
their desire for basic services, such as schools, grocery stores, and parks, to
make a more complete neighborhood. McNamara thinks that GNOBEDD
can address some of these community goals by raising revenues to invest
in amenities such as parks, but he believes the best way for GNOBEDD to
improve the neighborhoods within its footprint is by creating bioscience
and health care jobs and building education and training pathways to connect residents to these higher paying jobs.

Despite its ambitious goals, the viability and impact of GNOBEDD was
an open question in late 2010. It needed sustained political support and
financial resources to implement its agenda and avoid repeating the fate
of prior medical district economic development initiatives. Even if it suc-
ceeds in this respect, significant political, policy, and operational changes
among city, community, civic, and health institutions will be needed for
GNOBEDD to move beyond the government and health care sector's economic development agenda to become a vehicle to improve neighborhoods
and expand economic opportunity for poor residents.

Lower Mid-City Five Years after Katrina

Lower Mid-City was the most transformed neighborhood along Broad Street
at the end of 2010. In a purely physical sense, a large section of homes and
commercial buildings were converted into vacant land awaiting development

of the new VA hospital. A second large hospital redevelopment would soon follow. Economically, Lower Mid-City was in transition from a mixed neighborhood of homes, businesses, and health care institutions into one that will be increasingly devoted to the city's major health care institutions. While it will retain residential areas, a school, and businesses along its main commercial streets, two-thirds of Lower Mid-City—the section riverside of Canal Street—will be dominated by hospitals and health-related educational institutions once the two hospitals are completed. Further changes that reinforce an institutionally-oriented district may occur if the hospitals attract new medical office buildings and research laboratories.

Assessing residential recovery in Lower Mid-City is difficult, as the 2010 Census predated the housing demolition and population relocation that occurred to prepare the VA hospital site. Census data indicates that Lower Mid-City was repopulating at a faster rate than New Orleans. It had regained 86 percent of its 2000 population and 77 percent of its occupied housing units by spring 2010 (see Table 5.16). However, the hospital projects reversed this trend. According to their Environment Impact Assessments, the two projects eliminated 265 housing units and displaced 507 residents. When Census figures are adjusted for these impacts, the repopulation rate drops to 74 percent and occupied housing units are at 67 percent of the 2000 level. These figures are close to the 2010 citywide averages of 71 percent and 76 percent, respectively.

Census figures indicate that Lower Mid-City's racial composition shifted with the post-Katrina recovery, and these changes are likely to persist after the hospital redevelopment. It experienced a fourfold increase in Hispanic residents, 5 percent growth in its white population and, as found in all other neighborhoods, a loss of black residents (see Table 5.17). However, Lower Mid-City's 79 percent black repopulation rate was higher than other

Table 5.16. CHANGE IN LOWER MID-CITY POPULATION AND HOUSING UNITS, 2000–2010

	2000	2010	Total Change 2000–2010	Percent Change 2000–2010	2010 Recovery Rate
Population	4,234	3,649	−585	−13.8%	86%
Total housing units	1,934	1,878	−56	−2.9%	97%
Occupied housing units	1,583	1,222	−361	−22.8%	77%
Vacant housing units	351	656	305	+86.9%	NA

Table 5.17. CHANGE IN LOWER MID-CITY POPULATION BY RACE,
2000 AND 2010

Race/Ethnicity	Percent 2000	Percent 2010	Total Change 2000–2010	Percent Change 2000–2010
White	14.2%	17.5%	33	5.5%
Black	78.8%	72.5%	–690	–20.7%
American Indian and Native Alaskan	0.3%	0.5%	6	50.0%
Asian	5.0%	3.7%	–78	–36.8%
Hispanic	2.5%	18.0%	315	291.7%

Source: 2000 and 2010 US Census

neighborhoods, which ranged from 38 percent in Tremé to 73 percent in Mid-City. Black repopulation had a marked geographic profile: it doubled in Census Tract 60 (between Banks Street and the Pontchartrain Expressway) and declined 50 percent in the northeastern (lakeside) Census Tract 49 (see Table 5.18 and Figure 5.29). This corresponds to a 33 percent increase in rental housing within Census Tract 60 that resulted from a new multi-family housing development, including the conversion of the Falstaff Brewery near Broad Street and Tulane Avenue into 147 apartments. As in Mid-City, new rental housing development, financed with federal LIHTC incentives, was an important factor in allowing black residents to return. Both neighborhoods had new large apartment developments and achieved the highest levels of black repopulation across all six neighborhoods. As would be expected, they also contributed to high renter repopulation rates in Lower Mid-City. At the time of the 2010 Census, renter-occupied housing units had reached 83 percent of the 2000 amount, while owner-occupied housing stood at 55 percent (see Table 5.19).

Table 5.18. CHANGE IN LOWER MID-CITY POPULATION
AND HOUSING BY CENSUS TRACT, 2000–2010[1]

	Tract 49	Tract 60
Total population	–1,157	572
White	112	–79
Black	–1,359	669
Hispanic	–341	117

Source: 2000 and 2010 US Census
[1] The census data have a slight difference between total population change and sum of changes between renters and owners.

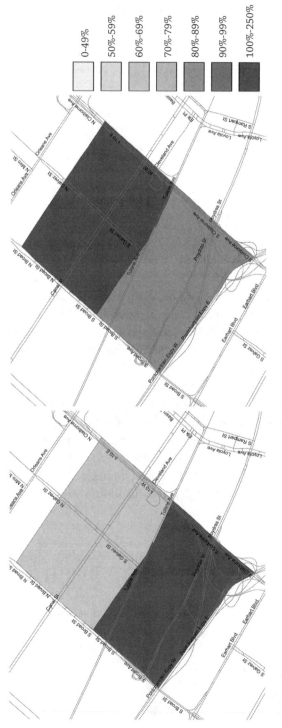

Figure 5.29.
Lower Mid-City African American (left) and white (right) repopulation rates by Census tract
Source: 2000 and 2010 US Census.

Table 5.19. SHARE AND CHANGES IN LOWER MID-CITY OWNER- AND
RENTER-OCCUPIED HOUSING UNITS, 2000 AND 2010

	Percent 2000	Percent 2010	Total Change 2000–2010	2010 Recovery Rate
Owner-occupied	19.3%	13.7%	–137	55%
Renter-occupied	80.7%	86.3%	–224	83%

Source: 2000 and 2010 US Census

Grassroots rebuilding in Lower Mid-City was more limited in scope
and did not generate the level of participation and influence achieved in
other neighborhoods. PNOLA and TCNDC primarily focused on repairing homes and building new ones. These efforts contributed to the neighborhood's recovery by helping to retain homeowners, addressing blighted
and abandoned properties, and supplying affordable housing for low- and
moderate-income families. However, with limited resident involvement and
resources, they did not spearhead efforts to create charter schools, build
libraries, and repair or add parks and playgrounds, as occurred in other
neighborhoods. While both groups provided a voice for local residents and
supported community organizing efforts after Katrina, a strong neighborhood organization did not emerge. Efforts to build a neighborhood identity
and social capital among residents who worked together to rebuild homes
were set back when many of these residents, like Bobbi Rogers and Kevin
Krause, were displaced by the VA hospital project.

Lower Mid-City was no longer a forgotten neighborhood in 2010. It was
now at the nexus of major plans for New Orleans' future: the focal point
for city, state, and federal plans to rebuild two hospitals with new and large
facilities and at the center of a new biosciences district designed to advance
a state and regional biomedical economic development strategy. Unlike
other New Orleans neighborhoods, in which a grassroots vision and activism defined recovery priorities, much of Lower Mid-City will be rebuilt by
the city and state in the service of regional heath care and economic development goals. Moreover, these projects are disconnected from residents
and the neighborhood's community-based organizations. Like Tremé in
past decades, city and civic urban renewal plans have displaced hundreds of
residents and numerous businesses and are transforming a neighborhood
with little consideration of residents' desires and needs, and with little
effort, thus far through the demolition phase, to link the benefits of these
large public investments to the many low- and moderate-income residents
of the adjacent neighborhoods.

VARIATIONS IN REBUILDING

As the four narratives show, these Broad Street neighborhoods had quite different rebuilding experiences after Hurricane Katrina. Table 5.20 summarizes the differences in population and occupied housing recovery, comparing 2010 and 2000 Census counts. Faubourg St. John recovered fairly quickly, particularly among homeowners who returned, rebuilt, and worked with their neighborhood association to implement a range of improvement projects. Its activists looked beyond their neighborhood to help launch initiatives to bring new parks, better schools, and a stronger economy to a larger geographic area. By 2010, 81 percent of its housing was reoccupied but with more white residents, a larger share of homeowners and far fewer black inhabitants. In Mid-City, community members joined with the Mid-City Neighborhood Organization to prepare their own neighborhood plan to guide rebuilding. From this plan, they worked with city government, private investors, and others to complete priority rebuilding projects that added new services and amenities. Mid-City also attracted new private development, which contributed to rebuilding the neighborhood, especially by adding new rental apartments, and brought changes to its population and business mix. With new housing development and homeowner activism, Mid-City achieved the highest recovery rates for both population and housing units. Large-scale rental development resulted in a higher recovery rate for rental housing than for homeowners and helped Mid-City

Table 5.20. FOUR NEIGHBORHOODS' 2010 POPULATION AND HOUSING RECOVERY RATES

Recovery Measure	Faubourg St. John	Mid-City	Tremé	Lower Mid-City (before hospital demolitions)	Lower Mid-City (after hospital demolitions)
Total repopulation	73%	84%	47%	86%	74%
White repopulation	117%	96%	173%	105%	Unknown
Black repopulation	53%	73%	38%	79%	Unknown
Recovery: All occupied housing units	81%	90%	56%	77%	67%
Recovery: Owner-occupied units	96%	78%	88%	55%	Unknown
Recovery: Renter-occupied units	73%	95%	47%	83%	Unknown

Note: Rates compare 2010 to 2000 US Census population and occupied housing counts retain a large black population and lower racial disparities in repopulation. Recovery in Tremé has been slower and more complex than in Faubourg St. John, Lower Mid-City, and Mid-City. Disjointed grassroots efforts have brought physical, cultural, and educational improvements, but they did not actively work to increase repopulation and the range of services and improvements needed to rebuild a complete neighborhood. Investment by new higher-income residents and outside aid helped to rebuild 88 percent of Tremé's owner-occupied housing, but less than 50 percent of its rental housing has returned. Consequently, it had regained only 47 percent of its 2000 repopulation and saw the number of its black residents drop by almost two-thirds. Tremé's recovery, echoing its past, was being shaped by large-scale urban renewal, through the Lafitte Public Housing Redevelopment, although this time driven by federal policies. Grassroots rebuilding was modest in its scope and impact in Lower Mid-City, largely focused on owner-occupied housing. Like neighboring Mid-City, it attracted new rental housing development, supported by GO Zone LIHTC incentives, and realized relatively high black repopulation rates. However, two major hospital projects reversed residential rebuilding and will shape the neighborhood's future development.

Each neighborhood followed a different path and realized different results shaped by the leadership and resources within the community but also influenced by government recovery policies, pre-Katrina conditions, and intersections between other agendas and grassroots rebuilding. None of these neighborhoods marshaled residents and resources to advance a shared rebuilding vision on the scale of Broadmoor and Village de L'Est. However, their diverse experiences reveal the complex factors that shaped neighborhood recovery.

Community Capital

Community-level resources and responses were critical to spurring rebuilding. Of particular importance was the presence of a core of homeowners who were committed to rebuilding and their ability to unite around common rebuilding goals. Faubourg St. John and Mid-City, the two neighborhoods with the largest concentration of homeowners, experienced high rates of housing recovery and greater success in advancing neighborhood rebuilding projects, including parks, gardens, and schools. Homeowners had a home they could return to, however badly damaged, and a financial stake in rebuilding this asset. With the decision to return, they had an interest in restoring nearby homes and ensuring that key facilities and services returned to make their neighborhood a good place to live. A large base of homeowners meant that more people were likely to return sooner; they also tended to live closer together to help each other and see evidence of rebuilding progress, and to provide a critical mass of residents to assume leadership roles and address rebuilding issues on a neighborhood scale. Much of the leadership, initiative, and labor for early neighborhood planning and improvement efforts across neighborhoods came from homeowners who returned in the first year after Katrina. Lower Mid-City and Tremé had fewer homeowners, and they tended to have lower incomes and fewer financial resources to rebuild. This slowed the number and pace at which residents returned and limited the human resources to tackle neighborhood scale needs. Lower Mid-City had the least success in this respect, as noted by one activist:

> Since there were very few people in the neighborhood and you didn't know whether they'd ever return [or] where they were, and [additionally] when people were just trying to survive, it was difficult to do much organizing.

Despite the efforts of PNOLA, St. Joseph's church and TCNDC, no sizable base of pre-Katrina homeowners emerged to provide the breadth of leadership and activism for rebuilding that was so central to the other neighborhoods.

Rebuilding progress also depended on the ability to coalesce around common goals and develop a strong voice for their neighborhood. Residents in Mid-City and Faubourg St. John rallied around their preexisting neighborhood association as the foundation for rebuilding, even those who had misgivings about their past leadership and priorities. Activists used these associations to organize residents to take on short-term projects, initiate neighborhood planning, advocate for city services and community facilities, and work to align private development with their plans and goals. Some of these activities occurred in Lower Mid-City and Tremé but did not reach the same scale and impact as in the other two neighborhoods due to weaker and divided grassroots organizations. Tremé had considerable activism but it was split among several organizations with separate priorities and different views of what constituted their neighborhood. These divisions limited the human resources that each organization could draw on and their political influence. With multiple groups and agendas, no organization tackled neighborhood-wide rebuilding—creating a neighborhood plan and working to reestablish and improve a broad range of neighborhood services. Instead, they worked on improvements (or opposing development) in a targeted area and focused on particular issues, such as crime, culture, and education. Rebuilding efforts in Lower Mid-City were less divided but PNOLA and TCNDC worked fairly independently after preparation of the Lambert neighborhood plan. Moreover, without a large resident base and limited resources, both organizations focused on repairing and building housing rather than a more comprehensive neighborhood rebuilding and improvement agenda.

Federal Recovery Policies

The design and administration of federal recovery aid was a ubiquitous influence on rebuilding throughout New Orleans, as discussed in chapter 2. It slowed the restoration of public infrastructure and facilities and shaped where and what type of housing was rebuilt. Although FEMA aid and Louisiana's allocation of CDBG funds favored the rebuilding of owner-occupied housing, federal policies had a much different impact in Mid-City and Lower Mid-City. LIHTC provided as part of the GO Zone recovery tax incentives contributed to hundreds of units of new rental housing. As a result these two neighborhoods achieved much higher recovery rates and repopulation of black residents through April 2010 than the other Broad Street neighborhoods, as well as Broadmoor and Village de L'Est.

Prior Conditions

Prestorm conditions also affected neighborhood recovery. As noted, socioeconomic conditions shaped rebuilding progress through the extent of homeownership and the financial resources that residents could marshal to rebuild, which in turn influenced who could return and how quickly they began to rebuild. Tremé and Lower Mid-City, as lower-income neighborhoods, had to overcome two critical barriers that impaired residential rebuilding—the supply of rental housing and households' limited financial resources. Housing in these less affluent neighborhoods, even among homeowners, tended to be in worse condition from deferred maintenance and repairs, further adding to the financial burden of rebuilding. Moreover, since economic status and race were intertwined, with poverty rates among blacks three times those for white residents, black New Orleanians faced greater barriers to returning and their population declined significantly across all four neighborhoods. In addition to economic factors, how each neighborhood responded after Katrina was prefigured by community civic capacity before Katrina. In the years before the storm, Lower Mid-City had

limited community organization, without an active neighborhood association, and thus lacked an established organization and leadership to drive
grassroots rebuilding. Organizational divisions within Tremé existed well
before 2005 and posed a challenge to creating a unified recovery effort.
Mid-City and Faubourg St. John each had a long-standing neighborhood
association with established political relationships and no major competing organizations, which facilitated their emergence as the rallying points
for grassroots rebuilding.

Geography

Geography influenced rebuilding through both the extent of flood damage and how each neighborhood's location attracted new development.
Although flood damage affected the cost and scope of investment needed
to rebuild, it proved a less critical determinant of recovery progress across
these four neighborhoods than other factors. This is seen in the different
recovery results for neighborhoods with similar flooding. Faubourg St John
and Tremé are both higher elevation areas that experienced limited flooding but the former recovered more quickly and broadly. Similarly, Mid-City
and Lower Mid-City both had widespread flood depths of 6 feet or higher.
Yet Mid-City, despite being more severely flooded, achieved greater rebuilding progress, including higher repopulation and housing recovery rates.

Geography exerted a powerful influence on rebuilding by attracting
new development interest and agendas. Three of the four neighborhoods
attracted new public and private sector development that will reshape their
development in significant ways. Neighborhood location, existing development and land use, and physical features were important in how and where
these rebuilding projects unfolded. The most far-reaching example is how
the new LSU and VA hospitals are altering Lower Mid-City. Government
decisions set the location of these projects but the neighborhood's existing
medical uses and proximity to downtown made Lower Mid-City an attractive place to site them. These advantages also attracted new affordable
multifamily housing to Lower Mid-City, which helped the neighborhood
repopulate, in particular to regain renter and black households. Tremé's
location adjacent to the French Quarter and downtown New Orleans, combined with its historic building stock, has drawn significant investor interest in restoring existing housing and some new development. This private
investment, which began before Katrina, is altering the neighborhood's
demographics, accelerated by the displacement impacts of Katrina. As the
home of the Lafitte housing development, HUD's decisions to demolish and

rebuild this large project has had the greatest impact on Tremé. At first it prevented the return of hundreds of low-income households, and its redevelopment has altered the neighborhood's physical fabric. Once completed and occupied by a planned 1,500 households, it will exert a major influence on the neighborhoods' economic, social, and cultural character. Mid-City has been less affected by large public projects but attracted considerable private investment along its main corridors to reuse properties left vacant after the storm. This investment accelerated repopulation and affected who lives in Mid-City by adding hundreds of new apartments, while increasing the number and diversity of businesses. With the reuse of the Lindy Boggs Medical Center underway, private investment also will bring a new nursing home and restored health services to Mid-City.

NEGOTIATING AGENDAS

A theme in all four neighborhoods was the opportunity for change with post-Katrina rebuilding needs and plans. The scale of destruction and widespread planning led to a reconsideration of where to locate and how to organize different services, institutions, and types of development. In this manner, Katrina was a transformative event that generated myriad opportunities and agendas for change. However, without a feasible city recovery plan that had broad political and civic support and lacking strong public sector leadership, neighborhood rebuilding emerged from a jumble of rebuilding agendas. Grassroots neighborhood groups established agendas to improve their communities through better schools, more parks and recreational activities, new stores and services, the reuse of abandoned and blighted properties, and, in some cases, better jobs and expanded economic opportunities for residents. Large institutions had plans for new, expanded, or consolidated facilities, as did many government agencies. Private and nonprofit developers proposed new development projects that were now feasible with incentives, federal funds, and other opportunities created after Katrina. Political and civic leaders had their own views on the most critical rebuilding projects for New Orleans, as well as plans to expand the tax base and leave their mark on the city's future.

The Broad Street neighborhoods, with their central location and major transportation corridors, often found themselves at the crossroads of competing plans and agendas. In these neighborhoods, to a far greater extent than in Broadmoor and Village de L'Est, a key part of the rebuilding process for neighborhood groups involved negotiating the competing agendas and projects that existed for their neighborhoods. Recovery results in these four neighborhoods depended on the effectiveness of grassroots organizations and other community members in shaping or stopping the rebuilding designs that other parties had for their neighborhood. Mid-City has been especially attentive to this challenge, beginning with Victory Real Estate's early proposal for a large retail development. MCNO provided a strong voice on development proposals, aided by the authority of a broadly supported neighborhood plan and its ability to mobilize community support. Although a shared vision and unified voice are important factors in a neighborhood's impact on proposed development projects, the power, values, and interests of the parties that control development can overshadow these factors, as occurred in the Lafitte and the VA hospital projects. New Orleans' political leaders viewed retaining the VA hospital as critical to the city's economy and decided, with state and federal officials, where and how to redevelop it without real opportunities for neighborhood input. Even if Lower Mid-City possessed the strong community voice and organization found in Mid-City, its capacity to reverse the decision was constrained by the strong intent by state and city political leaders to advance the project. Lafitte is more complex. On the one hand, HUD decided to close, demolish, and rebuild the development with little opportunity to alter this plan. On the other hand, HUD selected a nonprofit developer that valued community participation, sought to preserve the number of low-income units, and viewed the project as a means to more far-reaching neighborhood improvement. Consequently, there were more opportunities for residents and community organizations to influence the project within the demolition and redevelopment framework, and a willingness to use the Lafitte redevelopment to advance broader neighborhood goals such as expanded social services, resident employment, and removing blight.

THE EMERGENCE OF MULTINEIGHBORHOOD INITIATIVES

One aspect of neighborhood rebuilding within the Broad Street neighborhoods has been the emergence of multiple initiatives that span several neighborhoods. These initiatives are a promising development in the rebuilding process: they offer the potential to implement projects and address needs that transcend a single neighborhood. Despite the desire to build a complete neighborhood, some facilities and services cannot be feasibly addressed in each neighborhood. Health clinics, supermarkets, large retail districts, and major parks are examples of facilities that often need to serve several neighborhoods. Multineighborhood organizations, networks, and alliances can provide a mechanism to plan, negotiate, and implement such projects. Similarly, economic development and employ-ment initiatives often have to span several neighborhoods to connect residents in areas with limited or low-paying jobs to better opportunities in other parts of the city. Several initiatives discussed in this chapter are undertaking such projects that require action on a multineighborhood scale. The Lafitte Greenway project is building a new linear park and rec-reation area that traverses Tremé, Lower Mid-City and Mid-City. Broad Community Connections draws on groups from all four neighborhoods to revitalize Broad Street as a shared commercial center and community asset and is working to attract a supermarket that will serve several neigh-borhoods. Although the Greater New Orleans Biomedical Development District is by no means a community-based effort, it aspires to expand economic opportunity for residents and improve conditions in a large area that includes Lower Mid-City and Mid-City. A fourth initiative is the New City Neighborhood Partnership. This network convenes the leaders of over fifty organizations and funders undertaking projects in Tremé and Lower Mid-City to support each other's work and broaden their impact.[247] One of its first projects was commissioning a study on the feasibility of remov-ing part of the I-10 highway that bisects Tremé—the 1960s project that removed a vital community gathering place and green space while trigger-ing the decline on the Claiborne Avenue commercial district. The study, released in July 2010, concluded that replacing the overhead highway with an urban boulevard would provide sufficient transportation capacity and stimulate new commercial and cultural activity.[248] Based on this study, New Orleans received a $2 million federal grant to conduct a more detailed engi-neering study of this proposal.[249]

Although still fledgling, these multineighborhood initiatives offer promise to bring important changes to New Orleans' community devel-opment landscape. They can fill gaps in the capacity to plan, advocate for, and undertake district scale projects that service multiple neighborhoods. In uniting organizations across neighborhoods, they also provide a means to overcome past differences and build a stronger political voice for these neighborhoods, particularly the less influential low-income communities, to attract more government, civic, and philanthropic resources, and reduce the likelihood that future urban renewal projects will demolish and dis-place major sections of any neighborhood.

CHAPTER 6

✧

Neighborhoods and City Rebuilding

At the end of 2010, more than five years after Katrina and the flood
control system failures that decimated much of New Orleans, the
city's rebuilding was a work in progress with disparate results. Perhaps
the most telling statistic on New Orleans' progress was the population
count from the 2010 Census: New Orleans' population stood at 343,829,
71 percent of its 2000 level and 76 percent of the estimated population
just prior to Katrina.[1] Eighteen of the city's seventy-two neighborhoods
had regained over 90 percent of their 2000 population, while an almost
equal number (sixteen) had less than 60 percent of their population back.[2]
Uneven recovery is evident in the narratives of the six neighborhoods.
Broadmoor, Faubourg St. John, and Mid-City had rebuilt relatively quickly
and realized neighborhood improvement goals. Less than half of Tremé's
population had returned by 2010 and large sections of Lower Mid-City had
been demolished for new hospital development. For all six neighborhoods,
recovery was quite different across racial groups and between homeowners
and renters. Village de L'Est exemplifies these large disparities: repopulation reached 75 percent for Vietnamese American residents but 48 percent
for blacks; 85 percent of owner-occupied homes were back but only 44 percent of rental units were reoccupied.

Across this varied canvas, there were clear signs of progress. Economic
life had returned to New Orleans' central business district and tourism
economy. Major improvements to the flood control system were completed. New housing developments, schools, and health clinics had been
constructed. Yet major rebuilding challenges remained. Many poorer and

heavily flooded neighborhoods were only partially rebuilt. Widespread abandoned and blighted properties existed in many neighborhoods, even those with strong progress in rebuilding, such as Broadmoor and Mid-City. Important government and public facilities had still not been repaired or replaced, as evidenced by the large share of rebuilding funds that remained unspent.

Rebuilding a city after the scale of damage incurred by New Orleans is a long-term project in any circumstances and was particularly challenging given the city's economic, social, and political conditions in 2005. In their introduction to the 1977 comparative study of disaster recovery, *Reconstruction Following Disaster,* Kates and Pijawka presented a four-stage recovery model: (1) the emergency period of coping with and addressing the dead, injured, and large number of displaced and homeless persons; (2) the restoration period in which key public utilities, infrastructure, and buildings are restored and typical social and economic activities return; (3) the replacement–reconstruction period when the city rebuilds its capital stock to predisaster levels and regains its prior level of social and economic life; and (4) the commemorative, betterment, and developmental reconstruction period that focuses on memorializing the disaster and improving the city and preparing it for future development. In a later article, Kates et al. reported that the physical rebuilding of a city, its replacement-reconstruction phase, takes eight to eleven years.[3] Based on this standard, the rebuilding of New Orleans' neighborhoods at the five-year mark, as indicated by repopulation and housing restoration at close to 75 percent, appears to have progressed well and at a much faster rate than the reconstruction of infrastructure and major public facilities, as indicated by the rate of spending for CDBG recovery projects (36 percent) and the long delays in resolving FEMA PA funding for many facilities.

The progress in neighborhood rebuilding occurred in the context of a problematic official disaster recovery process. Multiple planning efforts delayed the creation of a citywide recovery plan to guide the investment for federal recovery aid and reduce uncertainty for residents, property owners, and businesses in making rebuilding decisions. Federal recovery assistance to both private parties and governments was slow to arrive, unpredictable, and poorly managed. Moreover, policies and rules meant that federal aid often did not match local rebuilding needs. The city government, hampered by state and federal bureaucracy and its own lack of implementation capacity, was either stymied or long-delayed in moving forward with many announced rebuilding programs, initiatives, and projects. The Soft Second Loan Program is a case in point. First proposed in May 2008, it was still not in place three years later. Moreover, there was no shared actionable civic

strategy to draw upon and align the collective resources among government, major businesses and institutions, the philanthropic community, and
grassroots organizations to advance rebuilding. In the absence of effective
leadership and governance of the city's recovery, grassroots organizations
worked to rebuild without effective governmental partners and supporting
civic infrastructure. These conditions magnified the importance and contribution of community-based initiatives to the city's rebuilding. However,
the fact that New Orleans firms, residents, and neighborhood organizations had to work around or compensate for poorly functioning government and civic institutions made their work more challenging and likely
slowed the recovery process. Better designed and executed federal policies,
a well-functioning city government, and a more collaborative rebuilding
process between the "grassroots" and "grasstops" would have served the
city much better.

The rebuilding experience across the six New Orleans neighborhoods
documented in the previous chapters provides insights into how grassroots
and neighborhood-scale rebuilding advances the postdisaster recovery of
a city and the value of achieving greater alignment between the work of
grassroots organizations and official government agencies. This final chapter synthesizes these insights and lessons on three issues: (1) the potential
contribution of community-based initiatives to rebuilding and the scope of
activities that neighborhood rebuilding can embrace; (2) how to undertake
grassroots rebuilding, particularly when strong staff-based community
organizations do not exist; and (3) the relationship between neighborhood
scale and citywide recovery and suggestions for coordinating and gaining
greater synergy between investments at both the neighborhood and citywide scales. The chapter first summarizes the contributions of grassroots
organizations to rebuilding New Orleans, arguing that their contribution
and the scope of neighborhood rebuilding have four essential components:
repopulation, creating more complete neighborhoods, economic development, and building civic capacity. This discussion then critically examines
the strengths and gaps in recovery efforts for each component. A second
section presents a simple framework for undertaking grassroots rebuilding in cities like New Orleans, where grassroots capacity is largely based
on volunteer organizations rather than on staff-based community development organizations. Since a city's recovery occurs on multiple scales, in
the conclusion's third section, the interrelationship between individual,
neighborhood- and city-scale rebuilding is considered, drawing on the positive and negative aspects of New Orleans' experience. I present a view of
city rebuilding that emphasizes the collective nature of rebuilding, leveraging grassroots initiatives, and using complete neighborhoods as a principle

to guide some citywide rebuilding decisions. I also argue for a "dual collab-orative" process to coordinate recovery investments across city functions and between sections of the city. Finally, in this chapter, I offer several pro-posals to address shortcomings in federal disaster recovery policies and to better align them with a more effective city rebuilding process that lever-ages grassroots initiative and capacities.

Although this book's purpose is to elucidate the major components of neighborhood rebuilding and their contribution to citywide recovery and not to explain varied outcomes across neighborhoods, a summary of the four critical factors that influenced rebuilding across the six neighbor-hoods is provided below. This section builds on the discussion at the end of chapter 5 to include Broadmoor and Village de L'Est and elaborates on the impact of government policies. It is exploratory in nature[4] and intended to aid other researchers in developing theories and hypothesis regarding post-disaster recovery. Further research and analysis across far more neighbor-hoods is needed to verify their importance and to better understand their dimensions, influence, and interaction.

FACTORS SHAPING NEIGHBORHOOD RECOVERY

Four broad factors influenced the rebuilding trajectory across the six neighborhoods: (1) pre-Katrina conditions; (2) geography; (3) government policies and decisions; and (4) neighborhoods' responses to rebuilding. No single factor determined the pace and nature of recovery; rather, multiple factors interacted to shape the rebuilding process and results. However, the first two factors are givens that cannot be changed, while the latter two fac-tors represent the social action taken to shape how neighborhoods rebuild. Consequently, the emphasis of this concluding chapter is on lessons and proposals in these two realms.

Pre-Katrina Conditions

Each neighborhood's circumstances before the storm and ensuing flooding influenced recovery in several ways. First, the level of income and poverty affected residents' ability to secure resources to return, including financial resources and a social network and support to help overcome rebuilding barriers.[5] A second important condition, closely associated with income and poverty levels, was the nature of its housing stock and the extent of homeownership. Higher income neighborhoods had a larger share of

Table 6.1. 2000 HOMEOWNERSHIP RATES AND 2010 RECOVERY
INDICATORS FOR SIX NEIGHBORHOODS

Neighborhood	2000 Homeownership Rate	2010 Repopulation Rate	2010 Housing Occupancy Rate
Broadmoor	48%	74%	69%
Village de L'Est	47%	62%	85%
Faubourg St. John	35%	73%	81%
Mid-City	28%	84%	90%
Tremé	22%	47%	56%
Lower Mid-City	19%	74%	67%

homeowners, which exerted a strong influence on recovery. As noted in chapter 5, homeowners were able to return more readily to start rebuilding, and returning homeowners often provided the leadership and volunteer core for communitywide grassroots rebuilding. Among the six neighborhoods, the four with the highest homeownership levels in 2000 achieved the greatest housing occupancy rates in 2010. Three also had the highest repopulation rates (see Table 6.1). A third influential prestorm condition was neighborhood organization and civic capacity, which affected the effectiveness of the neighborhood rebuilding response. In Lower Mid-City and Tremé, weaker and more fragmented community organization slowed recovery efforts while the other four neighborhoods benefited from established civic associations or strong church-based communities that provided the foundation for postdisaster grassroots rebuilding capacity.

Geography

Neighborhood geography shaped recovery in two ways. First, geography determined the level of flooding and thus the extent of damage to address. Flooding and property damage were the greatest in low-lying neighborhoods that had primarily been built later in the city's history, after the introduction of extensive drainage systems. At the extreme, this geographic factor had a powerful impact on recovery: many neighborhoods located on the city's high ground along the Mississippi River did not flood and recovered quickly, while heavily flooded areas such as the Lower Ninth Ward and New Orleans East had the city's lowest repopulation rates in 2010. Extensive flooding affected the loss of housing and slow repopulation rate in Village de L'Est and rebuilding in Broadmoor's eastern Area B. However, elevation and flooding were not always the primary determinants of rebuilding progress, since neighborhoods with comparable flood levels had very different outcomes. Broadmoor, despite its low elevation and widespread flood depths of 7 to 8 feet, repopulated at a faster rate than New Orleans overall, aided by favorable preexisting conditions and a strong neighborhood response. Despite Tremé's high elevation and limited flooding, it had the lowest repopulation rate across the six neighborhoods. Pre-Katrina conditions and government policies slowed rebuilding in Tremé, overwhelming the advantages of its higher elevation.

A second geographic influence was proximity to the city center and medical district: neighborhoods adjacent to these areas attracted public- and private-sector projects with a large impact on both the pace of recovery and form of rebuilding. Mid-City and Lower Mid-City attracted considerable new private multifamily rental housing that aided in repopulation, particularly for renters and black residents. These neighborhoods had the highest 2010 repopulation rates for renters (95 percent and 83 percent, respectively) and blacks (73 percent[6]) among the six neighborhoods. As discussed in chapter Five, the location of Lower Mid-City and Tremé contributed to the targeting of these neighborhoods for large-scale public-sector projects (the VA/LSU hospitals and Lafitte public housing redevelopment) that arguably have been the largest single factor in their post-Katrina rebuilding. In both cases, government policy and geography interacted to produce these results. On the other hand, rebuilding in the more remote neighborhoods of Broadmoor and Village de L'Est were not significantly affected by either new private development or large public-sector projects.

Government Disaster Recovery Policies and Decisions

Government policies and actions were a major influence on neighborhood recovery. These public policy impacts were shaped by four key processes: (1) federal disaster recovery policies and state government allocation of federal aid; (2) how recovery aid was administered and delivered; (3) the city's planning, coordination, and implementation of recovery efforts; and (4) specific government decisions around key projects and facilities. The broad impacts of the first three processes were discussed in chapter 2:

- Most recovery aid to private parties was used to restore owner-occupied housing with quite limited funding ($411 million) provided to New Orleans to implement its own recovery plans.
- The large provision of tax incentives favored larger-scale development and was difficult to utilize in New Orleans, especially following the global financial crisis.

- Poor management, extensive regulations, multiple layers of government bureaucracy, and financial barriers delayed and complicated the delivery of federal aid to governments and private parties.
- The multiple planning processes, absence of a grounded and feasible city recovery plan, and weak city government capacity to coordinate and implement rebuilding projects and programs added uncertainty to the recovery process and contributed to the slow pace of rebuilding investments.

These effects are observable across the six neighborhoods, but with variations that show the influence of other rebuilding factors. The emphasis on recovery aid to homeowners contributed to the larger repopulation and housing occupancy rates in neighborhoods with higher homeownership rates and the lower repopulation rates among rental households in Faubourg St. John and Village de L'Est. GO Zone housing tax credits facilitated the building of hundreds of new apartments in Lower Mid-City and Mid-City, increasing repopulation rates for renter and black household in these neighborhoods. They also funded a large part of the Lafitte redevelopment but did not contribute to rental housing recovery in the other three neighborhoods. All neighborhoods struggled with the slow pace in restoring public infrastructure and facilities and the barriers that residents and businesses faced in accessing recovery aid. Consequently, many grassroots efforts focused on accelerating public projects and overcoming barriers and limitations in recovery aid and influenced these outcomes. Residents and neighborhood associations initiated restoration projects in some cases: Alcee Fortier Park (Faubourg St. John), Keller Library (Broadmoor), and charter school projects in five neighborhoods. Advocacy efforts changed or accelerated public facility projects in Broadmoor, Mid-City, and Tremé. In Village de L'Est and Broadmoor, community groups addressed problems with business and homeowner recovery aid through case management services and partnerships to deliver supplementary aid. In all these cases, grassroots groups encountered a fragmented public sector recovery system in which they had to figure out and work separately with various bureaucracies to get individual projects and programs implemented.

Government decisions on how and where to rebuild specific projects had a major impact on two neighborhoods. The Housing Authority of New Orleans' (HANO) decision to close all public housing for many months and then to demolish and redevelop the Lafitte public housing complex shaped the pace and composition of repopulation in Tremé, while altering part of the neighborhood's physical character. Federal, state, and local government decisions converged to site the reconstruction of the VA and LSU hospitals in Lower Mid-City, displacing many residents and businesses and fundamentally transforming a large section of the neighborhood.

Given the importance of government policies and processes to postdisaster recovery, a large part of the discussion in this chapter concerns proposals to improve the impact of public policies on the rebuilding process. These proposals encompass expanded aid to rebuild rental housing, ways to better coordinate city recovery planning and investment, and changes in federal recovery policies to reduce regulatory and administrative barriers and support grassroots recovery.

Neighborhood Rebuilding Response

Community members shaped their neighborhood's recovery through their collective response to the rebuilding challenges after Katrina. While individual household, business, and property owner decisions were clearly an important part of the neighborhood response, these factors capture the collective organized response by community stakeholders to advance rebuilding. One aspect of a neighborhood's response was the rebuilding agenda pursued by grassroots organizations. Differences in recovery priorities across the six neighborhoods accounted for some variation in rebuilding outcomes: the focus on homeowner rebuilding in Broadmoor and Village de L'Est contributed to their repopulation outcomes; libraries were early priorities and ultimately successes in Mid-City and Broadmoor; the early attention to small business recovery and growth by MQVN Church and CDC helped restore and improve the community's stores and commercial centers. The next section addresses neighborhood recovery agendas and variations across the six neighborhoods in greater detail.

The effectiveness of a neighborhood's response played a far greater role in rebuilding outcomes than the recovery agenda itself. Effectiveness refers to the ability of grassroots organizations to implement projects and initiatives that contribute to repopulating their neighborhood and advancing other rebuilding priorities. It resulted from the neighborhood's leadership and civic capacity, success in forming partnerships to attract outside resources, and advocacy to shape public and private investments. Broadmoor and Village de L'Est benefitted from strong leaders who united a large part of their neighborhood behind shared goals and mobilized community resources to advance these goals. In these two neighborhoods, new CDCs also were created to expand the capacity to undertake rebuilding. Strong leadership and greater organizational capacity helped both neighborhoods form partnerships to garner resources and implement recovery projects and contributed to more effective advocacy. Mid-City and Faubourg St. John primarily relied on existing volunteer-based neighborhood associations to address rebuilding, drawing on newfound leadership and participation after Katrina, along with new partnerships. This resulted in effective advocacy and spurred several new projects and initiatives, such as the Lafitte Greenway and the Morris Jeff Community School, but limited the ability to provide organized communitywide rebuilding assistance to residents and businesses. Grassroots organizations in Lower Mid-City and Tremé, on the other hand, were less successful in uniting and mobilizing community members and resources behind a rebuilding agenda and in establishing partnerships to enhance their capacity and resources. The presence of less-established and divided community organizations contributed to this situation, as did leadership skills and values, the slower return of residents due to their greater poverty or renter status, and government policies.

The next two sections expand on the contributions of these grassroots neighborhood responses to disaster recovery and the foundations for this largely volunteer-based capacity. *Since this capacity is important in rebuilding neighborhoods and cities, it is critical to acknowledge and understand its role in the recovery process and to establish more effective public policies to support and utilize this capacity.*

GRASSROOTS NEIGHBORHOOD REBUILDING: CONTRIBUTIONS AND COMPONENTS

Grassroots rebuilding efforts differed in scope and impact across communities, but when viewed collectively they significantly contributed to neighborhood and citywide recovery. The breadth of these contributions indicates that community-based initiatives can play an important role in rebuilding neighborhoods after major disasters and provide a critical resource for citywide recovery, especially in the replacement-reconstruction phase. These contributions, as summarized in Table 6.1, are fourfold: (1) repopulation; (2) creating a more complete neighborhood; (3) economic development; and (4) civic capacity. Three neighborhoods had focused grassroots initiatives that helped to repopulate their community and the city. In Broadmoor and Village de L'Est, these included organized communitywide campaigns to encourage people to return, case management services to overcome obstacles, and the delivery of resources to help homeowners gut and repair their homes. Broadmoor Development Corporation also worked as a developer to rehab and build homes. Phoenix of New Orleans (PNOLA) and Tulane Canal CDC aided Lower Mid-City's repopulation by helping homeowners restore their homes and constructing new housing. The second, and most common, contribution was restoring or adding services and amenities that helped create more complete neighborhoods. Residents and community groups in every neighborhood restored or built new physical amenities, such community gardens, playgrounds and parks. Grassroots efforts to establish new charter schools occurred in five of the six neighborhoods. In Village de L'Est, Mid-City, and Broadmoor, groups worked with public agencies and private institutions to establish or restore libraries and health services.

Several community organizations aided New Orleans' economic recovery by helping small businesses to rebuild and grow and by working to revitalize commercial districts. This role was most pronounced in Village de L'Est, where MQVN CDC helped local businesses access rebuilding resources and branded and marketed the area to new customers as Viet Village, but it also occurred in BCC's work to improve Broad Street and DNIA's cultural district and other work on Bayou Road. Several groups pursued economic development through real estate projects, but these projects were quite challenging for grassroots organizations, and none had reached the construction stage at the five-year mark.

The final contribution was expanding organizational and civic capacities to undertake rebuilding in New Orleans neighborhoods. Although these capacities are not a direct rebuilding outcome, they enabled faster and more effective recovery by establishing shared goals and political support, creating new implementation capabilities, aligning activities and investments, and strengthening the ability to craft solutions to rebuilding challenges. It is the "how" of rebuilding that helps residents rebuild at the neighborhood level while creating a stronger partner for official recovery efforts and for philanthropic and nonprofit initiatives. Across the six neighborhoods, organizational and civic capacity improved in several tangible ways: plans were developed that established a shared vision and rebuilding priorities; new capacities were created with the formation of organizations and programs; more leaders and volunteers emerged to strengthen neighborhood organizations and to undertake projects and campaigns; and new partnerships and multi-neighborhood collaborations were established.

For neighborhood leaders, these four contributions (repopulation, complete neighborhoods, economic development, and capacity-building) suggest the areas of greatest impact for local activism: the main components of a neighborhood rebuilding agenda. Therefore, the following discussion offers critical insights into the implications for and lessons from this four-part neighborhood recovery agenda based on experiences across the six New Orleans neighborhoods. From the perspective of government and civic leaders, these four categories represent the most promising nexus for city-level recovery efforts and federal policies to leverage the capacities of grassroots rebuilding. The final sections of this chapter consider the connection between "top–down" and "bottom–up" recovery, with an eye toward how official policy, planning, and rebuilding can more effectively utilize and align with grassroots rebuilding capacities.

Repopulation

At its core, neighborhood rebuilding after a disaster is about repopulation—bringing people back to reclaim a neighborhood as their home. This may seem obvious but it was often overlooked—or perhaps taken for granted—in the official plans that concentrated on major projects and programs and in many grassroots efforts, which sought to improve neighborhoods for residents once they returned. There was no organized citywide initiative to contact displaced residents and assist them in returning and rebuilding, and there were limited neighborhood-based efforts to do so. This gap was reinforced by much of the financial assistance for rebuilding, which was delivered directly to individuals and households. This aid—FEMA Individual Assistance, SBA Disaster Recovery Loans, and the $8.8 billion state run Road Home Program (using federal CDBG funds)—emphasized the individual household decision on how and where to rebuild. Although rebuilding a neighborhood and city depends on these individual decisions, it is also a community project. It requires that many people, households, and businesses decide to return, and these decisions are influenced by the actions of neighbors and the aid and support provided on the ground to overcome the many obstacles to returning.

Broadmoor and Village de L'Est demonstrate the importance and power of treating repopulation as a communitywide commitment and project, and how grassroots organizing can facilitate it. Although the repopulation process in Broadmoor and Village de L'Est looks quite different—the former relied on a highly organized marketing campaign and block captain system and the latter used Sunday mass and strong ethnic social bonds— they shared some critical features. Leaders in each neighborhood tackled repopulation head-on through a sustained drive that began early and was central to their rebuilding efforts. Repeated highly visible affirmations of the communitywide commitment to rebuild also were important in both places. In Broadmoor, this affirmation occurred through the January 2006 rally and the proliferation of "Broadmoor Lives" lawn signs and banners. Weekly mass served a similar role for the Village de L'Est Vietnamese

Table 6.2. GRASSROOTS REBUILDING CONTRIBUTIONS ACROSS SIX
NEIGHBORHOODS

Contribution	Applicable Neighborhoods	Comments
Repopulation		
Organized repopulation effort	Broadmoor Village de L'Est	Community-wide effort to convince residents to return; assistance accessing rebuilding aid; case management to help residents return
Organized assistance and resources for home gutting and repair	Broadmoor Village de L'Est Lower Mid-City	BDC, PNOLA, and MQVN Church BDC had the most comprehensive program
Built or restored housing	Broadmoor Lower Mid-City	Unsuccessful effort by MQVN CDC to build senior housing
Complete Neighborhood		
Working with public agencies to accelerate rebuilding of public facilities	Broadmoor Village de L'Est Mid-City	MQVN CDC also worked with hospitals to establish health clinics
Sponsored/developed new charter schools	**Most neighborhoods** Broadmoor Village de L'Est Faubourg St. John Tremé Mid-City	DNIA also worked to improve existing schools in Tremé
Beautification/physical improvement projects	**All neighborhoods** Broadmoor Faubourg St. John Lower Mid-City Mid-City Tremé Village de L'Est	Included building or restoring playgrounds, parks, green spaces and community gardens, and completing cleanups
Economic Development		
Assisting small businesses to return, rebuild, and succeed	Tremé Village de L'Est	Greatest in Village de L'Est with MQVN small business development; some efforts in Tremé around Belles of the Bayou and business association in Mid-City

(Continued)

Table 6.2. CONTINUED

Contribution	Applicable Neighborhoods	Comments
Commercial district revitalization	Village de L'Est Faubourg St. John Lower Mid-City Mid-City Tremé	Viet Village initiatives Broad Community Connections
Real estate and workforce development	Tremé Mid-City Village de L'Est	Viet Village Urban Farm, Broad Refresh, St. Rose of Lima; none of these projects had begun construction within 5 years DNIA career development work with high schools
Rebuilding Capacity		
Preparing a neighborhood rebuilding vision or plan New organizational and program capacity	Broadmoor Mid-City All neighborhoods	Smaller scale efforts in Faubourg St. John and Village de L'Est Examples: BCC, BDC, Broadmoor Improvement District, MQVN CDC, PNOLA
Greater volunteer resident leadership and involvement	**Most neighborhoods** Broadmoor Village de L'Est Faubourg St. John Tremé Mid-City	New leadership and activism in neighborhood associations New generation of leadership in the Vietnamese American community Expanded civic awareness and participation in city governance and policy issues
Multifaceted partnerships and multineighborhood initiatives	**All neighborhoods** Broadmoor Faubourg St. John Lower Mid-City Mid-City Tremé Village de L'Est	Environmental justice coalition Broad Community Connections Lafitte Greenway NEWCITY Neighborhood Partnership

American community. In both cases, the visible communitywide nature of these actions helped convince others to return by showing that many of their neighbors were coming back and showed city political leaders that the neighborhood warranted future investment and political support. These collective grassroots approaches to repopulation removed a critical barrier to recovery by reducing uncertainty about the neighborhood's future.[7] Finally, each community secured resources to provide organized material and moral support to help households return and rebuild through case management, donated materials and labor, and assistance in accessing government and charitable rebuilding aid. This assistance was especially important for less well-off and marginalized residents for whom limited household assets prevented returning and language and cultural barriers hindered their access to rebuilding aid and funding.

While repopulation requires a balanced restoration of rental and owner-occupied housing, government policies and grassroots initiatives emphasized homeowner rebuilding. A telling statistic comes from a GAO report on federal financial assistance to restore permanent housing: 62 percent of storm-damaged homeowner units in Louisiana and Mississippi were awarded federal aid versus 18 percent of damaged rental properties.[8] FEMA's program to repair and restore damaged housing is targeted to individual homeowners and the agency decided that the Stafford Act did not allow for the funding to permanently restore rental housing.[9] Louisiana allocated the largest pot of discretionary rebuilding funds to homeowner assistance: funds allocated to the Road Home Program were almost six times that provided to restore rental housing.[10] Moreover, the state program to rebuild small rental properties was problematic since, at first, it required landlords to fund improvements themselves and then obtain state reimbursement. Since many small landlords lacked the financial resources or access to loans for the required upfront investment, the Small Rental Property Program was poorly utilized.[11] Community-based organizations also overlooked the rebuilding of smaller rental properties. The organized grassroots repopulation and housing repair efforts that occurred in Broadmoor, Village de L'Est, and to a lesser extent in Lower Mid-City focused on homeowners. No organized efforts were undertaken to contact and assist small landlords to rebuild their properties and help them access state financial assistance and volunteer rebuilding aid. State policies and grassroots priorities resulted in eleven times as many owner-occupied homes receiving state rebuilding grants as did small rental properties across all six neighborhoods. Moreover, homeowners in the six neighborhoods received $27 in state Road Home assistance for every dollar received under the Small Rental Assistance Program (See Appendix Tables A.1 and A.2).

Federal policies also affected rental housing recovery through public housing redevelopment and special allocations of low-income housing tax credits to finance rental housing projects. Both policies emphasized large new developments rather than restoring existing housing and smaller rental properties, which delayed the return of rental apartments. HUD and HANO's decision to keep many public housing units closed and then demolish and redevelop four of the largest developments reduced the supply of rental housing, especially apartments affordable to low-income families, in the initial years after Katrina. Large private multifamily projects had the advantage of replacing a large number of lost housing units to help renter and lower-income households return, as was the case in Mid-City and Lower Mid-City. On the other hand, large rental developments faced greater barriers than rebuilding existing small rental properties. These projects required large sites, which were not available in many densely developed New Orleans neighborhoods, were more likely to face resident and neighborhood association opposition, and were difficult to finance, especially after the 2008 financial crises. Problems raising capital with low-income housing tax credits contributed to the failure of MQVN CDC's senior housing project. Because of the challenges to completing LIHTC projects, on a citywide basis, only 38 percent of the New Orleans housing units allocated GO Zone credits were completed and in service by June 2009.[12]

The bias toward rebuilding owner-occupied housing was a major gap in the New Orleans rebuilding process; it biased who could return in the first five years after Katrina in favor of the higher-income and white households that were more likely to be homeowners in 2005. A critical lesson from this gap is that future disaster recovery efforts should place far greater attention and invest more resources in readily restoring the rental housing stock through effective public policies and grassroots initiatives. Moreover, these efforts will have to be far more balanced in two respects: between bringing back small rental properties, which can happen quickly, and building larger multifamily development; and between decisions to retain versus redevelop public housing. Federal policies can address this issue through expanding FEMA's housing repair programs to include small rental properties, while state and local governments should allocate more recovery resources to programs that provide both financing and case/project management assistance to small landlords. This aid should provide up-front repair funds to small landlords to accelerate rebuilding, using a combination of grants and loans. Nonprofit and grassroots organizations can play a role by expanding their outreach and case management services to small rental property owners, providing a critical bridge to help them access rebuilding resources.

The need for collective efforts at repopulation that encompass homeowners and renters begs the question of how to address future vulnerability to disaster as a city rebuilds. Scholars have noted the tension between the desire to rebuild quickly and the goal of rebuilding a better city that reduces future risk and overcomes past inequities.[13] This tension was central to New Orleans' early political conflicts regarding rebuilding and was linked to issues of racial justice, as many of the most vulnerable areas were primarily black and lower-income. Addressing risk is an example of the limits of neighborhood rebuilding. As Nelson et al. argue in their analysis of New Orleans rebuilding plans, some issues involve policy and investment trade-offs that should be addressed on a citywide scale[14]. The relationship and roles between neighborhood and citywide roles in rebuilding is a critical issue (taken up in a later section of this chapter), in which a more deliberative integration of neighborhood and city plans and addressing trade-offs on a multi-neighborhood scale are proposed as ways to help manage these tensions. However, even when new land-use policies and building codes affect where and how residents can rebuild, collective repopulation efforts are likely to be quite valuable in helping residents act in common to navigate and adapt to these changes and rebuild as a community.

Creating More Complete Neighborhoods

The second dimension of neighborhood recovery, creating a complete neighborhood, was pursued across all neighborhoods since it influenced residents' desire to return and their quality-of-life once back. As defined earlier, a complete neighborhood combines housing with an environment, goods, and services that support the health and well-being of community residents: public safety, good schools, health care services, parks and green space, entertainment and cultural activities, and stores and other businesses that address day-to-day needs. Building a complete neighborhood in the disaster recovery process is closely linked with repopulation; it increases a neighborhood's desirability and promises that residents will have access to what they need to get by, rebuild, and improve their lives if they return. It also helps tackle the "chicken and egg" nature of recovery in which the absence of key services deters residents from returning but uncertainty about repopulation prevents the needed investments to restore services.[15] The goal of a complete neighborhood was explicit in the formal vision and plans created by Broadmoor, Mid-City, and Faubourg St. John, and implicit in the rebuilding activities of other neighborhoods. Village de L'Est, for example, worked to establish a new health center, charter school, and community gardens, along with restoring its homes and businesses. The collective work among groups in Tremé sought to increase public safety, improve schools, add green space, expand businesses to serve residents, and restore its unique cultural life.

Creating a complete neighborhood encompassed both reconstruction and betterment aims: it sought to restore basic services and urban amenities but also tried through the rebuilding to overcome past deficiencies and create better places. The Broadmoor Redevelopment Plan was explicit in its goal to rebuild better through implementing many small improvements and pursuing some bigger ideas: it envisioned a Neighborhood Village Center built around an expanded library and new arts and cultural center to establish an active community center, provide expanded services, and promote community interaction.[16] Plans for the Wilson School extended beyond providing good elementary education to making it a resource for the entire community with year-round programs on health, recreation, adult education, and family social services, and as a community information and referral center.[17] Across the Broad Street neighborhoods, grassroots projects promoted physical, social, and economic changes: the goals of Lafitte Greenway included spurring reinvestment in adjacent neighborhoods, connecting neighborhoods and promoting cultural tourism;[18] Broad Community Connections hoped to transform Broad Street into a commercial and social connector for its four adjacent neighborhoods; DNIA worked to establish Bayou Road as a new arts and cultural center. Rebuilding in Village de L'Est evolved to encompass transformative goals: making the neighborhood an ethnic cultural destination and improving community environmental justice and health. Neighborhood groups pursued charter schools as a way to reform public education in five neighborhoods.

Progress in realizing betterment goals has been mixed. Neighborhoods have been successful in obtaining some new and improved facilities and amenities, such as libraries, playgrounds, green space, and expanded community-based health care. However, plans to change the character of commercial areas and bring greater diversity of goods and services to neighborhoods have seen far less success. Public education reform, one of the largest disaster recovery improvement efforts, which has been supported by substantial rebuilding investments in new school facilities and many neighborhood-based charter schools, has yielded mixed success. On the one hand, there has been real academic progress, with accelerating improvement in grade-level test scores after Katrina and fewer failing schools.[19] On the other hand, school performance ratings at the new charter schools in Broadmoor and Village de L'Est have been low. Moreover, the introduction of citywide school choice for most public schools after Katrina has weakened the connection between schools and their surrounding neighborhoods.[20]

The complimentary resources of grassroots organizations and larger public agencies and institutions were needed to advance projects that expanded neighborhood services. Local groups mobilized volunteer labor to help design and implement projects, secured some project funding, raised donations of materials and equipment to supplement public funding, identified and helped secure project sites, and advocated for projects and policy changes. For the reform initiatives for charter schools and community health centers, grassroots organizations were essential partners; they provided the impetus, leadership, and long-term governance of these new institutions. In some cases, they developed (or began the process to develop) facilities to house new schools and clinics. On the other hand, state and city agencies were often the key funders for community facilities and the decision makers on where to locate them. Hospitals and other large institutions have critical expertise and essential personnel to operate services such as health clinics and early education centers, and sometimes provide financial resources. As several projects demonstrated, restoring or expanding neighborhood services progressed most readily when collaboration and alignment existed between government agencies (or large institutions) and neighborhood organizations: the new Mid-City library, the Village de L'Est community health center, and Broadmoor's Wilson School. An important lesson from this experience is that partnerships between government agencies or large nonprofit institutions and community organizations provide an effective way to advance the rebuilding of key community facilities with mutual benefits to both parties. Institutions should pursue such partnerships as they begin recovery planning and when they site new facilities. While the immediate focus of these partnerships will be the restoration of damaged facilities, they can provide a foundation for developing deeper relationships and programs that can include resident employment initiatives, local business procurement, and community-based services,[21] such as the Diabetes Education in Vietnamese Americans program implemented by the Tulane Community Health Center New Orleans East in Village de L'Est. Grassroots organizations also should actively cultivate these partnerships and communicate the value that they offer as partners, i.e., political support, fundraising/access to additional funding sources, knowledge of community conditions and needs, improvements to service delivery, and the ability to demonstrate and help restore the market for services.

Post-disaster neighborhood recovery faces the challenge of balancing the goal of a complete neighborhood with the realities of population size and geography. Confronting this challenge requires sorting out which parts of a complete neighborhood can be provided in the immediate neighborhood, which are best addressed by adjacent neighborhoods sharing facilities on their borders, and when new multineighborhood projects are needed. A recovery planning and decision-making process should provide useful data to inform these decisions and incorporate conversations and collaborations across neighborhoods to work out these issues and guide citywide decisions on where to invest in and site schools, libraries, and other facilities. District scale investment plans that cover several adjacent neighborhoods provide a way to address this challenge if instead of combining priorities under neighborhood plans, as was often the case with UNOP, they sort out priorities, resources, and feasibility to increase access to critical services, and to coordinate rebuilding decisions across agencies. Reaching these decisions at a multineighborhood district scale should help craft a citywide facility investment plan that is responsive to resident and neighborhood priorities, feasible with available rebuilding resources, and completed in a time frame and manner that strengthens confidence in the city's recovery.

Economic Development

At the neighborhood scale, economic development initiatives make two contributions to a city's recovery: (1) restoring the small business base, especially enterprises that provide goods and services to local residents and the commercial districts that house them; and (2) reestablishing and improving employment and income generation opportunities for residents. However, with the exception of Village de L'Est, economic development was a low priority for neighborhood recovery efforts. One aspect of business recovery is providing assistance to help businesses rebuild—analogous to the repopulation assistance provided to residents.[22] Most neighborhood organizations lacked the financial and business expertise and administrative capacity to serve this function. Instead, several nonprofit business development organizations played this role and helped distribute loan and grant funds provided by the Louisiana Recovery Authority with federal CDBG funds. Since these business development groups typically operated on a citywide or regional scale, grassroots groups could add value through conducting outreach to identify and connect business owners to these business assistance services. Most neighborhood groups did not adopt this role, but when they did, as with MQVN CDC, local businesses received far more recovery assistance. Despite having far fewer businesses than the much larger Mid-City neighborhood, 70 percent more businesses in Village de L'Est received assistance under the state Business Recovery Small Loan and Grant program than in Mid-City, and their total financial awards were 48 percent higher (See Appendix, Tables A.4, A.5 and A.6). A lesson for neighborhood economic recovery is the need for grassroots organizations to include small business rebuilding in their agenda and for city and regional business development organizations to work with neighborhood organizations to build trust and extend their relationships with local business owners.

The second part of the neighborhood economic development agenda, improving the economic fortunes of residents, is as much an improvement goal as a recovery need; it seeks to build a better neighborhood and city where residents can earn a good income and poverty is reduced. Improving the economic well-being of residents is a community development goal and challenge in all cities, but it differs in two important ways in the context of disaster recovery. One difference is the greater opportunity to rethink and restructure the institutions and services that prepare residents for, and connect them to, jobs and business ownership. For example, rebuilding plans could include a vocational high school or a training center to better equip local residents for emerging jobs and/or establish new relationships with employers to hire and train neighborhood residents as they reestablish their workforces. Second, the extensive rebuilding investment creates a large demand for goods, services, and workers that does not exist under normal economic conditions. To capitalize on this opportunity, recovery efforts should integrate resident employment as an explicit rebuilding goal and devote cross-sector leadership and resources to implementing programs and services that connect and prepare residents for jobs created by citywide (and regional) rebuilding projects. This challenge requires a regional and citywide approach to be effective, since labor markets operate at a larger scale. However, grassroots and neighborhood groups can be important partners in designing and implementing such efforts: advocating to include and act on resident employment in city recovery efforts; providing knowledge of resident education levels, skills, and employment barriers; hosting or implementing new services required under such a reformed employment system; and connecting residents to new training, jobs, and business development opportunities.

Despite these economic opportunities and the need for jobs in all six neighborhoods—as each had a sizable low-income population—improving resident employment and income was not central to most rebuilding efforts. Village de L'Est was the exception, as locally owned businesses were an important source of resident income and viewed as vital to the neighborhood fabric. Consequently, MQVN Church and then the CDC made business assistance an early priority, helping business owners gain resources to return and reopen quickly, while generating important market and institutional changes for the Vietnamese American business community. These efforts expanded understanding of potential markets and organized initiatives to attract and serve customers beyond their traditional coethnic clientele. Institutionally, they created new business development capacity at the CDC and built connections between Vietnamese American businesses and regional sources of capital and technical assistance. These capacities and relationships have been important as the community worked to address a second economic shock from the BP oil spill.

In two other neighborhoods, increasing jobs and income for residents was a minor part of the grassroots rebuilding agenda. Broadmoor addressed this goal through adult education and work readiness programs at the Wilson School. By the BIA leadership's own admission, resident employment and economic development were not priorities in the first several years of its rebuilding plan. Resident employment received more attention in Tremé as a mandated policy under the Lafitte Redevelopment and through DNIA's work with John McDonough High School. The latter initiative is worthwhile but was limited to only one segment of the community—high school students. Lafitte demonstrates the potential to use rebuilding projects to expand resident employment: one-half of the construction jobs went to New Orleans residents and one-third to low-income workers. But the responsibility for achieving these goals fell on the developer and contractor, without a larger citywide strategy and systems to leverage the enormous rebuilding investments for local employment and economic development goals. HANO, for example, did not aggressively seek to use the $1 billion redevelopment of four major public housing projects as a job and career development initiative for public housing and other low-income residents. In their 2011 assessment of HANO, Gilmore Kean criticized HANO for lacking a resident employment strategy and failing to coordinate employment and training programs across the four projects and with other citywide initiatives.[23]

Neighborhood Rebuilding Capacity

For the past forty years, public policies, private sector initiatives, and philanthropic initiatives have focused on grassroots community-based organizations as a foundation to reverse disinvestment and revitalize urban neighborhoods. These efforts were rooted in building the capacity of resident-led community development corporations to organize their communities, undertake neighborhood planning, and implement a range of improvement projects and programs, with a strong emphasis on affordable housing development.[24] A combination of federal programs and policies, national community development intermediaries, and financial institutions developed funding streams to build housing and other real estate projects with supporting state and local government policies. In several cities, foundations, civic leaders, and local governments created funding and technical assistance resources to underwrite core operations, planning, and capacity-building for CDCs.[25] New Orleans followed other cities in working to improve its neighborhoods through creating CDCs and implementing supportive policies and resources during the 1990s. Since these efforts were not very successful, the city lacked CDCs with strong capacity and a robust system to finance community development projects and programs. As a result, neighborhood rebuilding could not rely on established community-based organizations with professional staff, project, and program implementation capacity and experience in accessing governmental, private, and national philanthropic funding. Neighborhoods, for the most part, created rebuilding capacity from the ground up through a combination of mobilizing their own human capital and forming partnerships with a range of volunteer, philanthropic, private sector, and government resources. The result was a model that relied more on resident civic engagement, a network of multi-faceted collaborations, and advocacy to align others' investments with the local rebuilding vision and goals, represented in Figure 6.1. The following paragraphs elaborate on how each component of this model worked across the six neighborhoods.

A shared vision is a core element of planning that is often cited as important to effective community development initiatives.[26] Since neighborhoods are complex places with varied residents and businesses and different interests and perspectives, all segments of a neighborhood are unlikely to embrace the same recovery vision. Moreover, all stakeholders may not be engaged in formulating this vision; this was especially true in the months after Katrina when many residents, property owners, and employees were displaced. For example, the charrette process used to formulate the initial vision for Village de L'Est had limited community participation, with most of the input from

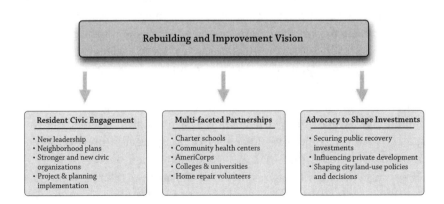

Figure 6.1.
Model of neighborhood rebuilding capacity.

the elderly population and business owners. Nonetheless, the ability to organize significant parts of a neighborhood around common recovery and improvement goals was vital to the rebuilding progress across the six New Orleans neighborhoods. In four neighborhoods, grassroots leaders were able to unify many returned residents and local organizations around a recovery vision that set priorities for rebuilding projects and initiatives, identified longer-term neighborhood improvements, and created a base of political support for responding to developers or others who proposed projects in their neighborhoods. In Village de L'Est and Faubourg St. John, the vision was at a general level: targeted areas for improvement; priority facilities to restore and build; and desired changes for key sites or corridors. Mid-City's vision included a more comprehensive neighborhood plan with proposals to address infrastructure, transportation, housing, schools, parks, historic preservation, crime, and youth services. It also was more explicit about priorities, phasing, and recommendations for city policy and actions. Broadmoor's vision was the most comprehensive and detailed; it was developed into an extensive plan with many urban design proposals, projects, programs, and implementation strategies. These visions informed the initial work and priorities regarding grassroots rebuilding efforts, but they often evolved in response to new needs, changes in market or other conditions, and as projects or activities become infeasible. This was the case with Broadmoor's plans for new housing development, which was scaled back and adjusted to emphasize improving existing properties due to market and financial factors.

Active resident leadership and engagement was vital to expanded rebuilding capacity in all neighborhoods except Lower Mid-City. New residents emerged to take leadership roles in neighborhood planning, repopulation efforts, physical improvement projects, establishing new charter schools, and restoring or expanding community services. Moreover, many projects and initiatives relied heavily or exclusively on neighborhood volunteers, either for their full implementation or to advance them until they could be implemented by public or private agencies. Neighborhood associations and neighborhood planning processes were often focal points for engaging new resident leaders and mobilizing an expanded cadre of volunteers to take on rebuilding projects. In other cases, such as PNOLA, the Mid-City Community Gardens, and the Belles of the Bayou, individual entrepreneurs and activists took initiative outside of existing organizations to launch rebuilding initiatives that then attracted support and involvement from others. In all these instances, residents' commitment to their neighborhood and city, matched with their investment of considerable time, effort, and skills, was a valuable rebuilding resource that official recovery policies and processes could have acknowledged and utilized to a far greater extent.

Neighborhoods implemented their recovery agenda through a network of partnerships that accelerated rebuilding when capacity in existing formal staffed organizations was quite limited. First, these partnerships allowed multiple volunteer-led projects to move forward as separate initiatives relatively quickly without relying on a single CDC (or other organization) to raise funds and hire the staff to implement them. This approach was used to establish charter schools in Mid-City and Broadmoor that were organized under separate resident-led boards. Laffite Greenway, Mid-City Community Garden, and Broad Community Connections are other cases in which distinct resident-led projects emerged to implement important parts of neighborhood rebuilding visions. Through the multipartnership approach, grassroots efforts also leveraged the expertise, resources, and capacities of many organizations beyond their neighborhood to implement and speed up rebuilding. A prime example was residential rebuilding in which neighborhoods used multiple partnerships to tap extensive volunteer labor and financial resources to gut and repair many homes. Broadmoor was especially proactive in this respect, collaborating with the Annunciation Mission to recruit hundreds of volunteers and create a dormitory to house and feed them. PNOLA did the same in Lower Mid-City, using the Internet for recruiting efforts, as well as staff from the AmeriCorps program to first bring in volunteers to gut homes and then to form a more extensive home repair program. Larger national organizations, such as Rebuilding Together and Habitat for Humanity, were important partners and intermediaries for the massive deployment of volunteer labor used to gut and repair homes following Katrina. Colleges and universities were another common partner in neighborhood rebuilding. They provided student volunteers to help gut homes; interns to help staff organizations; and technical expertise through faculty; classes and student projects that supported project, and program planning; landscape and building design; business plans; market analysis; fund-raising; and neighborhood information systems. Several universities, including Harvard, Bard, and MIT, established long-term partnerships with specific neighborhoods and organizations. Faculty and students at local universities, including Tulane University and the University of New Orleans, also provided ongoing planning support and technical assistance to many community-based organizations.

Even in Village de L'Est, where rebuilding was centralized around MQVN Church and CDC, myriad partnerships and networks were used. Much of the CDC's early staffing came from its partnerships with NAVASA and Catholic Charities, which provided Dan Than Fellows and case managers, respectively. Its business development work relied on partnerships with SEEDCO Financial Services, MIT, ASU Credit Union, and NAVASA. Tulane and Children's Hospital were critical to establishing new community health centers and expanding community health programs.

The third leg of neighborhood rebuilding capacity was advocating to incorporate (or protect) the neighborhood's vision and priorities in key decisions and investments made by government, large institutions, and private developers. As often occurs in cities, grassroots organizations worked to stop private and public sector decisions that they perceived as dangerous to the neighborhoods, e.g., operating the Chef Menteur Landfill, and the closure and demolition of Lafitte public housing. In the recovery context, advocacy also provided a way to garner rebuilding resources, particularly government-controlled investments to restore and improve community facilities. Examples include the BIA and MCNO efforts to shape decisions on restoring neighborhood library branches, residents' advocacy to alter the school facilities master plan, and the work by historic preservation and community organizations to move and preserve historic homes in the VA hospital footprint. Neighborhood organizations also fought to advance rebuilding goals in private-sector development decisions. This was most common in neighborhoods with strong development interests, especially Tremé and Mid-City, and focused on incorporating amenities, design changes, and desired business types in development plans. For neighborhoods without their own community-based development capacity, public and private sector advocacy was particularly important to realizing their rebuilding goals, since they could not directly build new community facilities, housing, or commercial space.

Although the use of volunteerism, partnerships, and advocacy in lieu of established community development spurred rebuilding progress, it also had some limitations. Neighborhoods that were less able to mobilize resident volunteers and attract resource-rich partners were at a disadvantage, and this was reinforced over time, as other neighborhoods became stronger advocates and built more capacity to research, design, and plan rebuilding initiatives. This argues for having stronger capabilities in city government and citywide or regional nonprofit organizations to offset weak grassroots capacity in some neighborhoods. Second, this capacity may decline or become less reliable if the number and enthusiasm of volunteers abates and partnership opportunities and resources shrink over time, after outside organizations move on to other disasters and priorities. Similarly, resident volunteer resources may diminish over time as the sense of crisis that initially motivates resident activism subsides. Consequently, the transition from a volunteer-driven to staffed organization may be important to sustain effective recovery efforts beyond the first five years, especially to tackle long-term challenges, such as addressing the substantial blighted properties in sections of Broadmoor and Tremé, revitalizing disinvested commercial areas like Broad Street, and transforming economic opportunities for low-income residents. Several such organizations emerged from grassroots efforts, but these are still fledgling entities that have not risen to the level of programmatic and development capabilities found in other cities with strong CDCs. Sustained resident leadership and a much stronger system of local government, foundation, and business community support will be necessary to leverage the full potential of this emerging community development capacity.

NEIGHBORHOODS IN THE CITY REBUILDING PROCESS

A city's recovery from any large-scale disaster extends beyond rebuilding its neighborhoods. Critical rebuilding needs that are citywide in scope include: repairing the infrastructure systems that underlie a city's functioning; restoring the economic base by bringing back businesses, workers, and the critical services that support economic activity; and reestablishing government, utility, and other basic services—e.g., education, health care, public transportation, and the like. Moreover, some critical spatial and policy decisions that affect where and how rebuilding can occur must be made on a citywide basis, including changes in land-use regulations and building codes to address ongoing disaster risks.[27] Given these needs and the compelling reasons to address recovery from a citywide perspective, what does the New Orleans case indicate about how neighborhoods fit into the rebuilding process? The following discussion addresses this question in three areas: (1) the significance of neighborhoods in overall recovery and its phasing; (2) the value and challenges in aligning neighborhood and citywide rebuilding efforts; and (3) the limitations of over-reliance on neighborhood-based recovery.

Cities are human settlements and, as argued above, repopulation is central to post-disaster recovery. Neighborhood conditions affect who can return and who chooses to return, and therefore they are the foundation for bringing people back. Broadmoor and Village de L'Est show that repopulation can be accelerated when residents are confident that their neighbors will return, that they will receive support and mutual aid to rebuild, and that effective efforts are in place to restore critical neighborhood services. An early and serious focus on rebuilding at the neighborhood-scale promises to accelerate the recovery process by convincing more residents, businesses, and property owners to return and invest in rebuilding. A positive feedback loop results from this acceleration: the labor force for rebuilding and service restoration is larger; decisions on where to site community facilities can be made more readily; and market demand increases to allow more businesses that serve local customers to reopen.[28] For these reasons, recovery work to create livable neighborhoods is part of the early reconstruction phase and should begin soon after the immediate task of restoring core infrastructure and essential services is underway.

Consequently, planning and organizing community capacity for neighborhood rebuilding should be a recovery priority after the emergency response is completed and restoration work is underway. New Orleans' initial recovery process did emphasize early neighborhood-scale plans, but political conflicts over the recovery framework and intergovernmental differences delayed its implementation for many months. Moreover, when neighborhood recovery planning got underway, it was not accompanied by investments in community outreach and organization to facilitate resident and other stakeholder participation, or combined with support for collective repopulation capacity, or connected to citywide planning to reconstruct infrastructure and community facilities.

Early attention to neighborhood recovery can provide better planning information and help coordinate investments, but it also presents challenges for integrating neighborhood and larger-scale plans. Through working closely with grassroots organizations as authentic partners in neighborhood recovery, planners and policy makers can tap into local knowledge, networks, and relationships to gain better information to inform analysis and decision-making. In the context of recovery, grassroots networks often have more accurate information on who has returned, who is planning to return, and local physical conditions. Evidence of this rich community-based information is found across the neighborhood narratives, from the Yahoo! group formed in Mid-City, to tight family and community relationships at MQVN Church, to the property database and neighborhood census created in Broadmoor. This information has a direct bearing on rebuilding decisions, such as the phasing of investments to reconstruct facilities and infrastructure, identifying sites for temporary housing, and identifying and addressing early recovery obstacles. Neighborhood groups also provide a valuable "second look" at the validity of decisions made by experts, as when Mid-City residents analyzed official projections to demonstrate the need for more schools than provided for in the initial School Facilities Master Plan. The inclusion and valuing of grassroots organizations in gathering information and deliberative decision-making should reduce distrust of government planning and decision-making that accompanies the rebuilding process.[29] To gain the benefits of community-level information and nurture the type of resident and neighborhood-level participation in recovery planning discussed below, dedicated funding and other support for community outreach and organization is needed. The final section proposes changes in FEMA programs to provide such support.

Neighborhood recovery plans provide a strategic tool to coordinate and guide the complex decisions that multiple public bureaucracies face in the rebuilding process. They supply a principle to inform these decisions: that facilities should be rebuilt to provide each neighborhood with access to schools, fire and police protection, health clinics, parks and recreational facilities, libraries, and other public services. Applying this principle means that multiple agencies need to look at how their rebuilding decisions will interact to shape specific neighborhoods (and future city recovery), rather than planning solely for the needs of their own system. Moreover, it requires public agencies to work more closely with neighborhood groups to consider how grassroots efforts influence their decisions and vice versa. Bringing multiple agencies together to look at how their actions interrelate and influence neighborhood recovery could foster consideration of options to more efficiently address rebuilding needs, e.g., co-locating schools and libraries in one facility. It also might clarify or alter the type of trade-offs being made. For example, the importance of rebuilding a community center or a library in a neighborhood where fewer schools are being restored might increase. Similarly, it would allow consideration of how to phase reconstruction investments or pool resources across agencies to accelerate repopulation, such as building "quick start" multiservice centers that might transition into a larger single-service facility after more people returned. This might require sacrificing the lowest cost option to restore a facility to provide more services sooner, thereby creating a healthier neighborhood and accelerating rebuilding. More flexible funding options and regulations under FEMA Public Assistance are needed to allow this type of coordinated and adaptive rebuilding of public facilities.

Dual Collaborative Rebuilding

Applying this principle in practice and achieving the necessary coordination is undoubtedly challenging. Ideally, it entails connecting place-based recovery plans for specific neighborhoods (and districts) with multiple "system"-level plans for schools, parks and recreation, public works, public safety, etc.. The term "dual collaborative" provides a shorthand phrase for describing this recovery approach: collaboration between official "top–down" planning and grassroots initiatives and collaborative recovery investment across multiple bureaucracies. It requires different government bureaucracies to share information, become less turf-oriented, collaborate with other agencies and parties in making decisions on which facilities should be reopened and rebuilt (and where), and explore options to share or co-locate facilities. It also envisions a partnership among public agencies, neighborhood organizations, and key nonprofit institutions to share information and deliberate about decisions on where and how to invest to rebuild facilities and restore services. This type of deeper engagement among community members, public managers, and nonprofit institutions allows for better understanding of the goals, priorities, and constraints faced by each party and exploration of solutions that can deliver better outcomes. Improved outcomes from dual collaboration might include: creative solutions for multiuse facilities, using volunteer efforts and new partnerships to reduce costs, and revealing neighborhood preferences that allow for more efficient and/or desired changes in where facilities are located and how resources are allocated. For example, if attracting a grocery store is a higher priority for a neighborhood than building a new playground, or if residents can mobilize their own labor and donations to get the playground built, then funds might be reallocated from parks to attract and finance a grocery store.

A dual collaborative process needs to proactively address the phasing of different projects and services, since every project cannot be built simultaneously. Phasing decisions that emerge out of priorities jointly developed with neighborhood residents based on a shared understanding of available resources and other constraints are more apt to gain political support and to foster confidence in the recovery process by showing when key facilities and services would return.[30] Phasing is informed by real funding constraints and what funding is feasible for different projects and programs. Linking phasing with funding is especially challenging in the early stages of recovery with the uncertainty about how federal aid will be distributed, what philanthropic commitments will be made, and when and what forms of private capital will be available. An evolving funding environment suggests that plans need to be adaptive and revisited as financial resources become more certain. Nonetheless, some proactive steps can be taken to address the funding conundrum. One is including more financial and funding expertise in the planning and implementation teams. Another is for federal aid agencies and philanthropies to provide funding and incentives to encourage more comprehensive and better integrated rebuilding plans. The School Facilities Master Plan is a great example of moving beyond individual project funding to look at the entire school system and awarding recovery funding for a systemwide plan. Under a dual collaborative process, a further step is to link and adapt this type of systemwide facility planning with neighborhood and district scale plans.

In practice, a dual collaborative approach will be messier and more incremental than the ideal of interagency and city–neighborhood partnership prescribed above. Consequently, political leaders and civic and neighborhood leaders need strategies that can advance these goals and realize some of the promised benefits in practice. One strategy is to drive the interagency process through creating a systemwide plan at one agency and then using this first plan as the basis to push coordination with other bureaucracies. The choice of which system should drive the process will depend on local factors—city politics, agency leadership, and agency planning capacity, among others—but public safety and schools are strong candidates given their importance in creating conditions for residents to return. Under this approach, schools would serve as anchors for investments to restore other facilities. Other agencies would be pushed and incentivized to link reconstruction of other public facilities with the rebuilt school. A "school plus" plan could incorporate additional services within the school building, e.g., childcare or a health clinic, and/or site other facilities near the school. A second strategy involves a sequential process whereby facility plans are first completed for separate systems (schools, libraries, health facilities, etc.) and these plans are then revised after the interrelationships (both conflicts and synergies) across system plans and with neighborhood and district plans are considered. Although this type of process might lengthen the time period for making decisions, the process also could be accelerated with more rapid damage assessment and stronger mayoral and political leadership to work collaboratively outside of traditional bureaucratic structures.[31]

The second critical bridging needed under dual collaboration is across the different perspectives and priorities of government agencies and neighborhood stakeholders. In New Orleans, from the grassroots perspective, residents were deeply committed to rebuilding their city and made large human and financial investments toward this end. These investments of time and energy were largely separate from, and at times in opposition to, official rebuilding efforts. Neighborhood residents invested considerable time in developing official plans that were not used and mobilized to push the city to invest in their priorities and to stop decisions that might undermine their recovery. From the city government perspective, residents and neighborhood organizations often had unrealistic expectations for what the city could accomplish and neither understood the legal and financial constraints that the city faced nor acknowledged the real tradeoffs that had to be negotiated. Consequently, community activists sometimes pressed for infeasible projects and hardened in opposition to proposals rather than engaging in problem solving.

With more information-sharing and deliberation among government recovery officials and grassroots leaders, the potential for greater trust exists and increased alignment between the actions of government and community-based organizations can be accomplished. With this trust and alignment, local activism can be redirected from fighting government decisions to repopulation and improvement efforts. Similarly, government agencies can gain political support for shared rebuilding priorities, leverage grassroots activism, and garner the resources to accelerate recovery. Several conditions and practices that contribute to building trust and collaboration between public officials responsible for recovery and neighborhood-based organizations include:

- A transparent recovery planning and implementation process with regular two-way communication between public officials and community groups.[32] Under this two-way communication, public officials can listen and learn about what neighborhoods need, want, and will act on and neighborhood leaders can get honest information about the legal requirements, resource constraints, and trade-offs faced by the city.
- A commitment by political leaders to an open participatory process and to partnerships with grassroots organizations for both recovery planning and implementation, along with a comparable willingness among community organizations and leaders to put aside past conflicts and work in partnership with city government.
- Employing new technologies and organizational structures to gather and share information and to establish opportunities for deliberation and collaborative decision-making.[33] For example, neighborhood residents can collect and transmit data on local property conditions and repair status using hand-held devices with data incorporated in both public agency and community databases.
- A willingness and commitment by government agencies that control rebuilding funds to invest in and build capacity among community-based organizations to implement appropriate recovery programs and projects.
- Creating mechanisms to hold both public agencies and grassroots groups accountable for fulfilling their respective parts in the recovery process, such as using implementation teams with staff and leadership from public agencies and community organizations.

Coordinating top–down and bottom–up recovery, like interagency collaboration, is quite challenging and requires creative strategies and ongoing learning to be effective. Neighborhoods have myriad divisions that pose barriers to internal coordination, let alone collaboration with external government and institutional initiatives. As evidenced in Tremé's recovery efforts, a neighborhood can have many organizations with different visions and priorities for recovery that speak for different segments of the community. These divisions can be especially difficult to bridge when they are racially based, as was often the case in New Orleans, or tied to narrow personal or political allegiances. As with crossagency collaborations, leadership and structures that encourage participation and deliberation among different groups, as occurred in Broadmoor, help build consensus on neighborhood priorities and facilitate a more effective partnership with the official recovery process.

Neighborhoods' recovery plans provide a practical way to link grassroots and citywide plans for land-use, infrastructure, and community facilities. They provide a tangible and operational platform for building agreement among groups and interests within a neighborhood and for deliberation and coordination between government and community-based decision-making. To achieve this purpose, plans must be far more grounded than the plans generated under UNOP; they must address real trade-offs and tackle difficult feasibility and implementation issues. They also require information-sharing and direct engagement by the public agencies and major institutions responsible for infrastructure and public facilities reconstruction. Further, they allow community-level information and priorities to inform decisions and help neighborhood groups make better informed plans for leveraging and complementing agency investments. Moreover, the aforementioned government–community partnerships that accelerate and enhance recovery projects are more likely to emerge from direct information-sharing and deliberation in preparing neighborhood plans.

Another approach is to link plans to a specific neighborhood recovery budget. This budget would be a rough approximation of the recovery funds available to rebuild community facilities and undertake new community-based initiatives, programs, and services rather than a fixed investment commitment. Although imprecise, the budget constraint would encourage more debate over trade-offs and substantive decisions to inform investment priorities for each neighborhood. It would encourage early and creative thinking about ways to augment and leverage public sector investments. The more grounded priorities and capacities that emerge from neighborhood plans could then be discussed and incorporated, when feasible, into systemwide infrastructure and facilities prepared by city agencies and large nonprofit institutions.

Implementing this dual collaborative rebuilding process—coordinating across multiple city agencies on the one hand and aligning city and grassroots activities on the other—requires strong political and civic leadership and trust between city residents and their government. Neither of these conditions existed in New Orleans after Katrina. If the crisis created an opportunity for new patterns of leadership and collaboration, they quickly dissolved with the lack of supportive state and federal policies and the elitist and expert-driven planning under the Bring New Orleans Back (BNOB) Commission. As time passed, public confidence in the official rebuilding system continued to erode due to repeated snafus in implementing promised projects and programs and decision-making on important issues by government leaders without community consultation. Under these circumstances, the grassroots response to rebuilding from the bottom up, pushing and pulling government to support their efforts when possible, was a feasible second-best strategy. However, it is far from the ideal. Political, civic, and grassroots leaders in other cities should strive for the dual collaborative process outlined above. Business and civic leaders have a responsibility to promote such a process and encourage more open and deliberative decision-making between government officials, major institutions, and grassroots organizations, recognizing its value in accelerating the city's recovery and potential to rebuild a city with healthier and more desirable neighborhoods.

Limitations of Neighborhood-Focused Recovery

Despite the benefits discussed above, there are real limitations in relying too heavily on neighborhood-based initiatives to drive a city's recovery. First, as demonstrated in the six narratives, considerable disparity exists in the rebuilding leadership, capacity, and resources across neighborhoods within a city. If reconstruction is driven solely by grassroots initiatives, then these differences in wealth, leadership, organizational capacity, and success or luck in building partnerships and attracting outside resources will heighten disparities in rebuilding outcomes. City policies and investments provide an important countervailing force to compensate for these resource and capacity differentials to shift the rebuilding trajectory toward more balanced results among neighborhoods. A second problem is that rebuilding based on neighborhood priorities mitigates consideration of the trade-offs across neighborhoods needed to achieve an efficient and balanced investment of limited resources to restore facilities and services across a city. An individual neighborhood's interest and advocacy focuses on restoring services and facilities for its community, not on citywide objectives. Despite the inherently political nature of distributing resources across neighborhoods, it is a city-level responsibility to decide how this should be done and to determine which goals, values, and policies should guide these decisions—e.g., what minimal level of services should be provided to every neighborhood, whether investment should follow repopulation or seek to stimulate it, and so on. Neighborhoods' narrow interests or concerns, such as "not in my back yard" opposition, also can stall or prevent the restoration of some critical services and facilities. These decisions cannot be left to neighborhood plans alone since some uses may be excluded from or heavily restricted in all such plans. Finally, some urban systems function at a city or regional scale (e.g., economic development and transportation) and recovery planning and investment must be done at this scale. However, the fact that controversial, unpopular, or regional facilities require city-, regional-, or state-level decision-making does not mean that these decisions should be made without an open and deliberative process. They still require transparency, communication, and participation with the affected neighborhoods, along with collaborative efforts to limit negative impacts and link the benefits from these investments to impacted residents and small businesses.

REFORMING FEDERAL DISASTER ASSISTANCE

New Orleans' recovery, for individual neighborhoods and citywide, was hampered by the design and delivery of federal disaster aid. One set of problems stems from policies that favor certain types of recovery investments and make more flexible and coordinated rebuilding difficult. Key federal recovery programs (FEMA Individual Assistance and the SBA Disaster Loan Program) target individual rebuilding decisions by homeowners and businesses with inadequate resources to reconstruct rental housing. The more recent trend toward using tax incentives to stimulate private-sector recovery investment favors large-scale projects in locations with stronger real estate markets and often funds projects that do not support recovery in disaster-impacted communities. FEMA Public Assistance (PA) is primarily designed to fund the restoration of preexisting facilities and places financial limits on using PA funds for alternative types of rebuilding.[34] These policies prevent widespread funding of the type of communitywide repopulation efforts undertaken in Broadmoor and Village de L'Est. They also make it difficult to restore rental housing, coordinate recovery investments across service areas (e.g., schools, day care and health clinics), and build new types of facilities and infrastructure that better serve postdisaster recovery needs. A second set of problems emanates from multiple layers of federal and state administration of critical recovery programs and the use of inappropriate rules and systems to deliver federal large-scale disaster recovery assistance. These problems lead to long delays (years in the case of New Orleans) in delivering federal assistance, confusion and mixed information on what could be funded (as in the Louisiana Road Home and New Orleans Soft Second Mortgage programs), and major constraints in cities' ability to direct federal aid to fit local conditions and priorities.

Significant reforms to this system are critical to improving the capacity of US cities and regions to respond and rebuild after large-scale disasters. This section proposes changes to federal long-term disaster recovery policy to address critical problems evident from New Orleans' experience[35] and to expand support for grassroots rebuilding capacity. Despite the many problems encountered with the short-term federal postdisaster response in New Orleans, the focus of this book and the discussion below is on long-term assistance for community rebuilding. These proposals address four aspects of federal disaster recovery policy that were problematic in the New Orleans case and are likely to impair recovery after future disasters: (1) the absence of a federal program to address large-scale disasters; (2) reliance on state governments to oversee federal rebuilding aid; (3) limited support to enhance and leverage local civic capacity; and (4) an emphasis on funding individual buildings rather than systemwide funding to restore public facilities. While these proposals are not a complete solution to these problems, they would shift federal policies toward delivering more effective support for local and regional rebuilding after massive disasters. They are presented to focus more attention on these problems and promote consideration of how to improve a system in dire need of reform before another disaster brings destruction on the magnitude faced by Gulf Coast communities in 2005.

Create a Federal Program for Large-Scale Disasters

Federal disaster programs have repeatedly proven insufficient to address the losses encountered in a large-scale disaster.[36] In such cases, entire communities or large sections of major cities need to be rebuilt. The required scale and forms of assistance extend far beyond the individual household assistance and public facilities restoration programs through FEMA and SBA under the Stafford Act. The large uninsured financial losses incurred by tens of thousands of households and businesses have to be addressed. Rental housing and leased commercial buildings need to be repaired and rebuilt. Families, businesses, and nonprofit organizations need help determining where and how to rebuild in a new and uncertain environment.

Cities must deal with a surge in abandoned and blighted properties. Finally, communities face a massively complex and multiyear task of planning for their rebuilding, on the one hand, and scaling up the capacity to coordinate and implement projects and programs at an order of magnitude beyond their normal level, on the other. These are all important components of large-scale rebuilding that are not institutionalized in federal disaster recovery programs administered by FEMA and other federal agencies. Although the Stafford Act, in theory, provides FEMA with broad authority to direct any federal agency to use its "authority and the resources granted it under Federal law … in support of state and local recovery efforts," FEMA has not exercised it to fund and initiate large-scale federal recovery assistance.[37] Instead, Congress has repeatedly addressed this limitation by passing ad hoc emergency legislation to provide resources—typically a combination of direct appropriations and special tax provisions—to respond to the special challenges of individual major disasters.

There are several problems with responding through ad hoc legislation. First, it pressures state and local governments to act quickly to "lock in" federal aid while rebuilding is still on the national agenda and the political will exists to pass special legislation. In this context, political leaders work to formulate the size of their ask and a framework for how the special funds will be used in the early weeks and months following the disaster, before the scope of the problem is well understood and effective strategies to address it can be formulated and tested. Moreover, it puts a premium on early consultation with people who have influence in Congress, often other politicians and business leaders, rather than a broader range of citizens and stakeholders whose trust, support, and actions are essential for the collective project of rebuilding a city. This urgency to secure federal rebuilding aid and to show the White House and Congress that it had a plan to spend this aid contributed to New Orleans' early failures under the BNOB process—choosing key leadership based on political connections rather than political legitimacy, relying on outside experts to shape key aspects of the plan, failing to learn from and engage residents across the city in crafting its initial plans, and not taking time to create effective ways to communicate what was being considered and why. If an established federal program that provided predictable forms of aid and delivered that aid after communities had undertaken well-grounded planning, civic engagement and capacity-building had existed at the time of Katrina, it would have provided incentives for New Orleans' leaders to approach long-term rebuilding through a better governed and participatory process supported by more extensive information and stronger collaborations among government, businesses, neighborhood groups, and the nonprofit sector.

Second, ad hoc legislation has used existing federal programs and tools that are ill-suited to deliver aid for large-scale rebuilding. As detailed in chapter 2, using the Community Development Block Grant Program to distribute this exceptional funding imposed legal requirements that often are irrelevant in disaster recovery situations and required a multilayered bureaucratic edifice to approve and administer funds. In some cases, preferred policy goals or mechanisms had to be altered to fit CDBG requirements (Road Home Program). In other cases, programs faced long delays to secure waivers and work out arcane regulatory issues (Soft Second Program). Although HUD has learned over time and made adjustments to adapt the CDBG regulations to disaster recovery situations, it is still trying to fit a square peg into a round hole. Congress also used existing tax expenditures on an ad hoc basis to stimulate private investments in rebuilding, including special allocations of Low-Income Housing tax credits (LIHTCs) and New Market tax credits (NMTCs) and other credits and deductions for impacted households and businesses to reduce their taxes. As with the CDBG program, these tax-based mechanisms are not always well-suited to recovery needs and may be far less efficient than other policy options. For example, because of the economics of LIHTCs and NMTCs, these programs attract investment in large multimillion-dollar projects but are not effective in restoring smaller rental housing and commercial properties—an important need after Katrina. Similarly, many small businesses incurred losses after Katrina. With losses, they had no tax liability and could not benefit from special tax credits or deductions. Tax expenditures have a role in offsetting losses and leveraging private investment to support rebuilding after major disasters, but these tax policies should be tailored to the specific needs of long-term recovery and based on sound evidence of their effectiveness.

The nation needs a federal program designed specifically to deliver assistance for communitywide recovery after large-scale disasters. This program should provide aid in forms and with guidelines that respond to the unique challenges of long-term rebuilding, and that will build the institutional knowledge, learning and relationships to foster the effective management of such a program.

Empower Local Governments to Directly Program and Manage Federal Rebuilding Funds

Most federal recovery assistance to localities flows through state government. This is true for disaster CDBG dollars and FEMA Public

Assistance—the two largest federal resources for community rebuilding. The reliance on state governments reduces the administrative burden on federal agencies. Moreover, Congress and federal executives may have more confidence in the state governments' ability to provide sound program and fiscal management, given their established role managing myriad federal programs and larger size compared to most municipalities. On the other hand, it adds an additional layer of bureaucracy in channeling aid to communities, and raises the potential for aid to get caught up in political or policy conflicts between state and local governments. Furthermore, state governments are not necessarily more capable managers of federal programs. In some program areas, such as infrastructure and housing, local governments may have more extensive and relevant program management capacity than their state government. Large cities in some states may have equivalent or better capabilities than state government. For example, when New York State received responsibility for overseeing recovery CDBG funds after the World Trade Center disaster, it had little experience with that particular program, while New York City had been managing CDBG funds for over two decades.[38]

Federal disaster recovery assistance, including FEMA PA and disaster CDBG funds (or the proposed replacement program), should allow funding for community-level rebuilding programs and municipal facilities to go directly to municipal governments. This policy would be consistent with the normal CDBG program that makes grants directly to entitlement cities (state governments only manage grants to small cities). This direct "municipal entitlement" would not apply to recovery aid designed to mitigate uninsured household or business losses, e.g., the Louisiana Road Home Program, which should be offered fairly and consistently across a state or region rather than under separate programs that differ across communities. It would provide direct grants to municipalities to fund collective programs, projects, and initiatives that address communitywide rebuilding priorities and agendas. A formula or detailed criteria would be used to distribute federal recovery funding between municipal grants and state-run programs.

While cities have a larger role in negotiating and deploying FEMA PA funds, this funding is still overseen by state governments, which adds procedures, delays the receipt of these funds, and increases their administrative costs. To reduce these delays and costs, FEMA should create an option to certify municipalities to directly receive and administer PA funds. FEMA could establish standards that local governments would need to meet to demonstrate their financial, information, and project management capacity to directly administer PA grants. Any municipality that received such certification would deal directly with FEMA to apply for, receive, administer, and report on PA funding without having to work through a second layer of state government oversight. Beyond its promise to reduce costs and delays, the certification process would create an incentive for local governments to develop the systems and capacity to administer FEMA PA funds and thus be prepared in advance for this critical part of the rebuilding process.

Support and Enhance Local Civic Capacity for Recovery

As the neighborhood cases demonstrate, and as elaborated earlier in this chapter, postdisaster recovery is a collective project that relies on the cooperation and effective deployment of resources across many sectors of a community. Grassroots organizations and neighborhood civic capacity are assets in the rebuilding process to advance both neighborhood-level and citywide recovery goals that include repopulation, reconstruction of community services and amenities, business recovery, and implementation of systemic reforms. Federal rebuilding assistance should nurture and support civic capacity as an important co-requisite to the effective use of federal funds. Beyond its established funding for rebuilding individual properties and public facilities, FEMA recovery assistance should consistently support the collective element of rebuilding by investing in civic capacity at a citywide, district, and neighborhood scale. The core of this support is funding and technical assistance to undertake recovery planning and to create an effective organizational infrastructure for rebuilding that incorporates multisector participation and collaborations among neighborhood, business, civic, and public sector organizations.[39] FEMA's Long Term Recovery Emergency Support Function (ESF #14) provides a foundation for this role, as it seeks to assist communities to create a postdisaster recovery vision and identify projects, funding, and implementation mechanisms to realize this vision. However, ESF#14 was envisioned as short- term in nature and emphasized recovery planning and project identification rather than long-term recovery capacity-building.[40] To provide more effective long-term recovery support to communities, FEMA needs to establish a separate unit to support community recovery planning and civic capacity-building with sustained and deeper assistance that encompasses the following elements:

- Encourages the creation of a broad recovery leadership "table" that includes multiple sectors and types of organizations and fosters their collaboration to both develop the recovery plan and coordinate action to implement it.

- Provides funding and support services for civic engagement and dialogue to gain broader support and legitimacy for rebuilding plans and to tackle difficult questions and trade-offs in making some of the hard decisions about rebuilding.
- Includes funding for grassroots organizing to build neighborhood-based recovery planning and capacity-building. This would support outreach to displaced residents and business owners to broaden participation in neighborhood and citywide planning, build organizational capacity to provide community-based repopulation/recovery assistance, and work on early community clean-up and rebuilding projects. This aid could be distributed in partnership with local community foundations.
- Serves as a resource for knowledge on what has proven to be effective in other places and builds connections to other resources that can help communities in their rebuilding efforts.

After the seriously flawed federal response following Katrina, the notion of helpful and supportive federal government that is also a repository of knowledge and advice on rebuilding may seem far-fetched. However, a federal government unit that reflects this notion already exists at the Pentagon. It is the Office of Economic Adjustment and its mission is to assist communities to make and implement plans to address the loss of a major military base or other defense department installation. This flexible, nonbureaucratic enterprise assists and advises communities in managing their adjustment process following the economic losses. It helps communities initiate the process in a productive way, provides easily accessible funding to undertake adjustment planning, and provides a repository of knowledge and experience from the scores of communities that have faced and successfully responded to this challenge. There is no reason why a similar type of office should not exist within the Department of Homeland Security.

Promote More Integrative and Systemwide Recovery Investment with FEMA PA Funding

As discussed earlier in this chapter, the rebuilding of community facilities creates an opportunity to rethink the location, scale, and interaction of these facilities with each other and in conjunction with neighborhood and district plans. To realize these opportunities, city leaders and facility planners must look beyond the reconstruction of individual predisaster facilities to plan for restoring services citywide and in conjunction with other plans. However, FEMA PA policies emphasize funding the repair or replacement of predisaster facilities rather than financing a more systematic reconstruction program that is adapted to the postdisaster condition and recovery strategy. With New Orleans' school system, however, FEMA made a major departure by supporting the formulation of a citywide School Facilities Master Plan and agreeing to provide $1.8 billion to help fund the plan. This valuable precedent should be applied in future disasters and extended to other public facility systems beyond schools. Moreover, FEMA should encourage information-sharing and deliberation across separate bureaucracies to promote more consistent plans and better integrated reconstruction plans across systems. They could also require (and provide support for) neighborhood input into systemwide facility plans and have the plans address their interaction and concurrence with neighborhood recovery. Since this type of systemwide, more integrative facilities planning will take time, a mechanism is also needed to rebuild some facilities on a "fast-track" basis where a clear and compelling need exists. The Quick Start Initiative, which delivered funds to rebuild five schools in advance of the overall facilities master plan, serves as an example for how this can be done.

FINAL WORDS

Large-scale disasters pose some of the most complex challenges to communities and governments, and these are challenges that places across the globe continue to confront. New Orleans' experience provides a rich learning opportunity along many dimensions. Two intertwined lessons are: the vital role that neighborhood rebuilding plays in citywide recovery and the potential for collective capacity at the neighborhood scale to accelerate and strengthen the recovery process and to nurture broader systemic improvements and reforms. Residents ultimately had to come home to reclaim and rebuild their city. When they organized and found common cause within their neighborhoods, they were able to shape and accelerate both their own and the city's recovery and to envision and act on new possibilities for New Orleans. The new vision, leadership, and capacity that emerged from grassroots rebuilding did not overcome the barriers to equitable recovery posed by long-standing economic, social, and racial problems. But it was an asset in the recovery process and continues to be as New Orleans works to become a better and more just city in the twenty-first century.

ACKNOWLEDGMENTS

As this book was the outgrowth of my courses and projects in New Orleans and entailed three years of research and writing, many people made it possible and contributed to its production. First, several professional colleagues introduced me to work in New Orleans and connected me to local organizations in 2006: Ivan Miestchovich, Long Nguyen, and Beth Siegel. Many community leaders and practitioners in New Orleans welcomed me and my students to work with their neighborhoods and organizations and shared their knowledge and insights about the city: Lisa Amoss, Robin Barnes, Hal Brown, James Bui, LaToya Cantrell, Phyllis Cassidy, Paul Ikemire, Jeanne Nathan, Hal Roark, Diem Nguyen, May Nguyen, Tuan Nguyen, Mary Tran, Father Vien The Nguyen, and Vera Warren-Williams. I am also appreciative of the dozens of other community leaders, planners, and practitioners who agreed to discuss their work with me, sharing their experiences, knowledge, and understanding of the recovery process. This book would not have been possible without their generosity and openness.

I received encouragement and support from many colleagues at MIT's Department of Urban Studies, both for my work in New Orleans and the writing of this book. As Department Head, Larry Vale provided encouragement and financial support for courses and student projects and sponsored and contributed to numerous department events and dialogues about the planning and recovery challenges in New Orleans. Amy Glasmeier, the next Department Head, continued and expanded DUSP's support for work in New Orleans, well after it had faded from public discourse and planning school studios. She planted the initial idea of writing this book, helped arrange for my research leave, and provided valuable advice and support in the book's final production. I benefitted from the advice, support, and knowledge of Susan Silberberg, Phil Thompson, and Cherie Abannat, who were partners and fellow travelers in New Orleans courses and projects. Phil Thompson, as DUSP's first deeply engaged faculty member in New Orleans, led the way for my work and helped with introductions, knowledge, and advice. Gus Newport, during his tenure as a Martin Luther King

Fellow, was another source of introductions, insight, and support for me and my students. MIT's Public Service Center, especially Sally Susnowitz and Alison Hynd, were generous and sustained supporters of my courses in New Orleans and of many student internships and projects in New Orleans. MIT's Co-Lab also provided financial and intellectual support for work in New Orleans and a space for many fruitful discussions and reflection, made possible by the leadership of Dayna Cunningham and the project management and convening skills of Amber Bradley and Dulari Tahbildar. Harriette Crawford provided valuable administrative support throughout the many years of my teaching, work, and research in New Orleans.

Numerous DUSP and MIT alumni who moved to New Orleans after graduation to contribute to the city's rebuilding helped keep me connected to the city and new developments, provided their own perspectives on the recovery process, and were a constant source of inspiration: Ore Alao, Jainey Bavishi, Will Bradshaw, Jackie Dadakis, Jeff Hebert, Ommeed Sathe, Lakshmi Siridan, and Sandi Stroud. I am especially appreciative of DUSP alumni and lifelong New Orleans residents, Seth Knudsen and Jeff Schwartz, who shared their knowledge of New Orleans, made valuable referrals and introductions, unlocked some important information sources, and introduced me to many good restaurants. Several of these alumni (and others) wrote Master's Theses on New Orleans that aided in my research and helped shaped my thinking about the city's recovery.

I received research, editorial, and production assistance from many people. Rob Olshanksy shared research materials and provided valuable feedback on chapter 2. Amanda Martin provided great research assistance on education issues, the biomedical district, and aspects of the Broadmoor chapter. Aditi Mehta assisted with early research on news coverage of city and neighborhood rebuilding. Lee Carpenter provided timely copy-editing and formatting assistance to prepare the final manuscript. Many of the book's graphics are the work of colleagues at MIT. Heather McCann produced the maps, while Duncan Kincaid and Jesse Kaminsky prepared several charts and diagrams. Dean Adele Santos and MIT's Humanities, Arts and Social Sciences Research Fund provided financial support for travel and research assistance.

Finally and most importantly, my wife, Deborah Becker, wore many hats and was an essential partner for this book in so many ways: participating in research interviews in New Orleans, preparing notes, conducting research on many topics, editing and proofreading, discussing all aspects of the book, and helping me to formulate my ideas. She was also a constant source of support and encouragement.

APPENDIX

Recovery CDBG and FEMA Public Assistance Funds Committed by Program for Six Neighborhoods, August 2010

HOUSING PROGRAMS

Table A.1. ROAD HOME PROGRAM

Neighborhood	Number of Awards, Option 1	Amount Awarded, Option 1	Number of Awards, Options 2 & 3	Amount Awarded Options 2 & 3	Total Number of Awards	Total Amount of Awards
Faubourg St. John	271	$23,173,000	6	$ 530,256	277	$23,703,256
Broadmoor	810	$78,927,344	39	$4,514,081	849	$83,441,424
Mid-City	811	$78,474,261	53	$5,287,383	864	$83,761,644
Tremé	391	$36,366,407	16	$1,446,307	407	$37,812,715
Lower Mid-City	169	$15,601,309	12	$ 1,136,108	181	$16,737,416
Village de L'Est	1812	$153,566,000	87	$7,431,507	1899	$160,997,507

Table A.2. SMALL RENTAL PROPERTIES PROGRAM (SRPP)

Neighborhood	Amount SRPP Awards	Number SRPP Units
Faubourg St. John	$1,485,675	40
Broadmoor	$2,649,001	54
Mid-City	$4,660,850	129
Tremé	$1,755,668	41
Lower Mid-City	$1,896,208	36
Village de L'Est	$1,888,350	31

Table A.3. ALTERNATIVE HOUSING PILOT PROGRAM (AHPP)

Neighborhood	Number of AHPP Units
Faubourg St. John	1
Broadmoor	31
Lower Mid-City	0
Mid-City	21
Tremé	10
Village de L'Est	0

ECONOMIC DEVELOPMENT PROGRAMS

Table A.4. SMALL FIRM LOAN AND GRANT PROGRAM

Neighborhood	Number of Grants and Loans	Amount of Grants and Loans
Faubourg St. John	13	$570,000
Broadmoor	7	$ 97,859
Mid-City	77	$2,615,107
Tremé	20	$528,820
Lower Mid-City	50	$1,617,625
Village de L'Est	131	$3,882,144

Table A.5. TECHNICAL ASSISTANCE TO SMALL FIRMS

Neighborhood	Number of Firms Assisted	Amount of Assistance
Faubourg St. John	32	$51,274
Broadmoor	20	$15,276
Mid-City	83	$204,091
Tremé	34	$87,426
Lower Mid-City	35	$40,164
Village de L'Est	117	$141,525

Table A.6. LOUISIANA BRIDGE LOAN PROGRAM

Neighborhood	Number of Loans	Amount of Loans
Faubourg St. John	2	$50,000
Broadmoor	0	$0
Mid-City	6	$145,570
Tremé	1	$25,000
Lower Mid-City	3	$75,000
Village de L'Est	0	$0

ADDITIONAL ECONOMIC DEVELOPMENT FUNDING

A $3,350,000 grant was made to the LSU Health Science Center (in partnership with the Tulane University Health Science Center) in Lower Mid-City under the Research Commercialization/Educational Enhancement Program to restore the economic impact of scientific and technology research facilities within higher education institutions in the most severely affected areas. The grant was for research on infectious diseases.

Table A.7. PUBLIC FACILITIES AND INFRASTRUCTURE

Neighborhood	Program	Amount Obligated	Amount Disbursed
Faubourg St. John	FEMA PA Total	$1,617,317	$198,149
	CDBG Infrastructure Total	$1,000,000	$ –
	Grand Total	**$2,617,317**	**$198,149**
Broadmoor	FEMA PA Total	$4,365,321	$1,465,903
	CDBG Infrastructure Total	$3,200,000	$180,344
	Grand Total	**$7,565,321**	**$1,646,247**
Mid-City	FEMA PA Total	$370,011,697	$149,100,020
	CDBG Infrastructure Total	$11,667,642	$1,633,067
	Grand Total	**$381,679,339**	**$150,733,088**
Tremé	FEMA PA Total	$28,791,107	$12,351,272
	CDBG Infrastructure Total	$16,895,634	$14,625,738
	Grand Total	**$45,686,741**	**$26,977,010**
Lower Mid-City	FEMA PA Total	$47,593,288	$29,514,277
	CDBG Infrastructure Total	$ –	$ –
	Grand Total	**$47,593,288**	**$29,514,277**
Village De L'Est	FEMA PA Total	$2,313,848	$785,527
	CDBG Infrastructure Total	$5,348,992	$5,252,867
	Grand Total	**$7,662,840**	**$6,038,394**

A $2,500,000 grant was made to educational institutions in Mid-City under the Workforce Recovery Program to train and place workers in critical recovery sectors that included construction, healthcare, transportation, cultural economy, advanced manufacturing, and oil and gas.

Data for all tables provided by the Louisiana Office of Community Development.

NOTES

CHAPTER 1

1. The description of Hurricane Katrina's development, path, and strength are from Richard D. Knabb, Jamie R. Rhome, and Daniel P. Brown, *Tropical Cyclone Report Hurricane Katrina 23–30 August 2005*, National Hurricane Center, December 20, 2005, updated August 10, 2006. A more detailed account of the storm's development, its monitoring by the National Hurricane Center, and communications with Louisiana and New Orleans officials in advance of the storm can be found in John McQuaid and Mark Schleifstein, *Path of Destruction* (New York: Little Brown and Company, 2006), pp. 161–186.

2. Katrina was likely a Category 4 storm just before landfall and may have impacted this part of the Louisiana coast with category 4 strength winds. See Knabb, Rhome, and Brown, pp. 6–7.

3. Fox and CNN News Broadcasts, August 29, 2005.

4. Dan Baum, *Nine Lives*, p. 219. This quote was written by Dan Baum based on his extensive interviews with Anthony Wells, one of the nine people whose stories are told in the book. Anthony Wells remained in his home in the Goose section of New Orleans East during Katrina.

5. See Pierce Lewis, *New Orleans: The Making of an Urban Landscape* (Santa Fe, NM: The Center for American Places, Inc., 2003), pp. 74–76 for a discussion of the Intracoastal Waterway and MRGO and their relationship to shipping and New Orleans Port development. The Intracoastal Waterway is part of a larger system of waterways extending from Texas to Florida.

6. Design and construction flaws in the levee system also were a leading reason for system failure and flooding of New Orleans; see UNOP Citywide Plan, Chapter 2, pp. 25–26 and McQuaid and Schleifstein, pp. 339–344. For example, a 1985 field test showed that water pressure on sheet pile in soft soil would lead the wall to bend away from its earthen base, resulting in fractures, but this flaw was not addressed and was an important factor in flood wall and levee failures.

7. A detailed animated explanation of the sequential levee breaches and flooding of the New Orleans region prepared by *The Times–Picayune* is at http://www.nola.com/katrina/graphics/flashflood.swf. The account in this paragraph is based on this graphic, which highlights the most significant breaches and flood events affecting New Orleans.

8. McQuaid and Schleifstein, p. 193.

9. Further flooding of New Orleans East and St. Bernard Parish resulted from the storm surge topping flood walls along Lake Pontchartrain and the Arpent Canal levee, respectively.

10. *UNOP Citywide Plan*, Chapter 2, p. 26.

11. *UNOP Citywide Plan,* Chapter 2; Knabb, Rhome, and Brown, *Tropical Cyclone Report Hurricane Katrina.*

12. Two accounts of the early days after the storm are McQuaid and Schleifstein, Chapters 10–15 and Douglas Brinkley, *The Great Deluge: Hurricane Katrina, New Orleans, and the Mississippi Gulf Coast* (New York: Harper Collins, 2006).

13. Joan Brunkard, Gonza Namulanda, and Raoult Ratard, "Hurricane Katrina Deaths, Louisiana, 2005," *Disaster Medicine and Public Health Preparedness,* August 2008. The authors reviewed death records and identified 986 deaths that could be attributed to Katrina and another 454 for which the cause of death was reported as being indeterminate. Consequently, they view 1,440, the total of 986 and 454, as the upper-bound of deaths that may have been caused by the storm.

14. Some estimates place the number of people who remained in New Orleans at 100,000. See GAO, *Transportation-Disadvantaged Populations: Actions Needed to Clarify Responsibilities and Increase Preparedness for Evacuations,* December 2006 (Report GAO-07-44), p. 1.

15. According to the 2000 Census, 51,435 households in New Orleans were without a vehicle; 48 percent of these were headed by a person 65 years of age or older, and 76 percent were headed by African Americans. Some of these households had access to the cars of friends and relatives, so could leave the city, but with 27 percent of all households lacking a car, the evacuation of the city through private transportation alone was not feasible.

16. One oversight that impacts particularly vulnerable residents is a gap in the federal medical emergency system to provide for the evacuation of nursing homes. See GAO, *Disaster Preparedness: Preliminary Observations on the Evacuation of Hospitals and Nursing Homes Due to Hurricanes,* GAO-06-443R (Washington, DC: February 16, 2006).

17. Robert B. Olshansky and Laurie A. Johnson, *Clear as Mud: Planning for the Rebuilding of New Orleans,* p. 4.

18. Editors of Time Magazine, *Hurricane Katrina: The Storm that Changed America* (New York: Time Inc., 2005).

19. *Hurricane Katrina: GAO's Preliminary Observations Regarding Preparedness, Response, and Recovery,* Testimony of David M. Walker, Comptroller General of the United States before the Senate Homeland Security and Governmental Affairs Committee, GAO-06-442T (Washington, DC, March 8, 2006); *Hurricane Katrina: The Storm that Changed America* (New York: Time Inc., 2005).

20. McQuaid and Schleifstein, pp. 287, 295.

21. Eric Lipton, Christopher Drew, Scott Shane, and David Rohde, "Breakdowns Marked Path From Hurricane to Anarchy," *New York Times,* September 11, 2005.

22. McQuaid and Schleifstein, pp. 229–230.

23. McQuaid and Schleifstein, p. 235.

24. McQuaid and Schleifstein, pp. 297–298. There were also mixed reports on the extent of crime in the Superdome and the Convention Center. Mayor Nagin and Police Chief P. Edwin Compass III stated that they believed murders occurred in the Superdome; New Orleans Swat Team Chief Captain Winn reported extensive violence and lawlessness in the Convention Center, including groups of 15 to 25 men terrorizing people, stealing jewelry and cash. In addition, there were police reports of murders and rapes (reported in Eric Lipton, Christopher Drew, Scott Shane, and David Rohde, "Breakdowns Marked Path From Hurricane to Anarchy,"

New York Times, September 11, 2005). McQuaid and Schleifstein reported that there were few instances of violent crime and that the National Guard were welcomed as "liberators" and had no problem establishing security once they arrived (pp. 312–313).

25. Editors of *Hurricane Katrina: The Storm that Changed America* (New York: Time Inc., 2005). The 42,000 figure for persons evacuated in these initial days is from Manuel Roig-Franzia and Spencer Hsu, "Many Evacuated, but Thousands Still Waiting: White House Shifts Blame to State and Local Officials," *Washington Post*, September 4, 2005.

26. A national Katrina hotline and website were established by the National Center for Missing & Exploited Children, which logged 34,112 phone calls involving separated families and missing persons, 5,192 cases of missing or separated children, and over 12,000 instances of missing adults.

27. Quoted from *National Center For Missing & Exploited Children Reunites Last Missing Child Separated By Hurricane Katrina And Rita*, March 17, 2006. Press Release by NCMEC.

28. *Gulf Coast Rebuilding: Observations on Federal Financial Implications*, Testimony of Stanley J. Czerwinksi, GAO Director of Strategic Issues, Before the Committee on the Budget, House of Representatives, August 2, 2007.

29. The task of pumping out the city was worsened and further delayed by additional rain and flooding that occurred with Hurricane Rita, which made landfall on September 24.

30. *UNOP Citywide Plan*, Chapter 2, p. 29.

31. *UNOP Citywide Plan*, Chapter 2, p. 33.

32. A combination of design flaws, construction problems, and sections of the design system that had not yet been constructed due to long delays in receiving congressional funding contributed to the flood control system failures, John McQuaid, "The Levees" in *City Adrift: New Orleans Before and After Katrina* (Baton Rouge: Louisiana State University Press, 2007), pp. 20–29. The system's performance was also undermined by rising sea levels and the compacting of soils from oil and gas extraction, as well as pumping out water to prevent flooding and to open up more city land for development. See Robert Giegengack and Kenneth R. Foster, "Physical Constraints on Reconstructing New Orleans," p. 25, in Eugenie L Birch and Susan M. Wachler, eds., *Rebuilding Urban Places After Disaster* (Philadelphia: University of Pennsylvania Press, 2006).

33. Olshansky and Johnson, pp. 7 and 11.

34. Jennifer Steinhauer, "Storm and Crises: Rebuilding; New Orleans Is Still Grappling With the Basics of Rebuilding," *New York Times*, November 8, 2005.

35. *UNOP Citywide Plan*, Chapter 2, pp. 40–41.

36. New Orleans had allocated $140 million for 550 miles of road repairs in 2004 following voter approval of a bond referendum.

37. *UNOP Citywide Plan*, Chapter 2, p. 41.

38. One early analysis of damages from Katrina across the three Gulf States estimated total damages to residential structure at $49.7 billion—over twice the estimate for commercial structures ($21.1 billion) and the highest among the eight damage categories analyzed. See Mark L. Burton and Michael J. Hicks, *Hurricane Katrina: Preliminary Estimates of Commercial and Public Sector Damages* (Huntington, WV: Center for Business and Economic Research, Marshall University, 2005), p. 6 . This pattern likely held (and may have been even more heavily weighted to res-

idential property damage) for New Orleans, with its extensive flooding and the predominance of residential properties in low-lying areas.

39. *Current Housing Unit Damage Estimates, Hurricanes Katrina, Rita and Wilma*, US Department of Housing and Urban Development, April 7, 2006. Severely damaged units met one of five criteria, including property inspections that found damage of $30,000 or more and remotely sensed flood depths of 2 feet or greater. Major damage was based on one of five criteria that included property inspections that found damage between $5,200 and $29,000 or remotely sensed flood depths of 1–2 feet. In practice, the damage losses in both categories were far higher. The SBS reported median property damage levels of $107,815 and $80,884 in New Orleans for severe and major damage, respectively.

40. Louisiana Office of Community Development, *Action Plan for the Use of Disaster Recovery Funds*, April 11, 2006. See p. 5 for the housing repair/rebuild/replacement cost estimate and Appendix 3 for statewide and Orleans Parish figures on major and severely damaged housing units.

41. *UNOP Citywide Plan*, Chapter 2, p. 44.

42. *UNOP Citywide Plan*, Chapter 2, p. 44. The school facilities Master Plan completed in 2008, three years after Katrina (with some repairs already made and six new schools built) projected $1.2 billion in school capital costs to repair and replace for 330 buildings, 77 of which were in poor or very poor condition, requiring either major renovation or replacement. See *A Blueprint for Building 21st Century Schools for New Orleans, New Orleans School Facilities Master Plan*, August 2008.

43. See Donna Fraiche, Testimony before the Subcommittee on Disaster Recovery, US Senate Committee on Homeland Security and Government Affairs, April 12, 2007, for a discussion of some of the challenges in and responses to bringing back health care practitioners.

44. *Status of the Health Care System in New Orleans and Difficult Decisions Related to Efforts to Rebuild It Approximately 6 Months After Hurricane Katrina*, US Government Accountability Office, March 2006.

45. A massive disparity and dispute over the rebuilding costs occurred, with FEMA estimating $12.4 million for University Hospital and $23.9 million for Charity Hospital to address only those repairs required to return the facilities to pre-disaster condition, and Louisiana State University's repair estimate of $117.4 million and $257.7 million, respectively. This cost estimate, at over 50 percent of the buildings' replacement value, supported LSU's argument that replacing the facilities, rather than repairing them, was the best option. See GAO, *Status of the Health Care System in New Orleans*, March 2006.

46. *UNOP Citywide Plan*, Chapter 2, p. 47.

47. Mark L. Burton and Michael J. Hicks, 2005.

48. Michael L. Dolfman, Solidelle Fortier Wasser, and Bruce Bergman, "The Effects of Hurricane Katrina on the New Orleans Economy," *Monthly Labor Review*, June, 2007, pp. 3–18.

49. Dek Terrell and Ryan Bilbo, *A Report on the Impact of Hurricanes Katrina and Rita on Louisiana Businesses: 2005Q2–2006Q4*, Tables 16 and 17. A *New York Times* article on April 5, 2006 reported that only 10 percent of businesses in New Orleans had reopened; see Gary Rivlin, "Patchy Recovery in New Orleans," *New York Times*, April 5, 2006.

50. See Rivlin, "Patchy Recovery in New Orleans," *New York Times*, April 5, 2006. A survey of 1,032 Gulf Coast businesses conducted in spring 2007, 18 months after the storm, still found labor availability and supply cost as highly ranked

challenges after insurance costs and red tape. Michael Turner, Robin Varghese, and Patrick Walker, *Recovery, Renewal and Resilience: Gulf Coast Small Businesses Two Years Later,* The Political & Economic Research Council, August, 2007.

51. Dolfman, Wasser, and Bergman, "The Effects of Hurricane Katrina on the New Orleans Economy."

52. Gary Rivlin, "After Two Storms, Cities Confront Economic Peril," *New York Times,* October 22, 2005.

53. Leslie Wayne, "Tax Bases Shattered, Gulf Region Faces Debt Crisis," *New York Times,* September 13, 2005.

54. Christine Hauser, "Mayor of New Orleans Announces Layoffs of City Workers," *New York Times,* October 5, 2005.

55. The exact language in Olshansky and Johnson is: "replanning, improvement and reconstruction of neighborhood and community centers and of areas or districts destroyed or seriously damaged by fire, earthquake, flood or other disasters."

56. Interview with Yolanda Rodriguez, City Planning Director, June 16, 2010.

57. Interview with resident who described conditions in New Orleans East upon return in September 2005.

58. Interview with resident on the conditions in Broadmoor and surrounding areas of New Orleans in early September 2005.

59. Emily Chamlee-Wright and Virgil Henry Storr, "There's No Place Like New Orleans: Sense of Place and Community Recovery in the Ninth Ward After Hurricane Katrina," *Journal of Urban Affairs,* 31(5), p. 623.

60. Kai Erickson and Lori Peek, *Hurricane Katrina Research Bibliography* provides an extensive listing of articles, books, and reports through October 2010, including over nine pages of citations on disaster recovery alone.

61. See for example, Marla Nelson, Renia Ehrenfeucht, and Shirley Laska, "Plans, Planning and People: Professional Expertise, Local Knowledge and Government Action in Post-Katrina New Orleans," in *Cityscape: A Journal of Policy Development and Research, 9* (3), pp. 23–52; Mafruza Khan, "The Color of Opportunity and the Future of New Orleans: Planning, Rebuilding and Social Inclusion after Hurricane Katrina" in Robert D. Bullard and Beverly Wright, *Race, Place and Environmental Justice after Hurricane Katrina* (Boulder CO: Westview Press, 2009, pp. 410–460). Karen Rowley, *The Role of Community Rebuilding Plan in the Hurricane Recovery* (Albany, NY: Rockefeller Institute of Government and Baton Rouge: Public Affairs Research Council of Louisiana, 2008) examines regional recovery planning in Mississippi and Louisiana and nine county and city plans in the two states.

62. This includes numerous reports by the US Government Accountability Office on the problems encountered with different federal recovery programs, a number of which are discussed in chapter 2; Donny R. Williams, *Far from Home: Deficiencies in Federal Disaster Housing Assistance after Hurricanes Katrina and Rita and Recommendations for Improvement,* Ad Hoc Subcommittee on Disaster Recovery of the Committee on Homeland Security and Governmental Affairs; Louise K. Comfort, et al., "Retrospectives and Perspectives on Hurricane Katrina: Five Years and Counting," (Public Administration Review, 70, no 5 (2010): 669–678), which calls for a stronger federal role in community-level recovery; Matthew O. Thomas and Peter Burns, *New Orleans Five Years Later: Key Questions in the Rebuilding of an American City,* (Washington, DC: Annual Meeting of the American Political Science Association, 2010) which highlights the differing roles of federal, state and local government policy and coordination in New Orleans recovery around

education, housing, economic development and policing. Jennifer Pike, *Spending Federal Disaster Aid Comparing the Process and Priorities in Louisiana and Mississippi in the Wake of Hurricanes Katrina and Rita* (Albany, NY: Rockefeller Institute of Government and Baton Rouge: Public Affairs Research Council of Louisiana, 2007) and Karen Rowley, *Three Years after Katrina and Rita, Challenges Remain* (Baton Rouge: Public Affairs Research Council of Louisiana, 2008), detail multiple barriers that state and local governments faced in utilizing federal recovery programs and the lack of coordination among federal programs.

63. Examples include Lisa A. Eargle, Ashraf M. Esmail, and Shyamal K. Das, "Disaster Impacts on Education: Hurricane Katrina and the Adaptation and Recovery of New Orleans-Area Colleges and Universities," in David L. Brunsma, David Overfelt, and J. Steven Picou, eds., *The Sociology of Katrina* (Lanham: Rowman & Littlefield Publishers, 2010); Davida Finger, "Public Housing in New Orleans Post Katrina: The Struggle for Housing as a Human Right," *Review of Black Political Economy*, 38 (4), pp. 327–337, 2011; Michelle Early Torregano and Shannon, Patrick, "Education Greenfield: A Critical Policy Analysis of Plans to Transform New Orleans Public Schools," *Journal for Critical Education Policy Studies*, 2009; Robert K. Whelan and Denise Strong, "Rebuilding Lives Post-Katrina: Choices and Challenges in New Orleans' Economic Development," in Bullard and Wright; Stephen Verderber, "The Unbuilding of Historic Neighborhoods in Post-Katrina New Orleans," *Journal of Urban Design*, 14(3), pp. 257–277; and the following articles in Amy Liu, et al., eds., *Resilience and Opportunity: Lessons from the U.S. Gulf Coast after Katrina and Rita* (Washington, D.C.: The Brooking Institution, 2011): Karen DeSalvo, "Delivering High Quality, Accessible Health Care: The Rise of Community Health Centers," Andre Perry and Michael Schwam-Baird, "School by School: The Transformation of New Orleans Public Education," Kalima Rose, "Bring New Orleans Home: Community, Faith and Non-profit-Driven Housing Recovery," and Nadiene Van Dyke, Jon Wood, and Lucia LeDoux, "Criminal Justice Reforms."

64. Examples include James R. Elliott, Amy Belone Hite, and Joel A. Devine, "Unequal Return: The Uneven Resettlement of New Orleans' Uptown Neighborhoods," *Organization & Environment* 22(4), pp. 410–421; Christina Finch, Christopher T. Emrich, and Susan L. Cutter, "Disaster Disparities and Differential Recovery in New Orleans," *Population and Environment*, 31(4), pp. 179–202; Elizabeth Fussell, Narayan Sastry, and Mark Van Landingham, "Race, Socioeconomic Status, and Return Migration to New Orleans after Hurricane Katrina," *Population and Environment*, 31(1–3), pp. 20–42; Rodney D. Green, Marie Kouassi, and Belinda Mambo, "Housing, Race and Recovery from Hurricane Katrina," *Review of Black Political Economy*, published online November 17, 2011; and Jonathan D. Stringfield, "Higher ground: an Exploratory Analysis of Characteristics Affecting Returning Populations after Hurricane Katrina," *Population and Environment*, 31(1–3), pp. 43–63.

65. Some articles address the role of universities in supporting neighborhood recovery efforts. See Jacob Wagner, Michael Frisch, and Billy Fields, "Building Local Capacity: Planning for Local Culture and Neighborhood Recovery in New Orleans," *Cityscape*, 10(3), pp. 39–56 and Kenneth M. Reardon, Rebekah Green, Lisa K. Bates, and Richard C. Kiely, "Commentary: Overcoming the Challenges of Post-disaster Planning in New Orleans: Lessons from the ACORN Housing/University Collaborative," *Journal of Planning Education and Research*, 28(3), pp, 391–400.

66. Farrah D. Gafford, "Rebuilding the Park: The Impact of Hurricane Katrina on a Black Middle Class Neighborhood," *Journal of Black Studies* 41(2), pp. 385–404, 2010.

67. Lisa K. Bates and Rebekah A. Green, "Housing Recovery in the Ninth Ward: Disparity in Policy, Process and Prospects," in Bullard and Wright, *Race, Place and Environmental Justice after Hurricane Katrina.*

68. James R. Elliot, Timothy J. Haney, and Petrice Sams-Abiodun, "Limits to Social Capital: Comparing Network Assistance in Two New Orleans Neighborhoods Devastated by Hurricane Katrina," *The Sociological Quarterly*, 51(4), pp. 624–648, Fall 2010.

69. For example, Lower Ninth Ward residents were one-third as likely to attend a neighborhood meeting or receive recovery assistance from community networks than Lakeview residents.

70. Michael Crutcher, Jr., Tremé: *Race and Place in a New Orleans Neighborhood*, pp. 114–126.

71. Karen J. Leong, Christopher A. Airriess, Wei Li, Angela Chia-Chen Chen, and Verna M. -Keith, "Resilient History and the Rebuilding of a Community: The Vietnamese American Community in New Orleans East," *Journal of American History*, December 2007.

72. Emily Chamlee-Wright, "Church Provision of Club Goods and Community Redevelopment in New Orleans East," Working Paper, Mercatus Center, George Mason University, 2007.

73. Eric Tang, "A Gulf Unites Us: The Vietnamese Americans of Black New Orleans East," *American Quarterly*, 2011.

74. Recent reviews and discussions of this literature include J. Steven Picou, David L. Brunsma, and David Overfelt, "Introduction: Katrina as Paradigm Shift: Reflections on Disaster Research in the Twentieth-First Century" in Brunsma, Overfelt, and Picou, *op. cit.* and Stewart Williams, "Rethinking the Nature of Disaster: From Failed Instruments of Learning to a Post-Social Understanding," *Social Forces*, 87(2), pp. 1115–1138. See E. L. Quarantelli, *The Disaster Recovery Process: What We Know and Do Not Know from Research*, 1999 for an earlier summary of disaster recovery research.

75. Picou, Brunsma, Overfelt, "Introduction: Katrina as Paradigm Shift: Reflections on Disaster Research in the Twenty-First Century" in Brunsma, Overfelt, and Picou, in eds., *The Sociology of Katrina* (Lanham: Rowman & Littlefield Publishers, 2010), pp. 16–17.

76. Anna M. Kleiner et al., "Using Research to Inform and Build Capacity among Community-Based Organizations: Four Years of Gulf Coast Recovery following Hurricane Katrina," in Brunsma, Overfelt, and Picou, eds., *op. cit.*, pp. 186–197. See Mark Pelling, *The Vulnerability of Cities: Natural Disasters and Social Resilience*, pp. 83–89 and 170–178 on the role of grassroots community organizations in addressing disasters in developing countries.

77. This definition is informed by Ronald F. Ferguson and Sara E. Stoutland, "Reconceiving the Community Development Field" in Ronald F. Ferguson and William T. Dickens, eds., *Urban Problems and Community Development*, (Washington, DC: Brookings Institution Press, 1999), and comprises their definition of level-zero organizations and nongovernmental level-one organizations with resident-based governance.

78. See Michael B. Tietz, "Neighborhood Economies and Regional Markets," *Economic Development Quarterly*, 3 (2), 1989, p. 114.

79. See http://www.gnocdc.org/def/neighborhood.html. The Greater New Orleans Community Data Center has largely adopted the city definitions with some minor changes noted on this website and used them to provide neighborhood scale data and maps. These maps were used to determine the neighborhood census tract and street boundaries that are used throughout the book.

80. Planning is often associated with the regulation of land-use, physical form, and design of places, but there are variations in planning by scale, field of interest, and approach. Patsy Healy, *Collaborative Planning Shaping Places and Societies* (Vancouver, BC: UBC Press, 1997) argues that planning has three main traditions: economic, spatial and public administration/policy. Eugenie J. Birch and Christopher Silver describe several different planning approaches as well as common themes in their brief overview of the first 100 years of the city planning field in "One Hundred Years of City Planning's Enduring and Evolving Connections," *Journal of the American Planning Association* 75(2), pp. 113–122. Another strand of planning, associated with Paul Davidoff, is advocacy planning that views planning as inherently political and values-based and argues for representation of all interests, particularly minorities and the poor in planning decisions. See Tom Angotti, *Advocacy and Community Planning: Past, Present and Future* at www.plannersnetwork.org/publications/2007_spring/angotti.htm for an overview of advocacy planning on its contemporary practice.

CHAPTER 2

1. Outside New Orleans, the nation dealt with providing aid and housing to the more than one million people evacuated by the storm who settled, at least temporarily, across 46 states, see "Fleeing Katrina" at http://www.epodunk.com/top10/diaspora/destination-map.html.

2. This discussion of the multiple recovery planning processes serves as background for understanding the context under which grass roots neighborhood rebuilding occurred. Therefore, it is based on existing research, especially Olshansky and Johnson, *Clear as Mud*, rather than original research by the author.

3. Mt. Auburn Associates, *World Trade Center Economic Recovery: Rebuilding the Economy of Lower Manhattan*, pp. 38–51 for detailed discussion of the formulation and content of this Action Plan.

4. Gary Rivlin, "New Orleans Executives Plan Revival," *New York Times*, September 10, 2005.

5. Olshansky and Johnson, p. 42.

6. Olshansky and Johnson, p. 42

7. Nelson, Ehrenfeucht, and Laska, "Plans, Planning and People: Professional Expertise, Local Knowledge and Government Action in Post-Katrina New Orleans," in *Cityscape: A Journal of Policy Development and Research*, 9 (3), pp. 23–52, 2007. See p. 29 for information on the City Council role in BNOB and the Advisory Committee.

8. The head of the New Orleans Business Council was quoted in *Newsweek* and the *Wall Street Journal* as stating that Katrina created an opportunity to build a city with fewer poor people, cited in Olshansky and Johnson, p. 26.

9. This committee is alternatively referred to as the City Planning Committee, Urban Planning Committee and Land-Use Committee. The Urban Planning Committee title is used in this discussion.

10. For example, students at Harvard Business School prepared preliminary proposals for the Economic Development Committee, and the consulting firm

Mt. Auburn Associates also worked with the committee on its report and recommendations. The author participated in this effort as a subcontractor to Mt. Auburn Associates.

11. Nelson, Ehrenfeucht, and Laska, pp. 28–30.
12. Olshansky and Johnson make this point in their discussion of the BNOB process, pp. 49–51 and 59–60.
13. Olshansky and Johnson, p. 43.
14. A *Rebuilding Strategy, New Orleans, LA.* November 12–18, PowerPoint Presentation and Draft Technical Report, December 10, 2005.
15. The ULI panel recommended that this corporation's board be appointed by the President, Governor, Mayor, and City Council, presumably to help establish it as a partnership with buy-in among all three levels of government.
16. This recommendation included dividing the city into three investment zones, A, B, and C based on their level of damage and corresponding level of rebuilding investment needed (pp. 47–51).
17. *ULI Draft Technical Report*, p. 7.
18. Olshansky and Johnson, pp. 44–46
19. Jeffrey Meitrodt and Frank Donze, "Plan Shrinks City Footprint," *The Times–Picayune*, December 14, 2005.
20. Olshansky and Johnson, pp. 46–47.
21. BNOB Urban Planning Committee, *Action Plan for New Orleans: The New American City*, January 11, 2006, p. 12. This report included five guidelines intended to inform the individual neighborhood plans. These guidelines proposed 5,000 to 10,000 people as an ideal neighborhood size and stated: "We should know that most residents are committed to return, at least half." A third guideline focused on neighborhood density and its impact on viable service delivery: "There should be enough people living close together (density) to permit the delivery of public infrastructure, services, and utilities in an efficient manner."
22. Base Flood Elevations are related to securing flood insurance under the National Flood Insurance Program (NFIP). For residents to have access to national flood insurance, New Orleans and Orleans Parish must enforce land-use and building regulations that require new structures (which includes existing structures undergoing renovations that cost more than 50 percent of the building's value) to be elevated above the Base Flood Elevations.
23. Olshansky and Johnson, pp. 55–56.
24. Olshansky and Johnson, pp. 57–58; Nelson, Ehrenfeucht, and Laska, pp. 29–30.
25. Olshansky and Johnson, p.60.
26. Interview with Father Vien The Nguyen, 11/5/10.
27. Michelle Goldberg. "Saving the Neighborhood," *Salon*, February 24, 2006, http://photos.nola.com/hurricane_katrina/2006/01/martin_luther_king_jr_day_events_1.html.
28. Mtangulizi Sanyika, "Katrina and the Conditions of Black New Orleans: The Struggle for Justice, Equity and Democracy," in Bullard and Wright, pp. 94–96; James Dao, "In New Orleans, Smaller May Mean Whiter," *The New York Times*, January 22, 2006.
29. See Sanyika, op. cit., pp. 91–92 and 96–100 for a discussion of AALP and its advocacy around the Citizens Bill of Rights and Neighborhood Rebuilding Equity Ordinance.

30. This policy was added to the National Response Plan in 2004 as Long-Term Community Recovery Emergency Support Function #14 (ESF 14). It was intended to support a process for creating a community-based vision for rebuilding after disaster, identify projects and funding strategies to achieve that vision, and create a mechanism to implement the project. See Olshansky and Johnson, pp. 30–31 for a discussion of ESM#14 and its initial implementation after Katrina.
31. Olshansky and Johnson, pp. 67–69.
32. Olshansky and Johnson, pp. 62–64.
33. Nagin presented a modified version of the BNOB plan on March 20, 2006, but without city council support the plan was not adopted. Moreover, without funding sources for its main proposals, there was no feasible basis for implementing it.
34. For example, the Health and Social Services Committee proposed a new system of neighborhood-based primary health care centers and the Economic Development Committee proposed a number of initiatives to reduce economic disparities and to use the rebuilding process to expand job opportunities for returning residents and create long-term regional competitive strengths.
35. Nelson, Ehrenfeucht, and Laska, p. 30.
36. Olshansky and Johnson (pp. 117–119) describe the Lambert plan process in more detail and illustrate how a community meeting worked in New Orleans East.
37. Olshansky and Johnson cite Paul Lambert as reporting that 400 to 500 people participated in each of the three meetings held outside New Orleans and that more than 7,500 residents attended the neighborhood meetings. See p. 115.
38. This list is culled from summaries in Olshansky and Johnson and Nelson, Ehrenfeucht, and Laska.
39. The cost for medium-term projects was $705 million, with $1.2 billion for long-term improvement projects.
40. Olshansky and Johnson, p. 97.
41. Olshansky and Johnson provided a very detailed treatment of these events in Chapter 4; see pp. 83–108.
42. The Greater New Orleans Foundation later agreed to provide another $1 million to fund the effort.
43. These RFQs were issued by the New Orleans Community Support Foundation with input from the City Planning Commission; see Olshansky and Johnson for a detailed discussion and chronology of the RFQ process, pp. 87–89 and 97–98.
44. The formal legal approval of the consultants and appointment of the CSO members occurred on August 31 at a board meeting of the New Orleans Community Services Foundation, the GNOF subsidary that received the funds for UNOP and was legally responsible for contracting for the plan. Olshansky and Johnson, p. 130.
45. In addition to the $3.5 million provided by the Rockefeller Foundation, the Greater New Orleans Foundation and Louisiana Disaster Recovery Foundation each provided $1 million for UNOP.
46. The description of the UNOP process is based on Olshansky and Johnson, pp. 127–129.
47. Olshansky and Johnson, p. 140.
48. Olshansky and Johnson, p. 132. AmericaSpeaks is a consulting firm specializing in the use of information and communications technologies to broaden citizen participation and decision-making. One of its highest profile efforts was

facilitating the large public meeting in July 2002 around planning to rebuild the World Trade Center site in New York City.

49. Olshansky and Johnson, pp. 146 and 152.

50. Details on the provisions and technology for the meeting are from Olshansky and Johnson, pp. 152–153.

51. See Olshansky and Johnson, pp. 155–157 for more details on the meeting participants, voting on different issues and rebuilding options, participants' evaluation of the event, and selected observer commentary.

52. Olshansky and Johnson, p. 177–178.

53. There were tensions between the citywide planning consultants and district level planners on how to address flood risk issues in district-level planning meetings. The citywide team felt it was critical for residents to have information on short- and long-term flood risks and discuss it as part of their rebuilding plans, but some district planners were resistant to this idea in part because it would raise residents' concerns about whether their neighborhood could rebuild or receive public services. See Olshansky and Johnson, pp. 148–149, 159–160.

54. District-level meetings reinforced this approach. Discussions at some meetings indicated that residents would consider elevating their homes or relocating if sufficient incentives were provided. See Olshansky and Johnson, p. 172.

55. UNOP, p. 72. Olshansky and Johnson discuss how planners arrived at these proposals, pp. 172–173.

56. Olshansky and Johnson, pp. 169–171 and *UNOP Citywide Plan*, pp. 59–68.

57. *UNOP Citywide Plan*, p. 72.

58. Formal city approval of UNOP was not completed until June 2007. Under the UNOP process, the final plan first needed to be approved by the New Orleans Community Service Foundation (NCSF) Board, which occurred on January 29, 2007. The plan then entered the city's public review and hearing process with the City Planning Commission (CPC) and the City Council, which took several months. CPC hearings were held on March 7 and 13 with Commission approval occurring on May 22. The transition to a new Office of Recovery Management and the need to convert the UNOP plan into a more detailed and feasible set of projects that could be implemented with available funding were major reasons for the delay. After CPC approval, a revised version of UNOP was approved by the City Council on June 21.

59. Projects were not only physical projects; they also included specific rebuilding policies and programs.

60. These goals are (1) Promote the integration of multilevel flood protection systems into rebuilding plans; (2) Renew the city's roads, utilities, public transit, and infrastructure in a sustainable and strategic fashion; (3) Ensure an adequate supply of affordable, rental, and public housing in an equitable manner; (4) Foster remedies to address blighted neighborhood conditions throughout the City; (5) Promote the strengthening and diversification of the economy; (6) Make significant, strategic investments in community facilities that will result in substantially enhanced community infrastructure and improved service delivery; and (7) Preserve New Orleans' culture, historic architecture and overall aesthetic character to the maximum extent possible while facilitating new development.

61. The UNOP plan used the term "recovery value" rather than priority level.

62. Blakely was a well-known planning educator and scholar who had experience in disaster recovery when he assisted Oakland in its response to the 1989 Loma Prieta earthquake and 1991 fire.

63. *UNOP Citywide Plan*, p. 139.

64. *UNOP Citywide Plan*, p. 136.

65. *UNOP Citywide Plan*, p. 166 cites 819 project worksheets submitted to FEMA for public assistance funding.

66. UNOP also emphasized the physical aspects of rebuilding. This was partly due to the bias in federal recovery aid toward buildings and physical assets but might also reflect the expertise and orientation of urban planners toward land use issues and the physical form of city development. For example, few proposed "projects" addressed the personal and social issues that people faced in returning, such as arranging child care or working out transportation if they lacked care, finding a trusted contractor, or overcoming the bureaucracy of dealing with and assessing aid programs and resolving insurance claims. Only one project in the housing sector for neighborhood recovery resource centers partly addressed this need. It was ranked low-priority and estimated at the lowest cost—by almost half the next smallest budgeted project among the seven housing sector projects. Similarly, a project for a citywide commercial corridor revitalization program addressed zoning, using public buildings to catalyze new development, streetscape improvements, and funds for private property owners to improve their buildings. It ignored the "soft" and people-focused aspects of creating a vibrant commercial corridor such as organizing, marketing, and special events and activities.

67. For example, the estimated cost for the slab-on-grade remediation program was $2.1 billion. At the start of the UNOP process, there was $645 million of uncommitted CDBG funding for community and infrastructure recovery projects, and it was unlikely that New Orleans would get all of these funds. According to Olshansky and Johnson, UNOP planning teams learned of this situation at a September 27 orientation meeting; see p. 139.

68. As quoted in *The Times–Picayune* article by Michelle Krupa, "Grand Plan: City Recovery Chief Envisions NO as a Hub for World's Growing Economies," February 1, 2007.

69. Interview with Earthea Nance, 6/15/10.

70. Michelle Krupa and Gordon Russell, "City's Post-K Blueprint Unveiled," *The Times–Picayune*, March 29, 2007.

71. Ibid.

72. Michelle Krupa and Frank Donze, "Leaders Stand United behind Recovery Plan," *The Times–Picayune*, March 30, 2007.

73. Krupa and Russell, op. cit.

74. Interview with Dr. Edward Blakely, 1/21/11.

75. The UNOP project summary sheets for each of the funded projects were included in an appendix.

76. Elisabeth Bumiller, "Bush Pledges Federal Role in Rebuilding Gulf Coast," *New York Times*, September 16, 2005. The role for federal assistance cited by Bush in this speech included providing the bulk of funds to rebuild the region's public infrastructure.

77. GAO Report 09-129, *Disaster Recovery: FEMA's Public Assistance Grant Program Experienced Challenges with Gulf Coast Rebuilding*, p. 7.

78. Bea, pp. 3–4.

79. http://www.fema.gov/news/newsrelease.fema?id=18686.

80. GAO Report 10-723, *Hurricanes Katrina and Rita: Federally Funded Programs Have Helped to Address the Needs of Gulf Coast Small Businesses, but Agency Data on Subcontracting Are Incomplete*, July 2010, pp. 5–6.

81. GAO Report 09-541, *Gulf Coast Disaster Recovery; Community Development Block Grant Program Guidance to States Needs to Be Improved*, June 2009, p. 6.
82. Congress also provided multiple tax incentives and credits to spur and support private rebuilding investment across damaged portions of the Gulf Coast, often referred to as Gulf Opportunity or GO Zone incentives. These included tax credits for employers to retain workers and assist with employee housing, bonus depreciation for new investment in the region, increased (expensing) of clean-up and demolition costs, an increase in tax credits to restore historic buildings, and special allocations of Low Income Housing and New Market tax credits.
83. Most CDBG funds go directly to "entitlement" cities, typically those with a population of 50,000 or more. State governments administer the part of the program that funds grants to small cities.
84. CDBG funds can be spent for purposes that advance two other national objectives: eliminating blight and addressing a pressing community need but at least 70 percent of CDBG funds must be spent on activities that benefit low- and moderate-income individuals. http://portal.hud.gov/hudportal/HUD?src=/program_offices/comm_planning/communitydevelopment/programs.
85. See Mt. Auburn Associates, 2005, pp. 78–79 and Seidman and Siegel, "Economic Recovery from the 9/11 disaster: Lessons from New York State's Response in Lower Manhattan," *Applied Research in Economic Development*, October 2008.
86. GAO Report 09-541, pp. 6–7. Several reports and articles have criticized these waivers for abandoning important public policy goals, reflecting a privatization of recovery policy and not allowing for public and community engagement in shaping how CDBG funds would be spent. See, for example, Kevin Fox Gotham and Miriam Greenberg, "From 9/11 to 8/29: Post-Disaster Recovery and Rebuilding in New York and New Orleans," *Social Forces*, 87(2) and Robert P. Stoker and Michael J. Rich, *Lessons and Limits: Tax Incentives and Rebuilding the Gulf Coast after Katrina*.
87. Waivers included requirements for holding a public hearing on the proposed action plan for how the CDBG funds would be spent, limits on state's direct administration of CDBG activities, requirements that funded housing activities comply with existing consolidated plans, annual reporting and HUD performance reviews (although states had to submit quarterly reports), and dollar-for-dollar match requirements on CDBG funds above $100,000 used for administration purposes.
88. GAO 04-72, *September 11: Overview of Federal Disaster Assistance to the New York City Area*, October, 2003, pp, 74–75; Gotham and Greenberg, p. 1049.
89. GAO 04-72, pp. 75–76.
90. GAO 08-913, *Gulf Opportunity Zone: States are Allocating Federal Tax Incentives to Finance Low-Income Housing and a Wide Range of Private Facilities,* 2008, p. 2; Gotham and Greenberg, p. 1053. Federal low-income housing tax credits provide tax credits to private developers that are then sold to investors, typically banks and large financial institutions, to provide a capital subsidy for low-income housing development. The complexity and large legal, accounting, and other transaction costs associated with using low-income housing tax credits mean that this subsidy is typically used for large projects undertaken by larger and experienced nonprofit and for-profit developers.
91. GAO 08-913, *Gulf Opportunity Zone: States are Allocating Federal Tax Incentives.*, pp. 10–11.

92. GAO 08-913, 2008, p. 28–29. The ten largest projects used up 76 percent of Louisiana's GO Zone tax-exempt bond authority, including two projects that received $1 billion each (p. 21). One factor that made it difficult for small firms and projects to use tax-exempt bonds was the high legal and transaction costs to issue the bonds.
93. GAO 08-913, 2008, p. 31.
94. Gotham and Greenberg, p. 1054.
95. Rebecca Mowray, "GO Zone bonds for Orleans Parish rebuilding now available to other parishes," The Times–Picayune, January 10, 2010.
96. GAO 08-913, 2008, p. 32
97. Gotham and Greenberg, p. 1054.
98. Leslie Eaton, "Gulf Hits Snags in Rebuilding Public Works," The New York Times, March 31, 2007.
99. Olshansky and Johnson, pp. 203–204.
100. Stoker and Rich, p. 16. Although Louisiana went the furthest in encouraging the creation of local recovery plans and allocating part of the recovery CDBG funds for local plan implementation, less than 7 percent of the state's recovery CDBG funding went to implement local recovery plans.
101. GAO 09-913, 2008, p. 5.
102. GAO 08-913, pp. 20–21.
103. Interview with Maggie Merrill, Mayor Nagin's policy advisor from 2007–2010.
104. Administrative responsibility for overseeing the spending went to the Office of Community Development, which ran the state's small cities CDBG program and thus was familiar with CDBG regulations and had existing relationships with HUD.
105. Hammer, "ICF's oversight of Road Home program Comes to an End," The Times–Picayune, September 28, 2009.
106. Paul Rainwater, "Louisiana Recovery Authority Looks to Match Investments to the Right Recovery Opportunities," Community Developments, Fall 2008, www.occ.treas.gov/cdd/newsletters/fall08/articles/landscape/cdn08fall03.htm.
107. The 58 percent share of the funds provided to New Orleans was based on damage assessments that indicated New Orleans incurred 58 percent of the state's losses from Katrina and Rita. Interview with Maggie Merrill. Although New Orleans Strategic Recovery and Redevelopment Plan anticipated a $442 million grant, the LRA ultimately awarded $411 million in CDBG funds to the city for its long-term recovery plan. Louisiana Recovery Authority, Progress Report, August 2008, p.3 and interview with Maggie Merrill, 9/9/10.
108. Hammer, "Road Home hits contract benchmark for first time," The Times–Picayune, September 2, 2007.
109. Meitrodt, "State Blasts Road Home firm," The Times–Picayune, December 24, 2006.
110. Hammer, "Road Home Hits Contract Benchmark for First Time," The Times–Picayune, September 2, 2007.
111. Two rounds of business recovery grants and loans were funded with CDBG dollars and provided through nonprofit organizations. The first grant round was begun in January 2007, with the second round started in April 2008. Rainwater, "Louisiana Recovery Authority Looks to Match Investments to the Right Recovery Opportunities," Community Developments, fall 2008, www.occ.treas.gov/cdd/newsletters/fall08/articles/landscape/cdn08fall03.htm.
112. Campbell Robinson, "Settlement Is Reached in Suit Over Katrina Grants," The New York Times, July 6, 2011. This difference in Road Home grants arose because

under the program's formula, the maximum grant was set to the lesser of either the pre-Katrina value of the home or the cost of repairs less insurance proceeds. Since home values were much lower in poorer neighborhoods with larger black populations, they typically received lower grant amounts despite a comparable financial gap in the repair cost. Bates and Green, pp. 236–247, discuss this problem and other factors that created racial disparities in program accessibility as well as grants awards.

113. Campbell Robinson, op. cit.
114. See GAO Report 09-541, pp. 13–21 for a detailed elaboration and discussion of the events and issues leading up to HUD's order and its final resolution.
115. An environment review entails reviewing a rehabilitation project for potential environmental impacts, providing for public notice and comment on the review, certifying compliance to HUD, and maintaining records of the environmental review.
116. One example of an environmental compliance cost, attributed to HUD officials in the GAO report, would be for a homeowner with an outdoor propane tank; HUD rules would require burying the tank or hardening the home to prevent damage to a home if the tank exploded. GAO Report 09–541, p. 11, footnote 18.
117. See GAO Report 09–541, pp. 22–26 for the details of this regulatory snafu.
118. Referred to prosaically in HUD regulations as sub-recipients.
119. When a homeowner decided to use the Road Home grant to relocate rather than to rebuild her or his pre-Katrina home, the state acquired the original home.
120. This account draws on documents related to the programs; an interview with Maggie Merrill (9/9/10), who was the staff person in Mayor Nagin's office who oversaw efforts to implement this program; an interview with NHS Executive Director Lauren Anderson (11/20/11); and press accounts.
121. Letter from LRA Executive Director Paul Rainwater to Mayor Ray Nagin dated May 27, 2008. This special approval or waiver was deemed necessary because the program planned to assist households with incomes (80 percent to 120 percent of area median income) above CDBG income limits for low- and moderate-income households, and to allow funds to be used for new construction.
122. *Federal Register*, 73(200), notice 61149, October 15, 2008.
123. Hammer, "New Orleans Neighborhood Housing Services to Run $20 Million Home Repair Effort," *The Times-Picayune*, August 18, 2009.
124. E-mail correspondence dated June 10, 2010 between New Orleans Program Delivery Unit, the Louisiana Office of Community Development, and Waggoner Engineering (a partner of Louisiana Solutions, a private firm hired to assist the state in administering recovery CDBG funds).
125. Hammer, "Audit Fault N.O. Housing Program," *The Times–Picayune*, November 2, 2010.
126. Hammer, "City Orders Housing Finance Agency to Pay 62 Home Loans," *The Times–Picayune*, November 4, 2010.
127. From the author's analysis of Louisiana OCD data on the www.rebuild.la.gov website.
128. A project worksheet may need to be amended if either the scope of work changes or construction bids differ from the estimated costs. These amended worksheets require state and FEMA approval.
129. GAO, pp. 7–11 for a description of the PA program and process. The 18-step diagram of the process is on pp. 10–11.

130. These problems are discussed in GAO Report 09-129, pp. 3–5.
131. Accurate cost estimation was also made more difficult with the increased costs for materials and labor triggered by the post-Katrina construction boom, GAO Report 09-129, pp. 3, 25.
132. Maggie Merrill interview, 9/9/10 and Maggi O'Dell, "City's $1 Billion Justice Complex Pie in the Sky," *The Times–Picayune*, August 25, 2008. Along with FEMA, the LRA questioned the need for and cost of the city's Criminal Justice facilities master plan.
133. GAO Report 09-129, *Disaster Recovery: FEMA's Public Assistance Grant Program Experienced Challenges with Gulf Coast Rebuilding*, first quote is from p. 4 and second quote is on p.5.
134. Chang, "FEMA Awards $1.8 billion to New Orleans Schools for Construction, Renovation Projects," *The Times–Picayune*, August 25, 2010.
135. Krupa, "Many FEMA Claims from Hurricane Katrina Remain Open," *The Times–Picayune,* August 30, 2010.
136. New Orleans Office of the Inspector General, *Review of City of New Orleans Professional Services Contract with MWH Americas, Inc. for Infrastructure Project Management*, April 21, 2010, pp. 23–24. The contract was later amended to allow its use for non-FEMA eligible project management costs. The city drew down $114.5 million of the line of credit for recovery projects from December 2007–January 2010.
137. GAO Report 09-129 p. 28. Congress had earlier reduced the local match requirement from 25 percent to 10 percent.
138. *UNOP Citywide Plan*, p. 166.
139. Krupa, "Many FEMA claims from Hurricane Katrina Remain Open," *The Times–Picayune,* August 30, 2010.
140. Data from www.rebuldla.gov website. The figure includes all Recovery CDBG Projects in Orleans Parish (97) and all obligated PA projects in Orleans Parish for the following applicants responsible for municipal level services: the City of New Orleans, New Orleans Water and Sewer Board, Housing Authority of New Orleans, Recovery School District, Orleans Parish Criminal Sheriff's Office, and the Regional Transportation Agency.
141. Mentioned in interviews with Ommeed Sathe, Director of Real Estate for NORA and Ellen Lee, former Deputy Executive Assistant to Mayor Nagin for Neighborhoods. Ed Blakely cited $20 million as the amount of unspent CDBG funds available when he was the city's recovery director.
142. HUD forgave the city for these funds and other audit findings in June 2007 in response to financial and other hardships faced by the city after Katrina. Letter from HUD Director of Community Planning and Development Gregory Hamilton to Donna Adkinson, New Orleans Chief Development Officer, dated June 15, 2007.
143. Katy Reckdahl, "HANO audits point to still-troubled agency," *The Times–Picayune*, September 6, 2009; Peter F. Burns and Mathew O. Thomas discussed these differences in their article, "A New New Orleans: Understanding the Role of History and the State-Local Relationship in the Recovery Process," *Journal of Urban Affairs*, 30(3), p. 263.
144. Ellen Lee interview.
145. Earthea Nance interview; Olshansky and Johnson, p. 192.
146. Lowe, *Case Studies of Community Foundation Support for Community Development Corporations*, Rutgers University PhD Dissertation, 2001, p. 93.

147. Interview with Ellen Lee, 8/10/10.

148. Nonprofit organizations, for example, played a critical role in economic recovery efforts after the WTC disaster; see Mt. Auburn report and SEEDCO documents. In fact, one of the CBOs that grew out of these efforts, SFS, created a New Orleans office and was active in business recovery efforts through its lending and TA programs.

149. The Preservation Resource Center had long-standing programs to evaluate rehab needs and finance restoration of historic homes and used volunteers to repair homes owned by the elderly, disabled, and low-income households, ultimately playing an important role in home rebuilding in several neighborhoods. See chapter 3.

150. See, for example, Nossiter, "New Orleans Picks Professor to Lead Efforts on Rebuilding," *The New York Times*, December 5, 2006.

151. Quoted in Nossiter, "New Orleans Picks Professor To Lead Efforts On Rebuilding," *The New York Times*, December 5, 2006.

152. Interviews with Ezra Rapport (9/2/10) and Ommeed Sathe (3/25/10).

153. Sathe interview.

154. Sathe interview.

155. Interviews with Rapport and Sathe.

156. Rapport interview.

157. Interview with Ezra Rapport; Mayor Ray Nagin, State of the City speech, May 28, 2008. The MWH contract was the outcome of a procurement process that initially included three separate RFPs issued on April 24, 2007—one for architectural design services, one for construction management, and the third for public infrastructure project management. The city selected seven firms for contract negotiations under these RFPs, including MWH, and decided to contract with only one of them, MWH, for services in all three categories. The contract with MWH was signed on December 21, 2007 to encompass 150 projects, with an estimated cost of $50 to $600 million. MWH's fees were capped at 8 percent of the design and construction cost. See New Orleans Office of the Inspector General, *Review of City of New Orleans Professional Services Contract With MWH Americas, Inc. for Infrastructure Project Management*, April 21, 2010, pp. 4–5.

158. Krupa, "City's Recovery Projects Go Online," *The Times–Picayune*, February 29, 2008.

159. This account of problems in implementing the new system draws on interview with Ed Blakely and Alexandra Norton (11/6/10).

160. One public example was the resignation of the city's Capital Projects Administrator Bill Chrisman over conflicts with chief technology officer and PDU head Harrison Boyd. Krupa, "Capital Projects Director Left after Long Dispute over Hurricane Recovery Spending," *The Times–Picayune*, March 8, 2010.

161. For example, interviewees reported that parts of the city's financial system still relied on punch-card computer systems run by a small set of employees.

162. Ezra Rapport interview.

163. The Veterans Administration hospital project is discussed in greater detail in chapter 5.

164. Ed Blakely interview.

165. Orleans Parish recovery CDBG project list from www.LArebuild.org and interview with Ed Blakely, 1/26/11.

166. Frank Donze, "Mayor Mitch Landrieu Expects Completion of 100 Recovery Projects in Three Years," *The Times–Picayune*, August 18, 2010.

167. Donze reported that the Nagin Administration had 655 recovery projects, of which 273 were completed or nearly finished, 138 were included among projects that the Landrieu Administration was committed to complete, and 186 were still under review.

CHAPTER 3

1. Broadmoor Neighborhood Snapshot, Greater New Orleans Neighborhood Data Center (GNOCDC) website, http://www.gnocdc.org/orleans/3/63/snapshot.html.
2. GNOCDC Broadmoor Neighborhood Snapshot, http://www.gnocdc.org/orleans/3/63/snapshot.html.
3. *The Redevelopment Plan for Broadmoor*, p. History-3 (the plan's pagination includes the chapter name). Flooding in heavy storms continued to be a problem for Broadmoor through 2002 when a major drainage regional flood control project, the Southeast Louisiana Urban Flood Control Project (SELA), brought improved drainage. See the *Broadmoor Plan*, p. History -7.
4. GNOCDC Broadmoor Neighborhood Snapshot, http://www.gnocdc.org/orleans/3/63/snapshot.html. *The Redevelopment Plan for Broadmoor*, p. History-4.
5. Some commercial activity and businesses are located at the neighborhood edges along Claiborne Avenue and the intersection of Broad and Washington Streets.
6. This account of planning for the rally is drawn from Esther Scott, *"Broadmoor Lives": A New Orleans Neighborhood's Battle to Recover from Hurricane Katrina (A)*, Kennedy School of Government Case Program, 2008, and interviews with LaToya Cantrell on 6/17/06 and Hal Roark on 6/14/10.
7. Scott, pp. 7–8; e-mail correspondence with LaToya Cantrell.
8. Interview with Timolyn Sams, New Orleans Neighborhood Partnership Network, 6/15/10.
9. *The Redevelopment Plan for Broadmoor*, p. History-4.
10. Interview with LaToya Cantrell, 6/17/10.
11. A *New York Times* article reported attendance at over 600. Kristina Shevory, "A New Orleans Neighborhood Rebuilds," *New York Times,* February 25, 2007.
12. For a more detailed description of the planning process and organizational structure used to prepare the *Broadmoor Plan*, see pp. Goals 16–28 of *The Redevelopment Plan for Broadmoor*, July 2006. The discussion of the planning process also draws on Scott, pp. Goals-16 to Goals-28.
13. Sub-area A was the northernmost mixed-income part of Broadmoor, bounded by Jefferson Davis Parkway, Washington Street, Fontainbleau and Broad Streets. The "B" sub-area was the lower-income eastern section between Napoleon Avenue and Toledano and south of Broad. Sub-group C was the western area between Napoleon and Nashville Avenues, bordered by Fountainbleau to the north and Claiborne Avenue to the south.
14. The Urban Planning Sub-committee's work was further divided into four areas: Housing, Urban Design, Flood Mitigation, and Community Development.
15. This section is based on interviews with Carolyn Wood on 8/3/10 and Doug Ahlers on 9/21/10 and Scott (A), pp. 15–18.
16. Isaacson was also head of the Aspen Institute and a former executive at CNN.
17. Ahlers also knew that Isaacson was friends with Harvard President Larry Summers and hoped Isaacson's support might also bring university resources to the table.

18. Interview with Ahlers, 10/21/10.
19. Interview with Ahlers, 9/21/10.
20. Descriptions of the planning process that inform this section are from *The Redevelopment Plan for Broadmoor*, pp. Goals 18–Goals 28 and Esther Scott, *"Broadmoor Lives": A New Orleans Neighborhood's Battle to Recover from Hurricane Katrina (B)*, Kennedy School of Government Case Program, 2008, pp. 3–6, 8–10.
21. The first Area meeting of Area C happened on January 30, 2006 with the final meeting for Area B on March 24.
22. Monthly meetings occurred from January through April and July, and two meetings occurred in May.
23. Cantrell's management of issues at community meetings and her handling of the bike path controversy are from Scott (B), p. 4.
24. When the overall priorities for different parts of the plan were done in May and June, addressing crime was deemed a high priority and bike paths a lesser priority.
25. The BIA hired the design firm of Eskew+Dumez+Ripple to prepare the visual components of this part of the plan, including maps and drawings to display the plan concepts and projects.
26. The nine sections are: Goals & Strategy, History, Conditions Pre-Katrina, Existing Conditions Post-Katrina, Future Vision, Education, Economic Development, Emergency Preparedness, and Implementation.
27. The nine goals were: (1) Support continued flood mitigation; (2) Repopulate and revitalize neighborhoods; (3) Create a safe and secure environment; (4) Build a central education & community corridor; (5) Rebuild housing and eliminate blighted properties; (6) Partner with Xavier University to bridge Broadmoor to Xavier's campus; (7) Work with the Church of the Annunciation Community to develop facilities and services on its campus; and (8) Redevelop Commercial Areas and (9) Become a partner in city revitalization.
28. The Goals and Strategy Section also details the process used to formulate the plan.
29. According to Hal Roark, the idea for the education corridor was based on a nexus model for education that was part of the BNOB plan.
30. The main national CDC intermediaries are the Local Initiative Support Corporation (LISC), which was created by the Ford Foundation in 1979; Enterprise Community Partners, founded in 1982 by real estate developer James Rouse and his wife to expand the supply of affordable housing; and NeighborWorks, a pilot initiative in the Nixon administration that was congressionally authorized in 1978 to promote reinvestment in older neighborhoods through partnerships between local financial institutions, residents, and local government. NeighborWorks organizations, initially known as Neighborhood Housing Services (NHS), first focused on helping homeowners buy and repair properties, but many NHS organizations have developed into CDCs.
31. New Orleans' efforts to create NONDC and its activities are detailed in Jeffrey Sheldon Lowe, *Case Studies of Community Foundation Support for Community Development Corporations*, Rutgers University PhD Dissertation, 2001.
32. Lowe, p. 93. In other cities, CDCs developed hundreds or thousands of housing units and ran other nonhousing programs.
33. Interview with Ellen Lee, 8/10/10.

34. Interview with Hal Roark, 6/14/10. The omission and subsequent inclusion of the Broadmoor Plan in the city council votes is also recounted in Olshansky and Johnson, p. 123.
35. This section is based on interviews with Doug Ahlers (9/21/2010) and Kelli Wright 11/4/10 and Scott 2008 (b), pp. 6–8.
36. These advantages were pointed out by Doug Ahlers in an interview on 9/21/10.
37. Ahlers interview, 9/21/10
38. Scott, 2008 A, p. 13.
39. This mailing worked to motivate residents and create awareness of rebuilding efforts, but it did not prove useful in gathering information on displaced residents and their plans.
40. This section is based on interviews with Hal Roark, 6/14/10, and LaToya Cantrell on 6/17/10.
41. Surdna's initial grant was for $50,000, but it was later extended for two more years at $75,000 per year for a total $200,000 grant over three years.
42. Interview with Hal Roark, 6/14/10.
43. For example, see McKnight and Kretzmann, *Mapping Community Capacity*, Institute for Policy Research, Northwestern University, 1996.
44. Scott, 2008 A, pp. 11–12.
45. Scott, 2008 B, pp. 10–11.
46. The mission was not exclusively for volunteers working in Broadmoor or working on rebuilding homes, although this was its largest use.
47. See Scott, 2008 B, pp. 14–15, for how the CGI commitment occurred and for information on Ahlers' role. The $5 million pledge could include both money and in-kind support.
48. *Five Years Later: Achievements, 2005–2010*, Broadmoor Improvement Association and Charter School Board Development Corporation. A total of $2.3 million was raised to renovate the library by July 2007.
49. Interview with LaToya Cantrell, 6/17/10.
50. Recovery School District Legislatively Mandated Plan, June 7, 2006, cited in Dulari Tahbildar, *Whose City? Whose Schools? A Case Study of Civic Engagement and Planning "from below" to Promote Educational Equity in New Orleans Public Schools*. Master's Thesis, MIT, June 2007.
51. New Orleans was one of the earlier southern school systems to desegregate but desegregation was marked by strong white resistance and conflict and with strong political and civic leadership supporting desegregation. White flight to the suburbs and the enrollment of many white students in private schools resulted in de facto segregated schools with 94 percent black enrollment in New Orleans public schools before Katrina. Lewis, pp. 99 and 127; Perry and Schwam-Baird, "School by School: The Transformation of New Orleans Public Education," pp. 32–33.
52. Paul Hill and Jane Hannaway, *After Katrina: Rebuilding Opportunity and Equity in the New New Orleans* (The Urban Institute, 2006).
53. Torregano and Patrick, "A Critical Policy Analysis of Plans to Transform New Orleans Public Schools," *Journal for Critical Education Policy Studies* 7(1) (2009), pp. 320–340. Under the law, the State Board of Elementary and Secondary Education (BESE) acts as the school board for "failing" schools taken over by the state.
55. At the time that Katrina hit, the RSD was operating five New Orleans schools, which the Louisiana Board of Elementary and Secondary Education had

transformed into charter schools. In spring of 2005, Mayor Ray Nagin proposed that the city take control of the 20 lowest-performing schools.

56. Tahbildar, 2007, p. 20.
57. Hill and Hannaway, 2006; Tahbildar, 2007.
58. The expanded definition included all schools scoring below the state's average School Performance Score and in school systems in "academic crisis" (R.S. 17:10.7).
59. Tahbildar, 2007.
60. The BDC minutes for 2007 to 2009 include repeated reports of delays and negotiations around the Keller Library but steady progress for the Wilson School project.
61. Scott, 2008 (Sequel), p. 1.
62. Pastorek, "Five New Schools to be Built in New Orleans" (no date), https://www.louisianaschools.net/lde/comm/five_new_schools.aspx, and Carr, "Five New School Sites Chosen for New Orleans," *The Times–Picayune*, September 12, 2007.
63. The Broadmoor Improvement Association and Plan were very explicit about the importance of a high-quality school as a means to reduce poverty. In a brochure summarizing the project, *The Broadmoor Improvement Association and the Wilson Charter School,* the BIA lists reducing poverty as a long-term impact from the schools through its role in increasing student achievement, access to state of the art computer technology, and helping prepare students for future jobs.
64. Interview with Will Bradshaw, 3/26/10.
65. The description of the Wilson School's green building features is from *Greening Charter Schools Andrew H. Wilson School Case Study,* Global Green USA, June 2010.
66. These include interpretative signs, a sun dial, a real-time Internet energy monitory system, vegetable garden plots created and maintained by students and faculty and a planned wetlands on the school grounds.
67. Enrichment programs include integration of the arts into the curriculum, ballet classes, a music ensemble, 4-H Club, chess club, and a summer enrichment program co-run by the YMCA and Bard College. This list is from the *Broadmoor Program Guide* and Wilson School enrollment brochure.
68. *Broadmoor Program Guide.*
69. EdisonLearning™ Case Study Louisiana models collaboration and achievement— Edison Learning, 2010. Wilson students also showed higher year-to-year average gains in reading and math proficiency than schools statewide during 2009.
70. Louisiana Board of Elementary and Secondary Education, *2009–10 School Performance Scores.*
71. Louisiana Board of Elementary and Secondary Education, *2011 School Performance Scores/Letter Grades.*
72. *NOLA By the Numbers: School Enrollment and Demographics,* Cowan Institute for Public Education Initiatives, Tulane University, March 2011.
73. Interview with Hal Roark, 6/14/10. Roark reported that Broadmoor's approach to work with the market and encourage a market-based recovery was embraced and supported by some foundations but not by others.
74. Interview with Roark, 6/14/10.
75. AmeriCorps is a program run by the Corporation for National and Community Service in which participants receive a modest living allowance and several

thousand dollars to apply toward repaying college loans or use in graduate education. They also have access to a federal loan forgiveness program. Part of these costs are paid with federal funds with limited costs for the host organization in which the AmeriCorps members work.

76. Interview with Karen Miller, 6/25/10. BDC's first office manager began in March 2007 with the expectation that she would work for a few months until the BDC set up a system to use volunteers to run the office. It soon became apparent that a volunteer system would not work and a regular full-time office staff person was needed. After taking a summer break, she started as the full-time office manager in September 2007.

77. Other AmeriCorps members worked elsewhere in Broadmoor, including at the Wilson School and Annunciation Mission.

78. Interview with Jonathan Graboyes, 6/22/10.

79. Esther Scott, *Broadmoor Lives: A New Orleans Neighborhood's Battle to Recover from Hurricane Katrina, Sequel,* Harvard Kennedy School of Government, 2008, p. 3.

80. This database and case management system grew out of the tracking of property and residents begun by Kelli Wright as part of the initial Repopulation Committee.

81. Scott, p. 3. BDC board meeting minutes, January 30, 2008 and April 30, 2008.

82. Interview with John Graboyes, 6/22/10. Broadmoor initially focused its case management system on connecting residents to C.A.R.E., a joint effort of the Salvation Army and Red Cross, but it fell through due to financial mismanagement and left many unfilled promises.

83. *Five Years Later: Achievements, 2005–2010,* Broadmoor Improvement Association and Charter School Board Development Corporation; interview with John Graboyes, 6/22/10.

84. See Richard Moe and Carter Wilkie, *Changing Place: Rebuilding Community in the Age of Sprawl* (New York: Henry Holt and Company, 1997), pp. 110–116, for a discussion of the PRC home repair and restoration programs and their impacts.

85. Rebuilding Together New Orleans, *Annual Report* 2009.

86. Before Katrina, Rebuilding Together focused on small-scale minor home repairs.

87. Interview with Jon Skvarka, 11/4/10. Rebuilding Together expanded from a staff of five in 2007 to 60 by fall 2010.

88. The BDC also secured a grant from the Greater New Orleans Foundation to fund a construction manager for Rebuilding Together projects in Broadmoor.

89. *Five Years Later: Achievements, 2005–2010,* Broadmoor Improvement Association and Charter School Board Development Corporation; interview with John Graboyes, 6/22/10. The BDC estimated the value of the volunteer labor from the Annunciation Mission and Rebuilding Together at $6.8 million dollars as of July 2010 based on 370,987 volunteer hours with a value of $18.75 per hour.

90. The BDC expects to repair 15 to 17 heavily damaged properties with these funds; interview with John Graboyes, 6/22/10.

91. Based on the 2000 Census, Broadmoor had 3,222 housing units. The 895 gutted units are 27.7 percent of these units. The LHFA, Annunciation Mission repairs, and Rebuilding Together repairs account for approximately 170 homes, which is 5.3 percent of the 3,222 pre-Katrina housing units.

92. Broadmoor's figures differ from those of the 2010 US Census but both show similar levels of vacant unused housing. Broadmoor's census counted buildings, not

individual units, while the US Census reported total and vacant housing units. Broadmoor's figures were 477 **properties** that were abandoned or not being rebuilt out of 2,225 properties—a 21.4 percent rate. The 2010 Census counted 3,183 **housing units**. Most of this discrepancy likely stems from properties with multiple housing units. From the US Census, Broadmoor had 980 vacant housing units but almost a quarter of these were for sale, for rent, under contract but not yet occupied, or seasonal units, thus likely to have been rebuilt or in the process of being rebuilt. The remaining 753 units, or 23.6 percent of Broadmoor's housing, were close to the 21.4 percent figure from Broadmoor's own data.

93. BDC e-mail correspondence to author (2/21/2011) and summary materials accompanying a January 26, 2011 letter to a funder.
94. E-mail correspondence with Doug Ahlers, 4/8/12.
95. This approach was outlined in materials submitted to funders and elaborated in conversations with Broadmoor's Executive Director Santiago Burgos.
96. Interview with Kelli Wright, 11/4/10.
97. Interview with Hal Roark, 6/14/10.
98. It would be preferable to compare the 2010 Census count to the population in 2005 prior to Katrina since Broadmoor's population likely changed between 2000 and 2005, but since the census is conducted every ten years, there are no neighborhood-level population figures for 2005.
99. Data are from *Five Years Later: Achievements, 2005–2010, Broadmoor Improvement Association and Charter School Board.*
100. UNOP District 3 Plan, pp. 5 and 9.
101. Broadmoor had a population of 7,232, with 3,222 housing units. Hollygrove's population was 6,919, with 2,981 housing units.
102. See Xavier De Souza Briggs, *Democracy as Problem Solving* (Cambridge, MA: The MIT Press, 2008), pp.13–14, which explores, through a series of case studies, the strategy and practice of creating civic capacity.
103. Interview with Jonathan Graboyes, 6/22/10.
104. Data provided by the Louisiana Office of Community Development. Through August 2010, $2.649 million in Small Rental Project Program funds had been invested in Broadmoor to rebuild 54 units.
105. These included a business development center, a microenterprise revolving loan fund, and training workshops for entrepreneurs.

CHAPTER 4

1. Lewis, pp 80–81,136–137, GNOCDC Pre-Katrina Neighborhood Snapshot, Village de L'Est (http://www.gnocdc.org/orleans/10/56/snapshot.html). See Mark J. Souther, "Suburban swamp: the rise and fall of planned new-town communities in New Orleans East," *Planning Perspectives*, 23(2) (2008), 197–219 for a more detailed history of planning and development of New Orleans East.
2. http://www.nasa.gov/centers/marshall/michoud/maf_capabilities.html.
3. Leong, et al., "Resilient History and the Rebuilding of a Community: The Vietnamese American Community in New Orleans East," *Journal of American History*, December 2007, p. 771.
4. Leong et al., p, 771.
5. Leong et al., pp. 775, Le, pp. 29–30.
6. Leong et al., p. 775.
7. Leong et al., p. 775.
8. Interview with Father Vien The Nguyen, 11/5/10.

9. New Orleans East had a large concentration of subsidized housing units. According to the *District 9-10-11 UNOP Plan*, it housed approximately 40 percent of New Orleans low-income residents that received section 8 housing subsidies (p. 4–4).

10. *Unified New Orleans Plan for Districts 9–10–11*, pp. c-2–c3.

11. The recovery assessment in the *District 9–10–11 UNOP Plan* completed in late 2006 reported that there was still visible debris in the district and that "debris pickup and removal is the most common problem" with city infrastructure and services (pp. 3–10).

12. Interviews with Tuan Nguyen, Mary Tran, and Trang Tu.

13. *District 9–10–11 UNOP*, pp. 3–10.

14. *District 9–10–11 UNOP*, pp. 3–10.

15. This section is based on interviews with Father Vien The Nguyen (11/5/10) and Trang Tu (9/21/10).

16. Interview with Father Vien The Nguyen, 11/5/10.

17. The main church had a large hole in the roof, the rectory had sustained water damage and was growing mold and the school was badly damaged on one side.

18. Volunteers hastily worked to cook more food to serve the many congregants. Interview with Father Vien The Nguyen, 11/5/10.

19. Interview with Trang Tu, 6/21/10.

20. This section is based on interviews with Father Vien Nguyen, Mary Tran, and Trang Tu.

21. The flood depth was important to know since the standard height for electric outlets was 16 inches and homes with flooding 1 or 2 inches below this depth could use power immediately without rewiring their home.

22. This account is based on interviews with Father Vien The Nguyen and Mary Tran from Sara Cantania, "Broken Promise," *The Gambit*, November 28, 2006.

23. The language from the lease agreement was quoted in Sara Cantania, "Broken Promise," *The Gambit*, November 28, 2006.

24. Sara Cantania's article in *The Gambit* quotes FEMA spokesman Ron Simpson to this effect and it is consistent with Father Vien Nguyen's account of FEMA's response. The determination of ineligibility was sometimes based on a resident moving into a temporary housing situation that FEMA deemed permanent. *The Gambit* article recounts the story of an 88-year-old deaf woman, My Huynh, who was first offered and moved into a trailer in Baton Rouge but was too isolated from her family and missed attending mass so she left Baton Rouge and moved into a two-room apartment without air conditioning or a working stove while she awaited a trailer. FEMA deemed her ineligible for a trailer, citing the apartment as permanent housing.

25. Interview with Father Vien and Sara Cantania, "Broken Promise," *The Gambit*, November 28, 2006.

26. The details and process for the organization plan is based on an interview with Trang Tu, 6/21/10. Father Vien confirmed that Tu had developed and presented a proposal to improve organization of recovery efforts.

27. This account of the design charrette is drawn primarily from an interview with Trang Tu, supplemented with information from interviews with Mary Tran, Tuan Nguyen, and Father Vien The Nguyen.

28. Trang Tu estimated that 60 to 80 people attended these two meetings. Input from these two meetings was incorporated into briefing materials provided to the design professionals who attended the charrette.

29. "Chef Menteur Landfill OK'd to C&D Accept Waste," Louisiana Department of Environmental Quality (LDEQ) Press Release, April 13. 2006. This estimate is also cited in Leslie Eaton, "A New Landfill in New Orleans Sets Off a Battle," *New York Times*, May 8, 2006.

30. Eaton, "A New Landfill in New Orleans Sets Off a Battle," *New York Times*, May 8, 2006. The state press release announcing approval of the Chef Menteur landfill stated that opening more landfills would reduce the required time for cleanup by 1.2 years with a second landfill and by 2 years if a total of three landfills were open.

31. J. Choi, A. Bhatt, and F. Chen, *In the Aftermath of Hurricane Katrina: The Chef Menteur Landfill and Its Effects on the Vietnamese-American Community*, Asian American Justice Center, August 2006, p. 7. The Gentilly landfill had been closed by the city in 1986 but was reopened after Katrina. See Eaton, "A New Landfill in New Orleans Sets off a Battle," *New York Times*,: May 8, 2006. It also posed environmental risk to the surrounding neighborhood and city since it was an older unlined landfill.

32. Choi et al., p. 8.

33. Tonda L. Hadley, *Congressional Inquiry, Landfill Cost Issues Relating to Disposal of Debris in the City of New Orleans*, Report DD-07-03, US Department of Homeland Security Memo, 12/15/2006, p. 2.

34. Hadley, p. 2.

35. Hadley, p. 2, J. Choi et al., p. 8.

36. Written testimony by Reverend Vien The Nguyen before the United States Senate Committee on the Environment & Public Works, February 26, 2007, p. 2.

37. The primary CDC staff person for the coalition was Leo Esclamado, a Dan Than Fellow who arrived in May 2006.

38. Tang, p. 124.

39. Tang, p. 129.

40. These include separating out material that could be recycled and reused and diverting potentially hazardous materials from the landfill. See testimony of Reverend Nguyen, pp. 2–3.

41. Interviews with Mimi Nguyen, 11/20/11 and James Bui, 10/25/10. Both reported that the 72-hour moratorium for testing was announced at the rally.

42. Testimony of Reverend Nguyen and Bruce Egger, "Landfill Testing Option Offered," *The Times–Picayune*, May 19, 2006.

43. Gordon Russell, "Chef Menteur Landfill Testing Called a Farce," *The Times–Picayune*, May 26, 2006; testimony of Reverend Nguyen; interview with James Bui, 10/25/10.

44. Testimony of Reverend Nguyen.

45. Interviews with Esclamado and Bui, 10/25/11.

46. Interview with Esclamado, 1/17/11.

47. Gordon Russell, "Second lawsuit Blasts East N.O. Landfill," *The Times–Picayune*, July 8, 2010.

48. Testimony by Reverend Nguyen. The city's position on the landfill was muddied when the city attorney sent a letter to LDEQ stating that the mayor did not necessarily oppose the landfill but only that WMI needed to get a local permit to continue to operate it. See Gordon Russell, "Chef Landfill to keep taking debris," *The Times–Picayune*, August 12, 2006.

49. Interview with Esclamado, 1/17/10.

50. From interview with Bui. 10/25/10.

51. Two volunteers, one from Boston and another from Southern California, worked with Village de L'Est teenagers to expand their role in the campaign, including meeting with City Councillors to gain their signatures to letters supporting closure of the landfill. Interview with Bui.

52. The creation of the coalition and changed relationship between the African American and Vietnamese American communities was cited in interviews with Diem Nguyen, Leo Esclamado, and Mimi Nguyen.

53. Interview with May Nguyen.

54. Interview with Esclamado.

55. Interview with Esclamado. These increased enforcement activities and the history of inaction regarding illegal dumping are discussed in Russell, "From Wetlands to Wastelands," *The Times–Picayune*, March 25, 2007.

56. The large effort devoted to the landfill campaign diverted some community time and resources from rebuilding projects, but on the other hand the strong role that elders played in the campaign heightened community support for developing the senior housing project. Interview with Bui, 10/25/10.

57. Enterprise was already working in New Orleans to support the efforts of Providence Community Housing, a new organization formed to develop affordable housing to bring residents back to New Orleans.

58. The students were undertaking this work as part of my spring 2006 Financing Economic Development class and were one of two teams working with the church on its business development goals. These projects emerged from discussions with Long Nguyen, Father Vien, and Trang Tu. A second team looked at options for organizing businesses to undertake revitalization of the commercial district and recommended forming a business association. I continued to work with MQVN CDC on economic development and community projects through 2010 as informal advisor to staff, through projects in my courses and the Chase Community Development Competition, and as a consultant to NAVASA.

59. It took close to one year for the CDC to obtain IRS approval for tax-exempt status (Tran Interview).

60. The six other members included several members of the church's pastoral council and business owners.

61. The bylaws provide for sole governance of the organization by the board of directors since the directors themselves rather than neighborhood residents and other stakeholders elect future directors of the CDC.

62. Neighborhood Works, a federally sponsored housing and community development intermediary, provided $100,000 for operating support, but these funds were not received until mid-2007.

63. Providence Community Housing, *Building Healthy Diverse Vibrant Communities*, May 2007.

64. The senior housing project description is from a grant application to Louisiana Economic Development.

65. Low-income tax credits provide ten years' worth of federal tax credits to private investors in low-income housing developments. The annual tax credit amount is equal to either 10 percent or 4 percent of the projects' total development costs, depending on the number of the low-income units developed and income level of the tenants housed in the project. States receive an annual amount of low-income tax credits from the federal government and then award these credits to developers for specific housing projects. The developer then relies on

a private syndication firm or nonprofit intermediaries to sell the tax credit to investors to raise funds for the housing development.

66. Interview with Tran.
67. Interview with Mimi Nguyen, 11/20/10.
68. According to the 2000 Census, Village de L'Est had 3,817 occupied housing units, of which 1,798 or 47 percent were owner-occupied. Total Road Home grants exceed 1,798, which may be due to new housing development and an increase in owner-occupied units between 2000 and 2005.
69. Harris, Mackin, Nafici, and Whitman, *Reaching Solid Ground: A Plan for a Faith-based CDC in Versailles*, May 2006. Report by student team in Financing Economic Development to Mary Queen of Vietnam Church.
70. This was possible because the business nodes were located on higher ground and had limited flooding.
71. Information on May Nguyen's family history and her initial business development work is from an interview with her on 11/18/10. During her tenure as Business Development Director and as a continuation of the work completed by my economic development class, I served as an informal advisor to her, providing suggestions and feedback on program and grant proposals. This firsthand knowledge also informs my description of MQVN CDC's business development work.
72. State government funds were for tourism promotion and were tied to marketing Village de L'Est to visitors from outside Louisiana.
73. Interview with Tuan Nguyen, 6/16/10.
74. The $12 million figure is from the MQVN CDC website, http://www.mqvncdc.org/page.php?id=14.
75. Interview with Dang, 11/4/10.
76. Other neighborhood priorities shared throughout New Orleans East were to reopen schools and hospitals and establish more community health centers. *UNOP District 9,10,11 Plan*, Chapter 6, and interview with Dang.
77. Quotes are from an interview with Dang, 11/4/10.
78. Interview with Bui, 10/25/10.
79. See the VAYLA website, www.vayla-no.org/home.
80. Interview with Dang, 11/4/10. MQVN CDC's outreach and leadership development work also led to a stronger support network for Vietnamese women in Village de L'Est.
81. Under the federal section 8 program, housing vouchers pay the difference between 30 percent of a tenant's income and the fair market rent in the area, as determined by HUD. A contract to provide these vouchers allowed the senior housing project to get fair market rent for its housing units.
82. Interviews with Tran, Tuan Nguyen, and Kelly.
83. This deadline applied to special LIHTC allocations provided under the 2005 GO Zone legislation, which were the tax credits awarded to the senior housing project.
84. Interviews with Tuan Nguyen and Kelly. The project in the Ninth Ward involved two separate developments, only one of which Christopher Homes expected to rebuild.
85. Nolan, "N.O. Priest Leaves Parish to Work for Church Tribunal," *The Times–Picayune*, June 30, 2010.
86. This account is based on interviews with Tran and Father Vien Nguyen.
87. From school description on MQVN CDC website: www.mqvncgc.org/.
88. Interview with Diem Nguyen, 1/14/11.

89. DeSalvo, *Community Health Clinics: Bringing Quality Care Closer to New Orleanians*, Brookings Institution, August 2010, p. 1.
90. This description of the problems in the New Orleans health care system and outcomes is from DeSalvo, pp. 2–3.
91. This body was appointed by Governor Blanco and worked in conjunction with the state Public Health Department (DeSalvo, pp. 4–5).
92. DeSalvo, pp. 5–9.
93. DeSalvo, pp. 10–11 and DeSalvo interview, 11/3/10. Federal policy looks toward Federally Qualified Health Centers (FQHC) as a means to deliver long-term funding for community-based health centers; it is not feasible for the dozens of new health clinics to obtain FQHC status within the next few years.
94. As of early 2011, all three hospitals remained closed, with plans to reopen Methodist Memorial in 2013. Interview with Diem Nguyen, 1/14/11.
95. Interview with Dang, 11/4/10.
96. Interview with DeSalvo, 11/3/10 and Diem Nguyen, 1/14/11. MQVN CDC had earlier initiated discussions with Touro Hospital about setting up a clinic in Village de L'Est. It was when these discussions dragged on without any action that Diem Nguyen sought out Tulane Medical School.
97. Interview with DeSalvo, 11/3/10.
98. Interview with DeSalvo, 11/3/10.
99. MQVN CDC web site. MQVN CDC also received a separate grant to provide community outreach and education around the prevention and early diagnosis of cervical cancer, which Vietnamese American women have at a rate five times that of non-Hispanic white women.
100. These vacant buildings were previously used as an auto repair shop and a nightclub.
101. Jacquelyn Dadakis, William Goodman, and Gerald Hunter, *Recommendations for Restoring Quality Healthcare to the New Orleans East Community*, MIT Department of Urban Studies and Planning, December 2008.
102. FQHC look-alike status provides the health center with enhanced reimbursement rates under Medicare and Medicaid, while full FQHC status also provides annual operating grants of $650,000 to provide care for the uninsured and federal torts claim protection for medical practitioners at the clinic. MQVN CDC applied for full FQHC status in December 2010.
103. Interview with Father Vien, 11/5/10.
104. The author was part of the NAVASA consultant team that advised Peter Nguyen on the urban farm project.
105. Interview with Diem Nguyen, 1/14/10.
106. Tang, p. 139.
107. Tuan Nguyen made this point in describing the numerous community residents who volunteered to provide translation services as part of assisting fishing and shrimp business owners hurt by the BP oil spill.
108. Chamlee-Wright, pp. 16–17.
109. Chamlee-Wright, pp. 17–19.

CHAPTER 5
1. On maps, the street is named Broad Avenue but residents refer to it as Broad Street.
2. Richard Campanella, *Bienville's Dilemma: A Historical Geography of New Orleans* (Lafayette, LA: Center for Louisiana Studies, 2008) p. 28.

3. Lewis, pp. 34–36.
4. This section draws on interviews with several neighborhood residents and activists: Lisa Amoss (3/24/2010), Keith Twitchell (11/13/2010), and Mary Jo Webster (11/12/2011), and materials from planning and rebuilding efforts by the Faubourg St. John Neighborhood Association.
5. UNOP District 4 Plan, pp. 25–27.
6. Property damage assessments are based on FEMA assessments conducted after Katrina. The figures summarized in this paragraph are based on the map from UNOP District Four Plan, p. 28.
7. Interviews with Lisa Amoss, 3/24/2010 and Keith Twitchell, 11/17/2010.
8. Anne Giseleson and Tristan Thompson, *How to Rebuild a City: Field Guide From a Work in Progress*, pp. 40–41.
9. Interviews with Mary Jo Webster 11/12/2010 and Keith Twitchell 11/17/2010.
10. Interview with Mary Jo Webster.
11. Joyce Rosenberg, "Small Businesses Ravaged by Katrina Struggle to Return: Coffeehouse Reopens Nearly Two Years Later," Associated Press, August 25, 2007, http://www.chron.com/business/article/Small-businesses-ravaged-by-Katrina-struggle-to-1816023.php; Gisleson and Thompson, op. cit, pp. 67–68.
12. Faubourg St. John Neighborhood Association website, www.fsjna.org, and interviews with Lisa Amoss 3/24/2010 and Keith Twitchell, 11/17/2010.
13. Strengths, Weaknesses, Opportunities. and Threats.
14. March 26, 2006 FSJNA Neighborhood Planning Meeting Notes.
15. The Vision Plan also stated the goal of restoring and rebuilding housing with increased home ownership and maintaining affordable housing.
16. FSJNA Neighborhood Planning Meeting Notes, April 8, 2006.
17. FSJNA Neighborhood Planning Meeting Notes, April 8, 2006.
18. Main Street districts are designated and funded through the Louisiana Main Street Office and are part of a larger national effort under the National Trust for Historic Preservation that promotes the revitalization of historic commercial districts through a four-part Main Street approach that involves design, promotion, organization and economic restructuring.
19. Friends of the Lafitte Corridor website, http://folc-nola.org/about.
20. Lolis E. Elie, "Public Parkway Through Tremé and Mid-City on the Drawing Board," *The Times–Picayune*, September 5, 2009.
21. Alex Woodward, "The Lafitte Greenway: Underway," *The Gambit,* March 15, 2011. The Design Workshop was originally selected to perform this work in November 2009, but its contract was terminated in January 2010 when HUD conducted an audit of CDBG funded projects. The contract was then rebid later that year and the Design Workshop was selected again. The contract with the Design Workshop faced some further delays but was signed in April 2011.
22. Interviews with Keith Twitchell, 11/17/2010, and Mary Jo Webster, 11/12/2010.
23. At the five-year anniversary of Katrina, Operation Playground had built or rebuilt 136 playgrounds. http://kaboom.org/about_kaboom/programs/operation_playground.
24. http://katrinafilm.wordpress.com/2008/01/21/olive-stallings-playground-renewal-2/.
25. Interview with Lisa Amoss, 3/24/2010.
26. Figures provided by the LA Office of Community Development. According to the US Census, there were 2284 housing units in FSJ in 2010, of which 712 were

owner-occupied. If vacant homes offered for sale are included, the utilization of Road Home Grants drops to 37 percent. Among businesses, 32 received technical assistance and 12 recovery grants or loans through state programs funded with federal CDBG recovery money.

27. Interviews with Lisa Amoss, 3/24/2010 and Keith Twitchell, 11/17/2010.
28. Recovery rates are the ratio of 2010 occupied housing units to 2000 occupied housing units from the US Census of Population and Housing.
29. Interview with Lisa Amoss, 3/24/2010.
30. The American Community Survey reports an increase in income based on pooled sample data from 2005 to 2009. This data is problematic since it uses data from the year of the storm and immediately after and thus may be under-counting lower income and rental households that were slower to return. Yet it shows the FSJ average household income increasing from $36,311 in 1999 to $54,570 (in 2009 dollars). In Census Tract 45, the 2005–2009 estimate for the average household income was $35,422, or 37 percent above the 2000 level.
31. The two bridges are the Cabrini Bridge, a historic 150-year-old iron bridge, and the Dumaine Bridge, built in 1951. FSJNA is collaborating with the New Orleans Regional Planning Commission and the City Department of Transportation to undertake these bridge improvement projects. Interview with Mary Jo Webster, 11/12/11.
32. Interview with Keith Twitchell, 11/17/10.
33. Interview with Mary Jo Webster, 11/12/11.
34. A concern over these disparities was expressed by some community activists, who hoped that the need for more rental and low-income housing would be addressed by large public housing redevelopments discussed later in the chapter.
35. Greater New Orleans Data Center Mid- City neighborhood snapshot, http://www.gnocdc.org/orleans/4/45/snapshot.html.
36. Lambert Advisory & SHEDO, Mid-City Neighborhood Planning District 4 Rebuilding Plan, page 3 and Ian McNulty, *A Season of Night: New Orleans Life After Katrina*, (Jackson: University Press of Mississippi, 2008) p. 31.
37. Interview with Jennifer Weisshaupt 6/16/2010.
38. Ian McNulty, *A Season of Night: New Orleans Life after Katrina*, pp. 31–32.
39. Interview with Jennifer Weisshaupt, 6/16/2010.
40. UNOP District Four Plan Chapter Three-Recovery Assessment, p. 26.
41. Lambert Advisory & SHEDO, p. 13 and UNOP District Four Plan Chapter Three-Recovery Assessment, p. 28.
42. Lambert Advisory & SHEDO, p. 13.
43. Bart Everson interview, 11/9/2010.
44. See MCNO website: http://mcno.org/about/.
45. The Lambert *Mid-City Neighborhood Planning District 4 Recovery Plan* describes it as the neighborhood's "policy statement and revitalization vision" that was created before the consultant team arrived, see p.5. Several verbatim parts of the vision statement posted by Everson are included in the Lambert Plan under the Recovery Vision and Goals section on p. 4.
46. Interviews with Jennifer Weisshaupt and Bart Everson; Lambert Advisory & SHEDO, p. 5, *Mid-City Recovery Plan Addendum*, December 7, 2006. The 12 committees were Housing, Governance, Green Space, Zoning, Economic Development, Transportation, Healthcare, Security and Crime Prevention, City Services, Hearts and Lives, Education.

47. Lambert Advisory & SHEDO, p. 5. and interviews with Jennifer Weisshaupt and Bart Everson.
48. This paragraph summarizes key aspects of the proposals presented on pp. 19–26. A fourth section discussed and proposed several citywide policies and programs to address housing needs.
49. Other medium-term park and green space proposals were planting trees and gardens along the neutral ground (meridian) of two boulevards (Jefferson Davis Parkway and Orleans Avenue), a redesign and new facilities at the St. Patrick Park, a new dog park, and four community gardens. Other medium-term proposals were a study on converting the closed Lindy Boggs medical complex into a community health center and senior housing and efforts to protect Mid-City's historic character.
50. MCNO also wrote and released its own separate text-only version of the Mid-City Recovery Plan, which can be found at http://thinknola.com/wiki/ Mid-City_Recovery_Plan. This summary of the addendum only addresses its major concerns. It also listed eight minor concerns, made revisions to the funding matrix, and listed corrections to seven "minor factual errors and typos."
51. These include proposals to study the development of the large transportation hub called "Midtown New Orleans" and for "open parking along the Jeff Davis corridor" that was included in the plan's concept for Comiskey Park.
52. Interview with Michael Holman, 11/15/2010.
53. The final draft of the resident's plan did include a proposal for a Mid-City Neighborhood Recovery Corporation but it was not pursued and implemented.
54. Memorandum dated July 17, 2006 from MCNO Education Committee to the New Orleans Public Library Board of Directors.
55. Interview with Jeanette Thompson, 11/4/2010.
56. This project was funded through the Gates Foundation.
57. The other five areas for these temporary libraries were the Lower Ninth Ward, New Orleans East, Algiers, Lakeview, and Broadmoor. *Rebuild: A Progress Report form the New Orleans Public Library Foundation,* Winter 2007.
58. Interview with Jeanette Thompson, 11/4/2010.
59. Interview with Jeanette Thompson, 11/4/2010.
60. Andrea Neighbours, "From Factory to Apartments in New Orleans," *New York Times,* March 26, 2000.
61. Review by Briana J. posted to Yelp on February 15, 2011.
62. Interview with Broderick Bagert, March 9, 2011; The Rebirth of Morris Jeff Community School, in *The New Orleans Tribune,* (Undated) http://theneworleanstribune.com/morrisjeff.htm.
63. The Rebirth of Morris Jeff Community School, in *The New Orleans Tribune,* (Undated) http://theneworleanstribune.com/morrisjeff.htm.
64. The phasing plan did not specify specific dates or time periods for each phase but it proposed completing all phases within 10 years—an ambitious schedule that depended on successfully securing $2 billion in funding. There were six phases for K–8 schools and five for high schools, so under the best scenario, phase two schools would not likely be built for at least 2 years. *A Blueprint: Building 21st Century Schools for New Orleans. School Facilities Master Plan for Orleans Parish,* Recovery School District and Orleans Parish School Board, August 2008, p. 66.
65. Interview with Broderick Bagart, 3/9/2011.

66. Mid-City Neighborhood Organization, Comments on the School Facilities Master Plan for Orleans Parish, September 30, 2010.

67. Sarah Carr and Darran Simon, "New Orleans Schools Set for Building Boom," *The Times–Picayune,* August 16, 2008.

68. Interview with Jeanette Thompson, 11/4/2010.

69. Interview with Broderick Bagert. According to Bagert, the details of the compromise were worked out at a meeting with Paul Vallas in January 2009. See also, Sarah Carr and Darran Simon, "New Orleans School Plans Receive Cautious Support: Costs, Campus Closures among Board Members' Concerns," *The Times–Picayune,* August 20, 2008.

70. State enrollment data from February 2011 has 138 students in kindergarten to grade 2, of whom 2 percent are Asian, 52 percent black, 2 percent Hispanic, 38 percent white and 5 percent mixed race. Sixty percent are considered at-risk (eligible for free or reduced cost lunches).

71. This account is based on interviews with Michael Holman, 11/16/2010 and Jeanette Thompson, 11/4/10.

72. Susan Finch, "Comiskey Park Project in Mid-City Vanishes," *The Times–Picayune,* June 1, 2008.

73. Susan Finch, "Comiskey Park Project in Mid-City Vanishes," *The Times–Picayune,* June 1, 2008.

74. Susan Finch, "Comiskey Park Project in Mid-City Remains in Limbo," *The Times–Picayune,* March 11, 2008.

75. Masako Hirsch and Gordon Russell, "Failed Comiskey Park Project Leaves City with $700,000 Bill," *The Times–Picayune,* August 23, 2010.

76. An audit report filed with the state film office and reported in an August 23, 2010 article by Masako Hirsch and Gordon Russell in the *The Times–Picayune* details payments of $923,765 for producers, executive producers, and production management along with a $529,000 public relations fee.

77. Lake Douglas, Jennifer Ruley, Daniel Samuels, Jacob Wagner, and Brown+Danos landdesign, inc., *The Lafitte Greenway: A Vision for the Lafitte Corridor,* December 2007.

78. McNulty, p. 82.

79. This description of Joseph Brock's work is based on an interview with him on November 3, 2010.

80. Alex Woodward, "Wise Words Community Garden: Mid-City Grows Another Urban Farm," *The Gambit,* January 22, 2010, and interview with Joseph Brock, 11/3/2010.

81. Interview with Joseph Brock, 11/3/2010.

82. Greg Thomas, "Giant Retail Project Planned for Mid-City," *The Times–Picayune,* March 31. 2007.

83. Kimberly Quillen, "Victory Real Estate wins demolition permit for Lindy Boggs Medical Center," *The Times–Picayune,* December 31, 2007.

84. MCNO economic development website (http://mcno.org/economic-development.

85. Interviews with Jennifer Weisshaupt, 6/16/2010 and Bart Everson, 11/9/10.

86. Bill Barrow, "St. Margaret's Daughters Pushes 2012 Opening of Nursing Home at Lindy Boggs Site," *The Times–Picayune,* February 8, 2011.

87. R. Stephanie Bruno, "Winn-Dixie Considers New Store on Carrollton Avenue in Mid-City," *The Times–Picayune,* January 24, 2011.

88. Rebecca Mowbray, "Winn-Dixie Will Anchor New Mid-City Shopping Complex," *The Times–Picayune*, June 10, 2011.

89. The full 15-point position statement is at http://mcno.org/mcno-takes-formal-position-on-mid-city-market-development/.

90. Robert Hand, RE/MAX Commercial Brokers, *Changing Industrial Warehouses to Affordable Apartments: A Story of How New Orleans is Bringing Residents Back*, undated, http://www.neworleansindustrial.com/admin/newsfiles/Changing percent20Industrial percent20Property percent20To percent20Affordable percent20Apartments.pdf.

91. Bruce Eggler, "City Planning Commission Approves Mid-City condos, Lakeview School," *The Times–Picayune*, February 11, 2010.

92. Interview with Joseph Brock, 11/3/2010.

93. Interview with Michael Holman, 11/16/2010.

94. Interview with Jennifer Weisshaupt, 6/16/2010.

95. The 864 Road Home grantees represent 53.1 percent of Mid-City's 1,626 owner-occupied housing units reported in the 2000 census and 68.5 percent of the 1,261 units counted in the 2010 census. If the number of homeowners increased from 2000 to 2005, as some sources suggested, then the percentage for 2005 may be slightly lower.

96. Planning commission staff cited examples of where MCNO opposition had stopped proposed projects and another agency mentioned MCNO as understanding and being willing to work out the trade-offs involved in city decisions.

97. Campanella, p. 28; Kiara Nagel, *Understanding Place after Katrina: Predatory Planning and Cultural Resistance in New Orleans Tremé Neighborhood*, (Master's Thesis, MIT, June 2006), p. 26; GNOCDC Tremé/Lafitte Neighborhood Snapshot, http://www.gnocdc.org/orleans/4/42/snapshot.html, cite a slightly later date of 1812.

98. Free people of color included the African American or mixed-race mistresses of white men and their offspring resulting from plaçage, as the long-term keeping of mistresses was known. See Crutcher, p. 23 and Ned Sublette, *The World that Made New Orleans From Spanish Silver to Congo Square* (Chicago: Lawrence Hill Books, 2009), p. 111.

99. Campanella, p. 28.

100. GNOCDC Tremé/Lafitte Neighborhood Snapshot, http://www.gnocdc.org/orleans/4/42/snapshot.html; Nagel, p. 27.

101. These laws arose out of fear that drumming and dancing might promote slave insurrections, Crutcher, pp. 27–28.

102. GNOCDC Tremé/Lafitte neighborhood snapshot; Sublette, pp. 281–283.

103. Crutcher, pp. 33–36 summarizes how these factors helped give birth to jazz and the significance of Tremé in this process.

104. Crutcher, pp. 37–40 describes the plans for, policies of, and impact related to the Municipal Auditorium project.

105. http://www.gnocdc.org/orleans/4/42/snapshot.html. New Orleans had a large network of public markets in the early decades of the twentieth century that were the primary source of fresh foods for city residents. See Jeffrey E. Schwartz, *Making Groceries, Food, Neighborhood Markets, and Neighborhood Recovery in Post-Katrina New Orleans*, (Master's Thesis, MIT, June 2008) for a longer discussion of public markets in New Orleans.

106. Campanella, p. 48.

107. Storyville had earlier become the target of federal anti-prostitution efforts and was closed down in 1917—Nagel, p. 36. Iberville's development involved the eviction of 800 families from Storyville.
108. Nagel, pp. 36–37.
109. Crutcher, p. 59.
110. Crutcher, pp. 53–57.
111. Crutcher, p. 60.
112. Crutcher, p. 60.
113. These figures on business activity are from a University of New Orleans PhD Dissertation by Daniel Samuels, *Remembering North Claiborne: Community and Place in Downtown New Orleans*, cited in Nagel, p, 40.
114. Crutcher, pp. 42–46, traces the evolution of the city's urban renewal program and plans for the cultural center project through the completion of the performing arts center.
115. Crutcher provides a detailed account of the long history of the efforts and controversies around the Performing Arts Center (pp. 37–49) and Louis Armstrong Park (pp. 66–81), including Tremé Community opposition to the latter. Plans for a second-phase development of Louis Armstrong Park continued into the early 1990s as sequential plans for a large-scale entertainment complex and a project in partnership with Copenhagen's Tivoli gardens failed. In the mid-1990s, the municipal auditorium had a short life as the temporary site for Harrah's New Orleans casino.
116. Figures on the number of families displaced by the cultural center/Louis Armstrong Park project vary in different accounts. Crutcher cites 122 families (121 nonwhite) living in the project area, 90 of whom had to be relocated in the 1964 plans for the project. Nagel cites a 1984 dissertation by Maria Donna Jones that reports 420 families were displaced, with 80 percent of them low-income blacks, and Richard Campanella in his timeline of New Orleans' development in Bienville's Dilemma says the project displaced over a thousand residents.
117. Crutcher, pp. 39–40, GNOCDC, Tremé neighborhood snapshot, http://www.gnocdc.org/orleans/4/42/snapshot.html.
118. Nagel, pp. 52–53.
119. Crutcher, pp. 5–6.
120. Crutcher, pp. 31–32.
121. Crutcher, pp 47–48.
122. Interview with Cheryl Austin, 11/16/2010; http://www.gnocdc.org/orleans/4/42/snapshot.html. Community activists and the Greater Tremé Consortium won several concessions from the casino project, including skills training and jobs for Tremé residents and a scholarship program for Tremé high school students, Crutcher, pp. 80–81.
123. Nagel, pp.47–48, "Veteran Activist Touted as Community Champion," Louisiana Weekly, August 10, 2010.
124. http://www.ujamaacdc.com/index.htm#.
125. Interview with Michelle Braden, 11/10/2010.
126. I heard differing accounts as to whether DNIA's founders left out of frustration with ERTCA or were expelled over differences about supporting the conversion of a firehouse into a senior center.
127. Tahbildar, pp. 35–36, interviews with Jeanne Nathan, 3/26/2010 and Robert Tannen, 11/8/2010.
128. Unified New Orleans Plan, District Four, p. 26.

129. Unified New Orleans Plan, District Four, p. 28.
130. Over 19 percent of Tremé's housing units were vacant in 2000, with the highest vacancy rate (25.8 percent) in the older Historic Tremé section between Claiborne Avenue and Rampart Street. John Skvarka of Rebuilding Together cited the conditions of Tremé housing that necessitated more costly repairs, November 5, 2010 interview.
131. This account of Greater Tremé Consortium's efforts is from an 11/16/2010 interview with Cheryl Austin.
132. Personal credit problems were common after Katrina, with the loss of income and personal property and emergency expenses that followed the storm.
133. Summary of the post-Katrina activities of ERTCA is from an 11/10/11 interview with association president Michelle Braden.
134. After the City Council approved the project in September 2010, it was halted by another action at the city's Board of Zoning Adjustments. At the end of 2010, the project appeared stalled, with its final resolution likely to be decided in court. See Stephen Babcock, "Esplanade Avenue Apartment Proposal Keeps Running into Roadblocks," *The Times–Picayune*, November 28, 2010.
135. Tahbildar, pp. 37–46 details the development of the DNIA Education Committee's initial post-Katrina education agenda and activities.
136. Sarah Carr, "Specialty High Schools Part of System Overhaul," *The Times–Picayune*, March 19, 2008.
137. Interview with Vera Warren-Williams, 11/18/2010.
138. This account of how the businesses reopened is based on an 11/18/10 interview with Vera Warren-Williams, and Oreoluwa Alao, *Rebuilding Plan Implementation in New Orleans, LA: A Case Study of Freret Street Commercial Corridor and Bayou Road Cultural Corridor*, pp. 44–47.
139. Alao, pp. 45–46, and interview with Robert Tannen 11/9/10.
140. http://www.crt.state.la.us/culturaldistricts/overview.aspx.
141. Interviews with Vera Warren Williams, 11/18/2010, and Hal Brown, 6/18/2010.
142. The account of HFTA's activities is based on an interview with Naydja Bynum on 11/8/2010, along with news and information from HFTA's website http://news.hfta.org/.
143. Joe's Cozy Corner was an established neighborhood bar, social hub, and one of Tremé's last jazz clubs, which was closed in spring 2004 following the revocation of its liquor license after a violent confrontation between Joe Glasper, the bar's owner and a street vendor. See Crutcher, pp. 1–6 and Rachel Breunlin, *Papa Joe Glasper and Joe's Cozy Corner: Downtown Development, Displacement and the Creation of Community*, Master's Thesis, Tulane University, 2004. Breunlin's thesis provides a detailed history of Joe's Cozy Corner and its role in the Tremé community.
144. Interview with Naydja Bynum, 11/8/2010.
145. Bruce Eggler, "Tremé Commercial Opportunities Increase under Zoning Change Approved by City Council," *The Times–Picayune*, August 18, 2010.
146. Bruce Eggler, "Apartment Complex Approved at Former site of St. Aloysius High School," *The Times–Picayune*, February 11, 2009, and Bruce Eggler "City Council Approves Mixed-Income Apartments on Esplanade Ave., but with Strings Attached," *The Times–Picayune*, April 3, 2009.
147. Rebuilding Together New Orleans, *Annual Report*, 2009.
148. Qatar Katrina Fund, 2007.

149. Assistance was for homeowners with income below 80 percent of median income for the metro area.

150. Isabelle Maret and Barbara Allen, "Tremé: The Challenges of an Equitable Recovery in New Orleans," *Projections: MIT Journal of Planning*, 8, pp. 203–207.

151. http://www.gnof.org/grantee-profiles/lillian-tinson-qatar-Tremé-lafitte-renewa l-project-2/.

152. http://www.prnewswire.com/news-releases/afl-cio-investment-trust-corporati on-and-local-coalition-partner-awarded-new-orleans-redevelopment-projects-5 6097082.html.

153. Interview with Jim Kelly, 8/18/2011.

154. Susan J. Popkin, et al., *A Decade of HOPE VI: Research Findings and Policy Challenges*, Washington, DC: The Urban Institute, 2004, pp. 7–11.

155. Popkin et al., ibid, pp. 14–15. Reducing the concentration of poverty was also addressed by helping public housing residents relocate to other neighborhoods.

156. Popkin et al., ibid., pp. 14–16.

157. Lewis, op. cit. pp. 134–136.

158. Lewis, p. 135, Popkin et al., pp. 39, 45.

159. US General Accounting Office, *HUD Takes over the Housing Authority of New Orleans*, Report GAO/RCED-96-67, Washington DC, 1996. The chronology of events through 1996 and the terms of the HUD–New Orleans Cooperative Endeavor Agreement also are drawn from this report.

160. GAO, 1996, pp. 11. HANO also had failed to spend most (82 percent) of the funding provided by HUD for operations and improvements and had unspent balances of almost $200 million (GAO, 1996, p. 12).

161. Katy Reckdahl, "HANO Audits Point to Still-Troubled Agency," *The Times–Picayune*, September 6, 2009.

162. Ibid.

163. Gilmore Kean, LLC, *Operational Assessment of the Housing Authority of New Orleans*, report to US Department of Housing and Urban Development, February 17, 2010.

164. Susan Saunly, "5,000 Public Housing Units in New Orleans Are to Be Raised," *New York Times*, June 15, 2006.

165. Ibid.

166. About 9,400 low-income households were living in private housing with HANO rental vouchers before Katrina and many of these families would also be seeking apartments along with displaced public housing residents (Liu, pp. 15–16), not to mention the tens of thousands of unsubsidized New Orleans households displaced and in need of housing.

167. According to its President Jim Kelly, Providence Community Housing not only sought to bring residents back but to bring them back to better and healthier neighborhoods. They pursued a three-prong strategy toward these ends that included brick-and-mortar development of new housing units, place-based community development to improve neighborhoods, and collaborating to help other nonprofit organizations build their capacity, one example of which was helping to form the Greater New Orleans Housing Alliance.

168. Interview with Jim Kelly, 11/18/2010.

169. Katy Reckdahl "Razing a Community," *The Gambit*, 10/31/2006. This article cited recent data from HUD's survey of fair market rents that showed a 45 percent increase in apartment rents in the year after Katrina.

170. Katy Reckdahl " Like Lots of Bricks" *The Gambit*, 10/16/2006.
171. Katy Reckdahl " Like Lots of Bricks" *The Gambit*, 10/16/2006.
172. According to Bob Tannen, quoted in Katy Reckdahl article, ibid.
173. *The Gambit*, October 31, 2006.
174. Coleman Warner, Michelle Krupa, and Gwen Filosa, "Demolition Protests Ignore Some Realities," *The Times–Picayune*, December 15, 2007. Adam Nossiter also quotes former resident Natasha Dixon as saying "If they're talking about redevelopment, I'm for it," in his December 26. 2006 *New York Times* article, "In New Orleans, Ex-Tenants Fight for Projects," although she wants to see redevelopment happen quickly and in phases.
175. Gwen Filosa, "HANO Gets OK to Raze 4,500 units," *The Times–Picayune*, September 22, 2007. HUD granted its approval for demolition in September 2007.
176. Katy Reckdahl, "Nagin OKs demolition of Lafitte housing complex," *The Times–Picayune*, March 25, 2008, City of New Orleans press release *Lafitte Housing Demolition Permit Approved* 3/24/2008, at http://www.nola.gov/en/PRESS/ City-Of-New-Orleans/All-Articles/LAFITTE-HOUSING-DEMOLITION-PERMI T-APPROVED.
177. These in-fill housing units will be built in both the Tremé and Lower Mid-City neighborhoods.
178. Interview with Jim Kelly, 8/18/2011, and Katy Reckdahl, "Lafitte Public Housing Residents Ordered to Leave at Once," *The Times–Picayune*, March 28, 2009.
179. Reckdahl, "Lafitte Public Housing Residents." This article also reported that a HANO manager told tenants that they had to leave several days early or face arrest.
180. Katy Reckdahl. "New Designs Hope to Avoid Past Problems in Public Housing Complexes," *The Times–Picayune*, May 12, 2009.
181. Providence Community Housing and Enterprise Community Partners, Homebuilding Plan for Tremé/Lafitte and Tulane/Gravier Community Development Approach, December 2007.
182. Reckdahl, "Like a Ton of Bricks," *The Gambit*, October 24, 2006.
183. Reckdahl, "New Designs Hope to Avoid Past Problems in Public Housing Complexes," *The Times–Picayune*, May 12, 2009 and Nicole Swerhun, *Record of Feedback Received: October 3–7, 2006 From Residents, the Public and Other Stakeholders*, report to Providence Community Housing and Enterprise, November 2006, pp. 3–4 and 10–13.
184. Swerhun, *Record of Feedback Received*, pp. 3–4.
185. Katy Reckdahl, "HANO commits to hiring locally for public housing construction," *The Times-Picayune*, February 24, 2011.
186. Contracting and employment data provided by HANO via e-mail correspondence on 12/16/2011. According to HANO, the figures cover the initial project construction start through the date the data was sent to the author. Since there was likely a time lag in reporting the figures to HANO they are likely through October or November 2011.
187. Doug MacCash, "Faubourg Lafitte, at a Glance," *The Times–Picayune*, February 13, 2011.
188. HANO e-mail, 12/16/11.
189. Both quotes are from a February 4 news report, "Residents Move into New Faubourg Lafitte Neighborhood," by Sabrina Wilson, on New Orleans Channel 8, Fox News.

190. Interviews with Hal Brown and Naydja Bynum. Food access was a problem for many other neighborhoods in addition to Tremé, as New Orleans, which had a low density of supermarkets before Katrina, saw the number decline from 30 to 20 between 2005 and 2010. http://www.americanprogress.org/issues/2010/03/food_after_storm.html.

191. These figures do not show when during the decade the growth in white and Hispanic residents occurred, but the large-scale decline in the black population is almost certainly a post-Katrina phenomenon.

192. Katy Reckdahl, "Tremé Anticipates life in 'Tremé' spotlight," *The Times–Picayune*, April 10, 2010.

193. These and other projects are listed in a brochure for the NewCity Neighborhood Partnership. Several are also included on Mayor Landrieu's 100 rebuilding projects announced in August 2010.

194. Frank Donze, "Streetcar Service along Rampart, St. Claude Is Getting a Green Light," *The Times–Picayune*, January 25, 2011. The Regional Transit Authority approved final design work for the streetcar line in January 2011.

195. Michele Krupa, "City Hall Gets $2 million to Study Claiborne Avenue, Possible Teardown of Elevated I-10," *The Times–Picayune*, October 20, 2011.

196. Interview with John Hankin, 11/10/2010; Bruce Eggler, "New Orleans African American Museum to Undergo Renovations," *The Times–Picayune*, January 10, 2011; www.marcmorial.com/Housing&Neighborhoods4.htm.

197. New Orleans had used federal CDBG funds to restore the Tremé Villa property for the museum and to cover its operating costs. The Nagin administration cut off this funding in 2003 when federal officials investigated the use of CDBG funds for the museum. A 2005 audit found that the use of CDBG funds to restore the museum buildings was appropriate but that museum operations were not an allowable use of CDBG funds and sought repayment of $1 million from the city. Eggler, op. cit.

198. Interview with John Hankin, 11/10/2011.

199. Eggler, op. cit.

200. The neighborhood was originally named for two prominent New Orleans families and property owners, Paul Tulane, who founded Tulane University, and Jean and Bertrand Gravier, who developed Faubourg St. Mary—the original American section of New Orleans (See http://www.gnocdc.org/orleans/4/46/snapshot.html). After Katrina, the Lower Mid-City name gained more prominence, as some residents sought to change the neighborhood's identity.

201. This overview of Lower Mid-City's development is from the GNOCDC Tulane/Gravier Neighborhood Snapshot http://www.gnocdc.org/orleans/4/46/snapshot.html.

202. Interviews with several past housing, community, and economic development officials; review of city archives on policies under the Marc Morial Administration; and state of city speeches by Mayor Ray Nagin in the years before Katrina did not turn up any examples of initiatives targeted to the Lower Mid-City neighborhood.

203. Interview with Sister Vera Butler, 11/18/2011.

204. http://www.stjosephchurch-no.org/history2.htm.

205. "Catholic Extension Presents 2006 Lumen Christi Award To Sister Vera Butler, PBVM." News story published on the Catholic Extension website, http://www.catholicextension.org/butler-story/. Sister Vera had a long history of working for greater social justice, starting with when she was in high school and first

joined the Presentation Sisters, a community of Catholic women with the mission of promoting greater justice and dignity for the poor and oppressed.

206. This account of the formation and early work of the Tulane Canal NDC is based on interviews with Sister Mary Louise Hoeller (11/15/2011) and Sister Vera Butler (11/18/2011).
207. Interview with Sister Vera Butler, 11/18/2011.
208. Ibid.
209. Interview with Paul Ikemire and Ryan Porcelli, 3/26/2010.
210. Ibid. and Sheila Stroup, "Rock 'n' Bowl Hosts a Bowl-A-Thon to Benefit The Phoenix of New Orleans," *The Times–Picayune*, April 14, 2009.
211. PNOLA web site, http://pnola.org/history.
212. Interview with Paul Ikemire and Ryan Porcelli, 3/26/2010, and http://pnola.org/about-pnola.
213. http://pnola.org/history.
214. Kate Moran, "Plans for LSU–VA hospital complex stir resentment," *The Times–Picayune*, February 23, 2008.
215. U.S. Department of Veterans Affairs, *Site Specific Environmental Assessment for Veterans Affairs Medical Center,* April 2010, pp. 3–3 to 3–4.
216. Kate Moran, "Plans for LSU–VA Hospital Complex Stir Resentment," *The Times–Picayune,* February 23, 2008.
217. Tulane / Gravier Neighborhood Planning District 4 Rebuilding Plan, pp. 19–20.
218. This alternative site was also closer to other downtown medical facilities.
219. Moran, "Plans for LSU–VA Hospital Complex."
220. Kate Moran and Frank Donze, "N.O. Seals Deal to Assemble Land for VA Hospital," *The Times–Picayune*, November 28, 2007, and Jennifer Farwell, "A New Orleans Hospital Has a Shot at Recovery," August 8, 2008, article on the National Trust for Historic Preservation website, www.preservation.org/story-of-the-week/200 8/a-new-orleans-hospital-has-a.html.
221. UNOP District 4 Recovery Plan, p. 80.
222. UNOP District 4 Recovery Plan, p. 96.
223. Moran and Donze, "N.O. Seals Deal to Assemble Land." The Department of Veterans Affairs issued a call for expressions of interest for sites for the medical center dated April 1, 2007, which is cited in the Site-Specific Environmental Assessments for Veterans Affairs Medical Center and Cooperative Endeavor Agreement between New Orleans and Louisiana.
224. Memorandum between the US Department of Veterans Affairs and the City of New Orleans 2007, Attachment C.
225. Bill Barrow, "Land for VA hospital Won't Be Ready until July: Feds Say They Won't Charge Nagin Administration Late Fees," *The Times–Picayune*, 11/2/2009. This included using over $70 million of the city's recovery Community Development Block Grant funds.
226. Moran and Donze, "N.O. Seals Deal to Assemble Land," and Memorandum between the US Department of Veterans Affairs and the City of New Orleans, 2007.
227. Orleans Parish recovery CDBG project list from www.LArebuild.org and Blakely interview, 1/26/2011.
228. Kate Moran, "Plans for LSU–VA hospital complex stir resentment," *The Times–Picayune,* February 23, 2008. In Interviews with several neighborhood residents and rebuilding activists, they all reported first learning of the new VA hospital site through media reports.

229. Interview with Bobbi Rogers, 11/18/2010.

230. Moran, 2/23/2008. Among the MOU provisions was a requirement for the city to pay penalties if it was late in preparing and transferring the site to the DVA.

231. Interview with Bobbi Rogers, 11/18/2011.

232. Ibid. Consideration of the Lindy Boggs site was also referenced in Farwell, 8/8/2008.

233. Bill Barrow, "Mid-City Hospital Complex Lawsuit Moved from D.C. to New Orleans Federal Court," *The Times–Picayune*, January 29, 2009.

234. Cain Burdeau, *Judge OKs Hospital Projects in New Orleans*, Associated Press, March 31, 2010, accessed at www. wwltv.com.

235. Bill Barrow, "Lawsuit: New Orleans Mayor Ray Nagin violated City Charter with VA hospital agreement," *The Times–Picayune*, July 14, 2009.

236. Kate Moran, "Plans for LSU-VA hospital complex stir resentment," *The Times–Picayune*, February 23, 2008

237. Bill Barrow, "State Expropriation for New Hospital Includes Those Who Rebuilt after Katrina," *The Times–Picayune*, November 29, 2009.

238. David Hammer, "Preservation Groups Want to Move Homes out of New Hospital Demolition Zone," *The Times–Picayune*, April 29, 2010.

239. Bill Barrow, "Historic Houses Being Moved from Mid-City Footprint for New VA Hospital," *The Times–Picayune*, September 10, 2010. Information on Providence Community Housing role is from interviews with Jim Kelley, 11/18/10, and Jeff Schwartz, 11/18/10.

240. This account is based on a November 18, 2010, interview with Bobbi Rogers and some additional information from a March 29, 2010, commentary piece in the *New Orleans Gambit* entitled "LSU/VA Complex Versus Lower Mid-City: Arrogant Indifference."

241. Eva Klein and Associates, Ltd., *New Orleans Medical District Economic Development Strategy, Issue Paper: Leadership and Management Strategy*, February 11, 2006, pp. 3–4.

242. Ibid. and N-Y Associates, *New Orleans Medical District Strategic Integration Plan Final Report*, March 2008, pp. 10–12. The Gene Therapy Consortium was established in 2000 with state funding. The BioInnovation Center was the result of a state effort to create three biotechnology incubators, one of which would be in New Orleans. Work on the New Orleans center began in 2002 but due to a series of setbacks construction of the center was not completed until 2011. See Kate Moran, "BioInnovation project poised to rise in New Orleans," *The Times–Picayune*, August 18, 2008, for more information on the BioInnovation Center history.

243. The legislatively mandated board for GNOBEDD provided representation for the district's educational institutions, city, and state government but not the district's neighborhoods. The 13-person board included one representative for each of the four universities, four mayoral appointees (one of whom had to be a city resident), four gubernatorial appointees, and one representative of a state economic development agency (Louisiana Economic Development).

244. Interview with James McNamara, 11/8/2010. This account of GNOBEDD's initial goal, approach and activities in 2009 and 2010 is based on this interview. A $650,000 legislative appropriation for GNOBEDD in 2008 was vetoed by Governor Jindal. In 2009, the Louisiana Recovery Authority provided $2.4 million for the master plan, a baseline economic analysis, and preparation of a study to recommend permanent revenue sources for the district.

245. Interview with James McNamara, 11/8/2010.
246. GNOBEDD's analysis indicated that the district needed 24 acres of new green space to increase tree coverage from 3 percent to 24 percent.
247. Interview with Jim Kelly, 11/18/2010.
248. Smart Mobility Inc. and Waggonner & Ball Architects, *Restoring Claiborne Avenue: Alternatives for the Future of Claiborne Avenue*, July 15, 2010, as summarized on the Congress for New Urbanism website, http://www.cnu.org/restoringclaiborne.
249. Bruce Eggler, "$2 Million Federal Grant Will Study Claiborne Avenue Revival, Possible Teardown of Elevated I-10," *The Times–Picayune*, October 20, 2010.

CHAPTER 6

1. The Census Bureau's April 1, 2005 population estimate for New Orleans was 454,863.
2. Author's analysis of neighborhood population data compiled from the US 2000 and 2010 Census by the Greater New Orleans Community Data Center. Neighborhood level population figures are not available for 2005.
3. Kates et al., "Reconstruction of New Orleans after Hurricane Katrina: A Research Perspective," *Proceedings of the National Academy of Sciences* 103 (40), 14653–14660. The authors reported in 2006 that New Orleans was behind schedule in its emergency phase and ahead in its restoration stage, based on progress in rebuilding levees.
4. A sample of six neighborhoods is too small to draw definitive conclusions, and no rigorous analysis was undertaken to control for and statistically test the range of factors that can influence a neighborhood's recovery.
5. Elliot, Haney, and Sams-Abiodun found that social networks of residents in a higher-income New Orleans neighborhood were more effective at providing recovery assistance than networks of residents in a low-income neighborhood.
6. The figure for Lower Mid-City is before the demolition for the two hospital sites.
7. Eugene J. Hass Robert W. Kates, Martyn J. Bowden, editors. *Reconstruction Following Disaster*. (Cambridge, MA: The MIT Press, 1977) mentioned reducing uncertainty about the future as a major way to improve rebuilding (p. xxvi).
8. GAO 10–17, p. 28.
9. Ad Hoc Committee on Disaster Recovery, US Senate Committee on Homeland Security and Government Affairs, *Far From Home: Deficiencies in Federal Disaster Housing Assistance after Hurricanes Katrina and Rita and Recommendations for Improvement*, p. 44.
10. Almost $8 billion was provided to Louisiana homeowners under the Road Home program, while $1.5 billion was budgeted for rental assistance programs, with $867 million of that for small rental properties. For both Louisiana and Mississippi, over ten times more federal dollars were awarded to restore homeowner units than rental units— GAO 10-17, p. 29.
11. Changes were made in 2008 that allowed the program to provide an option for upfront funding to assist landlords to repair rental units. GAO reported that 1,024 landlords had agreed to use this option as of November, 2009. See GAO, 10-17, p. 17.
12. GAO 10-17, p. 61.
13. This tension is discussed in Kates et al. (2006), Nelson et al., and Olshansky (2006).

14. Nelson, Marla, Renia Ehrenfeucht, and Shirley Laska. "Plans, Planning and People: Professional Expertise, Local Knowledge and Government Action in Post-Katrina New Orleans, in *Cityscape: A Journal of Policy Development and Research,* 9, no. 3 (2007): 23–52, see especially, pp. 25 and 43.

15. The interdependence of multiple aspects of recovery is noted in the 2009 report by the Pacific Northwest Preparedness Society, *A Review of a City's Efforts to Recover from Hurricane Katrina and Implications for Emergency Management in British Columbia,* pp. 7–8.

16. The Broadmoor Plan, p. 177.

17. The Broadmoor Plan, p. 296.

18. Lafitte Greenway Master Plan, pp. 1–2, 39, 45

19. Perry and Schwam-Baird, p. 41.

20. This observation and criticism of charter schools was made by several interviewees and noted in Perry and Schwam-Baird, p. 38.

21. There is growing interest and activity around "anchor institutions" partnerships with hospitals and education institutions to advance economic and community development ends, see for example, Initiative for a Competitive Inner City, "Anchor Institutions and Urban Economic Development: From Community Benefit to Shared Value," *Inner City Insight Findings,* June 2011.

22. Business recovery assistance also involved helping businesses adapt to changed market and economic conditions that exist in the aftermath of a large disaster.

23. Gilmore Kean LLC, p. 56.

24. See Sara E. Stoutland, "Community Development Corporations: Mission, Strategy and Accomplisnments." In Urban Problems and Community Development, edited by Ronald F. Ferguson and William T. Dickens (Washington, DC: Brookings Institution Press, 1999) and Avis Vidal, Rebuilding Communities: A National Study of Urban Community Development Corporations (New School for Social Research, Community Development Research Center, 1992) for an overview of the work of CDCs.

25. Lowe, 2001, 2007.

26. National Civic League, *The Community Visioning and Strategic Planning Handbook;* Keyes, et al., "Networks and Nonprofits: Opportunities and Challenges in an Era of Federal Devolution"; Seidman, *Revitalizing Commerce for American Cities.*

27. Haas et al. identified seven basic policy issues for post-disaster reconstruction—pp. 43–45, elaborated on pp. 46–59.

28. Lawrence Vale, "Restoring Urban Vitality." In *Rebuilding Urban Places after Disaster: Lessons from Hurricane Katrin,* edited by Eugenie L. Birch and Susan M. Wachter (Philadelphia: University of Pennsylvania Press, 2006). pp. 158–160 and Louise K. Comfort, Thomas A. Birkland, Beverly A. Cigler, and Earthea Nance. "Retrospectives and Perspectives on Hurricane Katrina: Five Years and Counting." Public Administration Review, 70, no 5 (2010), pp. 673–674, make similar points on the importance of neighborhood-scale rebuilding to citywide recovery.

29. Nelson et al. emphasized the importance of anticipating distrust and the need for experts and planners to build relationships to reduce distrust.

30. Nelson et al. also concluded that a more transparent, participatory, and deliberative planning process is necessary to gain resident support for official rebuilding policies; see pp. 44–45.

31. Comfort et al. argued for new "sociotechnical systems" to provide more rapid damage assessment and information sharing after larger disasters and working

more innovatively outside of normal agency operations, including "cross organizational and cross jurisdictional interaction" (p. 676). Naim Kapuchu and
Montgomery Van Wart. "Making Matters Worse: An Anatomy of Leadership
Failures in Managing Catastrophic Events," Administration & Society, 40, no. 7
(2008): 771–740. In their review of leadership failures after catastrophes, these
authors discussed the need for leaders to work outside traditional hierarchies
and create new systems and structures that change conventional reporting, bud-
geting, and the like (see pp. 714–716).

32. Nelson et al. emphasized the value of a participatory and deliberative process
and relationship-building to overcome distrust and build support for recovery
policies and decisions, pp. 44–46.

33. This point draws on findings by Comfort et al. and Kapuchu and Van Wart.

34. FEMA allows funding to be used for "alternative projects" when an applicant
determines that it is not in the public welfare to restore a facility or its function
to its predisaster design but limits its funding to 90 percent or 75 percent of the
federal share to rebuild the original damaged facility. FEMA also allows funding
for "improved projects" in which improvements or expansions are made to the
predisaster facility but FEMA limits its funding 90% of its share to rebuild the
same predisaster facility. See GAO Report 09-129, pp. 21–22 and footnote 12.

35. Some of the proposals also draw on the author's research on economic recovery
following the September 11 terrorist attacks, see Seidman and Seigel, "Economic
Recovery from the 9/11 disaster: Lessons from New York State's Response in
Lower Manhattan," *Applied Research in Economic Development*, October 2008.

36. This observation was also made by Comfort et al., p. 673. These authors note
the Stafford Act focuses on routine disasters and that, even with changes after
Katrina, current policies are oriented toward smaller-scale disasters and that
new policies and reforms have been made piecemeal without integrating different definitions and processes (pp. 674–675).

37. Stafford Act language quoted in Williams, *Far from Home*, p. 38. See pp. 43–45 for
discussion of FEMA's lack of use of its flexible powers to address housing needs
after Katrina.

38. Mt. Auburn Associates *World Trade Center Economic Recovery: Rebuilding the
Economy of Lower Manhattan*, 2005, p. 11.

39. Comfort et al. also called for longer-term federal support for postdisaster community planning, especially for planning that "can increase community resilience, improve mitigation and reduce vulnerability in the face of the next storm"
(p.674).

40. Olshansky and Johnson, on pp. 30–37, discussed the implementation of ESF#14
in Louisiana after Katrina.

Acronym Guide

AALP	African-American Leadership Project
A2E	Access to Equity
ACORN	Associations for Community Organizations for Reform Now
AHPP	Alternative Housing Pilot Program
ASI	Federal Credit Union
BCC	Broad Community Connections
BCSB	Broadmoor Charter School Board
BDC	Broadmoor Development Corporation
BESE	Board of Elementary and Secondary Education, state of Louisiana
BFE	Base Flood Elevations
BIA	Broadmoor Improvement Association
BNOB	Bring New Orleans Back Commission
CAO	Chief Administrative Officer, City of New Orleans
CDBG	Community Development Block Grant program, US federal government
CDC	Community Development Corporation
CGI	Clinton Global Initiative
CPC	City Planning Commission, City New Orleans
CSO	Community Support Organization
CSRRP	Citywide Strategic Recovery and Redevelopment Plan
DEVA	Diabetes Education in Vietnamese Americans
DNIA	Downtown Neighborhoods Improvement Association
DVA	US Department of Veterans Affairs, also referred to as the VA
ERTCA	Esplanade Ridge–Tremé Civic Association
ESF#14	FEMA's Long Term Recovery Emergency Support Function
FANO	Finance Authority of New Orleans
FEMA	Federal Emergency Management Agency, US Government
FOLC	Friends of Lafitte Corridor
FQHC	Federally Qualified Health Center
FSJNA	Faubourg St. John Neighborhood Association
GAO	US Government Accountability Office
GCR, Inc	Name of New Orleans planning firm
GNOBEDD	Greater New Orleans Biosciences Economic Development District
GNOCDC	Greater New Orleans Community Data Center
GNOF	Greater New Orleans Foundation
GTC	Greater Tremé Consortium
HANO	Housing Authority of New Orleans

HFTA	Historic Faubourg Tremé Association
HUD	U.S. Department of Housing and Urban Development
ICF	Name of private firm hired to administer the Louisiana Road Home Program
ICS	the Intercultural School in Village de L'Est
JOLI	Job Opportunities for Low Income Individuals program, US federal government
KSG	Kennedy School of Government, Harvard University
LDEQ	Louisiana Department of Environmental Quality
LEAN	Louisiana Environmental Network
LEED	Leadership in Energy and Environmental Design
LHFA	Louisiana Housing Finance Authority
LHW	Local Health Workers
LIHTC	Low-Income Housing Tax Credits
LISC	Local Initiative Support Corporation
LRA	Louisiana Recovery Authority
LSU	Louisiana State University
MCLNO	Medical Center of Louisiana at New Orleans
MCNO	Mid-City Neighborhood Organization
MOU	Memorandum of Understanding
MQVN	Mary Queen of Vietnam
MQVN CDC	Mary Queen of Vietnam Community Development Corporation
MREs	Meals Ready to Eat
MRGO	Mississippi River Gulf Outlet
MWH	Name of private engineering firm hired to oversee implementation of New Orleans recovery projects
NAVASA	National Association of Vietnamese-American Service Agencies
NCMEC	National Center for Missing and Exploited Children
NCSF	New Orleans Community Service Foundation
NFIP	National Flood Insurance Program
NMTC	New Market Tax Credits
NHS	Neighborhood Housing Services of New Orleans
NONDC	New Orleans Neighborhood Development Collaborative
NORA	New Orleans Redevelopment Authority
OCD	Office of Community Development, state of Louisiana
ORDA	Office of Recovery Development and Administration, City of New Orleans
ORM	Office of Recovery Management, City of New Orleans
PA	Public Assistance
PDU	Project Delivery Unit, City of New Orleans
PNOLA	Phoenix of New Orleans
PRC	Preservation Resource Center
QKF	Qatar Katrina Fund
RBT	Rebuilding Together
RFP	Request for Proposal
RFQ	Request for Qualification
RSDA	Recovery School District Act, state of Louisiana
RSD	Recovery School District, state of Louisiana
SBA	Small Business Association
SELA	Southeast Louisiana Flood Control Project

SRPP	Small Rental Properties Program, state of Louisiana
SWOT	Strengths, Weaknesses, Opportunities, and Threats
TCNDC	Tulane/Canal Neighborhood Development Corporation
ULI	Urban Land Institute
UNOP	Unified New Orleans Plan
VA	US Department of Veterans Affairs, also referred to as DVA
VAYLA	Vietnamese-American Young Leaders Association
WMI	Waste Management Incorporated
WRT	Wallace Roberts Todd planning firm

BIBLIOGRAPHY

PRIMARY SOURCE MATERIALS FROM ARCHIVES AND ORGANIZATIONS

New Orleans Public Library. Louisiana Division City Archive and Special Collections, Records of the Mayors of New Orleans, Marc H. Morial
Primary documents, Broadmoor Development Corporation
Primary documents, Faubourg St. John Neighborhood Association
Primary documents, Mary Queen of Vietnam Community Development Corporation
Primary documents, Mid-City Neighborhood Organization

INTERVIEWS

Lauren Anderson, November 22, 2010
Douglas Ahlers, September 22, 2010
Representative Jeffrey Arnold, September 10, 2010
Cheryl Austin, November 16, 2010
Lisa Amoss. March 24, 2010
Broderick Bagert, March 9, 2011
Edward Blakely, January 26, 2011
Michelle Bradden, November 12, 2010
William Bradshaw, March 25, 2010
Joseph Brock, November 3, 2010
Martha Broussard, November 5, 2010
Hal Brown, June 18, 2010
James Bui, October 25, 2010
Sister Vera Butler, November 19, 2010
Santiago Buros, November 9, 2010
Naydja Bynum, November 8, 2010
LaToya Cantrell, June 17, 2010
Nadiyah Morris Coleman, June 16, 2010
Mai Dang, November 4, 2010
Karen DeSalvo, November 3, 2010
Leo Esclamado, January 7, 2011
Danna Eness, November 17, 2010
Dan Etheridge, November 15, 2010
Bart Everson,, November 9, 2010
Ethan Frizzell, November 4, 2010
Ernest Gethers, September 16, 2010
Jonathan Graboyes, June 22, 2010

Councilwoman Kristen Gisleson Palmer, November 22, 2010
Julie Schwam Harris, June 18, 2010
John Hankins, November 8, 2010
Jeffrey Hebert, November 22, 2010
Sister Mary Louise Hoeller, November 15, 2010
Michael Holman, November 16, 2010
Paul Ikemire, March 27, 2010 and August 9. 2011
James Kelly, November 18, 2010 and August 18, 2011
Michelle Krupa, November 17, 2010
Ellen Lee, August 10, 2010
James McNamara, November 9, 2010
Maggie Merrill, September 9, 2010
Neal Morris, March 31. 2010
Earthea Nance, June 15, 2010
Jeanne Nathan, March 26, 2010 and August 16, 2011
Diem Nguyen, January 14, 2011
May Nguyen, November 17, 2010
Mimi Nguyen, November 20, 2010
Tuan Nguyen, June 16, 2010
Father Vien The Nguyen, November 5, 2010
Alexandra Norton, November 16, 2010
Ryan Porcelli, March 26, 2010
Evelyn Pugh, June 15, 2010
Ezra Rapport, September 2, 2010
Robert Rivard, June 17, 2010
Hal Roark, June 14 and 18, 2010
Yolanda Rodriguez, June 16, 2010
Bobbi Rogers, November 18, 2010
Ommeed Sathe, March 25, 2010
Timolyn Sams, June 15, 2010
Jeffrey Schwartz, November 18, 2010
Jon Skvarka, November 5, 2010
Lakshmi Sridaran, November 29, 2010
David Winkler-Schmit, November 5, 2010
Robert Tannen, November 9, 2010 and August 16, 2011
Keith Twitchell, November 17, 2010
Jeanette Thompson, November 4, 2010
Mary Tran, August 17, 2010
Trang Tu, September 21, 2010
Vera Warren Williams, November 18, 2010
Mary Jo Webster, November 12, 2010
Jennifer Weishaupt, June 16, 2010
Carolyn Wood, August 3, 2010
Kelli Wright, November 4, 2010

BOOKS

Baum, Dan, *Nine Lives*. New York: Random House, 2010.
Briggs, Xavier De Souza. *Democracy as Problem Solving*. Cambridge, MA: The MIT Press, 2008.

Brinkley, Douglas. *The Great Deluge: Hurricane Katrina, New Orleans, and the Mississippi Gulf Coast*. NY: Harper Collins, 2006.

Campanella, Richard. *Bienville's Dilemma: A Historical Geography of New Orleans*. Lafayette, LA: Center for Louisiana Studies, 2008.

Crutcher Jr., Michael E. *Tremé: Race and Place in a New Orleans Neighborhood*. Athens, GA: University of Georgia Press, 2010.

Editors of Time Magazine. *Hurricane Katrina: The Storm that Changed America*. New York: Time Inc., 2005.

Giselon, Anne, and Tristan Thompson, editors. *How to Rebuild a City: Field Guide From a Work in Progress*. New Orleans: Press Street, 2010.

Haas, Eugene J., Robert W. Kates, Martyn J. Bowden, editors. *Reconstruction Following Disaster*. Cambridge, MA: The MIT Press, 1977.

Hass, Edward F. *DeLesseps S. Morrison and the Image of Reform*. Baton Rouge, LA: Louisiana State University Press, 1986.

Lewis, Pierce. *New Orleans: The Making of an Urban Landscape*. Santa Fe, NM: The Center for American Places, Inc., 2003.

Lui, Baodong, and James M. Vanderleeuw. *Race Rules: Electoral Politics in New Orleans, 1965–2006*. Lanham, MD: Lexington Books, 2007.

McQuaid, John, and Mark Schleifstein. *Path of Destruction*. New York: Little Brown and Company, 2006.

McNulty, Ian. *A Season of Night: New Orleans Life After Katrina*. Jackson, MS: University Press of Mississippi, 2008.

Moe, Richard, and Carter Wilkie. *Changing Place: Rebuilding Community in the Age of Sprawl*. New York: Henry Holt and Company, 1997.

Nelson, Ashley. *The Combination*. New Orleans: Neighborhood Story Project, 2005.

Olshansky, Robert B., and Laurie A. Johnson. *Clear as Mud: Planning for the Rebuilding of New Orleans*. Chicago: American Planning Association Planners Press, 2010.

Sublette, Ned. *The World that Made New Orleans: From Spanish Silver to Congo Square*. Chicago: Lawrence Hill Books, 2009.

JOURNAL ARTICLES AND BOOK CHAPTERS

Bates, Lisa K., and Rebekah A. Green. "Housing Recovery in the Ninth Ward: Disparity in Policy, Process and Prospects." In *Race, Place and Environmental Justice after Hurricane Katrina*, edited by Robert D. Bullard and Beverly Wright. Boulder: Westview Press, 2009: 461–497.

Birch, Eugenie J. "Learning from Past Disaster." In *Rebuilding Urban Places after Disaster: Lessons from Hurricane Katrina*, edited by Eugenie L. Birch and Susan M. Wachter. Philadelphia: University of Pennsylvania Press, 2006: 132–148.

Brunkard, Joan, Gonza Namulanda, and Raoult Ratard. "Hurricane Katrina Deaths, Louisiana, 2005." *Disaster Medicine and Public Health Preparedness*, August 2008: 1–9.

Burby, Raymond J. "Hurricane Katrina and the Paradoxes of Government Disaster Policy: Bringing About Wise Governmental Decisions for Hazardous Areas." *Annals of the American Academy of Political and Social Science* 604 (2006): 171–191.

Burns, Peter F., and Mathew O. Thomas. "A New New Orleans: Understanding the Role of History and the State-Local Relationship in the Recovery Process." *Journal of Urban Affairs*, 30, no. 3 (2008): 259–271.

Chamlee-Wright, Emily. "Church Provision of Club Goods and Community Redevelopment in New Orleans East." Working Paper. Mercatus Center, George Mason University. 2007.

Chamlee-Wright, Emily and Virgil Henry Storr. "'There's No Place Like New Orleans': Sense of Place and Community Recovery in the Ninth Ward After Hurricane Katrina." *Journal of Urban Affairs*, 31, no. 5 (2009): 615–634.

Comfort, Louise K., Thomas A. Birkland, Beverly A. Cigler, and Earthea Nance. "Retrospectives and Perspectives on Hurricane Katrina: Five Years and Counting." *Public Administration Review*, 70, no. 5 (2010): 669–678.

DeSalvo, Karen. "Delivering High Quality, Accessible Health Care: The Rise of Community Health Centers." In *Resilience and Opportunity: Lessons from the U.S. Gulf Coast after Katrina and Rita*, edited by Amy Liu, Roland Anglin, Richard M. Mizelle, Jr., and Allison Plyer. Washington, DC: The Brooking Institution, 2011: 45–63.

Dolfman, Michael L., Solidelle Fortier Wasser, and Bruce Bergman. "The Effects of Hurricane Katrina on the New Orleans Economy." *Monthly Labor Review*, 139, no. 6 (June 2007): 3–18.

Eargle, Lisa A., Ashraf M. Esmail, and Shyamal K. Das, "Disaster Impacts on Education: Hurricane Katrina and the Adaptation and Recovery of New Orleans-Area Colleges and Universities," in David L. Brunsma, David Overfelt, and J. Steven Picou, eds., *The Sociology of Katrina*. Lanham, MD: Rowman & Littlefield Publishers, 2010: 227–250.

Elliot, James R., Timothy J. Haney, and Petrice Sams-Abiodun. "Limits to Social Capital: Comparing Network Assistance in Two New Orleans Neighborhoods Devastated by Hurricane Katrina." *The Sociological Quarterly*, 51, no. 4 (2010): 624–648.

Elliott, James R., Amy Belone Hite, and Joel A. Devine, "Unequal Return: The Uneven Resettlement of New Orleans' Uptown Neighborhoods," *Organization & Environment* 22, no. 4, (2009): 410–421.

Finch, Christina, Christopher T. Emrich, and Susan L. Cutter. "Disaster Disparities and Differential Recovery in New Orleans," *Population and Environment*, 31, no. 4, (2010): 179–202.

Finger, Davida. "Public Housing in New Orleans Post Katrina: The Struggle for Housing as a Human Right," *Review of Black Political Economy*, 38, no. 4 (2011): 327–337.

Fussell, Elizabeth, Narayan Sastry, and Mark Van Landingham. "Race, Socioeconomic Status, and Return Migration to New Orleans after Hurricane Katrina," *Population and Environment*, 31, no. 1–3, (2010): 20–42.

Gafford, Farrah D. "Rebuilding the Park: The Impact of Hurricane Katrina on a Black Middle Class Neighborhood," *Journal of Black Studies*, 41, no. 2 (2010): 385–404.

Giegengack, Robert, and Kenneth R. Foster. "Physical Constraints on Reconstructing New Orleans." In *Rebuilding Urban Places after Disaster: Lessons from Hurricane Katrina*, edited by Eugenie L. Birch and Susan M. Wachter. Philadelphia: University of Pennsylvania Press, 2006: 13–33.

Green, Rodney D., Marie Kouassi, and Belinda Mambo. "Housing, Race and Recovery from Hurricane Katrina." *Review of Black Political Economy,* published online November 17, 2011.

Haas, Edward F. "Political Continuity in the Crescent City: Toward an Interpretation of New Orleans Politics, 1874–1986." *Louisiana History: The Journal of the Louisiana Historical Association*, Vol. 39, No. 1 (Winter, 1998): 5–18.

Kapucu, Naim, and Montgomery Van Wart. "Making Matters Worse: An Anatomy of Leadership Failures in Managing Catastrophic Events." *Administration & Society*, 40, no. 7 (2008): 771–740.

Kates, R.W., C.E. Colton, S. Laska, and S. P. Leatherman. "Reconstruction of New Orleans after Hurricane Katrina: A Research Perspective." *Proceedings of the National Academy of Sciences* 103, no. 40 (2009): 14653–14660.

Keyes, Langley, Alex Schwartz, Avis C. Vidal, and Rachel G. Bratt. "Networks and Nonprofits: Opportunities and Challenges in an Era of Federal Devolution." *Housing Policy Debate*, 7, no. 2 (1996): 201–229.

Khan, Mafruza ."The Color of Opportunity and the Future of New Orleans: Planning, Rebuilding and Social Inclusion after Hurricane Katrina." In *Race, Place and Environmental Justice after Hurricane Katrina*, edited by Robert D. Bullard and Beverly Wright. Boulder: Westview Press, 2009: 410–460.

Leong, Karen J., Christopher A. Airriess, Wei Li, Angela Chia-Chen Chen, and Verna M. Keith. "Resilient History and the Rebuilding of a Community: The Vietnamese American Community in New Orleans East." *Journal of American History* (December 2007): 770–779.

Lowe, Jeffrey Sheldon. "Limitations of Community Development Partnerships: Cleveland Ohio and Neighborhood Progress Inc." *Cities*, 25 (2008): 37–44.

Maret, Isabelle, and Barbara Allen. "Tremé: The Challenges of an Equitable Recovery in New Orleans." *Projections: MIT Journal of Planning*, 8 (2008):190–211.

Nelson, Marla, Renia Ehrenfeucht, and Shirley Laska. "Plans, Planning and People: Professional Expertise, Local Knowledge and Government Action in Post-Katrina New Orleans." *Cityscape: A Journal of Policy Development and Research*, 9, no. 3 (2007): 23–52.

Olshansky, Robert B. "Planning after Hurricane Katrina," *Journal of the American Planning Association*, 72, no. 2 (2006): 147–153.

Perry, Andre and Michael Schwam-Baird. "School by School: The Transformation of New Orleans Public Education." In *Resilience and Opportunity: Lessons from the U.S. Gulf Coast after Katrina and Rita*, edited by Amy Liu, Roland Anglin, Richard M. Mizelle, Jr., and Allison Plyer. Washington, DC: The Brooking Institution, 2011: 31–45.

Piliawsky, Monte. "The Impact of Black Mayors on the Black Community: The Case of New Orleans's Ernest Morial." *Review of Black Political Economy*, 13, no. 4 (1985): 5–23.

Rainwater, Paul. "Louisiana Recovery Authority Looks to Match Investments to the Right Recovery Opportunities." *Community Developments* (Fall 2008). www.occ. treas.gov/cdd/newsletters/fall08/articles/landscape/cdn08fall03.htm.

Reardon, Kenneth M., Rebekah Green, Lisa K. Bates, and Richard C. Kiely, "Commentary: Overcoming the Challenges of Post-disaster Planning in New Orleans: Lessons from the ACORN Housing/University Collaborative." *Journal of Planning Education and Research*, 28, no. 3, (2009): 391–400.

Rose, Kalima. "Bring New Orleans Home: Community, Faith and Non-profit-Driven Housing Recovery." In *Resilience and Opportunity: Lessons from the U.S. Gulf Coast after Katrina and Rita*, edited by Amy Liu, Roland Anglin, Richard M. Mizelle, Jr., and Allison Plyer. Washington, DC: The Brooking Institution, 2011: 99–119.

Sanyika, Mtangulizi. "Katrina and the Conditions of Black New Orleans: The Struggle for Justice, Equity and Democracy." In *Race, Place and Environmental Justice after Hurricane Katrina*, edited by Robert D. Bullard and Beverly Wright. Boulder: Westview Press, 2009:153–209.

Seidman, Karl, and Beth Siegel. "Economic Recovery from the 9/11 Disaster: Lessons from New York State's Response in Lower Manhattan." *Applied Research in Economic Development*, 5: no. 2 (2008):5–20.

Souther, J. Mark, "Suburban Swamp: the Rise and Fall of Planned New-Town Communities in New Orleans East." *Planning Perspectives*, 23, no. 2 (2008).

Stoutland, Sara E. "Community Development Corporations: Mission, Strategy and Accomplishments." In *Urban Problems and Community Development*, edited by Ronald F. Ferguson and William T. Dickens. Washington, DC: Brookings Institution Press, 1999.

Stringfield, Jonathan D. "Higher ground: an Exploratory Analysis of Characteristics Affecting Returning Populations after Hurricane Katrina." *Population and Environment*, 31, no. 1–3, (2010): 43–63.

Tang, Eric. "A Gulf Unites Us: The Vietnamese Americans of Black New Orleans East." *American Quarterly*, 63, no. 1 (2011): 117–149.

Thomas, Matthew O. and Peter Burns, *New Orleans Five Years Later: Key Questions in the Rebuilding of an American City*. Washington, DC: Annual Meeting of the American Political Science Association, 2010).

Torregano, Michelle Early, and Patrick Shannon. "Education Greenfield: A Critical Policy Analysis of Plans to Transform New Orleans Public Schools." *Journal for Critical Education Policy Studies*, 7, no. 1 (2009): http://www.jceps.com/PDFs/07-1-13.pdf.

Vale, Lawrence. "Restoring Urban Vitality." In *Rebuilding Urban Places after Disaster: Lessons from Hurricane Katrina*, edited by Eugenie L. Birch and Susan M. Wachter. Philadelphia: University of Pennsylvania Press, 2006: 149–167.

Van Dyke, Nadiene, Jon Wood, and Lucia LeDoux. "Criminal Justice Reforms. In *Resilience and Opportunity: Lessons from the U.S. Gulf Coast after Katrina and Rita*, edited by Amy Liu, Roland Anglin, Richard M. Mizelle Jr. and Allison Plyer. Washington, DC: The Brooking Institution, 2011: 64–81.

Verderber, Stephen. "The Unbuilding of Historic Neighborhoods in Post-Katrina New Orleans," *Journal of Urban Design*, 14, no. 3 (2009): 257–277.

Wagner, Jacob, Michael Frisch, and Billy Fields. "Building Local Capacity: Planning for Local Culture and Neighborhood Recovery in New Orleans." *Cityscape*, 10, no. 3 (2008): 39–56.

Whelan, Robert K. "An Old Economy for the 'New' New Orleans? Post Hurricane Katrina Economic Development Efforts." In *There is No Such Thing as a Natural Disaster*, edited by Chester Hartman and Gregory D. Squires. New York: Routledge, 2006: 215–232.

Whelan, Robert K., and Denise Strong, "Rebuilding Lives Post-Katrina: Choices and Challenges in New Orleans' Economic Development. " In *Race, Place and Environmental Justice after Hurricane Katrina*, edited by Robert D. Bullard and Beverly Wright. Boulder: Westview Press, 2009: 362–409.

Wilkie, Curtis. "Politics." In *City Adrift: New Orleans Before and After Katrina*, edited by Jenni Bergal. Baton Rouge, LA: Louisiana State University Press, 2007: 96–110.

NEWSPAPER AND MAGAZINE ARTICLES

Babcock, Stephen. "Esplanade Avenue Apartment Proposal Keeps Running into Roadblocks." *The Times–Picayune*, November 28, 2010.

Barrow, Bill. "Historic Houses Being Moved from Mid-City Footprint for New VA Hospital." *The Times–Picayune*, September 10, 2010.

Barrow, Bill. "Land for VA hospital Won't Be Ready until July: Feds Say They Won't Charge Nagin Administration Late Fees." *The Times–Picayune*, November 2, 2009.

Barrow, Bill. "Lawsuit: New Orleans Mayor Ray Nagin Violated City Charter with VA Hospital Agreement." *The Times–Picayune*, July 14, 2009.

Barrow, Bill. "Mid-City Hospital Complex Lawsuit Moved from D.C. to New Orleans Federal Court." *The Times–Picayune*, January 29, 2009.

Barrow, Bill. "State Expropriation for New Hospital Includes Those Who Rebuilt after Katrina." *The Times–Picayune*, November 29, 2009.

Barrow, Bill. "St. Margaret's Daughters Pushes 2012 Opening of Nursing Home at Lindy Boggs Site." *The Times–Picayune*, February 8, 2011.

Bruno, R. Stephanie. "Winn-Dixie Considers New Store on Carrollton Avenue in Mid-City." *The Times–Picayune*, January 24, 2011.

Bumiller, Elisabeth. "Bush Pledges Federal Role in Rebuilding Gulf Coast." *New York Times*, September 16, 2005.

Burdeau, Cain. "Judge OKs Hospital Projects in New Orleans." *Associated Press*, March 31, 2010. Accessed at www. wwltv.com.

Carr, Sarah, and Darran Simon. "New Orleans School Plans Receive Cautious Support: Costs, Campus Closures among Board Members' Concerns." *The Times–Picayune*, August 20, 2008.

Carr, Sarah, and Darran Simon. "New Orleans Schools Set for Building Boom." *The Times–Picayune*, August 16, 2008.

Carr, Sarah. "Specialty High Schools Part of System Overhaul." *The Times–Picayune*, March 19, 2008.

Catania, Sara. "Broken Promises." *The Gambit*, November 28, 2006.

Chang. Cindy. "FEMA Awards $1.8 billion to New Orleans Schools for Construction Renovation Projects." *The Times–Picayune*, August 25, 2010.

Dewan, Shaila K. "Fatal Shootings Prompt Bar's Closing, and a Cultural Debate." *New York Times*, June 17, 2004.

Donze, Frank. "Mayor Mitch Landrieu Expects Completion of 100 Recovery Projects in Three Years." *The Times–Picayune*, August 18, 2010.

Donze, Frank. "Streetcar Service along Rampart. St. Claude Is Getting a Green Light." *The Times–Picayune*, January 25, 2011.

Eaton, Leslie. A New Landfill in New Orleans Sets Off a Battle. *New York Times*, May 8. 2006.

Eaton, Leslie. "Gulf Hits Snags in Rebuilding Public Works," *The New York Times,* March 31, 2007.

Eggler, Bruce. "Apartment Complex Approved at Former Site of St. Aloysius High School." *The Times–Picayune*, February 11, 2009.

Eggler, Bruce. "City Council Approves Mixed-Income Apartments on Esplanade Ave, but with Strings Attached." *The Times–Picayune*, April 3, 2009.

Eggler, Bruce. "City Planning Commission Approves Mid-City Condos, Lakeview School." *The Times–Picayune*, February 11, 2010.

Eggler, Bruce. "New Orleans African American Museum to Undergo Renovations." *The Times–Picayune*, January 10, 2011.

Eggler, Bruce. "Tremé Commercial Opportunities Increase under Zoning Change Approved by City Council." *The Times–Picayune*, August 18, 2010.

Eggler, Bruce. "$2 Million Federal Grant Will Study Claiborne Avenue Revival, Possible Teardown of Elevated I-10." *The Times–Picayune*, October 20, 2010.

Elie, Lolis E. "Public Parkway Through Tremé and Mid-City on the Drawing Board." *The Times–Picayune*, September 5, 2009.

Filosa, Gwen. "HANO Gets OK to Raze 4,500 Units." *The Times–Picayune*, September 22, 2007.

Finch, Susan. "Comiskey Park Project in Mid-City Remains in Limbo." *The Times–Picayune*, March 11, 2008.

Finch, Susan. "Comiskey Park Project in Mid-City Vanishes." *The Times–Picayune*, June 1, 2008.

Finch, Susan. "License of Tremé Tavern Revoked—Joe's Cozy Corner Scene of 2 Shootings." *The Times–Picayune*, April 27, 2004.

Fox and CNN News Broadcasts, August 29, 2005. See *Hurricane Katrina, Day 1 Vid 4 Fox CNN* http://www.youtube.com/watch?v=CXdEzMSvPAY&feature=channel& list=UL.

The Gambit. "LSU/VA Complex Versus Lower Mid-City: Arrogant Indifference." Editorial Commentary, *The Gambit*, March 29, 2010.

Hammer, David. "Audit Faults N.O. Housing Program." *The Times–Picayune*, November 2, 2010.

Hammer. David. "City Orders Housing Finance Agency to Pay 62 Home Loans." *The Times–Picayune*, November 4, 2010.

Hammer, David. "ICF's Oversight of Road Home Program Comes to an End." *The Times–Picayune*, September 28, 2009.

Hammer, David. "New Orleans Neighborhood Housing Services to run $20 Million Home Repair Effort." *The Times–Picayune*, August 18, 2009.

Hammer, David. "Preservation Groups Want to Move Homes out of New Hospital Demolition Zone." *The Times–Picayune*, April 29, 2010.

Hammer, David. "Road Home Hits Contract Benchmark for First Time." *The Times–Picayune*, September 2, 2007.

Hauser, Christine. Mayor of New Orleans Announces Layoffs of City Workers. *New York Times*, October 5, 2005.

Hirsch, Masako, and Gordon Russell. "Failed Comiskey Park Project Leaves City with $700,000 Bill." *The Times–Picayune*, August 23, 2010.

Krupa, Michelle, and Gordon Russell. "City's Post-K Blueprint Unveiled" *The Times–Picayune*, March 29, 2007.

Krupa, Michelle. "Capital Projects Director Left after Long Dispute over Hurricane Recovery Spending." *The Times–Picayune*, March 8, 2010.

Krupa, Michele. "City Hall Gets $2 Million to Study Claiborne Avenue, Possible Teardown of Elevated I-10." *The Times–Picayune*, October 20, 2011.

Krupa, Michelle. "City's Recovery Projects Go Online." *The Times–Picayune*. February 29, 2008.

Krupa, Michelle, and Frank Donze. "Leaders Stand United behind Recovery Plan." *The Times–Picayune*, March 30, 2007.

Krupa, Michelle. "Many FEMA Claims from Hurricane Katrina Remain Open." *The Times–Picayune*, August 30, 2010.

Krupa, Michelle. "Grand Plan: City's Recovery Chief Envisions NO as a Hub for World's Growing Economies." *The Times–Picayune*, February 1, 2007.

Lipton, Eric, Christopher Drew, Scott Shane, and David Rohde. "Breakdowns Marked Path From Hurricane to Anarchy." *New York Times*, September 11, 2005.

Louisiana Department of Environmental Quality (LDEQ). "Chef Menteur Landfill Ok'd to Accept C&D Waste." Press Release, April 13. 2006.

MacCash, Doug. "Faubourg Lafitte, at a Glance." *The Times–Picayune*, February 13, 2011.

Maggi, Laura. "O'Dell: City's $1 Billion Justice Complex Pie in the Sky." *The Times–Picayune*, August 25, 2008.

Maggi, Laura. "Six New Orleans Police Officers Indicted in Danziger Bridge Shootings." *The Times–Picayune*, July 14, 2010.

McCarthy, Brendan. "Five NOPD officers indicted in the Shooting, Burning of Henry Glover after Katrina." *The Times–Picayune*, June 11, 2010.

Meitrodt, Jeffrey, and Frank Donze. "Plan Shrinks City Footprint." *The Times–Picayune*, December 14, 2005.

Meitrodt, Jeffrey. "State Blasts Road Home Firm." *The Times–Picayune*, December 24, 2006.

Moran, Kate. "BioInnovation Project Poised to Rise in New Orleans." *The Times–Picayune*, August 18, 2008.

Moran, Kate, and Frank Donze. "N.O. Seals Deal to Assemble Land for VA hospital." *The Times–Picayune*, November 2, 2007.

Moran, Kate. "Plans for LSU–VA Hospital Complex Stir Resentment." *The Times–Picayune*, February 23, 2008.

Mowray, Rebecca. "GO Zone bonds for Orleans Parish rebuilding now available to other parishes," *The Times–Picayune,* January 10, 2010.

National Center For Missing & Exploited Children. "National Center For Missing & Exploited Children Reunites Last Missing Child Separated By Hurricane Katrina And Rita." Press Release, March 17, 2006.

Neighbours, Andrea. "From Can Factory to Apartments in New Orleans." *New York Times*, March 26, 2000.

Nossiter, Adam. "In New Orleans, Ex-Tenants Fight for Projects." *New York Times*, December 26, 2006.

Nossiter, Adam. "New Orleans Picks Professor To Lead Efforts On Rebuilding." *New York Times*, December 5, 2006.

Quillen, Kimberly. "Victory Real Estate Wins Demolition Permit for Lindy Boggs Medical Center." *The Times–Picayune*, December 31, 2007.

Reckdahl, Katy. "Down on the Corner—On Thursday, Joe's Cozy Corner May Be Serving Its Last Drink. Is the City Getting Rid of a Haven of Lawlessness—or Is It Losing a Priceless Community Center?" *The Gambit*, May 18, 2004.

Reckdahl, Katy. "HANO Audits Point to Still-Troubled Agency." *The Times–Picayune*, September 6, 2009.

Reckdahl, Katy. "HANO Commits to Hiring Locally for Public Housing Construction." *The Times–Picayune*, February 24, 2011.

Reckdahl, Katy. "Lafitte Public Housing Residents Ordered to Leave at Once." *The Times–Picayune*, March 28, 2009.

Reckdahl, Katy. "Like Lots of Bricks." *The Gambit*, October 16, 2006.

Reckdahl, Katy. "Nagin OKs Demolition of Lafitte Housing Complex." *The Times–Picayune*, March 25, 2008.

Reckdahl, Katy. "New Designs Hope to Avoid Past Problems in Public Housing Complexes." *The Times–Picayune*, May 12, 2009.

Reckdahl, Katy. "Razing a Community." *The Gambit*, October 31, 2006.

Reckdahl, Katy. "Tremé Anticipates Life in 'Tremé' Spotlight." *The Times–Picayune*, April 10, 2010.

Rivlin, Gary. "After Two Storms. Cities Confront Economic Peril." *New York Times*, October 22, 2005.

Rivlin, Gary. "New Orleans Executives Plan Revival." *New York Times*, September 10, 2005.

Rivlin, Gary. "Patchy Recovery in New Orleans." *New York Times*, April 5, 2006.

Roig-Franzia, Manuel, and Spencer Hsu. "Many Evacuated, but Thousands Still Waiting: White House Shifts Blame to State and Local Officials." *Washington Post*, September 4, 2005.

Russell, Gordon. "Landfill Testing Option Offered." *The Times–Picayune, May 19, 2006*.

Russell, Gordon. "Chef Menteur Landfill Testing Called a Farce." *The Times–Picayune*, May 26, 2006.

Russell, Gordon. "Chef Landfill to Keep Taking Debris." *The Times–Picayune*, August 12, 2006.

Russell, Gordon. "From Wetlands to Wastelands." *The Times–Picayune*, March 25, 2007.

Russell, Gordon. "Second Lawsuit Blasts East N.O. Landfill." *The Times–Picayune*, July 8, 2010.

Saunly, Susan. "5,000 Public Housing Units in New Orleans Are to Be Raised." *New York Times*, June 15, 2006.

Shevory, Kristina. "A New Orleans Neighborhood Rebuilds." *New York Times*, February 25, 2007.

Steinhauer, Jennifer. "Storm and Crises: Rebuilding; New Orleans Is Still Grappling With the Basics of Rebuilding." *New York Times*, November 8, 2005.

Stroup, Sheila. "Rock 'n' Bowl hosts a Bowl-A-Thon to Benefit The Phoenix of New Orleans." *The Times–Picayune*, April 14, 2009.

Tabak, Jonathan. "Our Pops, Who Art in Heaven, Hallowed Be Thy Horn: Kermit Ruffins." *Offbeat*, August 2000.

Thomas, Greg. "Giant Retail Project Planned for Mid-City." *The Times–Picayune*, March 31, 2007.

Thompson, A.C., Brendan McCarthy, and Laura Maggi. "New Orleans Police Department Shootings after Katrina under Scrutiny." *The Times–Picayune*, December 12, 2009.

Warner, Coleman, Michelle Krupa, and Gwen Filosa. "Demolition Protests Ignore Some Realities." *The Times–Picayune*, December 15, 2007.

Wayne, Leslie. "Tax Bases Shattered, Gulf Region Faces Debt Crisis." *New York Times*, September 13, 2005.

Wilson, Sabrina. "Residents Move into New Faubourg Lafitte Neighborhood." *New Orleans Channel 8 Fox News*, February 4, 2011.

Woodward, Alex. "The Lafitte Greenway: Underway." *The Gambit*, March 15, 2011.

Woodward, Alex. "Wise Words Community Garden: Mid-City Grows Another Urban Farm." *The Gambit*, January 22, 2010.

PLANS, REPORTS, STUDIES, AND GOVERNMENT DOCUMENTS

Bea, Keith. *Federal Stafford Act Disaster Assistance: Presidential Declarations, Eligible Activities, and Funding*, Congressional Research Service Report, August 29, 2005.

Bobo, James R. *The New Orleans Economy: Pro Bono Publico*. University of New Orleans, 1975.

Broadmoor Improvement Association. *The Broadmoor Improvement Association and the Wilson Charter School*, brochure. n.d.

Broadmoor Improvement Association. *The Redevelopment Plan for Broadmoor*, 2006

Broadmoor Improvement Association, Broadmoor Charter School Board, and Broadmoor Development Corporation *Five Years Later: Achievements, 2005–2010*. Brochure, 2010.

Brossy, Jackson, Sara Dabbs, and Rose Lindsay Finkenstaedt. *Broadmoor Teacher and First-Responder Homeownership Program*. MIT Department of Urban Studies and Planning. December 2008.

Burton, Mark L., and Michael J. Hicks. *Hurricane Katrina: Preliminary Estimates of Commercial and Public Sector Damages*. Center for Business and Economic Research, Marshall University, Huntington, West Virginia, 2005.

Choi, J. A. Bhatt, and F. Chen. *In the Aftermath of Hurricane Katrina: The Chef Menteur Landfill and Its Effects on the Vietnamese-American Community*. Asian American Justice Center, August 2006.

City of New Orleans. Bring New Orleans Back Commission Urban Planning Committee. *Action Plan for New Orleans: The New American City*, January 11, 2006.

City of New Orleans. *Unified New Orleans Plan, Citywide Strategic Recovery and Rebuilding Plan*, 2007.

City of New Orleans. *Unified New Orleans Plan, District Four Plan*, 2007.

City of New Orleans. *Unified New Orleans Plan for Districts 9–10–11*, 2007.

Dadakis, Jacquelyn, William Goodman, and Gerald Hunter. *Recommendations for Restoring Quality Healthcare to the New Orleans East Community*, MIT Department of Urban Studies and Planning, December 2008.

DeSalvo, Karen. *Community Health Clinics: Bringing Quality Care Closer to New Orleanians*. Brookings Institution, August 2010.

Douglas, Lake, and Jennifer Ruley, Daniel Samuels, Jacob Wagne, and Brown+Danos landdesign, Inc. *The Lafitte Greeenway: A Vision for the Lafitte Corridor*, December 2007.

Edison Learning. *EdisonLearning™ Case Study: Louisiana Models Collaboration and Achievement*, 2010.

Erickson, Kai, and Lori Peek. *Hurricane Katrina Research Bibliography*. Social Science Research Council Task Force on Katrina and Rebuilding the Gulf Coast, 2011.

Eva Klein, and Associates, Ltd. *New Orleans Medical District Economic Development Strategy, Issue Paper: Leadership and Management Strategy*, February 11, 2006.

Fraiche, Donna. *Testimony before the Subcommittee on Disaster Recovery*, US Senate Committee on Homeland Security and Government Affairs, April 12, 2007.

Friends of Lafitte Greenway and Brown+Danos landdesign, inc. *Lafitte Greenway Master Plan*, 2007.

Gilmore Kean, LLC. *Operational Assessment of the Housing Authority of New Orleans*. Report to US Department of Housing and Urban Development, February 17, 2010.

Global Green USA. *Greening Charter Schools: Andrew H. Wilson School Case Study*, June 2010.

Harris, J., D. Mackin, S. Nafici, and N. Whitman. *Reaching Solid Ground: A Plan for a Faith-Based CDC in Versailles*. MIT Department of Urban Studies and Planning, May 2006.

Hadley, Tonda L. *Congressional Inquiry, Landfill Cost Issues Relating to Disposal of Debris in the City of New Orleans*, Report DD-07–03, US Department of Homeland Security Memo, December 15, 2006.

Hill, Paul, and Hannaway, Jane. *After Katrina: Rebuilding Opportunity and Equity in the New New Orleans*. The Urban Institute. January 2006.

Knabb, Richard D., Jamie R. Rhome, and Daniel P. Brown. *Tropical Cyclone Report Hurricane Katrina 23–30 August 2005*, National Hurricane Center, December 20, 2005, updated August 10, 2006.

Lambert Advisory & SHEDO. *Mid-City Neighborhood Planning District 4 Rebuilding Plan*, 2006.

Louisiana Office of Community Development. *Action Plan for the Use of Disaster Recovery Funds*, April 11, 2006.

Louisiana Office of Community Development. *Proposed Action Plan for the Use of Disaster Recovery Funds Allocated by P.L. 109–235*, October 3, 2007.

Louisiana Recovery School District and Orleans Parish School Board. *A Blueprint for Building 21st Century Schools for New Orleans, New Orleans School Facilities Master Plan*, August 2008.

Mary Queen of Vietnam Community Development Corporation. Grant application to Louisiana Economic Development, 2006.

Mid-City Neighborhood Organization. *Mid-City Recovery Plan Addendum*, December 7, 2006.

Mt. Auburn Associates. *World Trade Center Economic Recovery: Rebuilding the Economy of Lower Manhattan*, 2005.

National Civic League. *The Community Visioning and Strategic Planning Handbook*. Denver, CO: National Civic League Press, 2000.

New Orleans Office of the Inspector General. *Review of City of New Orleans Professional Services Contract With MWH Americas, Inc. For Infrastructure Project Management*, April 21, 2010.

New Orleans Public Library Foundation. *Rebuild: A Progress Report*, Winter, 2007.

Nguyen, Reverend Vien The. *Written testimony before the United States Senate Committee on the Environment & Public Works*, February 26, 2007.

N-Y Associates. *New Orleans Medical District Strategic Integration Plan Final Report*, March 2008.

Pacific Northwest Preparedness Society. *A Review of a City's Efforts to Recover from Hurricane Katrina and Implications for Emergency Management in British Columbia*, 2009.

Pike, Jennifer. *Spending Federal Disaster Aid Comparing the Process and Priorities in Louisiana and Mississippi in the Wake of Hurricanes Katrina and Rita*, Albany: Rockefeller Institute of Government and Baton Rouge: Public Affairs Research Council of Louisiana, 2007.

Plyer, Allison. *Neighborhood Recovery Rates: Resiliency of New Orleanians Shown in Neighborhood Repopulation Numbers*, Greater New Orleans Community Data Center, July 1, 2010.

Popkin, Susan J., Bruce Katz, Mary K. Cunningham, Karen D. Bronw, Jeremy Gustafson, and Margery A. Turner. *A Decade of HOPE VI: Research Findings and Policy Challenges*, Washington, DC: The Urban Institute, 2004.

Providence Community Housing and Enterprise Community Partners. *Homebuilding Plan for Tremé/Lafitte and Tulane/Gravier Community Development Approach*. December 2007.

Providence Community Housing, *Building Healthy Diverse Vibrant Communities*. May 2007.

Rebuilding Together New Orleans. *Annual Report* 2009.

Rowley, Karen. *The Role of Community Rebuilding Plan in the Hurricane Recovery*, Albany: Rockefeller Institute of Government and Baton Rouge: Public Affairs Research Council of Louisiana, 2008.

Rowley, Karen. *Three Years after Katrina and Rita, Challenges Remain*, Baton Rouge: Public Affairs Research Council of Louisiana, 2008.

Scott, Esther. *Broadmoor Lives A New Orleans Neighborhood's Battle to Recover from Hurricane Katrina (A)*. Kennedy School of Government Case Program, 2008.

Scott, Esther. *Broadmoor Lives A New Orleans Neighborhood's Battle to Recover from Hurricane Katrina (B)*. Kennedy School of Government Case Program, 2008.

Seidman, Karl F. *Revitalizing Commerce for American Cities: A Practitioner's Guide to Urban Main Street Programs*. Washington, DC: Fannie Mae Foundation, September 2004.

Smart Mobility Inc. and Waggonner & Ball Architects. *Restoring Claiborne Avenue: Alternatives for the Future of Claiborne Avenue*, July 15, 2010 as summarized on the Congress for New Urbanism website, http://www.cnu.org/restoringclaiborne

Swerhun, Nicole. *Record of Feedback Received: October 3–7, 2006 From Residents, the Public and Other Stakeholders*, Report to Providence Community Housing and Enterprise, November 2006.

Terrell, Dek and Ryan Bilbo. *A Report on the Impact of Hurricanes Katrina and Rita on Louisiana Businesses: 2005Q2–2006Q4*, 2007.

Tulane / Gravier Neighborhood Planning District 4 Rebuilding Plan, 2006.

Turner, Michael, Robin Varghese, and Patrick Walker. *Recovery, Renewal and Resilience: Gulf Coast Small Businesses Two Years Later*. The Political & Economic Research Council, August 2007.

United State Department of Housing and Urban Development. *Current Housing Unit Damage Estimates, Hurricanes Katrina, Rita and Wilma*, April 7, 2006.

United States Government Accountability Office (US GAO). Report 10–17. *Disaster Assistance: Federal Assistance for Permanent Housing Primarily Benefitted Homeowners; Opportunities Exist to Better Target Rental Housing Needs*, January 2010.

U.S. GAO. Report GAO-06-443R. *Disaster Preparedness: Preliminary Observations on the Evacuation of Hospitals and Nursing Homes Due to Hurricanes*, February 16, 2006.

U.S. GAO. Report 09–129. *Disaster Recovery: FEMA's Public Assistance Grant Program Experienced Challenges with Gulf Coast Rebuilding*, December 2008.

U.S. GAO. Report 09–541. *Gulf Coast Disaster Recovery: Community Development Block Grant Program Guidance to States Needs to Be Improved*, June 2009.

U.S. GAO. *Gulf Coast Rebuilding: Observations on Federal Financial Implications*. Testimony of Stanley J. Czerwinksi, GAO Director of Strategic Issues, before the Committee on the Budget, House of Representatives, August 2, 2007.

U.S. GAO. Report 10–723. *Hurricanes Katrina And Rita: Federally Funded Programs Have Helped to Address the Needs of Gulf Coast Small Businesses, but Agency Data on Subcontracting Are Incomplete*, July 2010.

U.S. GAO. *Hurricane Katrina: GAO's Preliminary Observations Regarding Preparedness, Response, and Recovery*. Testimony of David M. Walker, Comptroller General of the United States before the Senate Homeland Security and Governmental Affairs Committee, March 8, 2006.

U.S. GAO. Report GAO-06-576R. *Status of the Health Care System in New Orleans and Difficult Decisions Related to Efforts to Rebuild It Approximately 6 Months After Hurricane Katrina*, March 2006.

U.S. GAO. Report 07–44. *Transportation-Disadvantaged Populations: Actions Needed to Clarify Responsibilities and Increase Preparedness for Evacuations*, December 2006.

U.S. GAO. Report GAO/RCED-96-97. *HUD Takes over the Housing Authority of New Orleans*, 1996.

Urban Land Institute. *A Rebuilding Strategy, New Orleans LA*. November 12–18, PowerPoint Presentation, December 10, 2005.

Urban Land Institute. *A Strategy for Rebuilding New Orleans, Louisiana* (Draft Report for Review Subject to Technical Editing), December 10, 2005.

US Department of Veterans Affairs. *Site Specific Environmental Assessment for Veterans Affairs Medical Center*, April 2010.

Vidal, Avis. *Rebuilding Communities: A National Study of Urban Community Development Corporations*. New School for Social Research, Community Development Research Center, 1992.

Williams, Donny R. *Far from Home: Deficiencies in Federal Disaster Housing Assistance after Hurricanes Katrina and Rita and Recommendations for Improvement*. Ad Hoc Subcommittee on Disaster Recovery of the Committee on Homeland Security and Governmental Affairs, February, 2009.

THESES AND DISSERTATIONS

Alao, Oreoluwa. *Rebuilding Plan Implementation in New Orleans, LA: A Case Study of Freret Street Commercial Corridor and Bayou Road Cultural Corridor*. Master's Thesis, MIT, 2008.

Breunlin, Rachel. *Papa Joe Glasper and Joe's Cozy Corner: Downtown Development, Displacement and The Creation of Community*. Master's Thesis, Tulane University, 2004.

Knudsen, Seth. *Answering the Bell: Rebuilding New Orleans around Neighborhood Schools*, Master's Thesis, MIT, 2008.

Lowe, Jeffrey Sheldon. *Case Studies of Community Foundation Support for Community Development Corporations*. Rutgers University PhD, Dissertation, 2001.

Nagel, Kiara. *Understanding Place after Katrina: Predatory Planning and Cultural Resistance in New Orleans Tremé Neighborhood*. Master's Thesis, MIT ,June 2006.

Perkins, Lyle Kenneth. *Failing the Race: A Historical Assessment of New Orleans Mayor Sidney Barthelemy, 1986–1994*. Master's Thesis, Louisiana State University, 2005.

Samuels, Daniel. *Remembering North Claiborne: Community and Place in Downtown New Orleans*. University of New Orleans Ph.D. Dissertation, 2000.

Schwartz, Jeffrey E. *Making Groceries: Food, Neighborhood Markets, and Neighborhood Recovery in Post-Katrina New Orleans*, Master's Thesis, MIT, June 2008.

Tahbildar, Dulari. *Whose City? Whose Schools? A Case Study of Civic Engagement and Planning "from below" to Promote Educational Equity in New Orleans Public Schools*. Master's Thesis, MIT, June 2007.

WEBSITES

http://www.americanprogress.org/issues/2010/03/food_after_storm.html.

Catholic Extension Presents 2006 Lumen Christi Award To Sister Vera Butler, PBVM. http://www.catholicextension.org/butler-story/

Joyce Rosenberg. "Small Businesses Ravaged by Katrina Struggle to Return: Coffeehouse Reopens Nearly Two Years Later, Associated Press, August 25, 2007

http://www.chron.com/business/article/Small-businesses-ravaged-by-Katrina-struggle-to-1816023.php

http://www.epodunk.com/top10/diaspora/destination-map.html

http://www.crt.state.la.us/culturaldistricts/overview.aspx

http://www.fema.gov/news/newsrelease.fema?id=18686

http://folc-nola.org/about Friends of the Lafitte Corridor

www.fsjna.org Faubourg St John Neighborhood Association

http://www.gnocdc.org/orleans/3/63/snapshot.html

http://www.gnocdc.org/orleans/4/42/snapshot.html

http://www.gnocdc.org/orleans/4/45/snapshot.html
http://www.gnocdc.org/orleans/4/46/snapshot.html
http://www.gnocdc.org/orleans/10/56/snapshot.html
http://www.gnof.org/grantee-profiles/lillian-tinson-qatar-treme-lafitt
    e-renewal-project-2/
http://kaboom.org/about_kaboom/programs/operation_playground
http://katrinafilm.wordpress.com/2008/01/21/olive-stallings-playground-renewal-2/
http://www.marcmorial.com/Housing&Neighborhoods4.htm
http://mcno.org/about/
http://mcno.org/economic-development
http://www.mqvncdc.org/
http://www.nasa.gov/centers/marshall/michoud/maf_capabilities.html
http://news.hfta.org/.
http://www.nola.gov/en/PRESS/City-Of-New-Orleans/All-Articles/LAFITTE-HOUSI
    NG-DEMOLITION-PERMIT-APPROVED
http://www.nola.com/katrina/graphics/flashflood.swf.
http://pnola.org/about-pnola
http://pnola.org/history
Jennifer Farwell, "*A New Orleans hospital has a shot at recovery,*" August 8, 2008 www.
    preservation.org/story-of-the-week/2008/a-new-orleans-hospital-has-a.html
    http://www.prnewswire.com/news-releases/afl-cio-investment-trust-corpora-
    tion-and-local-coalition-partner-awarded-new-orleans-redevelopment-project
    s-56097082.html
www.rebuild.la.gov
http://www.stjosephchurch-no.org/history2.htm.
http://thinknola.com/wiki/Mid-City_Recovery_Plan
http://theneworleanstribune.com/morrisjeff.htm *The Rebirth of Morris Jeff Community
    School*
http://www.ujamaacdc.com/index.htm#
www.vayla-no.org/home

OTHER DOCUMENTS CITED

Hand, Robert. RE/MAX Commercial Brokers, *Changing Industrial Warehouses to Affordable Apartments: A Story of How New Orleans is Bringing Residents Back*, n.d.
City of New Orleans, Mayor Landrieu's One Hundred Rebuilding Projects, August 2010.
Memorandum between the U.S. Department of Veterans Affairs and the City of New Orleans Regarding a Potential Acquisition and Transfer of Certain New Orleans Land by the City of New Orleans to VA for Construction and Operation of a New VA Medical Center, November 19, 2007.
NewCity Neighborhood Partnership Brochure.
Embassy of the State of Qatar, *The Qatar Katrina Fund*, 2007.
Review of Mid-City Library Branch by Briana J posted to Yelp on February 15, 2011.

INDEX

AALP. *See* African-American Leadership Project
Action Plan, 44, 46–47, 309n21
ad hoc legislation, 289–90
Advancement Project, 214
AFL-CIO Building Trust, 210
African-American Leadership Project (AALP), 26
African American Museum, 224
age distribution, 63*f*
Ahlers, Doug, 69–70, 81–82, 84
AHPP. *See* Alternative Housing Pilot Program
Alcee Fortier Boulevard, 132–33, 135–36, 136*f*, 148
Alcee Fortier Park, 167, 167*f*
Algiers, 3
All Communities Together, 218
Alternative Housing Pilot Program (AHPP), 298*t*
American Can Company, 174, 181, 181*f*
AmericaSpeaks, 31–32, 310n48
AmeriCorps, 93, 230, 321n75
Amoss, Lisa, 165–66
anchor institutions, 342n20
Andrew H. Wilson School
    as charter school, 89–91, 90*f*
    Education Committee and, 74, 83, 88
    math and reading proficiency at, 321n69
    rebuilding of, 61, 73–74, 77, 79, 83, 88–91, 90*f*, 103, 104*t*, 270, 274
Annunciation Mission Church, 75, 95
Army Corps of Engineers, 147
ASI Federal Credit Union, 134–35
Astrodome, 5

Back Street Cultural Museum, 225
Bagert, Broderick, 182, 332n69

Bagert, Jenny, 182
Baker, Richard, 26–27
Bard College, 84, 93
Base Flood Elevation (BFE), 25, 33, 309n22
Basin Canal, 227
Bates, Lisa K., 14
Bayou Road, 206–8, 207*f*
Bayou St. John, 159, 161, 163, 173
BCC. *See* Broad Community Connections
BCSB. *See* Broadmoor Charter School Board
BDC. *See* Broadmoor Development Corporation
Beard, Michael, 212
Belles of the Bayou, 207, 207*f*
BESE. *See* Board of Elementary and Secondary Education
BFE. *See* Base Flood Elevation
BIA. *See* Broadmoor Improvement Association
BioInnovation Center, 240, 340n242
Biosciences District, 240
Blakely, Edward, 35–38, 54–55, 311n62
Blanco, Kathleen, 5, 44
block captains, 81
BNOB Commission. *See* Bring New Orleans Back Commission
Board of Elementary and Secondary Education (BESE), 182
bonds, 42–44
Boyd, Harrison, 56, 317n160
BP oil spill. *See* British Petroleum oil spill
Brand Source, 184
brass band parades, 198–99
brewery district, 227

Bring New Orleans Back (BNOB)
   Commission
   Broadmoor and, 64–66, 69, 79
   "Citywide Framework for
      Reconstruction" of, 23–25, 24f
   formation of, 21
   opposition to, 24–27, 33, 64–65, 286
   planning by, 21–27, 24f, 34, 309n21
   UNOP and, 29–30
   Village de L'Est and, 120
British Petroleum (BP) oil spill, 156–57,
   274, 328n107
Broad Community Connections (BCC),
   166, 263
Broadmoor
   age distribution and, 63f
   AHPP and, 298t
   Andrew H. Wilson School, 61, 73–74,
      77, 79, 83, 88–91, 90f, 103, 104t,
      270, 274
   BDC rebuilding, 76–77, 82–84, 92–98,
      92t, 105, 131, 322n76
   BIA rebuilding, 64–66, 68f, 69–72,
      79–84, 89, 92–94, 105, 274, 278,
      321n63
   BNOB Commission and, 64–66, 69, 79
   Cantrell and, 64–67, 69, 71, 85–86,
      94, 107, 155
   CDBG and, 104, 104t, 131
   challenges facing, 106–7
   characterization of, 17
   citywide planning process and, 78–79
   civic capacity and, 105–6
   as complete neighborhood, 179, 265t,
      269–70
   economic development, 298t–299t
   educational reform and, 87–88
   FEMA and, 85–87, 89, 94
   first projects, 85–91, 86t, 90f
   five years later, 98–107, 99t–100t,
      101f, 102t–104t
   flooding, 60–61, 318n3
   geography influencing, 259
   government recovery policies influ-
      encing, 260
   grassroots contributions and compo-
      nents, 262–64, 265t–266t, 267
   Harvard and, 69–71, 84, 88, 179
   housing, 94–98, 96t–97t, 168, 210,
      322nn91–92

   implementation, 75–76, 78, 82–85
   Jefferson Parish and, 61
   Keller Library, 73, 77, 79, 83, 85–87,
      86t, 103, 104t
   Lambert Plan and, 29, 78–79
   leadership in, 155
   location of, 61, 62f, 79, 158
   Louisiana bridge loan program for, 299t
   market-based recovery, 321n73
   Neighborhood Improvement District,
      94, 105, 107
   neighborhood rebuilding capacity
      influencing, 261, 266t, 278–79
   New Orleans East and, 61
   organizing for, 64–68, 67f–68f
   PA Program and, 89, 104, 104t
   partnerships, 69–71, 75–76, 75f, 78,
      83–85, 95
   plan for, 69–78, 72f, 74t, 75f, 82, 96,
      99, 106–7, 179, 269–70
   prior conditions influencing, 249–50,
      258t
   problems with, 77–78
   public facilities and infrastructure
      funding, 299t
   race in, 64
   repopulation, 66, 79–82, 99–103,
      99t–100t, 101f, 102t–103t, 259,
      264, 265t, 267, 279
   residents' traits and, 62, 63t
   Road Home Program and, 94–96, 104,
      104t, 106, 168, 297t
   Roark and, 60–61, 64–66, 82–84, 93,
      95, 107, 155, 321n73
   Small Firm Loan and Grant Program
      and, 298t
   SRPP for, 298t
   street map and sub-areas, 67, 67f
   technical assistance to small firms in,
      298t
   uneven recovery in, 254
   Village de L'Est and, 113, 121, 128,
      131, 154–55
   vision for, 103–5, 104t
Broadmoor Charter School Board
   (BCSB), 88–89
Broadmoor Development Corporation
   (BDC)
   building capacity and, 92–94, 92t
   funding, 92t

rebuilding by, 76–77, 82–84, 92–98, 92*t*, 105, 131, 322n76
Broadmoor Improvement Association (BIA)
building capacity at, 64–66, 68*f*, 69–72, 79–84, 89, 92–94
rebuilding by, 64–66, 68*f*, 69–72, 79–84, 89, 92–94, 105, 274, 278, 321n63
Broad Street, 158, 159*f*, 164–66, 168, 270. *See also* Faubourg St. John; Lower Mid-City; Mid-City; Tremé
Brock, Joseph, 187–88, 191
Brunsma, David L., 15
Bui, Huy, 116
Bui, James, 126–27, 129
building capacity
BDC and, 92–94, 92*t*
BIA and, 64–66, 68*f*, 69–72, 79–84, 89, 92–94
MQVN CDC and, 128–32, 132*t*
Buros, Santiago, 93, 107
Bush, George W., 19, 27, 39, 42
business
challenges facing, 304n50, 342n21
damage to, 10–11, 303n33
Faubourg St. John, 161–62, 162*f*–164*f*, 266*t*
Lower Mid-City, 236, 239–41, 266*t*
Mid-City, 174, 187–90, 266*t*, 272
MQVN CDC and, 132–37, 134*f*, 135*t*, 136*f*
rebuilding, 10–12
Tremé, 200, 206–9, 207*f*, 221, 265*t*–266*t*, 274
Village de L'Est, 132–37, 134*f*, 135*t*, 136*f*, 265*t*–266*t*, 272–73
Business Recovery Small Loan and Grant program, 272
Butler, Vera, 227–29, 338n205
Bynum, Adolph, 208
Bynum, Naydja, 208–9

Canizaro, Joe, 22–23
Cantrell, LaToya
Broadmoor Neighborhood Improvement District and, 94
Broadmoor rebuilding and, 64–67, 69, 71, 85–86, 94, 107, 155
Cao, Joseph, 156
C.A.R.E., 322n82

Carnegie Corporation, 85
Carondelet Canal, 227
Carter, Karen, 94
Catholic Charities, 108–9, 129–31, 213–14, 277
Catholic Church, Vietnamese community and, 108–10, 129. *See also* Mary Queen of Vietnam Church
CDBG. *See* Community Development Block Grant
CDCs. *See* community development corporations
Center for the Performing Arts, 201
Central City, 214
CGI. *See* Clinton Global Initiative
Chamlee-Wright, Emily, 13–15
Charity Hospital, 142
charrette. *See* design charrette
charter schools, 320n55
Andrew H. Wilson, 89–91, 90*f*
BCSB and, 88–89
ICS, 140–42
John Dibert Community School, 184
Chef Menteur Highway
blighted properties on, 148, 149*f*
rebuilding of, 108, 121–22, 127, 137, 148, 149*f*, 152–53
Chef Menteur landfill, 122–28, 125*f*, 137–38, 325n48, 326n56
Chisom, Ron, 202
Chrisman, Bill, 317n160
Christopher Homes, 140, 327n84
Citizens' Committee (Comite des Citoyens), 202
Citizens for a Strong New Orleans East, 123–24, 126
City Center, 146
City Council, 27–29, 79, 209, 216, 236
city government, rebuilding and, 11
city infrastructure, rebuilding, 8, 13, 299*t*
City Park, 158, 163, 174, 178
City Planning Commission (CPC), 11, 30, 37, 311n58
City Planning Department, 16
city rebuilding process. *See also* grass-roots rebuilding, of neighborhoods
CDBG and, 28–29, 37, 40–49, 45*t*–46*t*, 53, 56–58
dual collaborative rebuilding in, 257, 281–86

city rebuilding process (*Cont.*)
  FEMA in, 26, 38, 40, 43–44, 49–52, 58
  funding for, 18–19, 35, 39–44, 58
  HUD and, 41, 44, 46–48, 53
  neighborhoods in, 279–94
  PA Program and, 40, 43–44, 49–52, 55, 59
  tension in, 311n53
"Citywide Framework for Reconstruction," 23–25, 24*f*
Citywide Strategic Recovery and Rebuilding Plan (UNOP), 34
Citywide Strategic Recovery and Redevelopment Plan (CSRRP), 37–39, 38*t*, 54, 56
civic participation
  in Broadmoor, 105–6
  enhanced, 292–93
  in Mid-City, 197
  in Tremé, 225
  in Village de L'Est, 137–38, 154
Claiborne Avenue, 199–200, 200*f*
Clear as Mud (Olshansky and Johnson), 14
Clinton, Hillary, 118
Clinton Global Initiative (CGI), 84
Cluster New Orleans Neighborhood Program, 34
CocoHut, 206
Comiskey Park, 178, 184–87, 186*f*, 332n69
Comite des Citoyens. *See* Citizens' Committee
commercial district marketing, in Village de L'Est, 132–37, 134*f*, 135*t*, 136*f*
Community Book Center, 206–8
community capital, 247–49
Community Development Block Grant (CDBG)
  Broadmoor and, 104, 104*t*, 131
  in city rebuilding process, 28–29, 37, 40–49, 45*t*–46*t*, 53, 56–58
  delays, 186
  distribution, 272, 290–91, 312n67, 313n83, 314n100, 314n104
  funding, 28–29, 37, 40–49, 45*t*–46*t*, 53, 56–58, 104, 104*t*, 131, 299*t*
  inappropriate use of, 53, 290, 338n197
  for infrastructure, 299*t*
  for Lafitte Greenway, 166
  Lower Mid-City and, 235, 237
  Mid-City and, 196

MQVN CDC and, 131, 134, 135*t*
  rate of spending, 255
  recovery policies, 249, 313n84
  reform, 290–91
community development corporations (CDCs), 76–78, 128, 319n30. *See also specific CDCs*
  bylaws, 326n61
  neighborhood rebuilding capacity and, 261–62, 275
community gardens, 187–88, 189*f*
community health center, in Village de L'Est, 142–46, 145*f*
community mobilization
  GNOBEDD and, 240–41
  in Village de L'Est, 122–28, 125*f*
Community Support Organization (CSO), 30
Compass, P. Edwin, III, 302n24
complete neighborhoods
  Broadmoor, 179, 265*t*, 269–70
  defined, 179
  Faubourg St. John, 179, 265*t*, 269
  grassroots rebuilding of, 265*t*, 269–72
  Lower Mid-City, 265*t*
  Mid-City, 179–80, 265*t*, 269, 271
  Tremé, 221, 265*t*, 269
  Village de L'Est, 179, 265*t*, 269–71
Congo Square, 198
Convention Center, 302n24
Covenant House, 210
Cowan, Scott, 141
CPC. *See* City Planning Commission
Crescent City Rebuilding Corporation, 22, 25, 27
Crescent Club, 191, 191*f*
Crutcher, Michael, 14
CSO. *See* Community Support Organization
CSRRP. *See* Citywide Strategic Recovery and Redevelopment Plan

Dang, Mai, 137–38
Dan Than Fellows, 116, 123, 129, 277
death totals, 3–4
Department of Homeland Security, 293
Department of Housing and Urban Development, US (HUD), 139, 316n142. *See also* Community Development Block Grant

in city rebuilding process, 41, 44, 46–48, 53
rental housing recovery and, 267–68
Tremé and, 212–13, 215–16, 218, 220, 252
Department of Veteran Affairs (DVA), 233, 235–36, 340n230
DeSalvo, Karen, 143–45
desegregation, 320n51
design charrette
GNOBEDD, 241
for Village de L'Est rebuilding, 120–22, 275–76
Design Workshop, 166, 186, 329n21
Digitas, 80
district scale decisions, 272, 311nn53–54
distrust, 280, 342n28, 343n31
DNA Creative Media, 185
DNIA. *See* Downtown Neighborhoods Improvement Association
Domain Companies, 188, 191
Donovan, Shaun, 219
Downtown Neighborhoods Improvement Association (DNIA), 203–8
dual collaborative rebuilding
city and neighborhood rebuilding in, 257, 281–86
conditions and practices for, 284
defined, 281
DVA. *See* Department of Veteran Affairs

economic development
Broadmoor, 298t–299t
Faubourg St. John, 266t, 298t–299t
funding, 298t–299t, 300
GNOBEDD and, 239–41, 253, 340nn243–44
in grassroots rebuilding of neighborhoods, 265t–266t, 272–74
HANO and, 274
Louisiana bridge loan program for, 299t
Lower Mid-City, 239–41, 266t, 298t–299t
Mid-City, 174, 266t, 272, 298t–299t, 300
Small Firm Loan and Grant Program for, 298t
technical assistance to small firms, 298t
Tremé, 265t–266t, 274, 298t–299t

Village de L'Est, 265t–266t, 272–73, 298t–299t
economy
losses from flooding, 6–11
viability of, 19
educational reform, 87–88, 270
Education Committee
DNIA, 205–6
MCNO, 180, 183–84
Wilson School and, 74, 83, 88
Emergency Support Function (ESF #14), 292, 310n30
Enrichment and Entrepreneurial Academy Program, 206
Entergy, 116–17
Enterprise Community Partners, 213, 217–18, 319n30
Environew, 97
environmental compliance cost, 47, 315n116
environment review, 41, 314n115
ERTCA. *See* Esplanade Ridge-Tremé Civic Association
ESF #14. *See* Emergency Support Function
Esplanade Ridge, 159, 203
Esplanade Ridge-Tremé Civic Association (ERTCA), 203–5
evacuation, 4–5, 302n15
Everson, Bart, 176–78, 181, 329n45

Fair Grinds Coffee House, 163, 164f
Fallon, Eldon, 236
families, separated, 4–6, 303n26
FANO. *See* Finance Authority of New Orleans
Faubourg Lafitte complex, 216–19, 217f
Faubourg St. John
agendas negotiated in, 251–52
AHPP and, 298t
Alcee Fortier Park in, 167, 167f
Amoss and, 165–66
businesses, 161–62, 162f–164f, 266t
community capital, 247–49
as complete neighborhood, 179, 265t, 269
economic development, 266t, 298t–299t
five years later, 170–74, 170t–171t, 172f, 173t

Faubourg St. John (*Cont.*)
 flooding in, 162, 250
 FSJNA in, 163–68, 165*f*, 173
 geography, 250–51
 government recovery policies influencing, 249, 260
 grassroots contributions and components, 265*t*–266*t*
 homeowners rebuilding, 168–70, 169*f*
 housing, 161, 161*f*, 168–70, 169*f*,
  193, 210, 246–47, 246*t*, 329n26
 Lafitte Greenway and, 166, 185–86
 location of, 158, 159*f*
 Lola's restaurant in, 187
 Louisiana bridge loan program for, 299*t*
 multineighborhood initiatives and,
  252–53
 neighborhood rebuilding capacity
  influencing, 262, 266*t*, 276
 planning and projects, 163–68, 165*f*,
  167*f*, 177, 179
 playgrounds in, 167–68
 prior conditions, 249–50, 258*t*
 public facilities and infrastructure
  funding, 299*t*
 race in, 161, 171, 171*t*, 172*f*, 174
 repopulation, 168–74, 169*f*, 170*t*–
  171*t*, 172*f*, 173*t*, 246–47, 246*t*
 residents, key traits of, 160, 160*t*,
  329n30
 Road Home Program and, 168, 297*t*,
  329n26
 schools, 182–83
 Small Firm Loan and Grant Program
  and, 298*t*
 snapshot of, 159–60, 160*t*
 SRPP for, 298*t*
 technical assistance to small firms in,
  298*t*
 uneven recovery in, 254
 variations in rebuilding, 246–51, 246*t*
 Vision Plan, 164–66, 165*f*
Faubourg St. John Neighborhood
  Association (FSJNA), 163–68,
  165*f*, 173
federal disaster assistance reform
 CDBG, 290–91
 empowerment of local governments,
  290–92
 FEMA, 281, 287–94

 government recovery policies, 290
 integrative and systemwide recovery
  investment, 293–94
 local civic capacity and, 292–93
 PA Program, 287, 291, 293–94
 program for large-scale disasters,
  288–90
Federal Emergency Management Agency
  (FEMA). *See also* Public Assistance
  Program; trailers, FEMA
 Broadmoor and, 85–87, 89, 94
 in city rebuilding process, 26, 38, 40,
  43–44, 49–52, 58
 ESF #14, 292, 310n30
 evacuation and, 5
 flood insurance standards, 18, 25, 33,
  309n22
 Hazard Mitigation Grant Program, 40,
  47, 52
 policies, 249, 343n33
 reform, 281, 287–94
 senior housing project and, 140
federally qualified health center (FQHC),
  145, 328n93, 328n102
FEMA. *See* Federal Emergency
  Management Agency
Finance Authority of New Orleans
  (FANO), 48–49, 56–57
Fine Arts and Wellness Center, 103
flood control system, 2, 7, 18, 301n6,
  303n32
flooding, of New Orleans
 in Broadmoor, 60–61, 318n3
 depth, 324n21
 economic losses, 6–11
 in Faubourg St. John, 162, 250
 in Gentilly, 3–4
 human catastrophe of, 3–6, 302n13
 in Jefferson Parish, 3
 Katrina and, 1–17
 in Lakeview, 3–4, 9
 in Lower Mid-City, 250
 in Lower Ninth Ward, 2–4, 9
 in Mid-City, 9, 176, 250
 in New Orleans East, 9
 physical losses, 6–11, 303n33,
  304n39
 reduced risk of, 33
 research after, 13–16
 St. Bernard Parish, 2–4

in Tremé, 203–4, 250
in Village de L'Est, 112–13
flood insurance
 claims, 40–41
 standards, 18, 25, 33, 309n22
FOC. *See* Friends of Lafitte Corridor
food access, 338n190
FQHC. *See* federally qualified health
 center
Free Church of the Annunciation, 84
French Quarter, rebuilding, 21
Friends of Lafitte Corridor (FOC), 166,
 186
FSJNA. *See* Faubourg St. John
 Neighborhood Association
funding, for rebuilding. *See also specific
 funding sources*
 in city rebuilding process, 18–19, 35,
  39–44, 58
 critical accomplishments in, 58
 economic development, 298t–299t, 300
 housing, 297t–298t
 infrastructure, 299t
 Keller Library, 86t, 103, 104t
 phasing and, 282
 private, 35, 70, 82, 85, 133
 problems with, 255, 305n62
 for public facilities, 299t
 repopulation and, 264
 state, 35, 43
 tortured road to, 39–44
 UNOP and, 312n67
Fyre Youth Squad, 206

Gafford, Farrah D., 14
gardens, community, 187–88, 189f
GCR, Inc., 8–9
Gene Therapy Consortium, 240,
 340n242
Gentilly
 Ahlers and, 69
 Broad Street and, 158
 flooding in, 3–4
 landfill, 122, 325n31
gentrification, 221–22
geography, rebuilding influenced by,
 250–51, 258–59, 271
GNOBEDD. *See* Greater New Orleans
 Biosciences Economic Development
 District

Gossett, Lou, Jr., 184
government recovery policies
 influence of, 249, 259–61, 267
 reform, 290
 repopulation and, 267
GO Zone tax incentives. *See* Gulf
 Opportunity Zone tax incentives
Grace Episcopal Church, 178
grassroots rebuilding, of neighborhoods.
 See also Broadmoor; Faubourg St.
 John; Lower Mid-City; Mid-City;
 Tremé; Village de L'Est
 accurate information in, 280
 complete neighborhoods, 265t,
  269–72
 contributions and components of,
  262–79, 265t–266t, 275f
 defined, 15–16
 development of, 19, 59, 256
 dual collaborative rebuilding and, 257,
  281–86
 economic development, 265t–266t,
  272–74
 factors shaping, 257–62, 258t
 lessons from, 256–57, 294
 limitations of, 286–87
 neighborhood rebuilding capacity
  influencing, 261–62, 266t,
  274–79, 275f
 overview of, 15–17
 pre-Katrina conditions influencing,
  257–58, 258t
 repopulation and, 264–69, 265t
 uneven recovery in, 254–55
 variations in, 246–51, 246t
Gravier, Bertrand, 338n200
Gravier, Jean, 338n200
Greater New Orleans Biosciences
 Economic Development District
 (GNOBEDD), 239–41, 253,
 340nn243–44
Greater Tremé Consortium (GTC), 202,
 204–5
Green, Rebekah A., 14
green building, 86, 89, 91, 97
Green Coast Enterprises, 190
GTC. *See* Greater Tremé Consortium
Gulf Opportunity (GO) Zone tax incentives, 139, 191, 249, 260, 313n82,
 314n92

Hankins, John, 224–25
Hannan, Phillip, 109
HANO. See Housing Authority of New
    Orleans
Harman, Damon, 185
Harvard, Broadmoor and, 69–71, 84,
    88, 179
Hayes, James, 202
Hazard Mitigation Grant Program, 40,
    47, 52
health care
    damage to, 9–10, 142
    at FQHCs, 145, 328n93, 328n102
    in Lower Mid-City, 227, 231–39,
        232f, 232t, 234f, 238f–239f,
        242, 299
    in New Orleans East, 143
    rebuilding, 9–10, 12
    Village de L'Est community health
        center and, 142–46, 145f
Historic Faubourg Tremé Association
    (HFTA), 204, 208–9
Hollygrove neighborhood, 102–3, 103t
Holman, Michael, 180–81, 184
HOPE VI, 211–13, 215, 218
housing. See also Department of
    Housing and Urban Development,
    US; Housing Authority of New
    Orleans; Low Income Housing Tax
    Credits; public housing; Road Home
    Program; senior housing
    AHPP for, 298t
    Broadmoor, 94–98, 96t–97t, 168, 210,
        322nn91–92
    damage, 8–9, 303n33
    Faubourg St. John, 161, 161f, 168–70,
        169f, 193, 210, 246–47, 246t,
        329n26
    funding, 297t–298t
    Lower Mid-City, 210, 226–31, 226f,
        242–47, 242t–243t, 245t–246t, 249
    Mid-City, 174–75, 175f, 187, 191–97,
        191f, 192t, 195t–196t, 246–47,
        246t, 333n95
    New Orleans East, 118, 149, 324n9
    rental, recovery of, 96, 96t, 104t,
        267–68, 298t
    Section 8 program for, 213, 327n81
    Tremé, 198–222, 198f, 217f, 220t–
        221t, 226, 246–47, 246t, 249–51,

260, 274, 335n130, 336n169,
    336nn166–67
Village de L'Est, 148–52, 149f–150f,
    150t–152t, 168, 193, 210, 220,
    327n68
Housing Authority of New Orleans
    (HANO), 336n160, 337n186
    economic development and, 274
    formation of, 199
    rental housing recovery and, 267–68
    Tremé and, 212–13, 215–16, 218–20,
        260
Housing Conservation District Review
    Commission, 215–16
HUD. See Department of Housing and
    Urban Development, US
human catastrophe, from flooding of
    New Orleans, 3–6, 302n13
Hurricane Katrina, 41–42, 116
    death totals, 3–4
    development of, 1
    flooding of New Orleans by, 1–17
    storm surges, 2
    strength of, 1–2, 4, 301n2
hurricane protection, 7
Hurricane Rita, 5–6, 41–42, 116

Iberville project, 199
ICS. See Intercultural Charter School
The Idea Village, 206–7
Ikemire, Paul, 229–31, 237
immigrants, 109–11, 110f, 111t
Industrial Canal, 2–3
infrastructure, rebuilding, 8, 13, 299t
insurance. See flood insurance
Intercultural Charter School (ICS),
    140–42
Intracoastal Waterway and Mississippi
    River Gulf Outlet (MRGO), 2,
    301n5
Isaacson, Walter, 69

Jarvis, Robin, 88, 141
jazz, 161, 198–99, 208–9, 335n143
JazzFest, 161
Jefferson Parish, 3, 61
Jindal, Bobby, 94
Job Opportunities for Low Income
    Individuals (JOLI), 136
Joe's Cozy Corner, 208–9, 335n143

John Dibert Community School, 184
Johnson, Laurie A., 14
JOLI. *See* Job Opportunities for Low Income Individuals
Jordan, Yashika, 206

KaBoom!, 167–68
Kates, R. W., 255
Katrina. *See* Hurricane Katrina
Katrina Survivors Association, 23
Keller Library. *See* Rosa F. Keller Library
Kelly, Jim, 213
Kennedy School of Government (KSG), 69–71, 88
King, John, 118
Koo, Doris, 120, 128, 213
Kramer, Jerry, 84
Krause, Kevin, 237–39
KSG. *See* Kennedy School of Government

Lafitte complex
    demolition controversy, 214–16
    Faubourg Lafitte, 216–19, 217*f*
    impact of, 250–51
    Tremé and, 199–211, 213–20, 217*f*, 247, 250–51, 260, 274
Lafitte Greenway, 166, 185–86, 189–90, 253
Lake Pontchartrain, 2–3, 8, 159, 227
Lakeview
    flooded, 3–4, 9
    personal networks in, 14
Lambert, Paul, 30
Lambert Plan, 27–30, 37
    Broadmoor and, 29, 78–79
    Lower Mid-City and, 230
    LSU hospital plans and, 233
    Mid-City and, 29, 178–79
landfills
    Chef Menteur, 122–28, 125*f*, 137–38, 325n48, 326n56
    Gentilly, 122, 325n31
Landrieu, Mary, 118
Landrieu, Mitch, 57, 166, 185, 219, 237, 318n167
Language Access Coalition, 137
large-scale disasters. *See also* Hurricane Katrina
    challenges of, 294
    program for, 288–90

LDEQ. *See* Louisiana Department of Environmental Quality
leadership, 155–56
LEAN. *See* Louisiana Environmental Network
legislation, ad hoc, 289–90
Leong, Karen J., 14
levees, 2, 7, 18, 301n6, 303n32
LHFA. *See* Louisiana Housing Finance Authority
LHWs. *See* local health workers
libraries, 180–82, 181*f. See also* Rosa F. Keller Library
Library Board, 85–86
LIHTC. *See* Low Income Housing Tax Credits
Lindy Boggs Medical Center, 174, 176, 188–90, 190*f*, 236, 251
LISC. *See* Local Initiative Support Corporation
local civic capacity, enhanced, 292–93
local governments, empowerment of, 290–92
local health workers (LHWs), 144
Local Initiative Support Corporation (LISC), 319n30
Lola's restaurant, 187
London Avenue Canal, 3
Long-Term Community Recovery Program, 37
Longwell, Kelly, 128
Louis Armstrong Park, 201–2, 201*f*, 334nn115–16
Louisiana Biomedical Research and Development Park, 239
Louisiana bridge loan program, 299*t*
Louisiana Department of Environmental Quality (LDEQ), 122–24, 126
Louisiana Environmental Network (LEAN), 123–24, 126
Louisiana Healthcare Redesign Collaborative, 142
Louisiana Housing Finance Authority (LHFA), 95, 130
Louisiana Parkway Area Association, 65
Louisiana Recovery Authority (LRA)
    creation of, 29, 44
    funding and, 30–31, 37–38, 43–44, 47, 54, 69, 272
    GNOBEDD and, 240

Louisiana State University (LSU), 227.
    See also LSU/Charity Hospital
Lower Mid-City
    agendas negotiated in, 251–52
    AHPP and, 298t
    businesses, 236, 239–41, 266t
    Butler and, 227–29, 338n205
    CDBG and, 235, 237
    community capital, 247–49
    as complete neighborhood, 265t
    economic development, 239–41, 266t,
        298t–299t
    FEMA trailers in, 228–29
    five years later, 241–45, 242t–243t,
        244f, 245t–246t
    flooding in, 250
    geography, 250–51, 259
    government recovery policies influenc-
        ing, 249, 260
    grassroots contributions and compo-
        nents, 262–63, 265t–266t
    health care in, 227, 231–39, 232f,
        232t, 234f, 238f–239f, 242, 299
    history of, 227
    housing, 210, 226–31, 226f, 242–47,
        242t–243t, 245t–246t, 249
    Lambert Plan and, 230
    location of, 158, 226
    Louisiana bridge loan program for, 299t
    LSU/Charity Hospital development in,
        231–39, 232f, 232t, 234f, 238f–
        239f, 260–61, 299
    multineighborhood initiatives and,
        252–53
    naming of, 338n200
    neighborhood rebuilding capacity
        influencing, 262, 266t, 276–77
    PNOLA and, 230–31, 237–38,
        248–49, 262–63
    prior conditions, 249–50, 258t
    Providence Community Housing and,
        214
    public facilities and infrastructure
        funding, 299t
    race in, 242–43, 243t, 244f
    repopulation, 242–47, 242t–243t,
        244f, 245t–246t, 262–63, 265t,
        267–68
    residents, key traits of, 160, 160t, 227
    Road Home Program and, 297t

St. Joseph's Church in, 227–29, 248
    Small Firm Loan and Grant Program
        and, 298t
    snapshot of, 159–60, 160t
    SRPP for, 298t
    TCNDC and, 227–30, 248–49, 262–63
    technical assistance to small firms in,
        298t
    Tulane-Gravier Neighborhood Plan
        for, 230, 233, 234f
    uneven recovery in, 254
    urban renewal in, 231–39, 232f, 232t,
        234f, 238f–239f
    VA complex in, 231–39, 232f, 232t,
        234f, 238f–239f, 260–61, 339n223,
        339n228
    variations in rebuilding, 246–47, 246t
Lower Mid-City Residents and
    Businesses, 235
Lower Ninth Ward
    attachment to, 13
    Catholic Charities in, 214
    community garden in, 188
    flooding in, 2–4, 9
    geography, 258
    march through, 26
    personal networks in, 14
    as Rebuild Zone, 37
    repopulation, 258
    senior housing in, 140
Low Income Housing Tax Credits
    (LIHTC), 42, 106, 130, 139, 327n83
    Mid-City and, 191, 195, 197
    policies, 249, 290, 313n90, 326n65
LRA. *See* Louisiana Recovery Authority
LSU. *See* Louisiana State University
LSU/Charity Hospital
    cost estimate, 304n45
    government policy and, 260–61
    in Lower Mid-City, 231–39, 232f,
        232t, 234f, 238f–239f, 260–61, 299
    plans, 233

Main Street districts, 166, 329n18
market-based recovery, 321n73
Mary Queen of Vietnam (MQVN)
    Church
    damage to, 113
    FEMA trailers and, 117–18
    landfill campaign and, 123–24, 127

Mass of the Resurrection at, 115
Nguyen, Nghiem Van, and, 140
Nguyen, Vien The, and, 113–18,
     120–21, 124, 127–29, 140–41,
     143–44, 147–48, 154–56
Village de L'Est rebuilding by, 110,
     112–20, 114*f*, 127, 151, 273
Mary Queen of Vietnam Community
     Development Corporation (MQVN
     CDC)
  BP oil spill and, 156–57
  building capacity and, 128–32, 132*t*
  business and, 132–37, 134*f*, 135*t*, 136*f*
  CDBG and, 131, 134, 135*t*
  challenges facing, 138–48, 145*f*, 147*f*
  civic participation and, 137–38
  New Orleans East and, 131
  Nguyen, May, and, 129, 132–35,
     327n71
  partnerships, 277
  rebuilding by, 123, 128–41, 132*t*,
     134*f*, 135*t*, 136*f*, 143–49, 145*f*,
     151–56, 263, 268, 273, 326n58,
     328n99
Mass of the Resurrection, 115
McDonough City Park Academy, 168
McDonough High School, 206, 274
MCLNO. *See* Medical Center of Louisiana
     at New Orleans
McNamara, James, 240–41
MCNO. *See* Mid-City Neighborhood
     Organization
McNulty, Ian, 187
McQuaid, John, 4–5
Medical Center of Louisiana at New
     Orleans (MCLNO), 10
Memorandum of Understanding (MOU),
     30, 340n230
Memorial Methodist Hospital, 113
Meridian development, 191
Michoud Boulevard, 132, 135, 148
Mid-City
  agendas negotiated in, 251–52
  AHPP and, 298*t*
  businesses, 174, 187–90, 266*t*, 272
  CDBG and, 196
  civic participation in, 197
  Comiskey Park in, 178, 184–87, 186*f*,
     332n69
  community capital, 247–49

community gardens in, 187–88, 189*f*
as complete neighborhood, 179–80,
     265*t*, 269, 271
development, 188–92, 190*f*–191*f*,
     266*t*, 272, 298*t*–299*t*, 300
economy, 174, 266*t*, 272, 298*t*–299*t*,
     300
Everson and, 176–78, 181, 329n45
five years later, 192–97, 192*t*–193*t*,
     194*f*, 195*t*–196*t*
flooding, 9, 176, 250
geography, 250–51, 259
government recovery policies influenc-
     ing, 249, 260
grassroots contributions and compo-
     nents, 263, 265*t*–266*t*
housing, 174–75, 175*f*, 187, 191–97,
     191*f*, 192*t*, 195*t*–196*t*, 246–47,
     246*t*, 333n95
individual initiative in, 187–88
Lambert Plan and, 29, 178–79
library, 180–82, 181*f*
LIHTC and, 191, 195, 197
Lindy Boggs Medical Center in, 174,
     176, 188–90, 190*f*, 236, 251
location of, 158, 159*f*, 174
Louisiana bridge loan program for,
     299*t*
MCNO rebuilding, 175–84, 187,
     189–91, 252, 331n50, 333n96
multineighborhood initiatives and,
     252–53
neighborhood rebuilding capacity and,
     261–62, 266*t*, 276, 278
Neighborhood Rebuilding Plan,
     177–80
planning, 175–80
prior conditions, 249–50, 258*t*
public facilities and infrastructure
     funding, 299*t*
race in, 9, 160, 174, 192–95, 193*t*,
     194*f*
repopulation, 192–97, 192*t*–193*t*,
     194*f*, 195*t*–196*t*, 246–47, 246*t*
residents, key traits of, 160, 160*t*
Road Home Program and, 168, 196*t*,
     297*t*, 333n95
schools, 182–84, 184*f*
Small Firm Loan and Grant Program
     and, 298*t*

Mid-City (*Cont.*)
  snapshot of, 159–60, 160*t*
  SRPP for, 298*t*
  technical assistance to small firms in,
    298*t*
  uneven recovery in, 254
  variations in rebuilding, 246–47, 246*t*
Mid-City Neighborhood Organization
    (MCNO)
  development and, 189–91
  Education Committee, 180, 183–84
  library built by, 180–82, 181*f*
  limitations of, 197
  planning by, 175–80
  rebuilding by, 175–84, 187, 189–91,
    252, 331n50, 333n96
  schools and, 182–84, 184*f*
Miller, Harvey, 4–5
Miller, Renee, 4–5
Mississippi River, high ground along, 3,
    159, 203
MIT, 84, 135, 145, 155, 166, 186, 210
Morial, Marc, 212–13
Morice, Mark, 66
Morris X. F. Jeff School, 182–83, 184*f*
MOU. *See* Memorandum of
    Understanding
MQVN CDC. *See* Mary Queen of
    Vietnam Community Development
    Corporation
MQVN Church. *See* Mary Queen of
    Vietnam Church
MRGO. *See* Intracoastal Waterway and
    Mississippi River Gulf Outlet
multineighborhood initiatives, 252–53
MWH, 55–57, 317n157

Nagin, Ray
  evacuation and, 4, 302n24
  landfill campaign and, 122–24, 126–27
  rebuilding and, 11, 21, 25–27, 29–30,
    36–37, 57, 77, 184, 216, 310n33,
    318n167, 338n197
  RSD and, 320n55
National Association of Vietnamese
    American Service Agencies
    (NAVASA), 116, 123, 126, 129, 136,
    146, 277
National Commission on Severely
    Distressed Public Housing, 211

National Flood Insurance Program
    (NFIP), 309n22
National Guard, 4–5, 60
National Trust for Historic Preservation,
    236
NAVASA. *See* National Association
    of Vietnamese American Service
    Agencies
Neighborhood Housing Services of New
    Orleans (NHS), 48–49
neighborhood rebuilding capacity,
    261–62, 266*t*, 274–79, 275*f*
Neighborhood Rebuilding Equity
    Ordinance, 26
neighborhoods. *See also* complete
    neighborhoods; grassroots rebuild-
    ing, of neighborhoods; *specific
    neighborhoods*
  boundaries of, 16
  in city rebuilding process, 279–94
  in multineighborhood initiatives,
    252–53
  neighborhood-scale planning and,
    280, 285
  rebuilding, 11–17, 26, 257, 261–62,
    266*t*, 274–79, 275*f*, 281–94
  recovery budgets for, 285
Neighbors for Morris X. F. Jeff School,
    182
NeighborWorks, 92, 92*t*, 319n30,
    326n62
New City Neighborhood Partnership,
    253
New Market tax credits (NMTCs), 290
New Orleans. *See also* flooding, of New
    Orleans; Housing Authority of
    New Orleans; rebuilding, of New
    Orleans; *specific neighborhoods*
  age distribution of, 63*f*
  City Council, 27–29, 79, 209, 216, 236
  City Planning Department, 16
  educational reform in, 87–88
  evacuation, 4–5
  FANO and, 48–49, 56–57
  jazz, 161, 198–99, 208–9, 335n143
  levees, 2, 7, 18, 301n6, 303n32
  NHS of, 48–49
  repopulation, in 2010 Census, 254
  residents, key traits of, 62, 63*t*,
    160, 160*t*

New Orleans East
  Broadmoor and, 61
  Citizens for a Strong New Orleans
    East and, 123–24, 126
  flooding in, 9
  geography, 258
  health care, 143
  housing, 118, 149, 324n9
  MQVN CDC and, 131
  race in, 124, 127
  as Rebuild Zone, 37
  repopulation, 151, 152t, 258
  UNOP and, 127
New Orleans Neighborhood
  Development Collaborative
  (NONDC), 77
New Orleans Neighborhood Rebuilding
  Plan. *See* Lambert Plan
New Orleans Redevelopment Authority
  (NORA), 54, 56, 97
New Orleans Regional Planning
  Commission, 56, 166
NFIP. *See* National Flood Insurance
  Program
Nguyen, Diem, 143, 328n96
Nguyen, Kim, 128
Nguyen, Long, 116
Nguyen, May, 129, 132–35, 327n71
Nguyen, Mimi, 131
Nguyen, Nghiem Van, 140
Nguyen, Peter, 146, 328n104
Nguyen, Tuan, 135, 154, 328n107
Nguyen, Vien The
  landfill campaign and, 124, 127
  in Village de L'Est rebuilding, 113–18,
    120–21, 124, 127–29, 140–41,
    143–44, 147–48, 154–56
NHS. *See* Neighborhood Housing
  Services of New Orleans
Nine Lives (Wells), 2
NMTCs. *See* New Market tax credits
No Child Left Behind, 87
NOLA Green Roots, 188
NONDC. *See* New Orleans Neighborhood
  Development Collaborative
NORA. *See* New Orleans Redevelopment
  Authority
North Vietnam, 109
Notre Dame, 84
nursing homes, 302n16

Office of Community Development
  (OCD), 47, 49
Office of Economic Adjustment, 293
Office of Recovery Development
  and Administration (ORDA),
  55–57
Office of Recovery Management (ORM),
  35–39, 54–55
Olive Stallings playground, 166–67
Olshansky, Robert B., 14
ORDA. *See* Office of Recovery
  Development and Administration
Orleans Parish Sheriff's Office, 196
ORM. *See* Office of Recovery
  Management
Overfelt, David, 15

PA. *See* Public Assistance
Parish Wide Recovery Committee, 35
parkland, proposed, 24f, 25, 27, 64,
  331n49
Parkway Bakery, 177
partnerships. *See also* dual collaborative
  rebuilding
  Broadmoor, 69–71, 75–76, 75f, 78,
    83–85, 95
  MQVN CDC, 277
  neighborhood rebuilding capacity and,
    277–78
  New City Neighborhood, 253
  PNOLA, 277
  Village de L'Est, 277–78
Passebon Cottage, 225
Paths of Destruction (McQuaid and
  Schleifstein), 4–5
Paul, Emelda, 215
Paul Davis National, 184
PDU. *See* Project Delivery Unit
personal networks, 14, 341n5
phasing decisions, 282, 331n64
Phoenix of New Orleans (PNOLA)
  Lower Mid-City and, 230–31, 237–38,
    248–49, 262–63
  partnerships, 277
  repopulation and, 262–63
physical losses, of flooding, 6–11,
  303n33, 304n39
Picou, J. Steven, 15
Pijawka, D., 255
place-based development, 239

planning, for rebuilding. *See also* Bring
New Orleans Back Commission;
Lambert Plan; Unified New Orleans
Plan
Action Plan, 44, 46–47, 309n21
approaches, 308n80
approval of, 36–39, 38*t*
in Broadmoor, 69–78, 72*f*, 74*t*, 75*f*,
82, 96, 99, 106–7, 179, 269–70
City Planning Department and, 16
CPC and, 11, 30, 37, 311n58
CSRRP, 37–39, 38*t*, 54, 56
in Faubourg St. John, 163–68, 165*f*,
167*f*, 177, 179
LSU/Charity Hospital, 233
in Mid-City, 175–80
neighborhood-scale, 280, 285
by New Orleans Regional Planning
Commission, 56, 166
by ORM, 35–39
problematic process of, 255–56
race and, 21, 26, 33
reasons for, 20–21
School Facilities Master Plan, 182,
278, 280, 282, 294, 304n42
shared vision in, 275
system-level, 281
Tulane-Gravier Neighborhood Plan,
230, 233, 234*f*
by Urban Planning Committee, 22–23,
64, 69, 79, 308n9
in Village de L'Est, 119–20, 179
playgrounds, 167–68
Plessy v. Ferguson, 202
PNOLA. *See* Phoenix of New Orleans
Preservation Resource Center (PRC), 95,
209
private funding, 35, 70, 82, 85, 133. *See
also specific funding sources*
Project Delivery Unit (PDU), 55–57
project worksheet, 50, 315n128
Providence Community Housing,
129–30, 139–40, 210, 213–18
Public Assistance (PA) Program
Broadmoor and, 89, 104, 104*t*
city rebuilding process and, 40, 43–44,
49–52, 55, 59
delays, 255
integrative and systemwide recovery
investment with, 293–94

for public facilities, 299*t*
reform, 287, 291, 293–94
public facilities
damage to, 9–10
funding for, 299*t*
public housing, 211–13. *See also* Lafitte
complex
Public Library Board of Directors, 180,
182
Puett, Cathy, 210

Qatar Katrina Fund (QKF), 209–10
Qatar Tremé/Lafitte Renewal Project,
210
QKF. *See* Qatar Katrina Fund
Quick Start Initiative, 89, 104, 294

race
in Broadmoor, 64
in Faubourg St. John, 161, 171, 171*t*,
172*f*, 174
housing damage and, 9
in Lower Mid-City, 242–43, 243*t*, 244*f*
in Mid-City, 9, 160, 174, 192–95,
193*t*, 194*f*
in New Orleans East, 124, 127
planning and, 21, 26, 33
repopulation and, 100, 100*t*, 101*f*,
102*t*, 338n191
Road Home Program and, 45,
314n112
schools and, 87, 91, 320n51
in Tremé, 198–201, 203, 206–7, 214,
221–22, 222*t*, 223*f*
in Village de L'Est, 111–12, 150–51,
151*t*
Rapport, Ezra, 55
"Razing a Community" (Reckdahl), 215
Rebuild Center, 229
rebuilding, of New Orleans. *See also* city
rebuilding process; dual collaborative rebuilding; funding, for rebuilding; neighborhoods; planning, for
rebuilding
businesses, 10–12
central questions of, 19
city capacity and coordination in,
52–58
city government and, 11
disparity in, 304n45

federal funding for, 18–19, 26
first five years of, 58–59
flood control system, 7, 18
French Quarter, 21
geography influencing, 250–51, 258–59, 271
government recovery policies influencing, 249, 259–61, 267
health care, 9–10, 12
infrastructure, 8, 13, 299*t*
Landrieu, Mitch, and, 57, 166, 185, 219, 237, 318n167
Nagin and, 11, 21, 25–27, 29–30, 36–37, 57, 77, 184, 216, 310n33, 318n167, 338n197
neighborhood rebuilding capacity influencing, 261–62, 266*t*, 274–79, 275*f*
profit from, 184–85
research on, 13–16
scale of, 6, 12, 255
schools, 9–10, 12, 51
tourism, 11
Rebuilding Together, 95, 209
Rebuild Zones, 37
Reckdahl, Katy, 215
Reconstruction Following Disaster (Kates and Pijawka), 255
recovery investment, integrative and systemwide, 293–94
Recovery School District (RSD), 87–89, 91, 131, 141
  Mid-City schools and, 182–84
  Nagin and, 320n55
  Tremé and, 206
Recovery School District Act (RSDA), 87
redevelopment scars, of Tremé, 199–202, 200*f*–201*f*
Redevelop Zones, 37
reform. *See* educational reform; federal disaster assistance reform
Reliant Center, 5
Renew Zones, 37
rental housing, recovery of, 96, 96*t*, 104*t*, 267–68, 298*t*
repopulation
  Broadmoor, 66, 79–82, 99–103, 99*t*–100*t*, 101*f*, 102*t*–103*t*, 259, 264, 265*t*, 267, 279
  Faubourg St. John, 168–74, 169*f*, 170*t*–171*t*, 172*f*, 173*t*, 246–47, 246*t*

funding and, 264
geography influencing, 258–59
government recovery policies and, 267
in grassroots rebuilding of neighborhoods, 264–69, 265*t*
importance of, 279
Lower Mid-City, 242–47, 242*t*–243*t*, 244*f*, 245*t*–246*t*, 262–63, 265*t*, 267–68
Lower Ninth Ward, 258
Mid-City, 192–97, 192*t*–193*t*, 194*f*, 195*t*–196*t*, 246–47, 246*t*
New Orleans, in 2010 Census, 254
New Orleans East, 151, 152*t*, 258
PNOLA and, 262–63
race and, 100, 100*t*, 101*f*, 102*t*, 338n191
Road Home Program and, 267
Tremé, 220–24, 220*t*–222*t*, 223*f*, 246–47, 246*t*, 259
Village de L'Est, 149–52, 150*t*–152*t*, 220, 254, 258, 264, 265*t*, 266–67, 279
Repopulation Committee, 66, 79–80, 83
rescue effort, 4
research, on rebuilding of New Orleans, 13–16
research and development parks, 239
Research Commercialization/Educational Enhancement Program, 299
Revitalizing Urban Main Streets program, 166
Rita. *See* Hurricane Katrina
Road Home Program, 33, 44–48, 46*t*, 237, 288, 290
  Broadmoor and, 94–96, 104, 104*t*, 106, 168, 297*t*
  disparities in, 314n112, 341n10
  Faubourg St. John and, 168, 297*t*, 329n26
  Lower Mid-City and, 297*t*
  Mid-City and, 168, 196*t*, 297*t*, 333n95
  race and, 45, 314n112
  relocation and, 315n119
  repopulation and, 267
  Tremé and, 210, 297*t*
  Village de L'Est and, 131–32, 132*t*, 297*t*, 327n68

Roark, Hal
  Broadmoor and, 60–61, 64–66, 82–84,
    93, 95, 107, 155, 321n73
  departure of, 93, 107
Robert T. Stafford Disaster Relief and
  Emergency Assistance Act, 39–40,
  288–89, 343n35
Rockefeller Foundation, 29–30
Rogers, Bobbi, 237–39
Rosa F. Keller Library
  funding for, 86t, 103, 104t
  rebuilding of, 73, 77, 79, 83, 85–87,
    86t, 103, 104t
Rouse, James, 213
RSD. *See* Recovery School District
RSDA. *See* Recovery School District Act
The Ruby Slipper restaurant, 187

Sachs, Ben, 144
St. Bernard Parish, 2–4
St. Joseph's Church, 227–29, 248
St. Margaret Daughters, 189–90
St. Rose of Lima church, 207, 224
Salvation Army, 97
Saussy, Virginia, 64, 66, 80–81, 155
Schell, Paul, 116
Schleifstein, Mark, 4–5
School Facilities Master Plan, 182, 278,
  280, 282, 294, 304n42
schools. *See also* charter schools;
    Recovery School District; *specific
    schools*
  damage to, 9–10
  educational reform and, 87–88, 270
  Faubourg St. John, 182–83
  Mid-City, 182–84, 184f
  poverty and, 321n63
  race and, 87, 91, 320n51
  rebuilding, 9–10, 12, 51
  Tremé, 205–6
Schwartz, Jeff, 166
Schwartz, Matt, 188
A Season of Night (McNulty), 187
Section 8 program, 213, 327n81
senior housing
  challenges of completing, 139–40
  in Lower Ninth Ward, 140
  in Village de L'Est, 118, 119f, 120–21,
    128–30, 139–40, 268
shared vision, in planning, 275

SHEDO LLC, 28, 178
Shinseki, Eric, 237
Sierra Club, 123
slaves, 198
Small Business Recovery Loan Program,
  134–35
Small Firm Loan and Grant Program, 298t
small firms, technical assistance to, 298t
Small Rental Assistance Program, 96,
  96t, 104t, 267
Small Rental Properties Program (SRPP),
  298t
Smith, Jerome, 203
social aid societies, 198
social networks, 14, 341n5
sociotechnical systems, 342n30
Soft Second Mortgage Program, 47–48,
  57, 59, 255–56, 288
Sojourner Truth Neighborhood Center,
  218
Southeastern Library Network Gulf
  Coast Libraries Project, 180
South Vietnam, 109
SRPP. *See* Small Rental Properties
  Program
Stafford Act. *See* Robert T. Stafford
  Disaster Relief and Emergency
  Assistance Act
state funding, 35, 43. *See also specific
  funding sources*
Stewart, Cortez, 6
storm surges, 2
Storr, Virgil Henry, 13
Storyville, 199, 334n107
student interns, 53, 70, 84, 88, 92–94
Superdome, 4–5, 302n24
system-level plans, 281

Tambourine and Fan, 202–3
Tang, Eric, 15
Target Recovery Zones, 37, 39, 53,
  56–57, 59
tax policies, 290
TCNDC. *See* Tulane/Canal Neighborhood
  Development Corporation
technical assistance, to small firms, 298t
Thompson, J. Phillip, 210
Thompson, Jeanette, 180
Thompson, Pam, 206
Thompson, Robert, 163

tourism, rebuilding, 11
Touro Hospital/Infirmary, 143
trailers, FEMA
  in Lower Mid-City, 228–29
  in Village de L'Est, 117–19, 119f, 130,
    324n24
Tran, Cam, 140–41
Tran, Mary, 116, 118, 121, 128–30, 135
transparency, 284
Tremé
  agendas negotiated in, 251–52
  AHPP and, 298t
  businesses, 200, 206–9, 207f, 221,
    265t–266t, 274
  civic participation in, 225
  community capital, 247–49
  Community Center, 203
  community-oriented projects, 224–25
  as complete neighborhood, 221,
    265t, 269
  DNIA and, 203–8
  economic development, 265t–266t,
    274, 298t–299t
  ERTCA and, 203–5
  five years later, 220–26, 220t–222t,
    223f
  flooding, 203–4, 250
  gentrification, 221–22
  geography, 250–51, 259
  government recovery policies influenc-
    ing, 249, 260
  grassroots contributions and compo-
    nents, 265t–266t
  GTC and, 202, 204–5
  HANO and, 212–13, 215–16, 218–20,
    260
  HFTA and, 204, 208–9
  history of, 197–203, 224
  housing, 198–222, 198f, 217f, 220t–
    221t, 226, 246–47, 246t, 249–51,
    260, 274, 335n130, 336n169,
    336nn166–67
  HUD and, 212–13, 215–16, 218,
    220, 252
  Lafitte complex and, 199–211, 213–20,
    217f, 247, 250–51, 260, 274
  location of, 158, 159f
  Louis Armstrong Park in, 201–2, 201f,
    334nn115–16
  Louisiana bridge loan program for, 299t

  multineighborhood initiatives and,
    252–53
  neighborhood rebuilding capacity
    influencing, 262, 266t, 278–79
  outside support and aid, 209–11
  preexisting organizations, 202–3
  prior conditions, 249–50, 258t
  Providence Community Housing and,
    210, 213–15
  public facilities and infrastructure
    funding, 299t
  race in, 198–201, 203, 206–7, 214,
    221–22, 222t, 223f
  redevelopment scars, 199–202,
    200f–201f
  repopulation of, 220–24, 220t–222t,
    223f, 246–47, 246t, 259
  residents, key traits of, 160, 160t
  Road Home and, 210, 297t
  schools, 205–6
  slow recovery of, 203–9
  Small Firm Loan and Grant Program
    and, 298t
  snapshot of, 159–60, 160t
  SRPP for, 298t
  technical assistance to small firms in,
    298t
  uneven recovery in, 254
  variations in rebuilding, 246–47, 246t
Tremé, Claude, 197
Tremé Community Improvement
  Association, 202
Tu, Trang, 115–16, 119–21, 128–29,
  324n28
Tulane, Paul, 338n200
Tulane/Canal Neighborhood
  Development Corporation
  (TCNDC), 227–30, 248–49, 262–63
Tulane-Gravier neighborhood. *See* Lower
  Mid-City
Tulane-Gravier Neighborhood Plan, 230,
  233, 234f
Tulane Medical School and Children's
  Hospital, 143–46, 145f
Tulane University Law School, 81
2010 Census, New Orleans repopulation
  and, 254

Ujamaa CDC, 128
ULI. *See* Urban Land Institute

Unified New Orleans Plan (UNOP)
  approval of, 311n58
  BNOB Commission and, 29–30
  Broadmoor Plan and, 77–78
  *Citywide Strategic Recovery and
    Rebuilding Plan* by, 34
  damage summarized in, 7
  funding and, 312n67
  LSU hospital plans and, 233
  meeting schedule and process, 31, 31*f*
  New Orleans East and, 127
  physical assets in, 312n66
  for rebuilding, 29–36, 31*f*, 37, 54, 58
  Village de L'Est and, 137
Urban Conservancy, 177
urban farm, in Village de L'Est, 146–48,
    147*f*
Urban Land Institute (ULI), 22–23, 34
Urban Planning Committee, 22–23, 64,
    69, 79, 308n9
urban renewal, in Lower Mid-City,
    231–39, 232*f*, 232*t*, 234*f*, 238*f*–239*f*
US Department of Housing and Urban
    Development. *See* Department of
    Housing and Urban Development, US
utilities, absence of, 176, 324n21

VA complex. *See* Veterans Affair complex
Vallas, Paul, 183, 332n69
VAYLA-NO. *See* Vietnamese American
    Young Leaders of New Orleans
Versailles Arms, 109, 148–49, 150*f*
Veterans Affair (VA) complex
  government policy and, 260–61
  in Lower Mid-City, 231–39, 232*f*,
    232*t*, 234*f*, 238*f*–239*f*, 260–61,
    339n223, 339n228
Victory Real Estate Investments,
    189–90, 236, 252
Vietnamese American Young Leaders of
    New Orleans (VAYLA-NO), 127, 138
Vietnamese community
  Catholic Church and, 108–10, 129
  national, 115–16
  NAVASA and, 116, 123, 126, 129, 136,
    146, 277
  research on, 14–15
  in Village de L'Est rebuilding, 108–48,
    110*f*, 114*f*, 150–56, 151*t*, 254, 264,
    266

  women in, 327n80, 328n99
Viet Village, 133, 134*f*, 137
Village de L'Est
  AHPP and, 298*t*
  BNOB Commission and, 120
  Broadmoor and, 113, 121, 128, 131,
    154–55
  Broad Street and, 158
  building implementation capacity and,
    128–32, 132*t*
  businesses, 132–37, 134*f*, 135*t*, 136*f*,
    265*t*–266*t*, 272–73
  challenges in, 138–48, 145*f*, 147*f*, 153
  characterization of, 17
  Chef Menteur Highway, 108, 121–22,
    127, 137, 148, 149*f*, 152–53
  Citizens for a Strong New Orleans
    East and, 123–24, 126
  citywide needs and, 118
  civic participation and, 137–38, 154
  commercial district marketing,
    132–37, 134*f*, 135*t*, 136*f*
  community health center, 142–46, 145*f*
  community mobilization in, 122–28,
    125*f*
  as complete neighborhood, 179, 265*t*,
    269–71
  damage, 9, 112–13
  decision to rebuild and, 113–15, 114*f*
  design charrette for, 120–22, 275–76
  early activism and organization,
    116–19, 119*f*
  economic development, 265*t*–266*t*,
    272–73, 298*t*–299*t*
  FEMA trailers and, 117–19, 119*f*, 130,
    324n24
  five years later, 148–57, 149*f*–150*f*,
    150*t*–152*t*
  flooding and, 112–13
  geography influencing, 258–59
  government recovery policies influ-
    encing, 260
  grassroots contributions and compo-
    nents, 262–63, 265*t*–266*t*
  housing, 148–52, 149*f*–150*f*, 150*t*–
    152*t*, 168, 193, 210, 220, 327n68
  ICS in, 140–42
  immigrants in, 109–11, 110*f*, 111*t*
  landfill campaign and, 122–28, 125*f*,
    137–38, 325n48, 326n56

leadership in, 155–56
location of, 108, 109*f*
Louisiana bridge loan program for, 299*t*
MQVN CDC rebuilding, 123, 128–41, 132*t*, 134*f*, 135*t*, 136*f*, 143–49, 145*f*, 151–56, 263, 268, 273, 326n58, 328n99
MQVN Church rebuilding, 110, 112–20, 114*f*, 127, 151, 273
neighborhood rebuilding capacity influencing, 261, 266*t*, 275–78
Nguyen, Vien The, and, 113–18, 120–21, 124, 127–29, 140–41, 143–44, 147–48, 154–56
organizing for, 116–20, 119*f*
partnerships in, 277–78
planning for, 119–20, 179
prior conditions influencing, 249–50, 258*t*
public facilities and infrastructure funding, 299*t*
race in, 111–12, 150–51, 151*t*
repopulation, 149–52, 150*t*–152*t*, 220, 254, 258, 264, 265*t*, 266–67, 279
residents' traits and, 110–11, 111*t*
Road Home Program and, 131–32, 132*t*, 297*t*, 327n68
senior housing, 118, 119*f*, 120–21, 128–30, 139–40, 268
Small Firm Loan and Grant Program and, 298*t*
SRPP for, 298*t*
technical assistance to small firms in, 298*t*
typical streets, 111, 112*f*
uneven recovery in, 254
UNOP and, 137

urban farm, 146–48, 147*f*
Vietnamese American community rebuilding, 108–48, 110*f*, 114*f*, 150–56, 151*t*, 254, 264, 266
Viet Village, 133, 134*f*, 137
vision for, 120–22
vision
for Broadmoor, 103–5, 104*t*
for Faubourg St. John, 164–66, 165*f*
shared, in planning, 275
for Village de L'Est, 120–22
Vitter, David, 118

waivers, 41, 43, 47–48, 52, 313nn86–87
Wallace Roberts Todd (WRT), 22
Warren-Williams, Vera, 206
Waste Management, Inc. (WMI), 122, 124–26
Weisshaupt, Jennifer, 187, 197
Wells, Anthony, 2, 301n4
West, Rod, 117
Wilson School. *See* Andrew H. Wilson School
Wise Words Community Gardens, 188, 189*f*
WMI. *See* Waste Management, Inc.
women, in Vietnamese community, 327n80, 328n99
Workforce Recovery Program, 300
World Trade Center disaster, 291, 317n148
Wright, Kelli, 66, 80–81, 155
WRT. *See* Wallace Roberts Todd

Xavier University, 174, 177

youth activism, 127, 138, 326n51

zoning, 209